RELIGIOUS PLURALISM IN INDONESIA

A volume in the series
Cornell Modern Indonesia Project
Edited by Eric Tagliacozzo and Thomas B. Pepinsky

A list of titles in this series is available at
cornellpress.cornell.edu.

RELIGIOUS PLURALISM IN INDONESIA

Threats and Opportunities
for Democracy

Edited by Chiara Formichi

SOUTHEAST ASIA PROGRAM PUBLICATIONS
AN IMPRINT OF CORNELL UNIVERSITY PRESS   ITHACA AND LONDON

First published 2021 by Cornell University Press

Library of Congress Cataloging-in-Publication Data

Names: Formichi, Chiara, 1982– editor.
Title: Religious pluralism in Indonesia : threats and opportunities for democracy / edited by Chiara Formichi.
Description: Ithaca [New York] : Southeast Asia Program Publications, an imprint of Cornell University Press, 2021. | Series: Cornell Modern Indonesia Project | Contributions from a conference held at Cornell University in April 2019. | Includes bibliographical references and index.
Identifiers: LCCN 2021007714 (print) | LCCN 2021007715 (ebook) | ISBN 9781501760433 (hardcover) | ISBN 9781501760440 (paperback) | ISBN 9781501760457 (epub) | ISBN 9781501760464 (pdf)
Subjects: LCSH: Religious pluralism—Indonesia—History— 20th century—Congresses. | Religious tolerance—Indonesia—History— 20th century—Congresses. | Pancasila—Congresses. | Religion and state—Indonesia—History—20th century—Congresses. | Religions— Relations—History—20th century—Congresses. | Indonesia—Religion— History—20th century—Congresses.
Classification: LCC BL2112 .R458 2021 (print) | LCC BL2112 (ebook) | DDC 201/.50959809045—dc23
LC record available at https://lccn.loc.gov/2021007714
LC ebook record available at https://lccn.loc.gov/2021007715

Contents

Acknowledgments

This volume is the outcome of the fifth conference in the Cornell Modern Indonesia Project's series "The State of the Field of Indonesian Studies," which was held at Cornell University in April 2019.

I am thankful to Eric Tagliacozzo, as director of CMIP, for giving me the opportunity to run this workshop. This was a most stimulating intellectual gathering that not only brought together colleagues from across the US, Europe, and Indonesia but also involved Cornell faculty and students across multiple departments as they joined in the organization, panels, and discussions. Michael Miller and Connor Rechtzigel, doctoral students in the Departments of History and Anthropology, respectively, supported us with tech and content. Panels were chaired by Alexandre Pelletier (an SSHRC and SEAP postdoctoral fellow) and by Seema Golestaneh (Near Eastern Studies), Kaja McGowan (History of Art and Visual Studies), Andrew Willford (Anthropology) and Marina Welker (Anthropology). Thomas Pepinsky (Government) presented the paper "Islam, Identity, and the Organizational Roots of Political Tolerance" (coauthored with Jeremy Menchick, Boston University), which was not included in this volume.

I would like to acknowledge the unswerving support of the Southeast Asia Program, especially in the persons of Abby Cohn, director, and Thamora Fischel, associate director. James Nagy and Divya Sriram, administrative assistants in the Southeast Asia Program, ensured that things were in place, that we were fed delicious food, and that everything ran smoothly. This was especially appreciated this time around—I returned to Ithaca from an unexpected overseas trip just a few hours before the beginning of the event, and it was reassuring to know that I didn't need to worry.

Generous financial support came from many corners of the Cornell campus. Thanks go to the Mario Einaudi Center for International Studies, the Southeast Asia Program, the Cornell Modern Indonesia Project, the Religious Studies Program, the Judith Reppy Institute for Peace and Conflict Studies, the Institute for the Social Sciences (now Cornell Center for Social Sciences), the Comparative Muslim Societies Program, the Department of History, the Department of Asian Studies, the Department of Anthropology, and the Department of Government, in collaboration with the American Institute for Indonesian Studies.

Last but not least, thanks go to Tsuguta Yamashita (PhD student in the Department of Asian Studies) for finalizing the manuscript, and to Sarah Grossman, the editor of SEAP Publications, and the editorial boards of SEAP Publications and Cornell University Press for publishing this volume.

Abbreviations

Bakorpakem	Badan Koordinasi Pengawas Aliran Kepercayaan Masyarakat (Coordinating Agency to Oversee People's Beliefs)
Banser	Barisan Ansor Serbaguna (Multipurpose Ansor Front)
BTP	Basuki Tjahaja Purnama, also known as Ahok, vice governor of Jakarta, 2012–14, governor, 2014–16
DI	Darul Islam
DPR	Dewan Perwakilan Rakyat (National Legislative Body)
DPRD	Dewan Perwakilan Rakyat Daerah (Regional House of Representatives)
FKUB	Forum Kerukunan Umat Beragama (Inter-religious Harmony Forum)
FPI	Front Pembela Islam (Islamic Defenders Front)
Gerindra	Gerakan Indonesia Raya (Great Indonesia Movement)
Golkar	Partai Golongan Karya (Functional Party)
HMI	Himpunan Mahasiswa Islam (Islamic Student Union)
HTI	Hizbut Tahrir Indonesia (Party of Liberation—Indonesia)
ISIS	Islamic State of Iran and Syria
KAGRI	Kementerian Agama Republik Indonesia (Indonesian Ministry of Religion)
KIP	Kartu Indonesia Pintar (Smart Indonesia Card, national program for public education)
KIS	Kartu Indonesia Sehat (Healthy Indonesia Card, national program for public health)
KJS	Kartu Jakarta Sehat (Healthy Jakarta Card, Jakarta program for public health)
Masyumi	Majelis Syuro Muslimin Indonesia (Consultative Body of Indonesian Muslims)
MMI	Majelis Mujahidin Indonesia (Council of Indonesian Mujahidin)
MPR	People's Consultative Assembly
MUI	Majelis Ulama Indonesia (Indonesian Ulema Council)
NKRI	Negara Kesatuan Republik Indonesia (Unitary National Republic of Indonesia)
NU	Nahdlatul Ulama (Renaissance of the Ulama)
PAN	Partai Amanat Nasional (National Mandate Party)

PAS	Parti Islam Se-Malaysia (All-Malaysia Islamic Party)
PBB	Partai Bulan Bintang (Crescent and Stars Party)
PD	Partai Demokrat (Democratic Party)
PDI-P	Partai Demokrasi Indonesia Perjuangan (Indonesian Democratic Party of Struggle)
Perda Syariah	Peraturan Daerah Syariah (Regional Regulation Based on Syariah)
PKB	Partai Kebangkitan Bangsa (National Awakening Party)
PKI	Partai Komunis Indonesia (Indonesia's Communist Party)
PKS	Partai Keadilan Sejahtera (Prosperous Justice Party)
PPP	Partai Persatuan Pembangunan (United Development Party)
SARA	*suku, agama, ras dan antar golongan* (ethnicity, religion, race, and intergroup [conflict])
SBY	Susilo Bambang Yudhoyono (former president and chairman of the Democratic Party)
UIN/IAIN	State Islamic University system

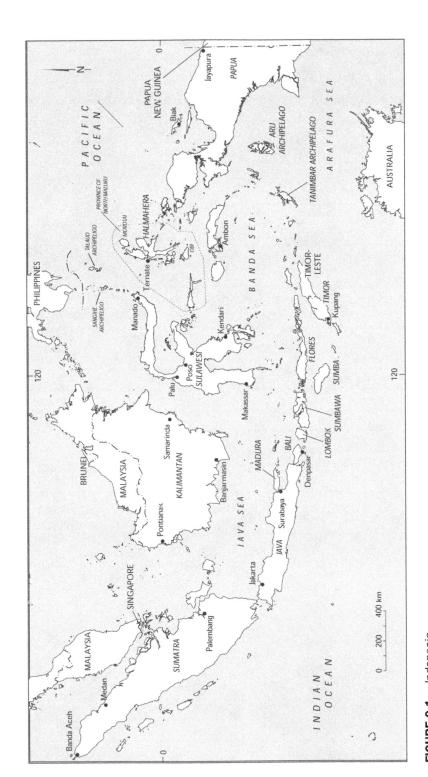

FIGURE 0.1. Indonesia

RELIGIOUS PLURALISM
IN INDONESIA

THE LIMITS OF PANCASILA AS A FRAMEWORK FOR PLURALISM

Chiara Formichi

Indonesia, a country of over 250 million people, made of 18,000 islands, 1,300 ethnic groups, and over 300 languages, built itself as an independent nation-state grounded on a commitment to "Unity in Diversity" (or *Bhinneka Tunggal Ika*). This motto, etched on each and every reproduction of the national emblem, was a match to the postcolonial republic's founding philosophy, illustrated by President Sukarno (1901–67) in 1945 and referred to as the Pancasila (i.e., the Five Principles of nationalism [*kebangsaan*], humanitarianism [*perikemanusiaan*], deliberation among representatives [*permusyawaratan-perwakilan*], social welfare [*kesejahteraan*] and the belief in One God [*ketuhanan*]).

Seventy years after the proclamation of independence, this edited volume opens a number of windows on how the Indonesian state, its government bodies, civil society groups, and individuals have experienced Pancasila as a framework for the attempted integration of minorities and majorities across the archipelagic state. Written by scholars of Indonesia belonging to a variety of disciplinary backgrounds including anthropology, sociology, history, political science, and religious studies, the chapters in this volume flesh out the identity of Pancasila as a philosophy and ideology that enabled postcolonial Indonesia to portray itself as an inclusive container for many different peoples—even if it meant molding Hinduism into the "one book, one prophet, one god" paradigm, thus arm-wrestling an established religious tradition into a "new form" that would fit under the framework. They also examine the historical and political trajectories that have brought about a less sophisticated and more contradictory situation, in which public discourses depicting Islam in Indonesia as localized and tolerant run parallel to the strengthening, and public affirmation of exclusivist majoritarian Islamism. The chapters offer analyses of contemporary phenomena (Islamist majoritarianism) and events (the Ahok trial); the changing legal and social status of certain minority groups (from local beliefs to Tamil Hindus, Confucianism, and non-Sunni Muslims); interfaith relations (in Bali and Maluku); and the role of Islam in Indonesia's foreign policy.

As the contributors to the volume explore the state of the Pancasila ideal and its contemporary implementation, the attention has been mostly attracted by its failures. Not only have Islamists been loud in voicing their concerns and fears about the threat of minorities but even so-called moderate Muslim groups who oppose calls to institutionalize Islam in Indonesia's politics have all the same stopped short when attacks have been directed to LGBTQI+ groups and non-Sunni Muslims, for example. Facing infringements of their human rights, some officially recognized minorities (Protestants, Catholics, Hindus, Buddhists, and Confucians) have been able to advocate for themselves with mixed success through the Pancasila framework, but others—from Ahmadi and Shi'i groups to atheists and followers of new religious groups—have been left without safeguards, proving the weakness of Indonesia's institutionalized pluralism.

Investigations into Indonesia's tolerance, the effective conditions of various minorities, and the role of the Pancasila ideology in politics remain productive themes of research. Karel Steenbrink has recently called Pancasila an "ambiguous" concept, "used to stimulate, [but] also to control various manifestations of religions and to prevent conflicts" (2015, 34); similarly, Leo Suryadinata (2018) has stressed how the "pluralist" Pancasila ideology has at the same time been both used by the government and challenged by conservatives since the 1940s. In *Contentious Belonging*, Greg Fealy and Ronit Ricci frame an exploration of how minorities "fit" in Indonesia; while they do not directly address the Pancasila framework, the institutional and cultural contexts covered throughout their volume were shaped by this founding ideology, as their observation that religious and ethnic minorities, differently-abled individuals, and LGBT communities "have variously been subject to condemnation or denigration . . . and in some cases have been target of violent attack" (2019, 2), is the inevitable outcome of the limited reach and impact of Pancasila on policy implementation today.

The Pancasila Framework

On June 1, 1945, Sukarno made his later-famous "Pancasila speech," illustrating his vision for an independent Republic of Indonesia, a vision that rejected the idea of an Islamic state and more generally the idea of giving Islam any "special" consideration in the constitutional text in favor of (supposedly) including all religions present in the Archipelago. In the subsequent weeks a compromise was attempted with representatives of the Islamic wing of the nationalist movement, suggesting the addition of the so-called Jakarta Charter which would have sanctioned "the obligation for Muslims to follow Islamic law" (Soekarno, Hatta, et al. 2006, 209–10). Shortly after, the "Jakarta Charter" was deleted from the constitution's preamble and Pancasila was enshrined as the ideological foundation of the new nation-state. To compensate for the loss, the principle of monotheism was given primacy (becoming listed as the first principle), and Islam was to function as the model; all recognized *agamas* (religions) had to have a prophet, a holy book, and a single deity. This inevitably created difficulties for the country's Hindus, Buddhists, and followers of local beliefs (*kepercayaan*).

In 1953, during a speech in Amuntai (South Kalimantan), Sukarno reinforced his initial approach, stating that "the state we want is a national state consisting of all Indonesia. If we establish a state based on Islam, many areas whose population is not Islamic, such as the Moluccas, Bali, Flores, Timor, the Kai islands, and Sulawesi, will secede" (Feith 1962, 218). Invoking the need to maintain the national boundaries as established by the Dutch, Sukarno continued to depict Pancasila as a cardinal pillar of the new, inclusive nation-state. A year later, Sukarno also further explained how the principle of monotheism should be understood to also be applicable to "the animist belief in spirits and ghosts" (Nasution 1965, 99). This latter statement was supposed to reinforce the inclusivist claims of Pancasila and dispel concerns among followers of *kepercayaan* (see Aragon, this volume) and non-Abrahamic religions (e.g., Hinduism—see Picard, this volume—but also Buddhism). But in fact it created even more of a backlash among certain groups of Muslims who understood this statement as endorsing "associationism" (*shirk*, commonly translated in English as polytheism), a severe breach of Islam's hard monotheism.

Groups within the nation's Muslim communities have been advocating for (or demanding) an explicit reference to Islam in the constitution ever since the June 1, 1945, speech. An early core of dissent was to be found in the Masyumi and Sarekat Islam parties and in the Darul Islam/Islamic State of Indonesia movement. With deep roots in colonial West Java, the Darul Islam had been shaped by S. M. Kartosuwiryo (1905–65), a nationalist journalist-*cum*-politician later seen as a rebel by Sukarno's republic; after two decades of participation in formal politics, Kartosuwiryo took the route of armed struggle and separatism in response to Sukarno's diplomatic engagement with the Dutch after their invasion of Sumatra and Java in 1948.

Challenges to the Pancasila continued through the 1950s. Masyumi politicians claimed that the nation's Muslims should only support the Islamic State of Indonesia and that those who did not do so were hypocrites (Formichi

2012, 91). During a visit to Aceh shortly after the Amuntai speech mentioned above, Sukarno was received with banners reading, "We love the president, but we love religion more" (Feith 1962, 346). If the insertion of Islam into the Indonesian constitution would have driven away non-Muslim regions, Sukarno's Pancasila state was having the opposite effect. The "Manifesto of the Atjeh Rebels" issued by Daud Beureueh (later an affiliate of Kartosuwiryo's Darul Islam) argued, "We shall therefore be the ones to secede from a state that is based upon nationalism" (Feith and Castle 1970, 212).

During Suharto's repressive New Order regime (1968–98) Pancasila rhetoric became a pillar of both anticommunism (as belief in religion was used as an antiatheist, and therefore anticommunist, measure) and nationalism (new policies in the 1970s forced all political groups to declare Pancasila as their founding principle, an approach sanctioned in 1983 with the *azas tunggal*, or "sole foundation"). All attempts at bringing Islam into formal politics were regularly suppressed. But as personal piety was instead fostered, Islam immediately resurfaced on the public sphere during *Reformasi* (referring to the reformation period that followed Suharto's resignation in 1998).

Religion and *Reformasi*

After the fall of Suharto, Islamic parties proliferated and during the 1999 parliamentary elections they received a third of the votes. The selection of Abdurrahman Wahid as president (1999–2001) reflected well the spirit of the time. On the one hand, as chairman of the largest Muslim organization, Nahdlatul Ulama (NU), Wahid matched the popular desire to see Islam represented at the top of the nation (it should be remembered that NU had been a political party in its own right until 1973). On the other hand, as a man committed to inclusivism—and I am careful here to connect Wahid and not NU at large to this commitment, as the role of NU youth groups in the post-1965 violence cannot be too easily brushed aside—Wahid also took a number of important steps in this era of reform: he recognized Confucianism as a sixth official religion; nominated renowned "liberal Muslims," secularists, and Christians to important cabinet roles; and promoted the establishment of the first non-Sunni civil society group, namely the All-Indonesian Assembly of Ahlul Bait [Family of the Prophet] Associations, (IJABI, Ikatan Jama'ah Ahlul Bait Indonesia), whose mission was to include "lovers of the *ahl al-bayt* regardless of their *madhhab*."[1] Wahid's term was however short-lived, as apparently was this spirit of inclusion.

In the early days of the presidency of Wahid's successor, Megawati Sukarnoputri (2001–4), while communal violence in Eastern Indonesia had just begun to subside (see Duncan 2013), parliament held discussions on the possibility of a constitutional amendment to include the Jakarta Charter. These failed, but in the following years attempts to Islamize the Indonesian state kept coming: the terrorist Acong exploded himself in the Sari Club on Kuta Beach on October 12, 2002, killing over two hundred people and claiming the memory of Kartosuwiryo's struggle for an Islamic state of Indonesia as inspiration; the Majelis Mujahidin Indonesia (MMI), established in the year 2000, advocated for the insertion of *shari'a* law in the penal code (Formichi 2012); the Indonesian branch of Hizbut Tahrir came out in the open and in 2007 hosted the first International Caliphate Conference, gathering about a hundred thousand Indonesians in Jakarta.

Despite general dissent against the establishment of Indonesia as a formal "Islamic state" (what that would look like remains contested and unclear), in the past twenty years *shari'a* laws have in fact made their way into the Indonesian legal corpus, largely within the post-Suharto framework of democracy and self-determination. An important mantra of the early years of *Reformasi* was "decentralization," a desire to diminish the power of Jakarta's authority not only over the rest of the archipelago's economy and natural resources but also over culture and education. Under this rubric, parliament passed the so-called Regional Autonomy Law as early as 2001. It did not take long before advocates of *shari'a* turned this law into a vehicle for Islamizing the legal corpus from the bottom up. Peraturan Daerah Syariah (*shari'a* -inspired regional regulations, also called *perda syariah*) have been implemented across the nation-state, enforcing social norms compliant with Islam: women have been required to wear headscarves and public servants have been tested for proficiency in Qur'anic recitation (Buehler 2016). It was this same umbrella law that allowed the promulgation of a *shari'a* -inspired code in post-tsunami Aceh (Feener 2013).

Islam is the majority religion in Indonesia, and Islam does tend to grab the headlines more than other religions when it comes to demands for its official inclusion in political, legal, or societal structures. But it should not be ignored that Indonesia also has areas with different demographics. Hence, Christian-majority regencies have also passed *perda injil* (local regulations inspired by the Bible), and since the 2002 Bali bombing, conservative Hindu groups in Bali have been making demands to protect Hinduism against encroaching Islamization and Christianization. While Muslim-majority Lombok is on the rise as an international *halal* tourism destination and the government has suggested that all goods traded in Indonesia should be *halal* certified, stakeholders in Hindu-majority Bali have called for Hindu *sukla* ("ritually pure") food stalls; in all cases, demographic majoritarianism was asserted as a prime aspect of policy-making at the expense of inclusivism, legitimation of diversity, and ultimately pluralism.

Pluralism

The Pancasila principle of "belief in one god" (*ketuhanan*) was first coined and then further elaborated upon as a framework to keep the Indonesian nation-state whole in the decolonization process, to avoid the secession of Christian, Hindu, and Animist areas. However, with the benefit of hindsight, one can see how the Pancasila framework created several problems in the following decades. Far from fostering a social and political environment conducive to pluralism, it instead encouraged religious belonging as a marker of exclusionary identity and the active marginalization of many Indonesian citizens across the archipelago.

The term "pluralism" is here deployed to refer to a condition of religious diversity in which all those present are validated as equally legitimate members of society. Echoing my previous engagement with the term (Formichi 2014b), I remain committed to this adoption of Michael Peletz's definition of "gender pluralism" as he illustrated it first in his seminal article "Transgenderism and Gender Pluralism" (Peletz 2006), and later expanded it in the monograph *Gender Pluralism: Southeast Asia since Early Modern Times* (Peletz 2008). The question of where this legitimation should emerge from remains murky, and scholars have explored various ways in which local communities, neighborhoods, or society at large have endeavored to validate minority groups through the frame of "living together" and "everyday pluralism."[2] This volume, however, is mostly concerned with exploring the impact of the Pancasila framework as a state ideology on the archipelago's religious diversity and the policies Pancasila has inspired since the mid-1940s. Let us then return to this framework to see how it has interfaced with this (possibly utopian) ideal of religious pluralism.

First of all, the phrasing of the principle of "The One and Only God" (*Yang Maha Esa*) created immediate epistemological difficulties for substantial numbers of citizens-to-be; these difficulties are further reinforced by the embracing of an Abrahamic religion as model for the definition of "godly-ness" (*ketuhanan*) and its related belief system. *Agama* became limiting as it came to mean "the peculiar combination in Sanskrit guise of a Christian view of what counts as a world religion, with a restrictive and prescriptive Islamic understanding of what defines a 'true' religion" (Picard, this volume). Hinduism and Buddhism both had to undergo major reforms to be recognized as *agama* by the Ministry of Religious Affairs.

Second, the stipulation of a list of officially recognized religions and the sanctioned obligation to declare affiliation to one of them marginalized—if not elided—from national consciousness all those citizens whose beliefs just did not fit with the *agama* paradigm. Their only choice was to either convert (at least nominally) to an official religion (usually Christianity—Catholic or Protestant—or Islam because of their universalistic claims, versus the ethnic connotations of Hinduism and Buddhism) or to remain at the margins of society, unable to take advantage of any of the public services provided by the state (e.g. public clinics and hospitals, schools, marriage and birth certifications, etc.). In the darkest days of the Suharto regime, they remained at risk of being accused of "atheism" and therefore communism (see contributions by Aragon and Duncan, this volume).

In the immediate post-*Reformasi* period, one of the first steps of the newly appointed president Abdurrahman Wahid was to expand the list from five to six religions, adding Confucianism; this was largely a symbolic sign of rapprochement toward Indonesia's Chinese ethnic citizens who had been the target of persecution in the post-1965 anticommunist purges (and in fact once again in 1997–98), after which they had been stripped of their cultural heritage and forced to assimilate to "mainstream" Indonesian culture for survival (changing names, not using the Chinese language, converting to Christianity or—less often—Islam). Confucianism and Buddhism remain the two smallest religious groups in the country and the only ones to not have a "majority area" (in comparison to, for example, Bali Hinduism), thus leaving their followers in a marginal and constantly challenged position (see Sutrisno, this volume, on Confucianism).

Third is the role of the bureaucratization and institutionalization of religions. Sukarno's vision of a Pancasila semisecular state was modeled on the example of Kemalist Turkey, and this he understood as a context in which the "flames of Islam" were being returned to society, freed from the control of the state (see Formichi 2013).[3] But similar to post-Ottoman Turkey, in Indonesia also the separation of state and "mosque" came along with a heavy bureaucratization of religion under the umbrella of the nation-state's administration. The emerging Indonesian state created the Ministry of Religious Affairs (KAGRI) in January 1946. Headed by a Muslim, KAGRI oversees and directs the activities of each religious group through dedicated offices. This structure ensured that all religions were being administered from one central place, supposedly allowing for equal treatment and policies, but Islam's primacy was nonetheless bound to surface.

Hence, the way that the Pancasila ideology took shape as a policy framework of the Indonesian nation-state came to undermine any possible aspiration to inclusivity and actual pluralism as an approach that promoted legitimation of diversity. Several groups of believers (and all nonbelievers) were excluded by definition from the required compliance to the concepts of *ketuhanan* and *agama*;

others were excluded by deliberate choice. The bureaucratization of religion also caused at least two further developments that negatively impacted the potential for religious pluralism in Indonesia. First, even though religious authority in Indonesia has always been diffused, held by local religious leaders, the existence of KAGRI's denominational offices as a nationwide official structure of reference has led to the popularization of the idea (and possibility) of a central and unique authoritative body for any given *agama*, de facto narrowing the spectrum of interpretative approaches. This is usually discussed within the scope of rising Sunni normativism, which since the early 2000s has been challenging the rights of Ahmadis and Shi'a, as well as other "alternative" groups (see Hamayotsu, this volume).[4] But as Picard explores in the context of Bali Hinduism and Vignato among the Tamil Hindus of Medan, control over orthodoxy is contested across the denominational spectrum. Second, consistently giving the highest KAGRI ministerial position to a Muslim stands as symbolic recognition of Indonesia's demographics; these long standing pro forma affirmations of Islam's primacy have enabled, and implicitly supported, the claims made in the name of Muslim majoritarianism on the national scale (see contributions by Hamayotsu, Jones, and Hefner) and their challenges to manifestations of pluralism (see Lohanda).

Institutionalized Intolerance

Religion emerged as a pervasive presence in post-*Reformasi* everyday life, as an aspect of the law, religiously conscious consumer culture, and more generally conservative attitudes (see van Bruinessen 2013). Although this has been a drawn-out and gradual transformation, a symbolic turning point can be identified with the activities of the Majelis Ulama Indonesia (MUI, Indonesia's Council of Ulama) in the early 2000s. Established in 1975 as a semiofficial body tasked with legitimizing the regime's policies in a religious frame, in the 21st century this fatwa-issuing council has taken on a life of its own, often even influencing decisions made by "secular" civil and criminal courts deliberating on accusations against Christians, atheists, and Muslim minority groups.

In 2005 MUI issued a fatwa calling for the closure of all Ahmadi places of worship and forbidding the sect from disseminating its teachings. This fatwa, in combination with another in 2007 that established guidelines to identify "heresy" (or *kesesatan*), triggered a wave of virulent violence against the Ahmadis. None of these arguments were new—in fact, MUI had already condemned non-Sunni Muslim groups in 1980. What had changed to enable sectarian violence was that the new fatwa was taken on by the government office in charge of religious minorities' affairs, de facto legitimizing MUI's opinion and translating it into local-level civil regulations (Crouch 2009; Hicks 2013). The pattern demonstrated here by the experience of the Ahmadiyyah was also lived by Indonesia's Shi'is a few years later; in the early 2010s, anti-Shi'a religious opinions were similarly translated into civil regulations, creating an environment conducive to violent expressions of dissent against this minority group (Formichi 2014b).

As illustrated by Kikue Hamayotsu in this volume, when branches of MUI create "intolerant coalitions" with local "civil society" groups and representatives of the political authority or security apparatus, local minorities—whether they are non-Muslims or non-Sunni Muslim groups—tend to become targets of persecution, sometimes violent, sometimes legal. Both Hamayotsu and Sutrisno, however, also point out that power brokers have the authority and ability to counter (or even prevent) intolerance.

In the mid-2000s, MUI also issued a fatwa condemning "Secularism, Pluralism and Liberalism" (dubbed SIPILIS), sealing the spirit of this time. According to this view, Western "viruses" threaten the aspirations and demands of Indonesia's Muslims; similarly, Islam was seen as marginalized, the result of the elevation of non (Sunni) Muslims to the same standing of (Sunni majority) Muslims, and "liberal" social norms, ranging from *seks bebas* (often translated as "free sex," referring to sexual relations outside of wedlock) to recognition of LGBTQI+ rights (Kersten 2015).

Uncivil Society and Its (Claimed) Antidotes

After years of gradual escalation of social tensions, by the second half of the 2010s, observers of Islam in Indonesia witnessed the affirmation of Islamist discourses in the public sphere. In late 2016 Muslim groups accused the Chinese Christian acting governor of Jakarta, Basuki Tjahaja Purnama (also known as BTP or Ahok), of blasphemy following the misrepresentation (and manipulation) of this politician's use of a verse of the Qur'an. A few months later, a civil court sentenced Basuki Tjahaja Purnama to two years in jail (see Lohanda, this volume). The "anti-Ahok" movement has become emblematic of the power of the exclusivist Islamists to bring the Muslim majority out onto the streets and influence juridical decisions based on the threat of violence and social instability (see contributions by Jones and Hefner in this volume).

Amid soaring exclusivism—what Hefner has in this volume referred to as "uncivil majoritarianism"—the government of Joko Widodo (also known as Jokowi) has attempted to come across as the voice of moderation and tolerance. In 2017 the Supreme Constitutional Court ruled that the requirement to list one's religion on identity cards is discriminatory; at the same time it also legitimized a new legal category for "native faiths." That same year, a presidential decree that targeted groups whose activities contradicted the spirit of Pancasila led to the banning of Hizb-ut-Tahrir. While Lorraine Aragon explores the limits of the Supreme Constitutional Court decision in her contribution to this volume, Sidney Jones explains how the presidential decree is also problematic, reminiscent of some New Order moves.

Another step taken by Jokowi, supposedly similarly aimed at fending off Islamist threats and promoting instead tolerance among Indonesia's Muslims, was his embrace of NU's Islam Nusantara ("Islam of the Archipelago"). Islam Nusantara rests on the historical narrative that Islam gained a foothold in Southeast Asia peacefully and gradually over time, hence blending with preexisting cultural and devotional forms and producing a "localized" form of Islam (Baso 2015; Azra 2015). Within this approach, Islam in Indonesia is portrayed as inherently more tolerant than the "pure" Islam of the Middle East (which within this perspective is univocally equated to Saudi Wahhabi or Salafi interpretations) and thus serves as an antidote to radical, jihadi groups (Hoesterey 2018). This narrative has resonated internationally, largely in conjunction with the fact that Indonesians appear to have been proportionally less involved in IS/Daesh activities than Muslims in other countries.

Presented by NU's intellectual elites as their 2015 Congress motto, this reading of Islam in Indonesia as local and tolerant has gained favor in Indonesia's government offices at home: antiterror government organizations promote it in their antiradicalization programs and the Ministry of Religion has embraced it as a way to teach Islam as a peaceful, moderate, and compassionate force (Widodo in Affan 2015).[5] Abroad, President Joko Widodo and Vice President Jusuf Kalla have openly endorsed it as a tool of diplomatic soft power, advocating for its export to other Muslim countries, notably the Middle East, to defuse the impact and reach of Islamic extremism (see Hoesterey, this volume).[6]

As we look ahead to the current state of pluralism and the position of religious minorities in the largest Muslim democratic country in the world, it seems that the political and religious establishments send mixed signals, but the final message is one of exclusion, othering, and marginalization. Joko Widodo, who in 2016–18 appeared as the voice of moderation against Islamist forces, won the 2019 electoral ticket with Ma'ruf Amin as vice president. Ma'ruf Amin might have been the supreme leader of NU (which claims to promote Islam as an inclusive and tolerant element in Indonesian society) but he was also the chairman of MUI when the council led major campaigns against the Shi'a and Ahmadis, overseeing the issuance of the SIPILIS fatwa, and he was the most authoritative spokesperson in the anti-Ahok campaign (Dewi 2018). The presidency embodies the contradictive reality of current discourses on tolerance and exclusivism and the ultimate emptiness of today's politics of tolerance in Indonesia.

Notes

1. Mission statement of the all-Indonesian Assembly of Ahlul Bait Associations (Ikatan Jama'ah Ahlul Bait).

2. The topic of religious pluralism has been explored by scholars working on a variety of geographical settings. Among them are Furnivall (1944, Southeast Asia), Hefner (2001, Southeast Asia), Eck (2001, North America), Connolly (2005, North America), Berger (2014, North America), Das (2006, South Asia), and Hasan and Roy (2005, South Asia)

3. The very fact that one of the principles was *ketuhanan* invalidates any attempt at defining the Pancasila state as "secular".

4. For an illustration of who the Ahmadis are, see Yohanan Friedmann, "Aḥmadīyah," in *The Oxford Encyclopedia of the Islamic World. Oxford Islamic Studies Online*, http://www.oxfordislamicstudies.com/article/opr/t236/e0036, accessed Jan 29, 2019.

5. NU's 2015 congress motto was *Meneguhkan Islam Nusantara untuk Peradaban Indonesia dan Dunia* ("Reinforcing Islam Nusantara for [the benefit of] Indonesia's and the World's civilization").

6. In May 2015 the Economic and Social Chamber of the United Nations hosted the seminar "Islam Nusantara: Diversity, Democracy and Modernity"; the following year NU itself sponsored an international conference (the International Summit of Moderate Islamic Leaders) with ulama from the US, Europe, and the Middle East to promote the idea of Islam Nusantara abroad (on this occasion Vice President Jusuf Kalla gave the opening speech).

References

Affan, Hayder. 2015. "Polemik di Balik Istilah Islam Nusantara [The polemics behind the concept of Islam Nusantara]." *BBC Indonesia*, June 15. www.bbc.com/indonesia/berita_indonesia/2015/06/150614_indonesia_islam_nusantara.

Azra, Azyumardi. 2015. "Islam Nusantara." *Republika*, June 18 and 25.

Baso, Ahmad. 2015. "Wawancara dengan Ahmad Baso Soal Islam Nusantara." Blog post. Accessed November 29, 2018. https://santripedia.wordpress.com/2015/04/27/wawancara-dengan-ahmad-baso-soal-islam-nusantara/.

Berger, Peter L. 2014. *The Many Altars of Modernity: Toward a Paradigm for Religion in a Pluralist Age*. Berlin: De Gruyter.

Bruinessen, Martin van. 2013. *Contemporary Developments in Indonesian Islam: Explaining the "Conservative Turn."* Singapore: ISEAS.

Buehler, Michael. 2016. *The Politics of Shari'a Law: Islamist Activists and the State in Democratizing Indonesia*. Cambridge: Cambridge University Press.

Connolly, William E. 2005. *Pluralism*. Durham, NC: Duke University Press.

Crouch, Melissa. 2009. "Indonesia, Militant Islam and Ahmadiyah: Origins and Implications." *ARC Federation Fellowship Background Paper Series* 4.

Das, Veena. 2006. *Life and Words: Violence and the Descent into the Ordinary.* Berkeley, CA: University of California Press.

Dewi, Sita W. 2018. "Who is Ma'ruf Amin, Jokowi's Running Mate?" *Jakarta Post*, August 9. http://www.thejakartapost.com/news/2018/08/09/who-is-maruf-amin-jokowis-running-mate.html.

Duncan, Christopher R. 2013. *Violence and Vengeance: Religious Conflict and Its Aftermath in Eastern Indonesia.* Ithaca, NY: Cornell University Press.

Eck, Diana L. 2001. *A New Religious America: How a "Christian Country" Has Now Become the World's Most Religiously Diverse Nation.* San Francisco: Harper San Francisco.

Soekarno, Hatta, et. Al. 2006. "Piagam Jakarta: Preamble to Undang-Undang Dasar Republik Indonesia 1945." In *Voices of Islam in Southeast Asia*, edited by Greg Fealy and Virginia Hooker, 109-10. Singapore: ISEAS Publishing.

Fealy, Greg, and Ronit Ricci, eds. 2019. *Contentious Belonging: The Place of Minorities in Indonesia.* Singapore: ISEAS Publishing.

Feener, R. Michael. 2013. *Shari'a and Social Engineering: The Implementation of Islamic Law in Contemporary Aceh, Indonesia.* Oxford: Oxford University Press.

Feith, Herbert. 1962. *The Decline of Constitutional Democracy in Indonesia.* Ithaca, NY: Cornell University Press.

Feith, Herbert, and Lance Castles, eds. 1970. *Indonesian Political Thinking, 1945–1965.* Ithaca, NY: Cornell University Press.

Formichi, Chiara. 2012. *Islam and the Making of the Nation: Kartosuwiryo and Political Islam in Twentieth-Century Indonesia.* Leiden: KITLV Press.

Formichi, Chiara. 2013. "Mustafa Kemal's Abrogation of the Ottoman Caliphate and Its Impact on the Indonesian Nationalist Movement." In *Demystifying the Caliphate: Historical Memory and Contemporary Contexts*, edited by Madawi Al-Rasheed, Carool Kersten and Marat Shterin, 95–116. London: Hurst.

Formichi, Chiara. 2014a. *Religious Pluralism, State and Society in Asia.* London: Routledge.

Formichi, Chiara. 2014b. "Violence, Sectarianism, and the Politics of Religion: Articulations of Anti-Shi'a Discourses in Indonesia." *Indonesia* 98, no. 1: 1–27.

Furnivall, John Sydenham. (1944) 1983. *Netherlands India: A Study of Plural Economy.* New York: AMS Press.

Hasan, Mushirul, and Asim Roy. 2005. *Living Together Separately: Cultural India in History and Politics.* New Delhi: Oxford University Press.

Hefner, Robert W. 2001. *The Politics of Multiculturalism Pluralism and Citizenship in Malaysia, Singapore, and Indonesia.* Honolulu: University of Hawai'i Press.

Hicks, Jacqueline. 2013. "Heresy and Authority: Understanding the Turn Against Ahmadiyah in Indonesia." (January 12). Available at SSRN: https://ssrn.com/abstract=2263855 or http://dx.doi.org/10.2139/ssrn.2263855.

Hoesterey, James Bourk. 2018. "Public Diplomacy and the Global Dissemination of Moderate Islam." In *Routledge Handbook of Contemporary Indonesia*, edited by Robert W. Hefner, 406–16. London: Routledge.

Kersten, Carool. 2015. *Islam in Indonesia: The Contest for Society, Ideas and Values.* Oxford: Oxford University Press.

Nasution, Harun. 1965. "The Islamic State in Indonesia: The Rise of the Ideology, the Movement for Its Creation and the Theory of the MASJUMI." Master's thesis, McGill University.

Peletz, Michael G. 2006. "Transgenderism and Gender Pluralism in Southeast Asia since Early Modern Times." *Current Anthropology* 47, no. 2 (April): 309–40.

Peletz, Michael G. 2008. *Gender Pluralism: Southeast Asia since Early Modern Times.* New York: Routledge.

Steenbrink, Karel. 2015. "Pancasila as an Ambiguous Instrument for Interreligious Harmony and Development in Indonesia, 1945–2015." *Bulletin of the Nanzan Centre for Asia-Pacific Studies* 10. 15–36.

Suryadinata, Leo. 2018. "Pancasila and the Challenge of Political Islam: Past and Present." ISEAS-Yusuf Ishak Institute.

2

ISLAMISM AND THE STRUGGLE FOR INCLUSIVE CITIZENSHIP IN DEMOCRATIC INDONESIA

Robert W. Hefner

In the more than three decades that I have done research in Indonesia, I can remember no period like today marked by so little consensus among researchers on the state of the field with regard to Islam, citizenship, and democracy in Indonesia. Certainly, in the immediate aftermath of the New Order's collapse in 1998–99, there were great theoretical disputes and higher anxieties as to where politics and society were going. After all, in the first three years of the transition, Dayaks were killing Madurese in Kalimantan (Davidson 2008), large portions of Maluku were in flames (Duncan 2014; Varshney et al. 2004), and it had become increasingly apparent that, whatever had happened in May 1998, it had not amounted to a sweeping regime change. The New Order's oligarchs remained largely in place and by 1999 they were learning to live comfortably with the new Indonesian democracy (Hadiz 2016; Winters 2013).

However, the policy and theoretical dissonance that characterizes Indonesian studies today has less to do with the general state of politics than it does something more specific: anxiety over the presence, scale, and future of Islamism in an ostensibly democratic Indonesia and its implications for citizenship in a country that, notwithstanding fifty years of Islamic resurgence, remains deeply if agonistically plural. Evidence of our theoretical disarray abounds, but let me quickly offer a small sampler of the range of opinion. On one hand, the Swiss-born and UK-based political analyst Michael Buehler has referred to the proliferation of shariah-influenced regional by-laws in Indonesia as one of the most significant Islamist advances in modern Indonesian history, a broad beachhead in the "Islamization of politics . . . via *democracy* itself" (Buehler 2016, 4). He underscores the significance of this development by noting that it is "one of the few tangible policy trends evident in a political system defined by clientelist rather than programmatic politics" (Buehler 2014, 159; cf. Buehler 2016). In a similar and no less sobering vein, analysts both in Indonesia and abroad have analyzed the so-called 212 movement's campaign against the Christian Chinese governor of Jakarta, Basuki Tjahaja Purnama ("Ahok"), in late 2016 and early 2017 as evidence of growing Islamist and Salafist influence (see Lohanda, this volume; IPAC 2018; Maarif 2017). The 212 movement took its name from the largest of the anti-Ahok demonstrations held in 2016, on December 2 (hence 2-12). The 212 figure was later adopted as the name for what was intended to become a long-term movement for the creation of political, social, and business networks promoting conservative, Muslim-first understandings of citizenship. Many Indonesian observers saw the movement as evidence of a decisive shift away from the Pancasila ideal of multireligious citizenship toward a differentiated, asymmetrical, and Muslim-supremacist citizenship.

Of course these high-anxiety judgments are not the only viewpoint on Muslim politics and Islamism in today's Indonesia. In a highly important book, Thomas Pepinsky, William Liddle, and Saiful Mujani (2018) draw on their survey of Muslim public opinion to analyze the interplay of Islamization and democratization in Indonesia, twenty years after the country's return to electoral democracy. The authors agree with most Indonesian analysts that there has been a notable uptick in piety in the post-Soeharto, *Reformasi* era. However, in contrast to the majority view, Pepinsky, Liddle, and Mujani discover what they describe as "a null finding" (2018, 3) with regard to piety and politics in Indonesia. To quote the authors, "Across various issue areas—support for democracy or Islamic law, partisan politics, Islamic finance, foreign relations—there is no evidence that the religious orientations of Indonesian Muslims have any systematic relationship with their political preferences or economic behavior . . . If we look across Indonesian Muslims, evidence that more religious Indonesian Muslims think or behave differently than their less religious counterparts simply does not exist" (2018, 3–4).

Although there are many shades of grey between the two, these viewpoints are illustrative of the striking lack of consensus among analysts on the state of the field with regard to politics, plurality, citizenship, and democracy in Indonesia. And it is against this background that I present my remarks in this chapter. I make four basic arguments.

First, part of the confusion with regards to the debate over Islamization and Islamism in Indonesia has to do with the theoretical incoherence of the concept of Islamization and the related notion of the "Islamization of Indonesian politics." The concept of Islamization is theoretically insightful only if made analytically and sociologically precise by highlighting first the heterogeneous and often contradictory normative projects that lie at its heart and second its rival carriers— carriers whose extrareligious interests always influence the forms and meanings of "Islamization" itself (cf. Ricklefs 2012). Rather than Islamization being defined for all times by certain features of *fiqh* or Qur'anic prescription, then, the process is situationally contingent, path-dependent, and agonistically plural (Daniels 2017; Hefner 2016; Peletz 2020).

Second, and notwithstanding Governor Ahok's electoral defeat in April 2017, I argue that, although the Islamist proponents of a Muslim supremacist citizenship have made some progress in recent years, they have still largely failed to secure a hegemonic base in the electoral arena. This electoral impasse stands in striking contrast to Islamist achievements in Turkey, pre-Sisi Egypt, northern Nigeria, and Tunisia. In reflecting on the Islamists' limited electoral success, I find myself in strong agreement with Pepinsky, Liddle, and Mujani's core thesis: the deepening pietization of Muslim society has had a far less decisive impact on electoral politics in Indonesia than is the case in many other Muslim-majority lands. This is one more reason why talk of a sweeping "Islamization of Indonesian politics" is premature and hyperbolic.

Third, notwithstanding my broader agreement with Pepinsky et al., I would take polite exception to these authors on two matters: first, although the "Islamic turn" may not have resulted in a marked differentiation of pious versus casual Muslims in electoral behavior, the Islamic turn has had a pronounced effect on the micro- and meso-politics of the quotidian, not least with regard to Muslim-non-Muslim interactions. The second and related qualification on the null-finding thesis is that, even if the growth in piety has not caused tectonic electoral shifts, it has affected the less formally organized but no less important Indonesian public sphere. In particular, the change has allowed Islamist political entrepreneurs (like those at the heart of the 212 movement's campaign against Governor Ahok) to push ethico-religious identities to the fore. This shift toward a Muslim-first identity politics has in turn provided cultural resources for Islamist minorities determined to frame national political problems as matters requiring enforcement of an Islamist majoritarian ethics. The outcome stands in striking contrast to the "null-finding" pattern seen in national elections.

Fourth and last, one consequence of the relative failure of Indonesia's Islamists in electoral politics but success in identity-politics mobilization has been a narrowing and refocusing of the Islamist project for citizenship and nationhood. The narrowing has been marked by a shift away from mobilizations for the establishment of an "Islamic" state and toward partial coexistence with the ideals of Indonesian nationhood. However, even as most Islamists have moderated their aspirations with regards to the NKRI state (Negara Kesatuan Republik Indonesia,

Unitary National Republic of Indonesia), they have pressed all the more firmly for a differentiated, asymmetrical, and Muslim supremacist citizenship. I argue that this "non-null-effect" contestation over citizenship and public ethics will figure prominently in Indonesian politics for some years to come.

As seen in the Constitutional Court's 2010 ruling affirming the right and obligation of the state to protect the religious sensibilities of the country's Sunni majority (Bagir 2013), this shift to a majoritarian understanding of Islam and state has serious implications for the proponents of a Pancasila-variety of plural-ist citizenship. However here too—in the processes of judicial review recently undertaken by Indonesia's Constitutional Court—there is evidence of "agonistic plurality" (Mouffe 2000), and, as of 2017 (see below), even a measure of pluralist hope.

Islamization's Agonistic Plurality

Let me now turn quickly to each of these points, beginning with the first, on the contingency and agonistic plurality of "Islamization" and "shariah." Since Indonesia's return to electoral democracy in 1998–99, there has been much talk of the deepening "Islamization" of politics, public culture, and subjectiv-ity in this Southeast Asian society (Buehler 2016). Whether in the widespread adoption of the *hijab* among Muslim women (Brenner 2011; Rinaldo 2013; Smith-Hefner 2007), the proliferation of Islamic study groups in urban neigh-borhoods (Howell 2008), the increase in Islamic programming on radio and television (Rakhmani 2016), or the displacement of syncretic village traditions by rituals of a more scripturalist nature (Cederroth 1996; Hefner 1987, 2011; Pranowo 1991), the influence of Islamic traditions in Indonesian society does indeed appear to have deepened dramatically since the early 1990s, and all the more since the dawn of the *Reformasi* ("Reformation") era in 1998–99.

Echoing arguments raised in other Muslim-majority countries (Peletz 2020; Schielke 2015), however, my first point in this chapter is that Islamization is never a unitary process but rather always a heterogeneous and agonistic plu-rality of normative and political projects. Certainly, Islamization projects may show family resemblance across cases by virtue of their claimed identification with values and practices deemed Islamic and shariah-based. However, to bor-row a phrase from poststructuralist scholarship, "the" shariah is in social reality a loosely-tethered, floating signifier, one given diverse and often contradic-tory meanings by different actors and movements. And, notwithstanding our understandable emphasis on a "conservative turn" in post-Soeharto Islam in Indonesia (van Bruinessen 2013a, 2013b; Sebastian et al. 2021), plurality and agonism have marked the various projects of Islamization and "shariatization" (Hasyim 2014) in the post-Soeharto period.

In his *Living Sharia: Law and Practice in Malaysia*, Timothy Daniels (2017) has vividly highlighted the floating meanings of shariah in contemporary Malaysia; the same mercurial effervescence has marked shariah politics and ethics in contemporary Indonesia. In the 1990s and early 2000s, I developed close ties with the prodemocracy and pro–Nurcholish Madjid wing of the Association of Indonesian Muslim Students (Himpunan Mahasiswa Indonesia, HMI) in Jakarta and Yogyakarta. These activists distinguished themselves from their conservative, "MPO"(Majelis Penyelamat Organisasi, Protector Committee of the Organization) rivals by referring to themselves as "HMI-DIPO" ("Dipo" referring to Jalan Diponegoro in Jakarta on which their main office was located). The HMI-DIPO activists all agreed that shariah is a vital and necessary feature of Islamic ethics and a Muslim way of life. However, in contrast to the MPO, they also emphasized that the ideals of citizen equality and freedom to which they as democratic activists aspired were entirely consistent with the "higher aims [*maqasid*] of the shariah." We hear much the same message among democracy-minded Muslim ethicists in the West, with reference to the *maqasid al-shariah* (see Auda 2008; Hefner 2016; Ramadan 2009). During these same two decades, however, the Salafi and Muslim-Brotherhood inspired activists whom I got to know at the Dewan Dakwah Islamiyah Indonesia (Indonesian Council of Islamic Propagation, DDII) headquarters on Jl. Kramat Raya in Jakarta Pusat were no less convinced that the positive-law, state-based, and overwhelmingly coercive variety of the shariah to which they subscribed was the only true variety of shariah, and the only proper compass for Indonesia's Islamization (cf. Lindsey 2012; Machmudi 2006).

Debates over the proper forms and meanings of shariah, then, have long been a feature of Muslim politics in Indonesia, and they have only increased in the *Reformasi* era. In the early *Reformasi* period, representatives in the People's Consultative Assembly (MPR) debated legislation that would require the state to enforce a state codified variety of Islamic law for all Muslim citizens, consistent with the ideals of the so-called Jakarta charter. Supporters of the proposed constitutional amendment like Ismail Yusanto of the now-banned transnational Islamist movement Hizbut Tahrir Indonesia (Party of Liberation, HTI) (Ahnaf 2011, 2017; Osman 2018) explained to me that "shariah is the solution" to Indonesia's ills and that its rules and meanings are clear, consistent, and irrefutable because unitary in their meaning (Elson 2013; Salim 2008). Here again, however, there was disagreement. Most scholars of shariah and *fiqh* in Nahdlatul Ulama, Muhammadiyah, and the State Islamic University system (UIN/IAIN) made clear that they did not share this unitarian understanding of shariah, particularly on the question of whether the shariah provides a fixed and finished blueprint for the form of the state or the status of religious minorities and citizenship.

At this early moment in the post-*Reformasi* period, it was clear that, although HTI provided new energy for the state-shariah campaign, the amendment's primary base of support was among old and rather tired political vehicles from the late New Order period, particularly the Dewan Dakwah Islamiyah Indonesia, the Crescent and Stars Party (PBB, Partai Bulan Bintang), and the United Development Party (PPP, Partai Persatuan Perbangunan), as well as an activist and non-liberal wing of the once influential ICMI (Ikatan Cendekiawan Muslimin Indonesia, Association of Indonesian Muslim Intellectuals; see Hefner 2000; Porter 2002). The dynamics of the shariah amendment mobilization reflected the positivist-minded approach to shariah ethics promoted by this rather established but tiredly ineffectual New Order Islamism, one which showed striking similarities with, but considerably less effectiveness than, the alliance of educators and bureaucrats that promoted shariatization in Aceh in these same years (Feener 2013).

At this early point in Indonesia's democratic transition, then, it was easy for the majority of Indonesia's observant Muslim leadership to take exception to unitary understandings of Islamization and shariah. Even if they had some sympathy for such efforts, most leaders of Muslim mass organizations were not convinced that they should position such claims at the top of their menu of political priorities. This latter point about priorities, I might add, figures prominently among the survey findings of Pepinsky, Liddle, and Mujani, and it is another important corrective to hyperbolic talk of the "Islamization of politics" in Indonesia. In a deeply important finding, Pepinsky and his coauthors report that, according to their survey data, the implementation of shariah is a top three priority for only 2.3 percent of their Muslim respondents. This figure compares poorly with the 61.7 percent who would prioritize increases in popular welfare, the 38.8 percent who foreground improving primary education, or the 37.1 percent who see reduction in unemployment as front-burner issues (Pepinsky et al. 2018, 92).

A rather half-hearted prioritization of statist shariah implementation was, in fact, a key feature of shariah politics in the early *Reformasi* period. This fact helps us to understand just why, in the period of 2000–2001, the National Assembly easily rebuffed Islamist efforts to change the constitution so as to require the state to implement a state-codified variety of Islamic law for all Muslim citizens. However, the effort failed not just because most pious individuals did not regard it as an urgent priority but also as a result of strong opposition from the leadership of Indonesia's two largest Muslim social welfare associations, the Muhammadiyah and Nahdlatul Ulama. In interviews I conducted during and after the amendment campaign, I heard repeatedly that opposition to the shariah amendment reflected the conviction among leaders in these organizations that the Pancasila is compatible with Islam and with a proper understanding of shariah (Elson 2013; Salim 2008). The opposition also reflected the fact that many if not all Muhammadiyah and NU scholars thought the amendment's proponents had a poor understanding of the shariah's "higher" aims (*maqasid*) and priorities on matters of governance and citizenship (Hefner 2016).

There is a broader theoretical lesson in these Indonesian realities concerning how we should understand such robustly polysemic concepts as "shariah" and "Islam." The contingency and polysemy of Islam—and, especially, Islamic legal traditions (see Abou El Fadl 2014; Daniels 2017; Lindsey 2012)—originate in the fact that the knowledge and habitus they express are not changeless or uniform but mediated through an array of social authorities, popular ethical imaginaries, and media of preservation and propagation. To borrow from Fredrik Barth's (1993, 177–236; 2002, 3) anthropology of knowledge, we can observe that not just Islam but all traditions of knowledge depend for their production and reproduction on an interplay of three social realities: first, "a corpus of substantive assertions and ideas about aspects of the world" (or what we might otherwise call an ontology); second, an array of media through which those assertions are "instantiated and communicated"; and, third, "a series of instituted social relations," which is to say authoritative organizations through which the tradition of knowledge can be "distributed, communicated, employed, and transmitted" (Barth 2002, 3). I would add to his triad a fourth social reality, one less exhaustively encompassed in the immediacy of a tradition's manifestation: namely, that for a tradition to remain resonant over time, the social powers and institutional assemblages with which it is associated must inspire and/or discipline actors so as to ensure a continuing identification with its forms of knowledge, the way of life in which they are embedded, and the distinctive ethical interests and concerns to which they give rise (Hefner 1985, 2018).

Contingencies of this sort help to explain why actors in Indonesia can have such different understandings of and commitments to shariah. As Michael Peletz has so vividly demonstrated in a recent study from Malaysia, the meanings of shariah, and the sociopolitical uses to which it is put depend not on a timeless text but on this discursive tradition's ever-evolving entanglement with identities, powers, and social organizations situated around and beyond the tradition of knowledge itself (Peletz 2020). In a brilliant study, the late Shahab Ahmed referred to this generative interaction within Islamic traditions in general and shariah in particular as the interplay of text, context, and pretext, where the pretext in particular refers to the habituated dispositions through which actors perceive, engage, and amend a tradition (Ahmed 2015).

In sum, to observe that Islamization is socially and epistemologically contingent is to say that its forms and meanings depend not on unchanging scriptural truths but on the ways in which the interaction between state, Muslim society, and Islamic traditions of knowledge succeed in stabilizing and focalizing an enduring commitment to a particular and hegemonic understanding and practice of Islam and an associated (and at times contradictory) array of shariatization projects (see Ahmed 2015; Hefner 2016). These and other facts should make us wary of attributing too unitary a meaning to the heterogeneous array of processes often grouped under the label "Islamization." When we do otherwise, we lose sight of what is one of the central foci of moral and intellectual contention in the late-modern Muslim world (An-Na'im 2008; Daniels 2017; Ramadan 2009). Here in Indonesia, "Islamization" in the minds of many mainstream Muslims is associated not with the formation of an Islamic state or the imposition of a differentiated citizenship pitting Muslims against non-Muslim *dhimmis* ("protected minorities" granted second-class standing on condition that they acknowledge Muslim suzerainty; see Emon 2012) but rather with the establishment of the rule of law, democracy (albeit usually of a largely non-liberal variety), and an inclusively multireligious citizenship, like that affirmed under the terms of the Pancasila.

All this duly acknowledged, the early *Reformasi* era's favoring of a non-Islamist understanding of shariah and public ethics also spurred Islamists to search for new strategies for pressing their campaign. This search would eventually bring a new shariah politics to the fore (cf. Buehler 2016) as well as a shift in the balance of power between the proponents of rival Islamization projects in districts across Indonesia.

Electoral and Legislative Vicissitudes

This brings me to my second and simplest point. It concerns the well-known fact, nicely highlighted by Pepinsky, Liddle, and Mujani, that the proponents of Islamism in Indonesia have consistently failed to secure electoral support for their more ideological programs, despite signs of growing piety and observance in Indonesian Muslim society. In the five national elections held since 1999, Islamist parties have never managed to secure any more than 20 percent of the vote, and depending on how one defines Islamist parties, they have consistently held less than 25 percent of the seats in the National Assembly. No less significant, Islamist parties have been able to maintain even that share of the vote only because, as with the Prosperous Justice Party (Partai Keadilan Sejahtera, PKS), they have downplayed any effort to establish an Islamic state or make shariah the law of the land in favor of promises of clean government and economic empowerment.

In their 2018 book, Pepinsky, Liddle, and Mujani rightly refer to the Islamist failure to gain greater electoral traction as one of the more glaring examples of the ways in which the growing piety seen among Indonesian Muslims has had a "null-effect" on political and economic life. I applaud what I believe are the two core theoretical contributions of Pepinsky, Liddle, and Mujani's research. The first is to dispel the myth that pietization always brings in its wake a heightened commitment to a unitary and narrowly Islamist variety of politics. Their second and no less significant contribution is their demonstration that in order to understand its political effects, "piety must be understood alongside the complex, multifaceted transformations that are concurrently underway in Muslim societies" (2018, 161). The latter of these ambitions, I would add, is consistent with what has become a garden variety theme in the contemporary sociology and anthropology of Islam in all Muslim societies: namely, that, as seen in their everyday ethics and social behavior, Muslims are not just "Muslim" in some sort of theologically invariant sense. Like those of people everywhere, the hopes and aspirations of Muslims—including those shaping their understanding of shariah—reflect an engagement with diverse social lifeways and the varied and even contradictory ethical currents through which they give the latter a more specific meaning (Hefner 2016; Schielke 2015; Simon 2014).

Shortcomings and Breakthroughs

This brings me to my third point, one which involves a gentle dissent from or qualification on the "null-finding" thesis, not least with regards to the issue of plurality and pluralism with which the chapters in this book are concerned. I have two concerns. First, to speak of a null-finding in politics and economics only makes sense if our understanding of the "political" is premised on a decidedly state-centric definition of politics—one that understands politics as operative only in relation to the formal institutions of state rather than as also involving processes of influence, hegemonization, and subject-formation pervasive across all domains of social life. For two generations now, feminist scholars have reminded us that gender relations are every bit as much a part of the political in this latter, socially diffuse sense as are national elections. And as anyone familiar with the research of Nelly van Doorn-Harder (2006), Kathryn Robinson (2009), Nancy Smith-Hefner (2019), or Syafiq Hasyim (2011), among many others, knows, gender relations in Muslim Indonesia have undergone tectonic shifts under the influence of new Islamic ideals since the 1980s-90s. Indeed, as Nancy Smith-Hefner (2019) has argued in a recent book, the "Islamization" of gender roles and intimacies in Muslim Indonesia over the past generation has arguably been far deeper and more pervasive in its social impact than have the changes associated with party politics. And we risk overlooking this fact when we speak indiscriminately of the "Islamization of Indonesian politics" or, conversely, null-findings with regard to pietization's sociopolitical impact.

The second qualification I would recommend with regard to Pepinsky, Liddle, and Mujani's otherwise compelling argument is that, in identifying public opinion surveys with what the authors believe is the essence of democracy, the account fails to highlight the social dynamics and impact of coalitions based in "civil-society" that emerged in the *Reformasi* era. This point requires a brief digression. Early on in their crisply argued book, Pepinsky, Liddle, and Mujani comment that "choices of mass publics constitute the essence of democratic politics" (2018, 1), a point they reiterate 158 pages later when they state that "our analysis rests on the basic assumption that the actions and choices of mass publics constitute the core of democratic politics" (2018, 159). In some principled sense these statements strike me as correct and even ethically laudable. However, as has become a commonplace theme in the literature on the "quality of democracy" and the "decline of democracy" in recent years (Hansen 1999; Diamond and Morlino 2005), and as was a theme four generations earlier in the writings of Max Weber and Joseph Schumpeter, real and existing democracy is never just about the actions and choices of mass publics. Democratic politics is as much about the intrigues and mobilizations of determined minorities—groups committed to the pursuit of a particular aim and willing to expend great economic and political capital for its realization, often in defiance of public opinion or behavior. When blocked from progress in the electoral domain, determined minorities often refocus their energies on less state-centric programs of identity politics, using whatever social media and nonlegislative instruments they have on hand. In today's Muslim-majority countries, such strategies might at first appear "post-Islamist" in Asef Bayat's (2013) sense of the term. However, as with the Muslim Brotherhood in pre-Sisi Egypt, such "civil-society" movements may well regard the turn to the public sphere as a temporizing strategy and one that aims eventually to scale the commanding heights of political society once more (see Brownlee, Masoud, and Reynolds 2015).

And it is this latter fact, I fear, that risks being overlooked in public opinion analyses and otherwise helpful statements about "null-findings" with regard to the impact of different varieties of piety on Indonesian politics and society today. However limited their progress in national elections, Islamist political entrepreneurs have exploited the new piety to give a more Muslim-majoritarian hue to Indonesia's public sphere, a shift that has in turn had serious political and legal consequences (cf. Fealy 2016; Lindsey and Pausacker 2016; Mietzner, Muhtadi, and Halida 2018).

To state my point differently, electoral outcomes and the public sphere dimensions of democracy don't always neatly align or converge, and they haven't here in post-Soeharto Indonesia. In the late 1990s, as a new and more politically assertive Muslim middle class was emerging, this class—forged in and still imbued with the values and organizational habits of the New Order (cf. Feener 2013, 186–88)— was so deeply factionalized along ideological and patronage lines as to impede the emergence of any broad-based Islamist electoral movement akin to that of the Muslim Brotherhood in Egypt or the AK Party in Turkey (Hefner 2000). Many moderately conservative but otherwise democratic-minded Muslims, including most of my Muslim friends active in the 1990s in ICMI and in the Muslim wing of the former ruling party, Golkar (Partai Golongan Karya), had expected such a united Muslim front to emerge and prevail in the first rounds of elections in the *Reformasi* era. The fact that it did not was not so much the product of a null effect but the result of the fractionalization of the Muslim electorate and the resulting failure of Islamists of any stripe "to win government or dominate the political opposition in the eras of both authoritarianism and democracy" (Hadiz 2016, 13). But fragmentation and setbacks in the electoral arena ultimately spurred a shift in Islamist strategies, and several rather more effective advances in politics and the public sphere.

From Islamic State to Differentiated Citizenship

This brings me to this chapter's fourth and final point. It is that as a consequence of the Islamists' inability to coalesce and prevail in the electoral arena we have witnessed a change in normativities and tactics: away from earlier schemes to establish a so-called Islamic state and toward coexistence with the ideals of the nation-state and a more or less capitalist economy. However, even as they have made these accommodations, Indonesia's post–New Order Islamists have pressed for the realization of a differentiated and asymmetrical rather than equal citizenship. In this sense, I might note, theirs is not a "post-Islamism" in Asef Bayat's sense of the term but merely a programmatically narrowed Islamism.

Evidence abounds of the course and consequences of this change of strategy, but let me draw on my own research to illustrate some of its dynamics. In the early post-Soeharto era, one of the more prominent movements seeking to rally a broad coalition of Muslims against democracy and for a shariah-based Islamic rather than Pancasila state was the Council of Indonesian Mujahidin (Majelis Mujahidin Indonesia; MMI). The MMI was founded in Yogyakarta in August 2000 by a core group of activists that included as spiritual leader Abu Bakar Ba'asyir of Jemaah Islamiyah fame and Irfan Awwas as executive director (Hasan 2006; ICG 2003). Although Ba'asyir was the undisputed spiritual leader (*amir*) of the organization, Awwas and others in the Yogyakarta-based MMI executive office ran day-to-day operations, including the movement's publishing wing. Awwas and the MMI executive leadership broke with Ba'asyir in 2008 over a host of issues including whether the MMI was to remain in full-blown opposition to the Indonesian state or if they should try to work within the existing state system on the model of the All-Malaysia Islamic Party (Parti Islam Se-Malaysia; PAS; see Liow 2009) in Malaysia. As Awwas explained in interviews with me in 2008 and 2009, he and the mainstream MMI were in favor of the latter approach (although they never reached a consensus as to whether they should support candidates in national elections), while Ba'asyir advocated a turn to a full blown antisystem struggle. The latter preference underlay Ba'asyir's decision in 2015 to swear a *bayat* (oath of allegiance) to the Islamic State in Iraq and Syria. As Awwas explained in a long conversation with me in August 2015, he and the MMI were bitterly opposed to ISIS, aligning themselves instead with the al-Nusra and other al-Qa'ida-linked organizations in Syria and the Middle East.

From 2001 through 2015, I conducted annual interviews in Yogyakarta with Awwas and his associates in an effort to trace the MMI's ideological evolution and its leaders' understandings of Islamization and Islamic law. The MMI's founding ambition was to create a broad coalition of organizations opposed to democracy and committed to a comprehensive implementation of shariah law across Indonesia. In our closed-circle discussions at their headquarters in Yogyakarta, Awwas and his colleagues stated repeatedly that, in their view, the shariah was not something that should or could be adjusted in light of national culture or citizenship. Awwas spoke disparagingly of the idea popular in some national-minded legal circles that Indonesia might be able to develop its own national school of Islamic law (*madhhab*; see Feener 2007; Hooker 2003). He was even more skeptical of modernizing reformists who sought not a literal application of an unreformed shariah but rather a variety premised on the "higher aims of the law" (*maqasid al-shariah*; Hefner 2016; Kamali 2008). In much the same spirit, Awwas made clear that Indonesia's Pancasila citizenship would have to be replaced by *dhimmihood* institutions, and non-Muslims were to be tolerated only if they acknowledged Muslim rule and accepted limits on their citizen rights, including not being allowed to serve in the military or assume positions of leadership over Muslims.

Over the course of these same years, I carried out some three hundred interviews with Muslim activists—ranging from vigilante-based Islamists to Muslim democrats—in Jakarta, Yogyakarta, Aceh, West Java, and South Sulawesi. A central question in my interviews had to do with the compatibility of shariah law with the ideals and practices of Indonesian nationalism and citizenship (Hefner 2016). One of the more striking findings to emerge from these discussions is that, in the years between the MMI's founding in 2000 and its decline in 2004–5, the movement's "anti-national" understanding of Islamic law caused growing unease among activists earlier aligned with the MMI coalition. Most interviewees commented that at first they had agreed with the MMI's one-size-fits-all view of Islamic law and Islamization. By 2005–6, however—and indeed at the very peak of Indonesian Islam's "conservative turn"—the tide of opinion in mainline Islamist circles had turned. Most shariah activists now took exception to the MMI's claim that the implementation of Islamic law required that Indonesia's constitution and nation-state framework be abolished. Even among Islamist conservatives in the ranks of the hardline militia, the Islamic Defenders Front (FPI; see Bamualim 2011; Pausacker 2013; Wilson 2006, 2008), interviewees who had once allied with the MMI were by 2005 telling me that they did not share the latter's opposition to Indonesian nationhood and, in particular, the long-central notion of a unitary Indonesian state (NKRI, Negara Kesatuan Republik Indonesia). Indeed, representatives of the FPI and the Makassar-based, neo-Salafi movement Wahdah Islamiyah ("Islamic Unity") with whom I conducted interviews in August 2006 and in 2010 were among the most vocal in taking exception to the MMI position on nationhood and cooperation with state officials.

Wahdah Islamiyah is a neo-Salafi movement founded in Makassar in the early 2000s that now has 120 branches across Indonesia (IPAC 2018). In a recent article, Chris Chaplin has observed that over the past several years the movement's leadership has begun to cooperate with the national police and other government agencies in various state programs. As a result of these interactions, those same leaders have "become adept at combining religious and national terminology in order to 'locate' themselves within nationally oriented narratives of Islamic revival" (Chaplin 2018, 209; cf. IPAC 2018). However, the accommodation is a still highly selective one, not least on two critical points: on the nature of the ethical values that should predominate in the public sphere, and on the question of citizen recognition, particularly with regard to whether non-Muslim citizens should be seen as equal with their Muslim compatriots or the bearers of a second-tier "differentiated citizenship." Chaplin rightly notes that Wahdah Islamiyah activists seek "to alter the membership boundaries of Indonesian citizenship so as to preference Muslims at the expense of non-Muslims" (ibid.).

Chaplin's insights are consistent with changes taking place not just in Wahdah Islamiyah but also in a broad range of Indonesian Islamist groups dedicated to a majoritarian and conservative Islamization of the public sphere and national identity. Indeed, the MMI's foundering over questions of nation and citizenship shows that the changes Chaplin reports in Wahdah Islamiyah actually began years earlier in many other Islamist organizations and involved a far larger number of networks and organizations than Wahdah Islamiyah alone. With the notable exception of transnational Islamist groups like Hizbut Tahrir Indonesia (Ahnaf 2011; Osman 2018), the shift away from antinational shariah projects and toward a new accommodation with nationhood and citizenship has been one of the most striking trends in Islamist circles since the peak period of the conservative turn from 2005–10. But equally striking is the fact that this shift retains and even deepens a commitment to a Muslim-supremacist citizenship at odds with mainstream understandings of Pancasila nationalism.

It is this tactical shift away from antisystem radicalism to Muslim-first nationalism that Vedi Hadiz has also sought to portray in his brilliant analyses of the rise of right-wing Islamist populism in post-Soeharto Indonesia. In his 2016 book and (even more clearly) in a 2018 article, Hadiz observes that "important strands of Islamic populism in Indonesia like . . . in . . . MENA [Middle East and North Africa] have now relegated the project of establishing a state based on Islamic law to the background" (Hadiz 2018, 566). He then goes on to make a point consistent with that which I am making here, namely that even as the majority of Islamists have adopted this new tack, right-wing populist Islamists have "developed increasingly anti-pluralist and illiberal characteristics," such as those "seen most dramatically in the mass mobilizations . . . against . . . 'Ahok'" (ibid.).

I think Hadiz's argument is entirely on mark. It also reminds us that "post-Islamism" here in Indonesia is often a temporizing strategy rather than an end-game scenario and it can have non-null finding effects even when Islamists don't make much headway in elections. And the strategy becomes more state-focused and "political" in Pepinsky and his coauthors' etatist sense when actors with oligarchic resources discover that it is in their interest to lend their support to Islamist campaigns.

The one issue that I would gently qualify in Hadiz's analysis has to do with his argument that the highlighting of religious symbolism and norms is essentially driven by the logic of political mobilization alone. Hadiz writes that "rather than just the durable elements of a traditional 'Islamism'" the turn to conservative religious themes "can be viewed as part of the intricate mechanisms by which the new Islamic populism mobilises a kind of identity politics as among an increasingly diverse *ummah* in order to forge social alliances that are, in effect, multi-class in nature for the purposes of contesting power and resources" (Hadiz 2016, 5–6). Certainly Hadiz is right to highlight the instrumentalization of conservative ethical issues and their benefits for transclass mobilization. However, one would want to immediately add that Islamic populism is, in Hadiz's words, "anti-liberal and anti-pluralist on social matters" (Hadiz 2018, 566), not just because such symbols are effective rallying cries for an identity politics but also because for the better part of fifty years the conservative wing of the Islamist movement has made them a central ingredient in the brand of majoritarian Islamization of which they have been the main proponents, typically against the Muslim supporters of a pluralist and inclusive practice of Pancasila citizenship. In this sense, Hadiz's claim that the new Islamic populism is best explained in terms of "a number of key themes *external* to that of the doctrines of the Islamic religion itself" (2016, 6) is unnecessarily binary: doctrinal themes internal to Islamic discourses do indeed figure in antiliberal Islamist mobilizations. There is thus no need to do as Hadiz recommends and "direct scholarly attention away from a focus on interpretations of Islamic doctrine in shaping Islamic politics or the effects of varieties of religious traditions on the behavior of social actors" (Hadiz 2016, 6). For more than two generations, scholars of political sociology and practice theory (Barth 1993; Daniels 2017; Giddens 1984; Hefner 1985) have rightly emphasized that the normative and epistemological can be structurally powerful where their cultural media are drawn into and fortify contests for political-economic hegemony.

Democracy and Uncivil Majoritarianism

What can we conclude from the Indonesian example and the seeming inability of Islamists to prevail in national politics while otherwise pressing forward in the public sphere and everyday living? For human rights activists like Andreas Harsono (2012), the Indonesian bureau chief for Human Rights Watch, the uptick in intimidation and violence of Ahmadis, Shi'a, Christian evangelicals, and others in contemporary Indonesia offers decisive proof that democracy in Indonesia is not really democracy at all—and surely *not* proof of the compatibility of Islam and democracy (cf. Human Rights Watch 2013; see Kikue Hamayotsu in this volume). Harsono is a friend whom I have known well since his prodemocracy activism in the 1990s. But I would politely dissent from his conclusion. I would suggest that much if not all of the institutional edifice we associate with modern democracy, at least in Schumpeter's procedural sense, has been significantly consolidated here in Indonesia. That infrastructure includes free elections, a free and sometimes outspoken press, labor unions, and freedom of assembly. It most certainly does not include the diminution of economic oligarchy or the establishment of a free and effective judiciary—two of the most serious shortcomings in the broader edifice of Indonesian democracy (Hadiz 2016; Winters 2013). But by most formal measures, including those of such international agencies as Freedom House (2020), Indonesia has a significant number of the ingredients we associate with modern democracy.

All this said, for many democratic theorists, and for scholars and activists of pluralist and egalitarian disposition, the uptick in discrimination and violence against religious minorities is a serious stain on Indonesia's post-Soeharto achievements. As Eve Warburton and Edward Aspinall have observed, "although public support for democracy as an abstract concept remains high, strong support does not extend to the institutions and values that underpin a liberal democratic order" (Warburton and Aspinall 2019, 257). This conclusion strikes me as correct and politically important. Placed in an even broader theoretical context, I would also argue that these antiplural developments are not so much evidence of flows against the currents of electoral democracy as they are an all-too-common example of how an illiberal majoritarianism can seep into citizenship contests in democratic settings (see also Jones in this volume). The latter is commonplace, not just in Indonesia but also in other democratic systems, including the United States of America under Donald Trump (Gorski 2017; cf. Mouffe 2005).

How are we to understand this? The idea and practice of a citizenship undifferentiated by religion, race, ethnicity, and gender is today almost universally identified by centrist, liberal, and left-leaning thinkers as part of the "package deal" required for a substantively effective democracy (Hall 1995; Hefner 1998). It is just such a package deal that Larry Diamond had in mind in his 1999 book when he argued that the consolidation of democracy in any society depends on not just a formal separation of powers and free elections but also the "internalization and habituation of democratic norms" with regards to an equal and inclusive citizenship (Diamond 1999, 73). I share and cherish those ideals. But I have never shared the empirical confidence that the operation of electoral democracy itself always or even typically generates such a package deal of inclusive ("liberal") citizenship. History provides many examples of electoral mobilizations that bring about a culture and practice of citizenship that is starkly majoritarian rather than inclusive and undifferentiated. Whether with the rise of right-wing Hindutva nationalism in India (Hansen 1999; Chatterji, Hansen, and Jaffrelot 2019), the Islamo-phobic and racist Ma Ba Tha movement in Myanmar (ICG 2017), or the explosion of anti-Muslim and anti-Semitic rage across Western Europe and the United States today (Beaman 2016; Gorski 2017; Whitehead, Perry, and Baker 2018), electoral competition often fuels populist and majoritarian appeals for a citizenship that is differentiated and hierarchized with regard to religion, race, ethnicity, and gender. Such majoritarian campaigns often begin in the public sphere rather than in democracy's formal institutions. But where they take deep root they inevitably feed back into elections and formal democratic processes.

As the anthropologist Thomas Blom Hansen has argued, in India since the early 1990s the back-and-forth of electoral competition spawned heightened civic participation and a proliferation of religion-based "civil society" organizations. However, the latter organizations were not inclined to cultivate Robert

Putnam's "bridging" habits-of-the-heart (Putnam 1994, 2001). Most were instead deployed to promote a Hindu-supremacist and Islamophobic citizenship (see Chatterji, Hansen, and Jaffrelot 2019). Tamir Moustafa's 2018 book, *Constituting Religion: Islam, Liberal Rights, and the Malaysian State*, details a less draconian but no less differentiating history of legislation and citizenship in Malaysia whereby Malays have laid claim to an ethnoreligiously differentiated citizenship, one that leaves Malaysia's large Chinese and Hindu minorities in a second class status (see too Kloos and Berenschot 2017). The paradox of democracy in modern times is thus not that it occasionally but rather that it regularly strengthens an "uncivil" majoritarianism in "civil" society, undercutting the package deal of democracy and inclusive citizenship Larry Diamond and others have described. Something similar, I would suggest, is being attempted by the Islamist flank of Muslim politics here in Indonesia, most recently under the auspices of the 212 movement that led the campaign against Governor Ahok.

Whither Muslim Politics in Indonesia?

I conclude this chapter on the politics of plurality in Indonesia with two highly conditional prognoses. The first is that, after an initial period of success, the 212 movement's campaign for a differentiated citizenship appears to be in some disarray, much as the movement for shariah implementation experienced after 2005. The drive for a religiously differentiated citizenship is being bitterly contested by Muslims in the Pancasila-pluralist wings of mainstream organizations like the Muhammadiyah and, even more strikingly, Nahdlatul Ulama (NU). NU and its Banser security force played a central role in the campaign—not always civil democratic in its tactics—to harass and ultimately ban the HTI in 2017 (Ahnaf 2017). For many of the NU activists I know, this campaign was informed by the conviction that the HTI was the one Islamist group vulnerable to challenge because of its vocal opposition to the principles of Indonesian nationalism. But there are other initiatives underway to slow or reverse the drive for a more vigorously differentiated citizenship, some even in unexpected locales like the Ministry of Religious Affairs and local branches of the Indonesian Council of Ulama.

But my second and last observation is equally important, and has to do with the lessons we might conclude from two decisions of Indonesia's Constitutional Court. The first decision was the court's 2010 ruling upholding Indonesia's blasphemy law and, with it, an affirmation of the right of the state to enforce Islamic orthodoxy as defined by the Indonesian Council of Ulama (MUI) and its associated religious organizations. The Court's 8 to 1 decision was the clearest judicial affirmation of an Islamist majoritarian illiberalism seen in the entire *Reformasi* period (Lindsey and Butt 2016). First issued as a presidential declaration in 1965, the blasphemy law (more accurately described as a law on religious "defamation") has long been invoked to justify discriminatory measures against non-conformist Muslims and others seen as deviating from state-sanctioned varieties of religion, including practitioners of *kepercayaan*-spiritualities and indigenous religions (*agama leluhur*) like the Marapu of Sumba (Maarif 2017). The court ruling in 2010 gave a green light to the policy begun during the presidency of Susilo Bambang Yudhoyono of the police and judicial system taking MUI opinions as grounds for legal prosecution in matters of religion (Assyaukanie 2009; Ichwan 2013; Sirry 2013). The MUI is an unelected, semigovernmental religious body and, as I hinted above, there are clear indications that efforts have been quietly underway during the Jokowi administration (2014 to today) to adjust the MUI's internal composition (Hasyim 2014; Olle 2009). Nonetheless, inasmuch as the police and the judiciary continue to defer to MUI judgments as grounds for prosecution of individuals and groups identified as "deviant" (*sesat*), politics in Indonesia violates what the late Al Stepan (2011) rightly emphasizes is one of the key prerequisites of modern democracy: not secularism, but the "twin tolerations" that prohibit religious authorities from exercising unilateral power over legislation and political affairs.

The fact that the Constitutional Court approved such arrangements is the single clearest sign that, notwithstanding what might appear to be a null-effect in electoral politics, other developments in the *Reformasi* era have favored a majoritarian drift toward differentiated citizenship. Even in such hallowed chambers as the Constitutional Court, however, there is evidence of ethical ambivalence and agonistic plurality—and perhaps even hopeful hints of pluralist progress. On November 7, 2017, the Constitutional Court issued a ruling (Putusan MK 97/ PUU/XIV/2016) in which it sided with petitioners from indigenous religious and *kepercayaan*-faiths and ruled that government policies preventing these groups from listing their faith as *kepercayaan* on their population identification cards as well as other documents related to marriage, birth, death, and religious classes in schools were unconstitutional (see Aragon in this volume). Prior to 2006, state regulations on religious identification were used to pressure individuals not affiliated with one of Indonesia's six state-recognized religions to choose a religion if and when they wanted access to some state-dependent resource, such as national education, wedding certification, or burial in a local cemetery.

As I myself witnessed in visits to *adat* villages and at the first International Congress on Marapu Religion in Tambolaka, West Sumba, in late June 2019, the impact of the Constitutional Court ruling has been nothing less than electrifying. It has stimulated a groundswell of hope in the *kepercayaan* and indigenous religious communities and initiated an organizational surge unthinkable several years earlier. No less astonishing, and as individuals long involved with providing social and legal support to Indonesia's indigenous religious communities have testified (Maarif et al. 2019), state officials in the Ministries of Internal Affairs, Education and Culture, and Religious Affairs have responded to earlier regulations and the 2017 court ruling by moving forward unhesitatingly with a series of implementation guidelines. These include the issuing of new national identity cards, marriage certificates, and teacher-training curricula for *kepercayaan* adherents across Indonesia. In late June and early July 2019, I had meetings in Java and Sumba with individuals from *kepercayaan* and indigenous religious communities from North Sumatra, West Java, Central Java, East Java, Sumba, and South Sulawesi. All without exception insisted that the impact of the court decision on their own communities has been positive and far-reaching (see Maarif et al. 2019). One must not read too far into these developments; powerful antipluralist currents remain at work in Indonesia as well. But one fact that has stood out in my interviews has been the large number of Muslim officials in state ministries—including, again, the Ministries of Religious Affairs and Education and Culture—who have lent their support to these efforts, on the grounds that the recognition of such minority religious communities is legally and morally incumbent.

Along with the outcome of the April 2019 elections, these latter developments suggest that the supporters of a revitalized variety of Pancasila citizenship have faced, and continue to face, serious challenge from their Islamist rivals. But they have by no means been defeated. The example also suggests that recent characterizations of Indonesian politics as a "patronage democracy" in which citizenship is the product of no more than informal negotiations between local politicians and vote-peddling brokers risk analytic hyperbole if they neglect to mention that in at least a few domains more is in contention with regard to citizenship and recognition than patronage peddling. In particular, coalitions linking the NGO advocates of inclusive citizenship to minority religious communities are alive and well (Maarif et al. 2019), and the Constitutional Court rulings indicate that at times—and especially where there is no vested oligarchic power pursuing an opposing political interest—the alliance can make a difference in the ideals and practice of citizenship in Indonesia.

None of this is to say that the future of Islam, democracy, and citizenship in Indonesia is clear. The struggle to define the proper form and practice of citizenship will be at the heart of Indonesian politics and society for many years to come. But the proponents of an inclusive variety of Pancasila citizenship have shown greater resilience than many Indonesian observers thought possible several years back. To the surprise of those inclined to see Indonesian politics as little more than patron-clientelism, some of these recent efforts appear to have won the conditional backing of important actors in the country's high courts and minis-tries. Some of these officials have acted as they have not for reasons of clientelism, but out of sympathy for, and love of, a remarkable Indonesian tradition of nation-alism and inclusive citizenship.

References

Abou El Fadl, Khaled. 2014. *Reasoning with God: Reclaiming Shari'ah in the Modern Age*. Lanham: Rowman and Littlefield.

Ahmed, Shahab. 2015. *What is Islam? The Importance of Being Islamic*. Princeton, NJ: Princeton University Press.

Ahnaf, Mohammad Iqbal. 2011. "From Revolution to 'Refolution': A Study of Hizb al-Tahrir, Its Changes and Trajectories in the Democratic Context of Indonesia (2000–2009)." PhD diss., Victoria University of Wellington.

Ahnaf, Mohammad Iqbal. 2017. "Where Does Hizbut Tahrir Go from Here." *New Mandala*, July 28. http://www.newmandala.org/hizbut-tahrir-indonesia-go/.

An-Na'im, Abdullahi Ahmed. 2008. *Islam and the Secular State*. Cambridge, MA: Harvard University Press.

Assyaukanie, Luthfi. 2009. "Fatwa and Violence in Indonesia." *Journal of Religion and Society* 11, no. 2: 1–21.

Auda, Jasser. 2008. *Maqasid al-Shariah as Philosophy of Islamic Law: A Systems Approach*. Herndon: International Institute of Islamic Thought.

Bagir, Zainal Abidin. 2013. "Defamation of Religion in Post-Reformasi Indonesia: Is Revision Possible?" *Australian Journal of Asian Law* 13, no. 2: 1–16.

Bamualim, Chaider S. 2011. "Islamic Militancy and Resentment against Hadhramis in Post-Suharto Indonesia: A Case Study of Habib Rizieq Syihab and His Islamic Defenders Front." *Comparative Studies of South Asia, Africa and the Middle East* 31, no. 2: 267–81.

Barth, Fredrik. 1993. *Balinese Worlds*. Princeton, NJ: Princeton University Press.

Barth, Fredrik. 2002. "An Anthropology of Knowledge." *Current Anthropology* 45, no. 1: 1–18.

Bayat, Asef. 2013. *Post-Islamism: The Many Faces of Political Islam*. New York: Oxford University Press.

Beaman, Jean. 2016. "Citizenship as Cultural: Towards a Theory of Cultural Citizenship." *Sociology Compass* 10: 845–57.

Brenner, Suzanne. 2011. "Private Moralities in the Public Sphere: Democratization, Islam, and Gender in Indonesia." *American Anthropologist* 113, no. 3: 478–90.

Brownlee, Jason, Tarek Masoud, and Andrew Reynolds. 2015. *The Arab Spring: Pathways of Repression and Reform*. Oxford: Oxford University Press.

Buehler, Michael. 2014. "Elite Competition and Changing State-Society Relations: Shari'a Policymaking in Indonesia." In *Beyond Oligarchy: Wealth, Power, and Contemporary Indonesian Politics*, edited by Michele Ford and Thomas B. Pepinsky, 157–75. Ithaca, NY: Cornell University Press.

Buehler, Michael. 2016. *The Politics of Shari'a Law: Islamist Activists and the State in Democratizing Indonesia*. Cambridge: Cambridge University Press.

Cederroth, Sven. 1996. "From Ancestor Worship to Monotheism: Politics of Religion in Lombok." *Temenos* 32: 7–36.

Chaplin, Chris. 2018. "Salafi Islamic Piety as Civic Activism: Wahdah Islamiyah and Differentiated Citizenship in Indonesia." *Citizenship Studies* 22, no.2: 208–23.

Chatterji, Angana P., Thomas Blom Hansen, and Christophe Jaffrelot, eds. 2019. *Majoritarian State: How Hindu Nationalism is Changing India.* Oxford: Oxford University Press.

Daniels, Timothy P. 2017. *Living Sharia: Law and Practice in Malaysia.* Seattle: University of Washington Press.

Davidson, Jamie S. 2008. *From Rebellion to Riots: Collective Violence on Indonesian Borneo.* Madison: University of Wisconsin Press.

Diamond, Larry. 1999. *Developing Democracy: Toward Consolidation.* Baltimore: Johns Hopkins University Press.

Diamond, Larry, and L. Morlino, eds. 2005. *Assessing the Quality of Democracy.* Baltimore: Johns Hopkins University Press.

Duncan, Christopher R. 2014. *Violence and Vengeance: Religious Conflict and Its Aftermath in Eastern Indonesia.* Singapore: NUS Press.

Elson, Robert E. 2013. "Two Failed Attempts to Islamize the Indonesian Constitution." *Sojourn: Journal of Social Issues in Southeast Asia* 28, no. 3: 379–437.

Emon, Anver M. 2012. "Religious Minorities and Islamic Law: Accommodation and the Limits of Tolerance." In *Islamic Law and International Human Rights Law: Searching for Common Ground?*, edited by Anver M. Emon, Mark S. Ellis, and Benjamin Glahn, 322–43. Oxford: Oxford University Press.

Fealy, Greg. 2016. "The Politics of Religious Intolerance in Indonesia: Mainstream-ism Trumps Extremism?" In *Religion, Law and Intolerance in Indonesia*, edited by Tim Lindsey and Helen Pausacker, 115–31. New York: Routledge.

Feener, R. Michael. 2007. *Muslim Legal Thought in Modern Indonesia.* Cambridge: Cambridge University Press.

Feener, R. Michael. 2013. *Sharīʿa and Social Engineering: The Implementation of Islamic Law in Contemporary Aceh, Indonesia.* Oxford: Oxford University Press.

Freedom House 2020. "Freedom in the World 2020: Indonesia." At https://freedomhouse.org/country/indonesia/freedom-world/2020. Accessed March 20, 2020.

Giddens, Anthony. 1984. *The Constitution of Society: Outline of the Theory of Structuration.* Berkeley: University of California Press.

Gorski, Philip. 2017. "Why Evangelicals Voted for Trump: A Critical Cultural Sociology." *American Journal of Cultural Sociology* 5, no. 3: 338–54.

Hadiz, Vedi R. 2016. *Islamic Populism in Indonesia and the Middle East.* Cambridge: Cambridge University Press.

Hadiz, Vedi R. 2018. "The 'Floating' Ummah in the Fall of 'Ahok' in Indonesia." *Trans: Trans-Regional and National Studies of Southeast Asia* 1, no. 1: 1–20.

Hall, John A. 1995. *Civil Society: Theory, History, Comparison.* London: Polity Press.

Hansen, Thomas Blom. 1999. *The Saffron Wave: Democracy and Hindu Nationalism in Modern India.* Princeton, NJ: Princeton University Press.

Harsono, Andreas. 2012. "No Model for Muslim Democracy." *New York Times*, May 21. http://www.nytimes.com/2012/05/22/opinion/no-model-for-muslim-democracy.html.

Hasan, Noorhaidi. 2006. *Laskar Jihad: Islam, Militancy, and the Quest for Identity in Post-New Order Indonesia.* Ithaca, NY: SEAP Publications.

Hasyim, Syafiq. 2011. "The Council of Indonesian Ulama (Majelis Ulama Indonesia, MUI) and Religious Freedom." *Irasec's Discussion Papers*, no. 12. Bangkok: IRASEC.

Hasyim, Syafiq. 2014. "Council of Indonesian Ulama (Majelis Ulama Indonesia, MUI) and Its Role in the Shariatisation of Indonesia." PhD diss., Freie Universität Berlin.

Hefner, Robert W. 1985. *Hindu Javanese: Tengger Tradition and Islam.* Princeton, NJ: Princeton University Press.

Hefner, Robert W. 1987. "Islamizing Java? Religion and Politics in Rural East Java." *Journal of Asian Studies* 46, no. 3 (August): 533–54.

Hefner, Robert W., ed. 1998. *Democratic Civility: The History and Cross-Cultural Possibility of a Modern Political Ideal*. New Brunswick: Transaction Press.

Hefner, Robert W. 2000. *Civil Islam: Muslims and Democratization in Indonesia*. Princeton, NJ: Princeton University Press.

Hefner, Robert W. 2011. "Where Have All the *Abangan* Gone? Religionization and the Decline of Non-Standard Islam in Contemporary Indonesia." In *The Politics of Religion in Indonesia: Syncretism, Orthodoxy, and Religious Contention in Java and Bali*, edited by Michel Picard and Remy Madinier, 71–91. Abingdon: Routledge.

Hefner, Robert W. 2016. "Shari'a Law and the Quest for a Modern Muslim Ethics." In *Shari'a Law and Modern Muslim Ethics*, edited by Robert W. Hefner, 1–34. Bloomington: Indiana University Press.

Hefner, Robert W. 2018. "Introduction: Indonesia at the Crossroads—Imbroglios of Religion, State, and Society in an Asian Muslim Nation." In *Routledge Handbook of Contemporary Indonesia*, edited by Robert W. Hefner, 3–30. New York: Routledge.

Hooker, M. Barry. 2003. *Indonesian Islam: Social Change through Contemporary Fatawa*. Honolulu: University of Hawaii Press.

Howell, Julia Day. 2008. "Modulations of Active Piety: Professors and Televangelists as Promoters of Indonesian 'Sufism.'" In *Expressing Islam: Religious Life and Politics in Indonesia*, edited by Greg Fealy and Sally White, 40–62. Singapore: Institute for Southeast Asian Studies.

Human Rights Watch. 2013. *In Religion's Name: Abuses Against Religious Minorities in Indonesia*. New York: HRW.

ICG. 2003. "Jemaah Islamiyah in South East Asia: Damaged but Still Dangerous." *International Crisis Group*, August 26. https://www.crisisgroup.org/asia/south-east-asia/indonesia/jemaah-islamiyah-south-east-asia-damaged-still-dangerous.

ICG. 2017. "Buddhism and State Power in Myanmar." *Asia Report*, no. 290, September 5. Brussels: International Crisis Group.

Ichwan, Moch Nur. 2013. "Towards a Puritanical Moderate Islam: The Majelis Ulama Indonesia and the Politics of Religious Orthodoxy." In *Contemporary Developments in Indonesian Islam: Explaining the "Conservative Turn,"* edited by Martin van Bruinessen, 60–104. Singapore: ISEAS.

IPAC. 2018. "After Ahok: The Islamist Agenda in Indonesia." *IPACReport*, no. 44. Jakarta: Institute for Policy Analysis of Conflict.

Kamali, Mohammad Hashim. 2008. "Maqasid al-Shari'ah Made Simple." Kuala Lumpur: International Institute of Advanced Islamic Studies.

Kloos, David, and Ward Berenschot. 2016. "Citizenship and Islam in Malaysia and Indonesia." In *Citizenship and Democratization in Southeast Asia*, edited by Ward Berenschot, Henk S. Nordholt, and Laurens Bakkereds, 178–207. Leiden: Brill.

Lindsey, Tim. 2012. *Islam, Law and the State in Southeast Asia. Vol. I: Indonesia*. London: Tauris.

Lindsey, Tim, and Simon Butt. 2016. "State Power to Restrict Religious Freedom: An Overview of the Legal Framework." In *Religion, Law and Intolerance in Indonesia*, edited by Tim Lindsey and Helen Pausacker, 19–41. New York: Routledge.

Lindsey, Tim, and Helen Pausacker, eds. 2016. *Religion, Law and Intolerance in Indonesia*. New York: Routledge.

Liow, Joseph Chinyong. 2009. *Piety and Politics: Islamism in Contemporary Malaysia*. New York: Oxford University Press.

Maarif, Samsul. 2017. *Agama Leluhur dalam Politik Agama di Indonesia: Pasang Surut Recognisi*. Yogyakarta: CRCS.

Maarif, Samsul, Husni Mubarok, Laela Fitriani Saharoni, and Dyah Roessusita. 2019. "Merangkul Penghayat Kepercayaan Melalui Advokasi Inklusi Sosial: Belajar dari Pengalaman Pendampingan." *Edisi II, Laporan Kehidupan Beragama di Indonesia*. Yogyakarta: CRCS.

Machmudi, Yon. 2006. "Islamising Indonesia: The Rise of Jemaah Tarbiyah and the Prosperous Justice Party (PKS)." Ph.D. diss., Faculty of Asian Studies. Canberra: Australian National University.

Mietzner, Marcus, Burhanuddin Muhtadi, and Rizka Halida. 2018. "Entrepreneurs of Grievance: Drivers and Effects of Indonesia's Islamist Mobilization." *Bijdragen tot de Taal-, Land- en Volkenkunde* 174, No. 2/3, pp. 159–87.

Mouffe, Chantal. 2000. "Deliberative Democracy or Agonistic Pluralism." *Political Science Series No. 72*. Vienna: Institute for Advanced Study.

Mouffe, Chantal. 2005. "The 'End of Politics' and the Challenge of Right-Wing Populism." In *Populism and the Mirror of Democracy*, edited by Francisco Panizza, 50–71. London: Verso.

Moustafa, Tamir. 2018. *Constituting Religion: Islam, Liberal Rights and the Malaysian State*. Cambridge: Cambridge University Press.

Olle, John. 2009. "The Majelis Ulama Indonesia versus 'Heresy': The Resurgence of Authoritarian Islam." In *State of Authority: The State in Society in Indonesia*, edited by Gerry van Klinken and Joshua Barker, 95–116. Ithaca, NY: Cornell Southeast Program Publications.

Osman, Mohamed Nawab Mohamed. 2018. *Hizbut Tahrir Indonesia and Political Islam: Identity, Ideology and Religio-Political Mobilization*. New York: Routledge.

Pausacker, Helen. 2013. "Morality and the Nation: Pornography and Indonesia's Islamic Defenders Front." PhD diss., University of Melbourne.

Peletz, Michael G. 2020. *Sharia Transformations: Cultural Politics and the Rebranding of an Islamic Judiciary*. Oakland: University of California Press.

Pepinsky, Thomas B., R. William. Liddle, and Saiful Mujani. 2018. *Piety and Public Opinion: Understanding Indonesian Islam*. New York: Oxford University Press.

Porter, Donald J. 2002. *Managing Politics and Islam in Indonesia*. London: Routledge.

Pranowo, Bambang. 1991. "Creating Islamic Tradition in Rural Java." PhD diss., Monash University.

Putnam, Robert. D. 1994. *Making Democracy Work: Civic Traditions in Modern Italy*. Princeton, NJ: Princeton University Press.

Putnam, Robert. D. 2001. *Bowling Alone: The Collapse and Revival of American Community*. New York: Simon and Schuster.

Rakhmani, Inaya. 2016. *Mainstreaming Islam in Indonesia: Television, Identity and the Middle Class*. New York: Palgrave Macmillan.

Ramadan, Tariq. 2009. *Radical Reform: Islamic Ethics and Liberation*. Oxford: Oxford University Press.

Ricklefs, Merle C. 2012. *Islamisation and Its Opponents in Java: c. 1930 to the Present*. Singapore: NUS Press.

Rinaldo, Rachel. 2013. *Mobilizing Piety: Islam and Feminism in Indonesia*. New York: Oxford University Press.

Robinson, Kathryn. 2009. *Gender, Islam and Democracy in Indonesia*. London: Routledge.

Salim, Arskal. 2008. *Challenging the Secular State: The Islamization of Law in Modern Indonesia*. Honolulu: University of Hawaii Press.

Schielke, Samuli. 2015. *Egypt in the Future Tense: Hope, Frustration, and Ambivalence before and after 2011*. Bloomington: Indiana University Press.

Sebastian, Leonard C., Syafiq Hasyim, and Alexander R. Arifianto, eds. 2021. *Rising Islamic Conservatism in Indonesia: Islamic Groups and Identity Politics*. London: Routledge.

Simon, Gregory. M. 2014. *Caged in on the Outside: Moral Subjectivity, Selfhood, and Islam in Minangkabau*. Honolulu: University of Hawaii Press.

Smith-Hefner, Nancy J. 2007. "Javanese Women and the Veil in post-Soeharto Indonesia." *Journal of Asian Studies* 66, no. 2: 389–420.

Smith-Hefner, Nancy J. 2019. *Islamizing Intimacy: Gender, Sexuality, and Youth in Contemporary Indonesia*. Honolulu: University of Hawaii Press.

Sirry, Mun'im. 2013. "Fatwas and Their Controversy: The Case of the Council of Indonesian Ulama (MUI)." *Journal of Southeast Asian Studies* 44, no. 1: 100–117.

Stepan, Alfred. 2011. "The Multiple Secularisms of Modern Democratic and Non-Democratic Regimes." In *Rethinking Secularism*, edited by Craig Calhoun, Mark Juergensmeyer, and Jonathan VanAntwerpen, 114–44. Oxford: Oxford University Press.

Van Bruinessen, Martin, ed. 2013a. *Contemporary Developments in Indonesian Islam: Explaining the "Conservative Turn."* Singapore: ISEAS.

Van Bruinessen, Martin. 2013b. "Introduction: Contemporary Developments in Indonesian Islam and the 'Conservative Turn' of the Early Twenty-first Century." In *Contemporary Developments in Indonesian Islam: Explaining the "Conservative Turn,"* edited by Martin van Bruinessen, 1–20. Singapore: ISEAS.

Van Doorn-Harder, Nelly. 2006. *Women Shaping Islam: Indonesian Muslim Women Reading the Qur'an*. Urbana-Champaign: University of Illinois Press.

Varshney, Ashutosh, Mohammad Zulfan Tadjoeddin, and Rizal Panggabean. 2004. *Patterns of Collective Violence in Indonesia, 1990–2003*. Jakarta: UNSFIR.

Warburton, Eve and Edward Aspinall. 2019. "Explaining Indonesia's Democratic Regression: Structure, Agency, and Popular Opinion." *Contemporary Southeast Asia: A Journal of International and Strategic Affairs* 41, No. 2, pp. 255–85.

Whitehead, Andrew L, Samuel L. Perry, and Joseph O. Baker. 2018. "Make America Christian Again: Christian Nationalism and Voting for Donald Trump in the 2016 Election." *Sociology of Religion* 79, no. 2, pp. 147–71.

Wilson, Ian Douglas. 2006. "Continuity and Change: The Changing Contours of Organized Violence in Post-New Order Indonesia." *Critical Asian Studies* 38, no. 2: 265–97.

Wilson, Ian Douglas. 2008. "'As Long as It's Halal': Islamic *Preman* in Jakarta." In *Expressing Islam: Religious Life and Politics in Indonesia*, edited by Greg Fealy and Sally White, 192–210. Singapore: ISEAS.

Winters, Jeffrey A. 2013. "Oligarchy and Democracy in Indonesia." *Indonesia* 96: 11–33.

3

THE RISE OF ISLAMIST MAJORITARIANISM IN INDONESIA

Sidney Jones

The optimism about Indonesia's democratic consolidation that marked many analyses of Indonesia in the early 2000s has given way to pessimism about majoritarianism from the Islamist right. In the 2016 campaign to bring down the Christian governor of Jakarta by accusing him of blasphemy (see Lohanda in this volume), Islamists managed to draw hundreds of thousands onto the streets not only to portray the majority religion as being under threat from the governor but also to assert their claim to control how Islam should be interpreted. The majoritarian arguments were in full force in local elections in June 2018 in West Kalimantan and North Sumatra, both areas with large non-Muslim populations, and again in the bitterly polarizing presidential election of April 2019, where the incumbent president Joko Widodo (Jokowi), himself an observant Muslim, was portrayed as a danger to majority Muslims because of his alleged support for secularism and Communism.

It is no coincidence that majoritarianism increasingly comes up in political analyses of developments in two of the world's largest democracies—Indonesia and India. In India, it is the Hindu right that has increasingly tried to assert its right to dominate and subject non-Hindu groups to its will, threatening the Gandhian vision of a secular state where all were to be treated equally regardless of ethnicity, religion, or caste. In Indonesia, it is the Islamist right that claims a privileged position for Muslims over other citizens and would like to see the inclusivist state ideology, Pancasila, reinterpreted to back its views. In both, the privileged majority portrays itself as under threat—from minorities, foreigners, and international conspiracies. In both, activists on the right claim to speak for the larger community, especially on matters of morality and orthodoxy. And in both, the majoritarians have a long-term goal of trying to stack legislatures and courts to ensure that their values are enshrined in law.

Indonesia and India are not the only Asian examples of majoritarianism at work. In Myanmar, Sri Lanka, and Thailand, minorities have accused the governments of practicing a Buddhist version, with particularly lethal consequences in 2017 for the Muslim minority in Myanmar's Rakhine State. None of the three, however, could be held up as shining examples of multiethnic democracies, whereas Indonesia and India are routinely referred to as such (Stepan 2016).

Majoritarianism in this sense is unquestionably a threat to a cornerstone of liberal democracy: the concept of equality of all citizens under the law. The fear of Indonesia's non-Muslims that they could become second-class citizens in their own country was reflected in one stark statistic from exit polls in the 2019 election: 97 percent of non-Muslims backed Jokowi, whose only rival was associated with hardline Islamist groups (Wijaya 2019).

But in belatedly deciding to stand up to the majoritarian threat, the Indonesian government risks reviving repressive tools and tactics that could undermine some of the hard-won civil liberties that reformists secured after Indonesia's authoritarian president Soeharto stepped down in 1998. In this paper, I argue that while the Islamist right in Indonesia has managed to build itself into a forceful political lobby, the "cure" could raise as many problems as the disease. The challenge is to come up with a more strategic response.

What Is Majoritarianism?

In multiethnic, multicultural societies, majoritarianism has come to mean a political stance that rejects constitutional guarantees of equality of all citizens and argues that the dominant group and its norms and values should prevail. As one writer puts it, "Majoritarianism insists on different tiers of citizenship. Members of the majority faith and culture are viewed as the nation's true citizens. The rest are courtesy citizens, guests of the majority, expected to behave well and deferentially" (Kesavan 2018). Where religion becomes the main identity marker, the enemy of majoritarians is religious pluralism. In India, the organizations making up the Hindu right

> collectively promote the ideology of Hindutva, which posits Hinduism not simply as a religion but as a nation and a race that is indigenous to India. Muslims and Christians are posited as outsiders to the history

of the nation because their faiths are said to have originated outside of India. This logic has allowed the ideologues of the Hindu Right to construct Muslims and Christians as foreigners, aliens, and invaders and their religious presence in the country as a threat to the Hindu nation. (Kapur 2014, 111)

Similar elements have crept into the Indonesian Islamist version of majoritarianism. The following statements have come up in various campaign speeches and social media postings:

Pluralism, liberalism, and secularism are in direct contradiction to Islamic teachings. This antidemocratic "principle" of majoritarian thought came to national attention as a fatwa of the Indonesian Ulama Council (Majelis Ulama Indonesia, MUI) on July 28, 2005, signed by K.H. Ma'ruf Amin, who in 2019 was to be elected vice president (Eramuslim.com 2020). At the time, it was seen as "illiberal but not intolerant" (as one scholar put it), but in hindsight, it marked the beginning of the rise of a much more politically active role for the MUI, one dominated by conservative ulama (Bush 2015, 239–57; Menchik 2007).

Muslims have 90 percent of the population so they should get 90 percent of the jobs in the civil service. Variations on this theme are common; this iteration came from Aminuddin, leader of the "alumni" of the December 2016 anti-Ahok rally (Jones 2019, 261). The implication is that all citizens are not equal and Muslims as the majority should receive preferential treatment.

Only Muslims should be allowed to govern Muslim majority areas. Muslims can take part in democratic elections but they have an obligation to vote only for Muslim candidates and for those who will defend the interests of the umma *(the Muslim community).* When the Indonesian Ulama Council issued a fatwa on October 11, 2016, that Ahok had committed blasphemy, it cited a Qur'anic verse, Surah al-Maida 51, as "explicitly forbidding Christians and Jews [from being] leaders" of Muslims and therefore as the basis for banning non-Muslims from governing Muslims (Kami 2016).

Christians and Jews are the natural enemies of Islam. This tenet, long accepted by Salafis citing Qur'anic references, gained broader currency after communal conflicts between Christians and Muslims erupted in eastern Indonesia (Ambon and Poso) in 1999–2000. It surfaces periodically in campaigns against "Christianization"—fears that the Muslim majority is under threat from Christians, especially evangelical Protestants (International Crisis Group 2010 and BAZNAS 2018). Jews regularly appear as a pariah group in public opinion surveys designed to test intolerance, despite the tiny size of Indonesia's Jewish community. A survey by the Wahid Foundation in late 2017 ranked Jews third, after LGBT individuals and communists, as the group respondents most disliked (Triyogo 2018).

Indigenous Muslims (pribumi*) have systematically lost out to non-Muslims and especially to ethnic Chinese, and it is time to redress the imbalance.* In October 2017, the newly installed governor of Jakarta, Anies Baswedan, raised a firestorm when he spoke of how "indigenous" Indonesians (*pribumi*, which his Indonesian listeners almost all interpreted as "Muslim") had been oppressed and now it was time for them to become masters in their own home. His remarks were widely seen as being directed against ethnic Chinese, although he said he was merely referring to colonial oppression (BBC News Indonesia 2017).

The privileged position of Islam in the Constitution was hijacked by secularists at the time of independence and it is now time to restore the real meaning of Pancasila. As I will discuss below, this theme was the dissertation topic of Habib Rizieq Syihab, founder of the Islamic Defenders Front (Front Pembela Islam, FPI), and has become a favorite topic of Islamist preachers.

The West is seeking to destroy Islam by stealing our resources, corrupting our youth, and weakening our economy, so we need to guard against its encroachment and strive for self-sufficiency. This became one of the themes of the anti-Jokowi campaign in 2019 but it had long been the idée fixe of Hizbut Tahrir Indonesia (HTI), an influential Islamist group that played a major mobilizing role in the anti-Ahok campaign and was particularly strong on Indonesian university campuses. The Indonesian government banned HTI in 2017 for advocating a caliphate, but as of mid-2020 its activities were largely undiminished.

The state should be the guardian of Islamic norms and if it fails in this responsibility, the people will take the law into their own hands. Examples abound of mobs putting this tenet into practice. In 2010, for example, a mob pulled down a modern sculpture of three women in ethnic Sundanese dress that Islamists found offensive (International Crisis Group 2010, 8–9).

The state should also protect Muslims from deviance and apostasy, hence pressure for a ban on the Ahmadiyah sect and use of the blasphemy law to defend Sunni orthodoxy. The government of Soesilo Bambang Yudhoyono (2004–14) capitulated to this pressure, allowing an anachronistic department within the attorney general's office, the Coordinating Agency to Oversee People's Beliefs (Badan Koordinasi Pengawas Aliran Kepercayaan Masyarakat, known by its acronym Bakorpakem), to weigh in on defining religious "deviance." This concern about "deviance," like regular warnings about the "latent threat" of communism, are examples of the way majoritarians stoke fear that their privileged position is in jeopardy.

Communism is on the rise, and only communists would try to argue against a greater role for religion in society. The danger of communism remains a favorite theme of majoritarians, despite the fact that the ideology remains banned in Indonesia following the annihilation of the Communist Party of Indonesia (Partai Komunis Indonesia, PKI) in the purge of 1965–67. In January 2019 as the presidential campaign got underway, Jokowi felt obliged to publicly deny fake news spread by his political opponents that he had links to the PKI, stirred up in part by his government's prosecution of leading Islamist figures involved in the anti-Ahok campaign (Tempo.co 2018; see also Hefner and Lohanda, respectively, in this volume).

The sense of being persecuted is very much part of the majoritarian viewpoint. As Felix Siauw, an Indonesian hardline cleric, writes,

> If the majority of the Hindu people elect someone of their own faith, it's democracy. If Muslims look for someone of their own faith, it's intolerance. If Buddhists practice their beliefs, based on scripture, that's being religious. If Muslims wish to uphold their holy book, it's radicalism. . . . If tribes in the interior wear no clothes, that's their culture, but if young women want to cover their *aurat*, that's called going Arab, watch out, it's a sign of extremism. The disgusting practice of homosexuals is called normal, we must accept it as part of diversity. But the ideas of Islamic law and the caliphate are considered terrorism. Rebels who carry guns are labeled as armed criminals, while those who carry the flag of *tauhid* [oneness of God] are considered rebels. . . . If you're a Muslim, you must be guilty in the name of diversity, tolerance and democracy. As long as you call yourself a nationalist, you can be the most brutal criminal ever (Siauw 2018).

The concern among more inclusivist Indonesians is that even if the Islamist alliance that brought down the Jakarta governor fails to stay united, its various grassroots components have a sufficient base to marshal the political resources necessary to promote regressive policies on everything from laws banning sodomy to rejection of measles vaccines. And they can always reunite if another common goal appears.

A word on nomenclature: in this paper, I sometimes use the terms "majoritarian" and "Islamist" interchangeably. I would argue that most Islamists—politically active Muslims who aim for a greater role of Islam in society and government and a wider application of Islamic law—are majoritarian, but not all majoritarians are Islamists. Some of the Christian groups in eastern Indonesia—notably the Evangelical Church in Indonesia (Gereja Injili di Indonesia, GIDI), a denomination based in Papua province and closely linked to the provincial power structure—exhibit strong majoritarian characteristics at a local level.

Turning Points

In retrospect, several policy decisions and events were key turning points that gradually transformed the Islamists from a largely invisible fringe population into a political force to be reckoned with. One was the creation of a civilian militia, FPI, in August 1998, one of many vigilante groups formed by the police and military to counter student protestors who threatened to bring down the first post-Soeharto government. Led by religious teachers of Yemeni descent but recruiting initially among the urban poor, FPI carved out a niche in what Ian Wilson has called "morality racketeering" by working in partnership with local officials and, in particular, the police (Wilson 2014).

Thanks to that partnership, FPI grew beyond its initial Jakarta boundaries to become a national organization, with local branches using their antivice credentials to become an important element of local alliances with other hardline groups, whether to obstruct the construction of churches or to take down statues considered offensive to Muslims (see Evi Sutrisno's contribution in this volume). The FPI was never Salafist—that is, linked to the ultrapuritan stream of Islam that looked to clerics in Saudi Arabia and Yemen for guidance—but as it grew in size, it came to define for itself a role in protecting Islamic moral values and fighting deviance that was very much in line with more ideological groups. Without police protection, it could not have expanded the way it did, and without the FPI the Islamist alliance would have lacked a critical grassroots mobilizing force.

Another important event for the rise of Islamist influence was the outbreak of communal conflict in Maluku, North Maluku, and central Sulawesi from January 1999 to February 2002. Some 6,500 people died, and several massacres of Muslims became iconic examples of Christian brutality, helping cement the notion of *kafir* as enemy (Duncan 2013; McRae 2013; Barron et al. 2012). The conflicts drew Salafist Muslims into active participation in the conflict together with other Muslim groups; demonstrated the mobilizing power of the Internet and online information networks; helped translate the idea of an international Christian-Zionist alliance against Islam into a local setting; and provided a rationale for an antiseparatist alliance between Islamist hardliners and nationalists in the Indonesian military (Hasan 2006). They may have convinced some groups that mobilizing for political power was a survival strategy. The circulation of information on deaths and atrocities via the Islamic media network (Isnet), websites, and CDs in 1999 anticipated the much more sophisticated use of social media two decades later by an alliance that in many important ways was shaped by the Ambon experience.

But the Ambon and Poso conflicts left another legacy as well. They showed what can happen when communal tensions get out of hand. For Indonesian officials and the security apparatus, it is this kind of eruption that must be avoided at all costs. The Islamists have skillfully exploited these fears both to inject an implicit threat of violence into mass demonstrations—as if to say, "We will ensure that these protests are peaceful but you'd better give us what we want"—and to persuade many officials that compromise is better than confrontation, because confrontation can lead to communal conflict, as in the past.

A third watershed was the introduction in June 2005 of direct local elections for district and provincial-level executives. These local elections gave a new role to hardline civil society, enabling them to seek the patronage of local leaders in exchange for mobilizing support from conservative constituencies. It also gave them new scope for political lobbying, demanding promises from candidates in conservative Muslim districts to ban the Ahmadiyah sect or close brothels or curb the sale of alcohol. Another key building block of the Islamist alliance, Forum Umat Islam (FUI), was born in August 2005, the brainchild of Muhammad al Khaththath, with a specific objective of implementing the MUI's fatwa against pluralism, liberalism, and secularism. In an atmosphere where the newly elected President Yudhoyono was already reaching out to religious conservatives, mobilizing at the local level could now produce concrete political outcomes (Bush 2015).

The phenomenon of *penolakan* (rejection) became popular around the same time, where groups like FPI and Hizbut Tahrir Indonesia (HTI) would organize residents into a coalition, usually with the word "Forum" in the title, to reject a new church or seal off an Ahmadiyah mosque. Sana Jaffrey points out that the notion of neighborhood residents gathering to defend their values or make demands on local officials gave the action a legitimacy that it might have lacked if seen as having been organized by outsiders (Jaffrey 2019). Local social media networks took on a new importance as well. These tactics, tested most frequently in West Java and the greater Jakarta metropolitan area but also elsewhere and increasingly used from 2005 onwards, became critically important as the Islamists moved onto the national stage (on antiminority violence in West Java see Hamayotsu in this volume).

The jump in support for the Prosperous Justice Party (Partai Keadilan Sejahtera, PKS), an Islamist party associated with the international Muslim Brotherhood movement, in the 2009 elections may have also convinced the Salafists and other hardline groups that a pro-shari'a agenda could be achieved through democratic participation. By and large, Islamists saw democracy as antithetical to Islam because only God, not elected representatives, could be the source of law. Many were therefore highly critical of a fatwa issued by the MUI prior to the 2009 election requiring all Muslims to vote—as long as they chose candidates who were of the same faith, devout, honest, trustworthy, strategic (*aspiratif*), capable, and ready to defend the interests of the Muslim community (Gufron 2009). Felix Siauw of HTI, for example, was one of the outspoken critics of that ruling (Siauw 2012). But by 2012, many prominent Islamists were citing the fatwa, especially the last point about defending the interests of the *umma*, as a basis for encouraging followers to vote against or in favor of specific candidates and using their mobilizing power to get voters to the polls accordingly (CNN Indonesia 2018). It was not just recognition that participation could produce benefits, but also that it was necessary to get out and defeat candidates seen as liberal, secular, or pluralist.

The final part of the puzzle was to draw in the pious middle class, aided by media-savvy preachers, urban religious study groups and educational networks, and politicians who saw the sponsorship of religious activities as a useful part of their support base. One example is Yudhoyono's use of Majelis Zikir Nurus-salam during the 2004 presidential campaign and later as a vehicle to support his son's unsuccessful bid to become Jakarta governor (IPAC 2018). Mietzner and Muhtadi noted how national survey data showed growing education and income levels for those expressing intolerant views (Mietzner and Muhtadi 2018). The popularity of after-work religious study as a new form of social activity for the affluent may have been a factor.

The elements that enabled the majoritarians to turn themselves into a national force were thus all in place by 2012. First were the institutional building blocks: civil society groups committed to an Islamist agenda and shaped by the Ambon and Poso conflicts. Second was proven experience in coalition-building at the local level in support of Islamist goals; this enabled the groups to build up a grassroots base connected by social media networks. All they needed was a focus for a national show of force, and Ahok provided it. The scale of the mobilization against Ahok on December 12, 2016, could not have happened, however, without convincing a large segment of the Muslim mainstream that Islam was under attack. This was achieved at least in part through the tactical decision to use mosque-based campaigning and appeal to the *umma* directly through sermons at Friday prayers.

The story of how the governor was brought down and how the focus shifted to an anti-Jokowi campaign has been told in detail elsewhere (IPAC 2018, 2019; see also Lohanda, this volume). The important takeaway is that the success of the Islamists in getting Ahok arrested and convicted and their own candidate elected as Jakarta governor changed the political landscape in important ways. It suggested that that the ability to turn people out into the streets could change policy by convincing those in power (and those who wanted to be in power) that the risk of standing up to the masses was higher than capitulation. With the FPI in particular severing ties with the police because they had other donors and new, loftier goals, the police came to see the Islamist coalition as an existential threat.

Three Majoritarian Issues

The Islamist agenda is long and growing, and even though there are serious differences among groups on long-term institutional goals (Islamic state from the top down? Islamized society from the bottom up?), there is general agreement on the need to infuse government policy with the values of conservative Islam and give the ulama a greater role in decision-making. In this section I present three issues that help define the majoritarian stance. The first, promoting a revisionist view of Pancasila, reflects a classic tactic of majoritarian groups to set the historical context for their claims. The second, exhorting Muslims to only vote for other Muslims and for those who will defend the interests of the Muslim community, provides the basis for political alliances and future patronage. It works particularly well as a subject for mosque-based campaigning at election time, one reason why the pro-Jokowi police insisted on the neutrality of houses of worship during the 2019 campaign. The third is a morality issue—in this case a draft bill to prevent sexual violence that the Islamists are interpreting as an invitation to debauchery, but we could equally have chosen the efforts to outlaw homosexuality or ban sales of alcohol. All debates over morality offer an opportunity to draw in the less ideological mainstream and frame the issue as one that pits "good" Muslims against sinners.

The Hijacking of Pancasila

The Islamists, led by Habib Rizieq Syihab, who wrote his dissertation on the subject of Pancasila, argue that Sukarno and Hatta unilaterally hijacked the "true" Pancasila—five principles for the basis of an independent state that were first outlined by Sukarno himself in June 1945—from a consensus that had been reached between the nationalists and Islamists in July 1945. This version, to be included in the preamble to the new constitution, included seven words, collectively known as the Jakarta Charter (*piagam Jakarta*), that would have made the first principle of Pancasila read, "Belief in God, with the obligation of Muslims to carry out Islamic law" (Salim 2008). On 18 August 1945, however, the seven words were deleted in the interests of national unity and the first principle became "Belief in Almighty God" (for the implications of this principle on believers of non-Abrahamic religions, see Aragon, this volume). Islamists have been angry ever since. "It is very ironic," Syihab notes in his dissertation, "that Hatta took out the words to avoid disappointing the Christian minority, when the result was to create even bigger disappointment in the Muslim majority" (Syihab 2012, 74).

Syihab and others argue that this betrayal by secular nationalists of a hard-won consensus shows that the true representatives of independence were the Islamists. If some now portray Islam as being antithetical to nationalism and a threat to the unitary state of Indonesia (Negara Kesatuan Republik Indonesia, NKRI), the Islamists portray themselves as being the true nationalists and therefore deserving of the greatest share of power (IPAC 2019), echoing claims advanced by S. M. Kartosuwiryo since the late 1920s and his Darul Islam movement in the 1940s (Formichi 2012). In a classic majoritarian statement, Lutfi Fathullah of Majelis Pelayan Jakarta, a group involved in the 212 movement, said, "We don't have a problem with NKRI, but we say our NKRI is better than yours. The majority has to rule, it's like that everywhere. It's not right that the majority is ruled by a minority. In certain areas, okay, but in matters of state, no way. And we have to have the biggest portion, don't just give us the small change."[1]

Support for an inclusivist interpretation of Pancasila is likely to remain high, particularly given the explicit rejection of the Jakarta Charter by both Nahdlatul Ulama and Muhammadiyah, although the Islamist version may be gaining ground. One survey suggested that support for Islam rather than Pancasila as the ideological basis of the Indonesian state had grown from 4.6 percent in 2005 to 13.2 percent in 2018 (Kabar24 2018).

The reality may be that it is not either-or any longer—even without adopting Syihab's version of Pancasila, many Indonesians may see no incompatibility in supporting Pancasila as the basis for the state while also desiring a higher level of commitment to Islamic values from state officials, as many Muslim political leaders did in the 1950s. A survey in 2017–18 of over five hundred randomly selected local legislators from thirty-one of Indonesia's thirty-four provinces showed most were oriented more to Pancasila than to Islam, but that many saw no contradiction between supporting Pancasila and hoping that their parties would allow Islam to play a greater role. The authors of the survey conclude, "Taken together, the results suggest that many of the provincial parliament (DPRD) members [legislators] we interviewed do not see Pancasila as necessarily implying a commitment to the implementation of secularist policies" (Aspinall et. al. 2018).

This also suggests that lip service to Pancasila as the antidote to intolerance will not be enough to prevent the majoritarian view from gaining ground. I will return to this point in the conclusion.

Islam and Elections

If majoritarians believe they have a right to rule based on their own norms and values without any nod to acceptance of minority rights or equality of all citizens under the law, they are adamant that Muslims are obliged to vote for fellow Muslims. Many Islamists remain convinced that democracy is *haram* but the majoritarians see it as a necessary evil to consolidate their position. The Qur'anic verse that the Islamists and MUI used to bring down Ahok became a theme in Friday prayer sermons throughout Jakarta during the 2017 election for governor and was used by gubernatorial candidates in local elections, notably in North Sumatra and West Kalimantan, in June 2018. The Idul Fitri sermon in Pontianak on June 15, 2018, less than two weeks before the election for governor that pitted a Muslim Malay against a Christian Dayak, was a case in point. The preacher repeated most of the themes of the anti-Ahok campaign (IPAC 2018).

He said that choosing a leader was an obligation for all Muslims, especially if by failing to vote, leadership could fall to a non-Muslim. Not using one's right to vote is acceptable only if the welfare of the Islamic community is not threatened, but if there is a danger that the Muslim candidate might lose if Muslims do not vote, then not voting is forbidden. He said that only Muslims fulfill the requirements to become leaders according to Islamic jurisprudence. Islam absolutely forbids non-Muslim leaders, he warned. This is nonnegotiable. Allah forbids adultery through five verses of the Qur'an, prohibits drinking liquor through three verses, prohibits eating pork through four verses, but forbids choosing non-Muslim leaders in nineteen verses. One such verse is Surat Al Maidah 51. Muslims who choose non-Muslim leaders should be seen as having left Islam. If they choose Jews as leaders, they should be considered Jews. If they choose Christians, they should be considered Christian. If those who betray Islam in this fashion die, we are no longer obliged to pray over their bodies.

Those arguments are deeply persuasive for audiences with little religious knowledge, but they work only in the relatively rare cases in which Muslims are contesting non-Muslims for public office. (In Pontianak, identity politics determined the outcome and the Muslim candidate won, but he was also far and away the better candidate.) The harder task is to convince Muslim worshipers that of two Muslim candidates, one will defend the interests of the *umma* more than the other. This is where majoritarians try to portray their conservative values as being the "true" Islam.

The Bill to Prevent Sexual Violence

The Islamist campaign against a bill to prevent sexual violence is emblematic of Islamist efforts to get the state to play a greater role in enforcing morality—or one set of moral standards.

A bill to prevent sexual violence, placed on the priority list of the DPR in 2015 and formally introduced in 2016, became the target of Islamists who claimed it reflected secular values and would encourage adultery. The most contentious part of the bill was the definition of sexual violence in Article 1: any form of assault inflicted upon the "body, sexual drive and/or reproductive functions . . . that make the [victim] incapable of giving his/her consent freely due to imbalance in power and/or gender relations . . ." The Islamists argued that this definition suggested that any form of sexual relationship was acceptable as long as someone consented, meaning it implicitly condoned adultery, premarital sex, sodomy, and other acts forbidden by Islamic law (Nahimunkar.com 2018). One critic said sexual violence was indeed a growing problem, but only the full application of Islamic law would stop it (MuslimahNews.com 2019).

The bill became a cause célèbre for the leaders of the 212 Movement, whose members killed an earlier bill on gender equality. The Alliance for Family Love (Aliansi Cinta Keluarga, AILA), an organization linked to Bachtiar Nasir's Salafi network, sent delegations of women around to various cities to give talks in the hope of rallying local opposition, using the grassroots *penolakan* tactics that the Islamists perfected. Despite the fact that the Gerindra (Gerakan Indonesia Raya [Great Indonesia Movement]) party initially backed the law and the niece of Jokowi's rival Prabowo Subianto, an elected Gerindra legislator, was a strong supporter, the bill was targeted as anti-Islamic and it was withdrawn from the legislative priority list in July 2020.

The protest against the bill was only one of many such morality campaigns, directed most systematically against the LGBT community but also against everything from topless statues to a Lady Gaga concert, where the threat of violence forced its cancellation in 2012. They are the easiest way to draw in the mainstream because no one wants to take a stand in support of immoral behavior or be tarred as a bad Muslim. But they also become an important vehicle for extending the influence of Islamists who claim to represent the majority of the Indonesian population.

The Government Response

Mietzner notes that governments historically have had three ways of handling above-ground populist movements: repression, appeasement, and "civilizing pressure." Repression to be effective must be rooted in "militant democracy" or measures that are based on "strict adherence to the rule of law," he writes, continuing, "Any misuse of legal regulations by incumbent governments— through arbitrary criminalization, for instance—carries the risk of devaluing and damaging the democracy that the strategy was designed to defend" (Mietzner 2018, 265).

He suggests that the Yudhoyono government made the mistake of appeasing the Islamists, allowing them to develop the organizational capacities that made the 2016 mobilization possible. The Jokowi government, led by the police, began with accommodation but then went increasingly overboard in the other direction, bringing dubious charges against Islamist leaders and banning one organization— HTI—entirely, though in an ineffective and potentially counterproductive fashion (Mietzner 2018; IPAC 2018). While HTI continued to operate as though nothing had happened, state universities and government offices began to systematically remove employees suspected of HTI sympathies (Okenews 2018).

The repression only increased as the 2019 election got closer, with the police banning opposition rallies on flimsy grounds, criminalizing legitimate expression as defamation, and encouraging the perception that Islamism is one step away from terrorism. In doing so, they relied on broadly worded laws and regulations that raised alarm among human rights activists. These included Law 11/2008, which prohibits the dissemination of broad categories of electronic information.

At the same time, the Jokowi government tried to put forward a "moderate," inclusivist vision of Islam that was a direct challenge to the majoritarians. It did so by embracing Nahdlatul Ulama and its concept of "Islam Nusantara" and "humanitarian Islam" (Scott 2019). By embracing one organization, however, it created resentment in others about lack of access to resources and patronage.

Police Crackdown

Initially, the moves against the Islamist leaders could be seen as an effort to belatedly confront a potential security problem. Continued mass mobilization that brought economic activity in the capital to a halt and sent images around the world of an increasingly intolerant Indonesia was bad enough, but as noted above, it carried with it the implicit threat of violence. If even a small fraction of the hundreds of thousands out on the streets began rioting, the situation could quickly get out of control. Police therefore began moving against the organizers, most notably the FPI leader Rizieq Syihab, whom they forced into exile in Saudi Arabia, then arrested after his November 2020 return (IPAC 2019).

But as the 2019 campaign began heating up with most of the major leaders and institutions from the 212 movement in the camp of Jokowi's rival Prabowo, the police took a much more aggressive stance. Senior police officials in private conversations suggested three reasons why.[2] First, according to one official, radical Islamists were now one of Indonesia's largest security threats, and Prabowo could not be relied on to stop them, since he was deeply tied into their networks. Second, the Islamists were only a step away from terrorists, and they both believed in a caliphate; if the influence of hardline groups was allowed to expand, the enabling environment for terrorism would also grow. Third, a Prabowo victory would open the door to further encroachment of the military into internal security at the expense of the police, but since some members of the military are closely allied with the Islamists, this could also serve to increase the latter's influence.

Until November 2016, the police believed that they controlled FPI: "Give them money, keep them busy, that's how you keep them in line," said one official, who faulted Ahok for confronting FPI members instead of accommodating them.[3] But that accommodation, which often involved the police using FPI members as a kind of civilian auxiliary, also allowed FPI to grow into a more sophisticated political organization that was less willing to accept the role of junior partner. The anti-Ahok campaign may have triggered its defection and given it new sources of patronage, but with high national visibility and a grassroots urban base, it was a matter of time before FPI turned on its former master. There is no question, though, that senior police officials were seriously shaken by the size of the anti-Ahok demonstrations and became genuinely concerned about a threat to the Indonesian state.

The police were convinced that Prabowo was inviting violent extremists into his campaign, in part because one member of the campaign team in central Java, Ustadh Mu'inudinillah (Ust. Mu'in, for short), was the brother of one of the most senior Indonesian ISIS fighters in Syria, a man known as Abu Walid (killed in an airstrike in January 2019). A video circulated by police leaves the impression of a direct link between Ust. Mu'in and ISIS, and states that his role in the campaign was specifically to draw in Solo-based extremists. It ends with a warning: "The Indonesian people must be aware that Prabowo-Sandi will use any means to win the presidential election, even if the NKRI has to be mortgaged to extremists who want to change the NKRI." The video, entitled "BPN Prabowo-Sandi Rekrut Jaringan Teroris" (The Prabowo-Sandi Campaign Team Recruits A Terrorist Network), is in the possession of the author.

Despite Ust. Mu'in's family ties, there was little evidence that the Islamists involved in above-ground political activity in Indonesia supported pro-ISIS groups (and plenty to suggest that they did not) or that violent extremists recruited from Islamist organizations. But the labeling of Islamists as extremists added to the majoritarian anger and their feeling of being under attack from the state.

It is difficult to tell whether the police seriously believed that a Prabowo victory would facilitate the growth of terrorist cells or whether they were also reflecting their own institutional interests. Several political analysts believed that if Prabowo won, he would encourage the army to expand its influence at police expense (Laksmana 2019). The former commander of the Indonesian armed forces General Gatot Nurmantyo made no secret of his own political ambitions, though he lost out early on in his bid for a vice presidential slot. Gatot began systematically courting the Islamist organizations as early as 2016 with a concept of "proxy war" that tallied very well with majoritarian views in its portrayal of Indonesia as a nation under siege, surrounded by enemies using proxies to weaken it from within (Nurmantyo 2017). Gatot may not have represented a majority faction within the Army (Tentara Nasional Indonesia, TNI), but his activism helped reinforce a perception among the Islamists of the TNI as friend and the police as foe. The belief of many in the army and the Islamists that communism is on the rise also brought the two together—an alliance which the abandonment by the police of any semblance of neutrality in the 2019 campaign can have only reinforced.

A combination of convictions, then—that Islamists constituted an existential threat to the Indonesian state, that a Prabowo victory would allow them to grow in influence, and that their own institutional interests were at risk—may explain why the police engaged in such repressive tactics during the election campaign. The danger is that the overly broad language of the laws now in place has serious implications for freedom of association and expression more broadly.

One postelection example was the issuing of a joint ministerial decree on November 12, 2019, by eleven ministers and agency heads, most of them newly appointed, on "Preventing Radicalism in the Context of Strengthening National-ism in the Civil Service" (Ministry of Administrative and Bureaucratic Reform 2019). The decree encourages citizens to report on anyone they believe has exhib-ited indications of intolerance or sentiments that are deemed anti-Pancasila, against the state, or threatening the unity of the nation.

The decree, which nowhere defines radicalism, proceeds to outline a list of examples so broad and far-reaching that almost anyone could get caught. They include expressing opinions in any form (oral, written, text message, audio, video, or photo) that suggests hatred toward Pancasila, the constitution, diversity, national unity, or the government; any communication on social media express-ing hatred toward an ethnicity, religion, race, or other group; using mechanisms like share, retweet, repost, or broadcast to do the same; spreading misleading information via social media; taking part in activities, getting involved in organi-zations, or using signs or symbols that could defame, incite, provoke, or inculcate hatred toward Pancasila, the constitution, diversity, national unity, or the govern-ment; or denigrating national symbols.

A website was set up to receive reports that will then be assessed by a task force in the Ministry of Communication and Information, with recommendations for ongoing actions. "Radicalism" may be the target, but the wording was reminis-cent of Soeharto-era tactics to punish political dissent.

None of the repressive tactics get at the heart of the problem, which is that Indonesian citizens who are not Sunni Muslims, or those who are but do not share the conservative values of the majoritarian Islamists, are increasingly being forced to bend to Islamist concerns.

Embracing NU

Jokowi and his advisers made a decision early on to embrace Nahdlatul Ulama as the government's main ally in facing down the Islamists (Fealy 2018). Shortly after winning the presidency in 2014, Jokowi declared October 22 as "National Santri Day," a move not only designed to reach out to Muslims in the aftermath of a divisive campaign but also calculated to appeal in particular to NU boarding schools (*pesantren*) and their students, known as *santri*. NU's promotion of a nationalist, inclusivist Islam coincided with Jokowi's own views. Its strongholds in Java were part of his natural political base and it was deeply opposed to the "transnational Islam" of the Salafists and HTI (IPAC 2019). If he had not been assiduous in courting NU before the 212 demonstration, he more than made up for it afterwards, dispensing patronage on a lavish scale.

The support for NU took many forms, but one was encouragement of the NU militia, Barisan Ansor Serbaguna (Banser), to try and seize the momentum from the Islamists by mobilizing its forces to prevent or disrupt "radical" meetings, which it occasionally succeeded in doing. The problem was controlling the spin, and NU was no match for the Islamists on social media. The debacle over a flag-burning incident was but one example: on October 22, 2018, a few dozen youths from Banser NU in Garut, West Java, seized and burned a HTI flag that appeared during a celebration of National *Santri* Day in the town square in Limbangan, Garut. As HTI was now a banned organization, no one in Banser foresaw a problem, nor, initially, did the police, who confirmed that the flag was HTI's symbol.

The flag in question consists of a black background with words of the declaration of the Islamic faith written in white in Arabic script and was carried by HTI in all the anti-Ahok rallies. This time, however, HTI denied that it had an official flag, and the word went out over social media that Banser members had burned the "flag of *tauhid*," desecrating an Islamic symbol. An edited video of the burning went viral. A petty act of vandalism was deliberately turned into a perceived attack on the faith, with all Islamist groups, many of whom do not like HTI, taking up the call and demanding that the perpetrators be arrested. On October 25, police arrested the man who had carried the flag into the rally on the grounds of disturbing public order. Later the same day the two Banser members who appeared on the video setting fire to the flag sought the protection of the Garut police as the manufactured anger mounted. Mob pressure forced the police to formally arrest them on charges of creating a disturbance, and the two were sentenced to ten days in prison in November 2018. Once again, the Islamists used the threat of violence to impose their will.

Once reelected, Jokowi began a more systematic campaign against "radicalism" with full support from NU and, opinion polls indicated, much of the Indonesian public. Measures included banning FPI by executive decree in December 2020, prosecuting top FPI leaders on the grounds of violating health protocols at mass events, and stepping up efforts to link FPI to terrorism. All this left the Islamists temporarily on the defensive by mid-2021, but the scale of the country's COVID disaster quickly wiped everything else off the national agenda.

Majoritarianism presents a risk to Indonesian democracy to the extent that it seeks to privilege one group of citizens above others. It is closely tied to the rise of

Islamism as a political movement, particularly with a series of developments that followed the resignation of Soeharto in 1998, but it was not until the anti-Ahok campaign that its size and scope became clear. It is not something that can be fought with band-aid tactics. Several of the most important majoritarian groups have their own school networks from kindergartens on up, and there is a reason: to inculcate a set of values, one has to start young.

The only way Islamist majoritarianism can be effectively challenged is to rethink the education system from the elementary school level up, developing new books and new programs aimed at promoting an inclusivist notion of citizenship as well as retraining teachers, including religious teachers, in a way that counters the majoritarian arguments listed at the beginning of this paper. That means the allocation of major resources. Rhetoric about Pancasila is not enough. Any such effort through the schools, led by the president, is certain to create an Islamist backlash against pluralism, and the government needs to try to anticipate it, head it off, or be prepared to stand up to it.

The majoritarians have made hugely effective use of social media, especially WhatsApp networks, to mobilize around particular causes. Various civil society groups are trying to mount their own crowd-sourced initiatives to challenge false information and demonstrate support for alternative viewpoints, but it is an uphill battle. As with populism in Western countries as well, the ability of leaders to communicate directly with their followers without being mediated by representative political institutions makes those institutions weaker—and Indonesia's legislatures were not strong to begin with.

Where morality campaigns have been successfully challenged, it has been on economic grounds—concerns that a ban on alcohol would affect tourism or the hotel industry, for example. In some cases, quiet lobbying has proven more effective than frontal challenges: the worst provisions of a revised criminal code that would have outlawed homosexuality were at least temporarily pushed back, but any public defense of the LGBT community in the current climate would be political suicide. There is a role for arrests and prosecution in challenging majoritarianism, but it is in punishing clear crimes—acts of vandalism by FPI mobs, for example—not in the repression of legitimate dissent or sacking university lecturers for allegedly "radical" views.

Islamists themselves remain a minority bloc in the political system. But their majoritarian values appear to be increasingly shared, in a way that has long-term negative consequences for Indonesian democracy.

Notes

1. Lutfi Fathullah, interview by Nava Nuraniyah for Institute for Policy Analysis of Conflict (IPAC), Jakarta, November 3, 2017.

2. Indonesian National Police (officer requested anonymity), interview by Sidney Jones, IPAC, March 25, 2019.

3. Indonesian National Police (officer requested anonymity), interview by Sidney Jones, IPAC, November 18, 2015.

References

Aspinall, Edward, Diego Fossati, Burhanuddin Muhtadi, and Eve Warburton. 2018. "Mapping the Indonesian Political Spectrum." *New Mandala*, April 24. https://www.newmandala.org/mapping-indonesian-political-spectrum/.

Barron, Patrick, Muhammad Najib Azca and Tri Susdinarjanti. 2012. *After the Communal War: Understanding and Addressing Post-conflict Violence in Eastern Indonesia*. Yogyakarta: CSPS Books, 10.

BAZNAS (Badan Amil Zakat Nasional). 2018. *Indeks Rawan Pemurtadan*. Jakarta: Pusat Kajian Strategis BAZNAS.

BBC News Indonesia. 2017. "Mengapa Istilah 'Pribumi' dalam Pidato Anies Baswedan Memicu Kontroversi?" October 17. https://www.bbc.com/indonesia/trensosial-41648172.

Bush, Robin. 2015. "Religious Politics and Minority Rights during the Yudhoyono Presidency." In *The Yudhoyono Presidency: Indonesia's Decade of Stability and Stagnation*, edited by Edward Aspinall, Marcus Mietzner and Dirk Tomsa, 239–57. Singapore: ISEAS—Yusof Ishak Institute.

CNN Indonesia. 2018. "Al Khaththath Ingatkan Kembali Fatwa MUI Memilih Pemimpin." November 22. https://www.cnnindonesia.com/nasional/20181122195743-32-348554/al-khaththath-ingatkan-kembali-fatwa-mui-memilih-pemimpin.

Duncan, Christopher R. 2013. *Violence and Vengeance: Religious Conflict and its Aftermath in Eastern Indonesia*, Ithaca, NY: Cornell University Press.

Eramuslim.com. 2020. "Fatwa MUI Tentang Haramnya Pluralisme, Liberalisme, dan Sekulerisme Agama." Accessed July 17, 2020. https://www.eramuslim.com/berita/tahukah-anda/fatwa-mui-tentang-pluralisme-liberalisme-dan-sekulerisme-agama.htm#.XxErgigzYdV.

Fealy, Greg. 2018. "Nahdlatul Ulama and the Politics Trap." *New Mandala*, July 11. https://www.newmandala.org/nahdlatul-ulama-politics-trap/.

Formichi, Chiara. 2012. *Islam and the Making of the Nation: Kartosuwiryo and Political Islam in 20th Century Indonesia*. Leiden: KITLV Press.

Gufron. 2009. "Fatwa Penggunaan Hak Pilih Dalam Pemilu." BA thesis, Institut Agama Islam Negeri Walisongo, Semarang. http://eprints.walisongo.ac.id/5144/1/2102240_lengkap.pdf.

Hasan, Noorhaidi. 2006. *Laskar Jihad: Islam, Militancy, and the Quest for Identity in Post-New Order Indonesia*. Ithaca, NY: Cornell Southeast Asia Program.

IPAC. 2018. "After Ahok: The Islamist Agenda in Indonesia." Report no. 44, April 6.

IPAC. 2019. "Anti-Ahok to Anti-Jokowi: Islamist Influence on Indonesia's 2019 Election Campaign." Report no. 55, March 15.

International Crisis Group. 2010. "Indonesia: 'Christianisation' and Intolerance." Asia Briefing no.114, November 24, 2010.

Jaffrey, Sana. 2019. "Leveraging the Leviathan: Politics of Impunity and the Rise of Vigilantism in Indonesia." PhD diss., University of Chicago.

Jones, Sidney. 2019. "Manipulating Minorities and Majorities: Reflections on 'Contentious Belonging.'" In *Contentious Belonging: The Place of Minorities in Indonesia*, edited by Greg Fealy and Ronit Ricci, 255–65. Singapore: ISEAS—Yusof Ishak Institute.

Kabar24 2018. "Survei LSI: Pendukung Pancasila Turun 10%, Pro NKRI Bersyariah Naik", https://kabar24.bisnis.com/read/20180717/15/817421/survei-lsi-pendukung-pancasila-turun-10-pro-nkri-bersyariah-naik.

Kami, Indah Mutiara. 2016. "MUI Nyatakan Sikap Soal Ucapan Ahok Terkait Al Maidah 51, Ini Isinya." October 11. https://news.detik.com/berita/d-3318150/mui-nyatakan-sikap-soal-ucapan-ahok-terkait-al-maidah-51-ini-isinya.

Kapur, Ratna. 2014. "A Leap of Faith: The Construction of Hindu Majoritarianism through Secular Law." *South Atlantic Quarterly* 113, no. 1: 111. https://papers.ssrn.com/sol3/papers.cfm?abstract_id=2402555.

Kesavan, Mukul. 2018. "Murderous Majorities." *New York Review of Books*, January 18. https://www.nybooks.com/articles/2018/01/18/rohingya-murderous-majorities/.

Laksmana, Evan. 2019. "Is Indonesia's Military Eyeing the Republic?" *New York Times*, April 11. https://www.nytimes.com/2019/04/11/opinion/joko-widodo-indonesia-military.html.

McRae, Dave. 2013. *A Few Poorly Organized Men: Interreligious Violence in Poso, Indonesia*, Leiden: Brill.

Menchik, Jeremy. 2007. "Illiberal But Not Intolerant." *Inside Indonesia* 90, Oct–Dec. https://www.insideindonesia.org/illiberal-but-not-intolerant.

Mietzner, Marcus. 2018. "Fighting Illiberalism with Illiberalism: Islamist Populism and Democratic Deconsolidation in Indonesia." *Pacific Affairs* 91, no. 2 (June): 261–82. https://doi.org/10.5509/2018912261.

Mietzner, Marcus, and Burhanuddin Muhtadi. 2018. "Explaining the 2016 Islamist Mobilisation in Indonesia: Religious Intolerance, Militant Groups and the Politics of Accommodation." *Asian Studies Review* 42. no. 3: 479–97. https://doi.org/10.1080/10357823.2018.1473335.

Ministry of Administrative and Bureaucratic Reform. 2019. "Tangani Radikalisme ASN, Pemerintah Bentuk Taskforce dan Portal Aduan ASN." November 12, 2019. Accessed July 18, 2020. https://www.menpan.go.id/site/berita-terkini/tangani-radikalisme-asn-pemerintah-bentuk-taskforce-dan-portal-aduan-asn.

MuslimahNews.com. 2019. "Perempuan Butuh Syariat Islam, Bukan RUU PKS." January 30. https://www.muslimahnews.com/2019/01/30/perempuan-butuh-syariat-islam-bukan-ruu-pks/.

Nahimunkar.org. 2018. "RUU P-KS (Penghapusan Kekerasan Seksual) Dinilai Menjerat Aturan Agama dan Berpotensi Melegalkan Prostitusi, Aborsi dan Suburkan LGBT." December 20. https://www.nahimunkar.org/ruu-p-ks-penghapusan-kekerasan-seksual-dinilai-menjerat-aturan-agama-dan-berpotensi-melegalkan-prostitusi-aborsi-dan-suburkan-lgbt/.

Nurmantyo, G. 2017. "Memahami Ancaman, Menyadari Jati Diri Sebagai Modal Membangun Menuju Indonesia Emas." Jakarta [publisher not identified]

Okenews. 2018. "Undip Berhentikan Profesor Suteki yang Diduga Dukung HTI." June 6. https://news.okezone.com/read/2018/06/06/512/1907519/undip-berhentikan-profesor-suteki-yang-diduga-dukung-hti.

Salim, Arskal. 2008. *Challenging the Secular State: The Islamization of Law in Modern Indonesia*, Honolulu: University of Hawai'i Press.

Scott, Margaret, 2019. "Indonesia's New Islamist Politics." *New York Review of Books*, April 18. https://www.nybooks.com/articles/2019/04/18/indonesias-new-islamist-politics/.

Siauw, Felix. 2012. "Fatwa Golput: Isyarat Gagalnya Demokrasi," February 16. https://www.facebook.com/permalink.php?story_fbid=501165230000458&id=496620087121639&__tn__=K-R (accessed April 19, 2021).

Siauw, Felix. 2018. "Ust. Felix Siauw: Mayoritas Rasa Minoritas." Eramuslim.com, January 16. https://www.eramuslim.com/berita/analisa/ust-felix-siauw-mayoritas-rasa-minoritas.htm.

Stepan, Alfred. 2016. "Democracies with Large Muslim Populations: Reflections on Indonesia, India, Senegal and Tunisia." Lecture at School of Oriental and African Studies, London, April 18. Video at https://www.soas.ac.uk/politics/events/18apr2016-democracies-with-large-muslim-populations-reflections-on-indonesia-india-senegal-and-tunis.html.

Syihab, Al-Habib Muhammad Rizieq bin Husein. 2012. "Pengaruh Pancasila Terhadap Penerapan Syariah Islam di Indonesia." PhD thesis, Malaya University, Kuala Lumpur.

Tempo.co. 2018. "Kembali Bantah Terlibat PKI, 4 Pidato Jokowi yang Singgung PKI." *Tempo*, October 26. https://nasional.tempo.co/read/1140030/kembali-bantah-terlibat-pki-4-pidato-jokowi-yang-singgung-pki.

Triyogo, Arkhelaus Wisnu. 2018. "Survei Wahid Foundation: Komunis dan LGBT Paling Tak Disukai." *Tempo*, January 29. https://nasional.tempo.co/read/1055349/survei-wahid-foundation-komunis-dan-lgbt-paling-tak-disukai/full&view=ok.

Wijaya, Callistasia. 2019. "Siapa saja yang memilih Jokowi dan Prabowo berdasarkan exit poll dan quick count?" *BBC Indonesia*, April 24. https://www.bbc.com/indonesia/indonesia-48019930.

Wilson, Ian. 2014. "Morality Racketeering: Vigilantism and Populist Islamic Militancy in Indonesia." In *Between Dissent and Power*, edited by Khoo Boo Teik, Vedi R. Hadiz and Yoshihiro Nakanishi, 248–74. IDE-JETRO Series. London: Palgrave Macmillan.

4

MAKING THE MAJORITY IN THE NAME OF ISLAM

Democratization, Moderate-Radical Coalition, and Religious Intolerance in Indonesia

Kikue Hamayotsu

Since the mid-2000s, rising religious conservatism and intolerance across the archipelago has posed a major challenge to religious pluralism and pluralistic foundations of the religiously divided nation in democratic Indonesia (Van Bruinessen 2011; Van Bruinessen 2013; Feillard and Madinier 2011; Hamayotsu 2014, 2015). Conservative Islamist movements and religious elites benefited from political liberalization and newly introduced democratic and decentralized institutions to organize and mobilize collective sentiment and action against religious minorities, be they Muslim or non-Muslim. As a result, aggressive and assertive religious conservativism and radicalism has put moderate, secular, and liberal elements of civil society on the defensive (Hamayotsu 2013). Presently, the quality of Indonesia's hard-fought democracy and the effective functions of democratic institutions to protect the fundamental constitutional rights and freedom of religious and secular communities appears to have deteriorated to an alarming level (Künkler 2018). What has contributed to the rising religious intolerance and what are the theoretical and policy implications for the protection of religious pluralism, minority rights, and freedoms for believers (and nonbelievers) in a Muslim-majority democracy such as Indonesia?

This chapter focuses on the religious authority of traditional religious elites (ulama or *kiai*) and their strategic coalition with radical Islamists in order to account for religious intolerance. I argue that collective intolerance is likely to escalate and persist when traditional clerical elites forge this kind of coalition with radical Islamists to consolidate the former's religious authority and domination at the grassroots level. I call this an "intolerant coalition." When intolerant coalitions dominate state-sponsored religious institutions and policymaking, political elites and the state apparatus are not willing, nor likely, to interfere in religious conflict to protect minority communities. In contrast, when religious elites forge coalitions with other segments of civil society (such as minorities or secular and liberal groups) to prevent radicals from expanding their spheres of influence and authority, collective intolerance is likely minimal and more effectively mitigated. This is called a "tolerant coalition." In this situation, tolerant coalitions are likely in control of state-sponsored religious institutions and policymaking and are thus able to offer an informal channel to help minority communities mediate with the state apparatus and political elites and protect them against radical adversaries.

The province of West Java offers an ideal case study to answer questions pertinent to religious tolerance and pluralism. Bordering Jakarta, the national capital, West Java is a political, business, and educational center and the most populous and industrialized province of Indonesia's thirty-six provinces. The province is also traditionally known as a stronghold of Islamism due to its connection as the birthplace of some of the most prominent Islamist movements, including Darul Islam (DI) in the 1940s–50s, Hizbut Tahrir Indonesia (HTI), and the Justice and Prosperous Party (PKS) in the 1980s–90s. Since the mid-2000s, the province has experienced the most prominent and the largest number of cases of collective violence against religious minorities—what I call collective intolerance.

Despite these province-wide sociocultural and political similarities and shared historical legacies, districts such as Kuningan and Tasikmalaya have experienced more severe and persistent antiminority violence than neighboring districts such as Cirebon and Garut. The diverging levels of antiminority violence between Tasikmalaya and Garut—and the ways in which religious conflict is mitigated—is especially puzzling. Both regions were once a stronghold of the Darul Islam movement and remain susceptible to penetration by radical Islamism as well as the politicization of religion by elected Muslim officials seeking state powers. Yet Tasikmalaya gained national and international prominence as an intolerant district thanks to consistent and severe attacks by Muslim groups against religious minorities, especially the Ahmadiyah sect. In contrast, Garut remains relatively peaceful. Against our expectations, Garut's Ahmadi communities were integrated into the local Muslim community relatively peacefully and were thus able to continue their religious activities during the same period. Why and how did such striking variation emerge within the same province, known for its strong Islamist tradition and activism?

This chapter adopts paired comparison of two similar districts in the West Java province, Tasikmalaya and Garut, in order to explain the rise (and reduction) of religious intolerance. The comparative case studies of collective intolerance against religious minorities at the district level are methodologically beneficial for several reasons. First, it is important to note that collective intolerance is typically limited to a specific locality or a district, as is usually the case in large-scale communal violence (e.g., Varshney 2002, Wilkinson 2004). Hence my case studies take violence at the district and city level as the unit of comparative analysis instead of violence at the national and province level.[1] Even within provinces where many incidences of violence or intolerance are recorded, such as East Java, West Java, and Aceh, many districts and cities remain relatively peaceful and tolerant of religious minority communities despite being under structural, political, and sociocultural conditions that are said to be a cause of collective intolerance.

Second, West Java has experienced collective intolerance not only against the most prominent Muslim minority target, Ahmadiyah, but also against the most prominent Christian minority target, the Protestant congregations. This allows us to look closely into the mechanisms of antiminority mobilization, examining how violence is justified to mobilize the Muslim population and on what grounds. Scholars are divided not only in the categorization of violence but also regarding motivation. Are these incidents politically and materialistically motivated, as the instrumentalist position asserts, or ideologically or doctrinally motivated and hence characterized as religious and sectarian? (For an overview of these approaches see Duncan 2013.)

Third, my empirical focus on antiminority violence in West Java, particularly against the Ahmadiyah Muslim sect, critically assesses other prominent explanations and untested assumptions, especially "Christianization" or "secularization" of the Muslim community, penetration of radical Islamism, and electoral incentives of Muslim politicians. It also addresses the question of temporal variation: why does collective intolerance grow and escalate at a particular time?

The religious coalition I propose as a primary explanatory variable also accounts for the state's approach to minorities and their involvement in religious conflict. Extant studies of communal conflict in Indonesia and beyond tend to regard religious conflict primarily as a security, legal, or policy issue, thereby attributing state security and coercive apparatuses (e.g., the police, courts, laws), government policies (e.g., regional regulations), or the state's partnership with vigilante groups as the primary cause of communal violence (e.g., Crouch 2014; Tajima 2008, 2014). However, my empirical observations in selected localities across Indonesia suggest that formal institutions, laws, and policies introduced by the government are rarely (or poorly) enforced because of lack of state will or capacity to enforce them. It is still unclear why the state is sometimes willing to implement particular policies or laws to interfere in religious conflict and protect some religious minorities at the district level.

Area experts and large-N statistical analyses demonstrate that local enforcement officers and state officials typically rely on locally influential communal/ religious leaders and informal institutions to maintain social and public order, security, and peaceful relations among various religious communities at the grassroots level (De Juan, Pierskalla, and Vüllers 2015; Jaffrey 2019; Tajima 2014). Furthermore, minority religious communities opt to build relationships with dominant religious organizations and leaders as well as with state officials to defend their interests, communities, and faith according to a given local condition. For them, friendly relations with local religious leaders is essential. They do not simply remain silent as powerless victims in a democratized Indonesia.

My comparative case studies demonstrate that when an intolerant coalition is forged to dominate institutions of religious authority and policymaking to assert their shared majority identity against targeted minorities, political elites as well as security and legal apparatuses tend to be unwilling to actively interfere in conflict before, or when, violence escalates. By contrast, state and security officials are willing to provide support and protection to targeted minority communities when the dominant religious coalition is eager to protect a moderate and pluralistic local community and ensure peaceful religious and social order to prevent the penetration of radicals. The following sections offer two empirical case studies in Tasikmalaya and Garut to support my theoretical propositions.

Theories and Debates: Democracy, Religious Intolerance, and Religious Pluralism

One of the major challenges to religious pluralism in an Indonesian democracy, whether interpreted as a social condition or a political ideology, is from religious intolerance, or collective violence against religious and secular minorities. Religious intolerance violates the individual and communal rights of religious and secular citizens; but as underscored by scholars of modern democracy (Dahl 1986, 1991; Stepan 2007), these are fundamental rights and conditions that a modern constitutional democracy should protect. The problems of religious tolerance and religious freedom (and lack thereof) are not new or unique social and political phenomena across the globe (Grim and Finke 2011; Künkler and Shankar 2018; Lerner 2013; Sullivan et al. 2015). The recent upsurge of religious fundamentalism, nationalism, and collective violence against religious (and secular) communities, however, raises valuable questions about the quality and future of democracy in deeply divided emerging democracies such as Indonesia. Against expectations, religious conflict has significantly increased in the process of democratic consolidation against the backdrop of growing religious fundamentalism and politicized religious identity (Almond, Appleby, and Sivan 2003; Juergensmeyer 2017; Toft, Philpott, and Shah 2011), a phenomenon also evident in Burma/Myanmar, Egypt, Greece, Malaysia, Pakistan, and Poland, for example.

To differentiate religious intolerance from other political and sociocultural phenomena or general attitudes that scholars and observers have referred to as a "conservative turn" (Van Bruinessen 2013; Feillard and Madinier 2011; Platzdasch and Saravanamuttu 2014), I adopt a typology of collective violence (Tilly 2003) to conceptualize religious intolerance and term it "collective intolerance." More specifically, collective intolerance is defined as "abuse of religious minorities by individuals or groups in society for acts perceived as offensive or threatening to the majority faith of the country" based on the definition commonly used by international organizations and think-tanks (Pew Research Center 2014). According to this definition, collective intolerance encompasses abusive and aggressive *actions* against other religious communities based on religious affiliation, identity, belief, or practice. It is collectively motivated and mobilized and analytically differentiated from individual or group *attitudes* toward religious minorities, as advocated by other scholars to assess (in)tolerance (Menchik 2016; Fish 2011, 69–108). Such acts of collective intolerance take a variety of forms, ranging from damaging a place of worship and religious symbols to discrimination, prohibiting worship, protest, reporting to the police, public shaming, condoning practices considered religiously offensive, and legal accusation and criminalization.

According to the Setara institute, a Jakarta-based prodemocracy human rights organization, incidents and acts of assault, abuse, intimidation, and harassment against minority communities have increased dramatically since the mid-2000s and persist today, as shown in figure 4.1. The institute recorded 135 cases of such incidents of violence in 2007, 265 cases in 2008, 200 cases in 2009, 216 cases in 2010, 244 cases in 2011, 264 cases in 2012, 222 cases in 2013, and 134 cases in 2014. The latest data in 2016 reports 208 cases of violent incidents.[2]

According to this dataset, West Java consistently experienced the largest rate of violence since 2007, and the trend appears to continue. The major target of violence is the Ahmadiyah community, a Muslim sect considered by many Muslim groups as "heretical" or "unorthodox" because of their controversial doctrinal position on prophethood, contested by several mainstream Sunni groups in Indonesia (Burhani 2014), Pakistan, and elsewhere. The second largest target is

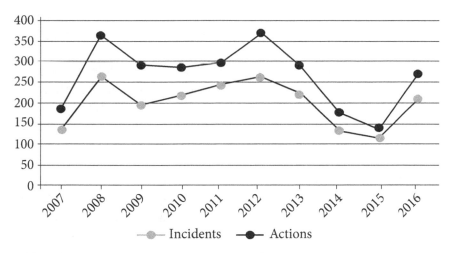

FIGURE 4.1. Level of religious intolerance (2007–2016)

Christian (primarily Protestant) communities. Datasets from local NGOs such as the Setara Institute, KontraS (KontraS 2012), and the Wahid Institute (The Wahid Institute 2010) and my own confidential communications and surveys with targeted religious communities between 2012 and 2017 indicate that collective intolerance was especially high and persistent in some districts (such as Bogor, Kuningan, and Tasikmalaya). In contrast, other neighboring districts (such as Cirebon and Garut) remained relatively peaceful and tolerant despite the presence of similar conditions, including legacies of Islamism, influential traditional religious boarding schools (*pesantrens*) and *kiais*, and a socioeconomically rural environment. In short, collective intolerance is not a nation- or province-wide but rather a district-specific trend.

Seeking Explanations for Religious Intolerance in Democratic Indonesia

My theoretical argument and empirical findings based on this controlled comparison and paired case studies provide an alternative assessment of and explanation for religious intolerance in Indonesian democracy. First, my argument is focused on religious institutions and authorities, questioning the function of secular politicians and officials and their instrumentalist use of religion—be they symbols, institutions, or resources, all of which are said to be the primary determinants for rising radicalism and conservativism. For example, some scholars consider religious policies (e.g., shari'a-influenced bylaws) and resource distribution (e.g., collection and distribution of zakat) as a policy instrument for secular politicians to cultivate broader support base and clientelistic relations in the Muslim community (Buehler 2008, 2016; Soedirgo 2018; Wilson 2014). According to this instrumentalist perspective, ultimately it is the electoral incentives of secular elites that will enable radical and conservative Islamism to flourish because both need one another in order to gain access to state power and patronage. Generally, religion is understood as an epiphenomenon of other materialistic interests.

Provinces such as West Java seem to be an ideal place for such relations to thrive, facilitating religious intolerance and conservativism, allegedly because of historically strong radical Islamism in civil society and pious Muslim populations whom aspiring politicians could capitalize on to cultivate popular support and win state offices (Rahman Alamsyah and Hadiz 2017). However, my empirical findings in West Java suggest that "marriages of convenience" between secular elites and radicals do not always take place despite the former's potential susceptibility to societal pressures from radicals. Nor have radical legacies or pressures resulted in religious intolerance throughout the province. For example, so-called shari'a-influenced bylaws were mostly intended to promote and defend piety and morality (e.g., regulation of alcoholic beverages, compulsory dress codes, or Quran classes), and were widely introduced across the province and the archipelago more broadly. And yet, collective intolerance was minimal in a large number of districts. In other words, the penetration of radical Islamism is not even across the province, as demonstrated by a study of the most famous radical group, the Islamic Defender's Front (FPI), whose influence is centered largely around Jakarta (Wilson 2014) and who has no connection to historical legacies. In Garut, the birthplace and stronghold of DI, there is no strong presence of FPI or other major radicals despite the district's historical ties to radical Islamism and its geographical and cultural proximity to Tasikmalaya. According to local leaders and civil society activists, the radicals in the region are weak, with more than one man claiming to be the leader of FPI Garut, and few local leaders or residents care to take them seriously.[3]

Second, my study indicates that the political influence of radical Islamism as civil society and social movement actors on policymaking is generally overrated, especially for new and fringe vigilante groups such as FPI. Radical Islamists indeed have grown and managed to foster mutually beneficial short-term relations with opportunistic secular politicians and/or state apparatuses (e.g., the police) and they seem to have gained unprecedented power to influence policymaking in the realm of religion, especially in urban areas such as Jakarta (Wilson 2014). However, we should not assume that these overzealous "born again" Muslim young men could go out and achieve their intended goals on their own without regard to other local conditions and institutions.

The influence and authority of traditional religious and communal elites remain essential at the grassroots level in maintaining social order and security in rural Indonesia, as aptly demonstrated by Sana Jaffrey's comparative study of vigilante violence (Jaffrey 2019) and Rizal Panggabean and Ihsan Ali-Fauzi's study of religious conflict (Panggabean and Ali-Fauzi 2015). The authority and what social movement theorists call "certification" of recognized elites (Tilly 2003; Tilly and Tarrow 2007, 74–78) are often needed by secular politicians and the security apparatus, not only in the latter's selfish quest for state powers and material payoffs but also, and more important, in their daily efforts to manage local conflict and maintain social order and peaceful religious society. This is especially true when it comes to the question of religion, as David Kloos and Mirjam Künkler reiterate in their study of local religious authority (Kloos and Künkler 2016). We must note that theological expertise and cultural and doctrinal capital are essential sources of local authority for the production and management of religious conflict. In fact, the expansion of radical Islamism has posed a threat to the domination and authority of traditional religious leaders who were already on the defensive in the context of the perceived threat of secularism, liberalism, and pluralism (ideological left) and Wahhabism/Salafism (ideological right), as well as consolidation of secular political powers in the democratic state.[4]

Furthermore, the religious market in democratic Indonesia has become more competitive and politicized among various religious organizations as a result of political liberalization and thriving new religious movements and leaders of all stripes who are aggressive claimants of religious authority (e.g., Hamayotsu 2011a; Hasan 2006, 2007; Hoesterey 2015). Mainstream Islamic movements and elites such as Nahdlatul Ulama (NU) and Muhammadiyah are searching for a strategy to deal with these new challenges and rivals, both ideological and political, to retain their religious authority and domination against the backdrop of their declining political clout in formal democratic institutions and electoral politics (Fealy and Bush 2014; Hamayotsu 2011b, 2012; Hamayotsu and Nataatmadja 2016; Pelletier forthcoming).

Finally, it is still unclear if and how structural transformations such as "secularization" "Christianization," or "Islamization" per se have contributed to religious conflict in civil society as some scholars and studies seem to indicate (e.g., Crouch 2014; Duncan 2013). There is indeed a widespread fear of secularization or Christianization in the Muslim community, especially among religious elites and officials. In the context of politicized religious identity, organizations and individuals perceived as representing or promoting secular, liberal, and plural-istic interests, are often considered to be "un-Islamic" and "anti-Islam," thereby easily framed as a threat to the Muslim community and Islam at large.

However, such a threat of secularism and Christianization is not entirely new or unusual in Indonesian history and society.[5] Hence we should not assume that such a fear, real or perceived, is automatically translated into collective violence against vulnerable minorities. It is still not clear why and under what condi-tions the perception of such a threat can lead to collective hatred and action to eliminate vulnerable Muslim communities such as Ahmadiyah or Shi'a, if Chris-tianization or secularization is the major concern. These communities mostly lived peacefully alongside surrounding Muslim communities for many decades, despite their theological discord (Beck 2005).

Even in West Java, there was significant variation in terms of the level and persistence of collective intolerance, despite the widespread perception of secu-larization and Christianization among religious elites across the board. It is also important to realize that it was largely *pesantrens* and ulama culturally and socially identified with NU (a movement generally associated with syncretic Islamic tra-ditions, moderation, and toleration) that have actively endorsed and promoted violence against other religious communities, especially Ahmadiyah, in the prov-ince. In contrast to theoretical propositions proposed by Jeremy Menchik that some religious organizations (e.g., Persis) are more intolerant than others (e.g., NU) (Menchik 2016), I have observed almost no active involvement of religious violence in West Java by Muhammadiyah or Persis, Islamic movements gener-ally categorized as more intolerant to other religious communities known for moderate and syncretic traditions. Quite the contrary: a Persis leader in Garut, for example, insisted that Persis were willing to join force with other groups, NU and Muhammadiyah, to fight against radicals and their common enemies to maintain a moderate community. She justified this position in the following way: "We, Persis, are finally accepted by the majority community to gain access to state and resources now. We were disliked, excluded and traumatized for a long time as an enemy of the state [*negara*] in the community, because of our past association with Masyumi [Majelis Syuro Muslimin Indonesia, political party identified with radical Islamism] and Islamist rebellion [DI] against the state."[6] Analytically, we need a model that can operationalize abstract concepts like "secularization" and "Christianization" as variables that could be linked causally to collective intoler-ance as an outcome. The case studies below help to fill the theoretical gaps I have identified and systematically investigate under what conditions, and how, a per-ceived threat among religious elites and organizations is cultivated and translated into collective action against targeted minority communities.

Democratization, Religious Conservativism, and Radicalism

The fall of authoritarian rule and the transition to democracy in 1998 opened up a range of opportunities and outlets for Islamic organizations and religious elites to pursue their interests and advance a vision of a more Islamically compliant society. Islamic organizations and religious elites viewed the regime transition as an opportunity to gain access to state power and patronage while elevating the position of Islam and promoting their respective corporate interests. The conditions under which the regime's transition and consolidation took place, however, differed considerably from conditions prior to the regime transition in at least three respects. This further accelerated a sense of insecurity and threat among Islamic organizations and elites, who had mostly been stripped of their political and legislative powers prior to the transition.

First, it was a transition from brutal military-dominant authoritarianism to democratic rule that occurred against the backdrop of a global push toward religious fundamentalism and transnational Islamism and security concerns among the US and allied countries to counter this push after 9/11. In order to counter transnational jihadism and terrorism, the US (and some other Western countries) strategically promoted so-called liberal and progressive Islamic movements and civil society groups in order to cultivate religious moderation and pluralism in the Muslim world. At the same time, as competition among various Islamic movements and actors intensified, the top echelons of mainstream organizations such as NU and Muhammadiyah considered transnational Islamism—and Wahhabism and Salafism in particular—to be a major ideological threat to their own religious traditions and identities and to organizational cohesion and domination.[7]

Second, the democratic transition allowed for the establishment of numerous religious parties connected to Islamic organizations and elites. However, Islamist organizations and elites determined to establish the constitutional superiority of Islam and build the state following shari'a-derived regulations were largely marginalized at the national level. In the parliamentary debate on the constitutional amendment, Islamist parties such as the United Development Party (PPP), Prosperous Justice Party (PKS), and Crescent Star Party (PBB) were easily defeated (Elson 2013). Furthermore, Islamic parties with parliamentary representation steadily declined after the inaugural elections of 1999 or altered their ideological position to appeal to broader Muslim constituencies and ensure political survival (Hamayotsu 2011b; Liddle and Mujani 2007; Pepinsky, Liddle and Mujani 2012).

Finally, a new democratic Indonesia saw the ascent of elites and organizations to executive and legislative positions, especially those whom Islamists generally regard as proponents of liberal, secular Christian and minority interests. The first post-*Reformasi* president, Abdurrahman Wahid (1999–2001), was an exceptionally progressive and liberal cleric and the former chairman of NU; he was elected president sponsored by an ad-hoc coalition of Islamic parties and leaders, including his own National Awakening Party (PKB) (Liddle 2001). But in contrast to the expectations of these religious parties and elites that Wahid would cater to their Islamic interests and elevate the position of Islam and the Muslim community in the democratic state, Wahid put in place extremely controversial policies, an approach that was perceived as a betrayal and overall detrimental to Islam and the Muslim community. These policies included: adding Confucianism (the cultural ritual connected to the Chinese community) as the sixth official religion sanctioned by the state (alongside Islam, Protestantism, Roman Catholicism, Hinduism, and Buddhism); lifting restrictions against communism (Leninism/Marxism) and other political leftist ideologies; removing discriminatory practices against ethnic/cultural minorities, especially the Chinese; and opening Indonesia's diplomatic relations with Israel.[8] Wahid, with his young and active civil society allies—most notably represented by the youth wing of NU, the Gerakan Pemuda Ansor (Youth Movement Ansor, GP Ansor)—were also strong advocates of religious minorities, religious pluralism and toleration, and liberal Islamic groups.[9]

Wahid's Indonesia not only reaffirmed the constitutional superiority of Pancasila as a pluralistic national ideology and as the foundation of the democratic state, but also allowed liberal Islamic groups and leaders, most prominently the Liberal Islamic Network (Jaringan Islam Liberal, JIL), to thrive. He encouraged liberal democrats to openly assert their progressive visions of Islam and civil and political rights and to demand religious freedom and pluralism. Wahid's liberal policies gained him popularity and admiration among the secular nationalist and minority communities as well as international communities. Yet his government was perceived by others as overtly privileging liberal, secular, minority, Christian, and Chinese interests, which a large segment of Islamic organizations and elites tended to regard as threats to the superiority and authority of the majority Muslim interests and of Islam more generally, under the new democratic regime (Waskito 2010).

Megawati Sukarnoputri's sudden ascent to power in 2001 further reinforced ambivalence and uncertainty among religious elites regarding the place of Islam and the majority community in the regime and state. The Indonesian Democratic Party of Struggle (PDI-P) chaired by Megawati adopted an explicitly secularist position regarding relations between state and religion, which they insisted be separate. PDI-P was a staunch opponent of the Islamist attempt to establish the constitutional superiority of Islam over Pancasila (Elson 2013, 410).[10] Moreover,

over 30 percent of PDI-P members of the DPR (Dewan Perwakilan Rakyat, national legislative body) were Christian and Hindu, while other secular parties such as Golkar and Democratic Party (PD) were predominantly Muslim (Kompas 2005, 2010). PDI-P was traditionally supported by minority communities and elites, especially Christian and Chinese, as a defender of their political, economic, and cultural interests in the state, thereby further contributing to suspicion and hostility toward the party—as well as minority communities—among conservative Muslim elites.[11]

It is against this backdrop that conservative Islamic elites sought and gained access to state and semistate organizations, especially the Indonesian Council of Ulama (Majelis Ulama Indonesia, MUI), to pursue political prominence and religious authority at the highest echelon of policymaking since the mid-2000s. Through these institutional and informal channels, conservative clerics and religious leaders sought to suppress and criminalize groups and individuals they categorized as enemies of Islam or infidel—most prominently, groups that promoted secularism, liberalism, and pluralism. In 2005, MUI issued a series of fatwas (Islamic decrees) to this end; a fatwa declaring the Ahmadiyah sect "heretical," and another one declaring religious pluralism, liberalism, and secularism "deviant" (sesat).[12]

Another equally prominent religious institution sponsored by the government during this period that ended up further fueling collective intolerance is the Inter-religious Harmony Forum (Forum Kerukunan Umat Beragama, FKUB). Following the issuing of the joint ministerial decree by the Ministries of Religious Affairs and Home Affairs (Peraturan Bersama Menteri Agama dan Menteri Dalam Negeri, No. 9 2006/No. 8 2006), FKUB offices were newly established at the provincial and district levels across the archipelago in order to regulate places of worship among religious communities.[13] Despite its intention to maintain harmonious interreligious relations, however, in reality FKUB has allowed dominant religious organizations and leaders in a given district to exercise considerable influence in religious policymaking, especially pertinent to the regulation of religious minorities and proselytization as discussed in the case studies below (see the contributions by Aragon and Duncan in this volume for more on this).

Islamic conservativism and religious intolerance at the national level grew more prominent after Susilo Bambang Yudhoyono was elected president in 2004. In stark contrast to his relatively pluralist predecessors, Yudhoyono not only appointed conservative leaders from Islamist parties in the highest positions in the government but also actively sponsored MUI and their discriminatory policies to revitalize the institutional power and authority of conservative ulama in the Muslim community, thereby fostering hostile environments against religious minorities (Hamayotsu 2013).[14] Moreover, his government is seen among the Muslim community as well as by Indonesia observers to be more amenable to radical Islamism, especially FPI—hence, some observers argue, legitimizing radical and violent actions and fueling religious intolerance and antiminority violence since the mid-2000s (Bush 2015; Platzdasch 2011).

Collective Intolerance in West Java

Such macrolevel political conditions and a deep-seated sense of suspicion and hostility toward secular, liberal, and Christian interests, reinforced under the various presidents, have not however automatically translated into collective action against religious minorities at the local level. As outlined at the onset of this chapter, collective intolerance was restricted to and more pronounced and persistent in some of West Java's districts, including Kuningan and Tasikmalaya (against Ahmadiyah) and Bogor (against the Protestant Church, Yasmin). By contrast, other districts such as Cirebon and Garut managed to keep collective intolerance minimal despite the presence of equally sizable Ahmadiyah communities and similar socioeconomic and political conditions.

West Java has consistently endured the highest level of collective intolerance across the archipelago between 2007 and 2018, and the pattern appears to continue today. Ahmadiyah remains a chief target of violence, intimidation, and harassment. The province is not only demographically and socioeconomically diverse but also highly fragmented politically and religiously. There is no single powerful religious or political organization that dominates the province (such as NU in East Java or Muhammadiyah in Yogyakarta and Central Java), making the political and religious markets even more competitive in the context of decentralized democratic institutions. Moreover, the province is traditionally known for radical and conservative Islamism thanks to the prominent Islamist movement Darul Islam, which built a strong support base in the southeastern region (locally called Priangan Timur) in the 1940s (Formichi 2012; Horikoshi 1975). In 2008, an Islamist politician from the PKS, Ahmad Heryawan, was elected as governor. Additionally, the province—alongside at least around half (twelve) of the province's districts—enacted a decree (Regulation No. 12/2011) prohibiting Ahmadiyah from proselytizing among Muslims; this was just one among several conservative and discriminatory policies that local authorities introduced. Despite these province-wide conditions, the level of collective intolerance differed considerably across districts.

My comparative case studies in the province demonstrate that the level of collective intolerance—and the ways in which it is managed—is primarily dependent on dominant religious elites (ulama or *kiais*) and institutions (*pesant-rens*) in a given locality and the pattern of coalition they forge with other civil society actors. In contrast to other studies, my empirical findings suggest that certification of established elites was essential for collective intolerance to grow. Vigilante radicals were only able to penetrate and integrate into the lower echelons of religious policymaking within a dominant coalition when dominant religious elites relied on and authorized the former's coercive powers to achieve their shared goals enforcing religious policies, regulations, and practices.

It is important to note that the intolerant coalition is based on mutual benefits and payoffs; radical vigilantes provide religious elites informal coercive powers (i.e., intimidation, criminalization, punishment) to attain popular compliance with the latter's policies and regulations. The services provided by radical vigilantes are useful for religious elites running state-sponsored religious organizations such as MUI and FKUB because these bodies are officially representative of civil society in a given district and not an arm of the formal state religious bureaucracy. They are unequipped with adequate coercive and jurisdictive functions, nor do they have administrative and financial means to enforce fatwa, directives, or policies.

When dominant religious elites and institutions forge coalitions with vigilante Islamists to dominate state-sponsored religious institutions (e.g., MUI, FKUB) and gain access to policymaking (e.g., regulation of places of worship), collective intolerance tends to rise and persist. Under this condition, intolerant coalitions target and attempt to eliminate symbolic groups and/or individuals they categorize as "un-Islamic," "heretical," or "infidel"—a common threat to their Islamic tradition and doctrinal authority and cohesion. The targets may range from Muslim fringe groups (Ahmadiyah and Shi'a) to foreign pop icons (Lady Gaga was banned from holding a concert in 2012 by MUI) and political leaders (e.g. Basuki Tjahaja Purnama, see the contribution by Lohanda in this volume), to name just a few prominent examples. Moreover, political elites and the state apparatus are not willing to interfere in religious conflict to protect minority communities when local dominant religious elites are united with and supportive of radicals in the name of Islam and defending the Muslim majority.

When dominant religious elites and institutions forge a coalition with moderate, secular and liberal civil society to fight radicals, however, collective intolerance is likely to be low and less persistent. In this situation, tolerant religious coalitions take charge of state-sponsored religious institutions and policymaking while offering an informal channel to mediate effectively with political elites and the state apparatus to accommodate and protect minority communities against radical adversaries.

In order to demonstrate how these patterns of coalition making have resulted in collective intolerance, the final section below offers empirical findings from two comparative case studies of anti-Ahmadiyah violence in the Priangan Timur area, the former stronghold of Darul Islam: Tasikmalaya and Garut.

Tasikmalaya: Conservative *Pesantrens*, Intolerant Coalitions, and Collective Violence

Tasikmalaya is identified as one of the districts that have experienced the most persistent antiminority violence, especially against the Ahmadiyah community. The region is comprised of two administrative units, Kotamadya Tasikmalaya (city) and Kabupaten Tasikmalaya (regency), and it is popularly dubbed *Kota Santri* (City of the Pious) thanks to the presence of vibrant *pesantren*s and religious communities deeply embedded in the local community, economy, and politics.[15] Ahmadiyah communities are mostly located near Cipasung, Singaparna, the regency capital. They have mostly lived peacefully alongside the surrounding communities for decades until the sudden surge of attacks and harassment involving local radical groups such as FPI and the Taliban began in the mid-2000s.[16] According to my observations and interviews with Ahmadiyah leaders there in July 2016, they still lived in fear and were not able to practice openly because of the inadequate protection and security provided by the community, government agencies, and police forces. Ahmadiyah leadership categorized Tasikmalaya as one of the "red-zones" where their community and members were still at risk, even though the level of physical violence had receded considerably.[17]

One of the key attributes that sets Tasikmalaya apart from other tolerant West Java districts is that dominant religious leaders and *pesantren*s have actively supported and integrated radical vigilante groups, FPI in particular, into the lowest echelons of the structures of religious policymaking and influence to coordinate and work together in the name of "defending Islam and the *umma* (Islamic community)." MUI Kota Tasikmalaya, headed by the prominent cleric KH. Achef Noor Mubarok, together with other influential religious leaders such as KH. Asep Maoshul Affandi, have openly endorsed FPI, whose national leader, Muhammad Rizieq Shihab, has called for a united front in order to achieve their shared goals: the creation of an Islamic state of Indonesia guided by shari'a laws and the eradication of un-Islamic, liberal, and secular elements from Tasikmalaya and Indonesia, including the Ahmadiyah sect.[18]

Asep Maoshul Affandi's authority and influence among *pesantren* communities was essential in instigating antiminority sentiment and mobilizing young people, especially students, to take action against Ahmadis. He is the son of

KH. Choer Affandi, the head of one of the most prestigious *pesantrens* in Tasik-malaya, the Pesantren Miftahul Huda in Manojaya, and also a deputy executive board member of a prominent Islamist organization, the Majelis Mujahidin Indonesia (Council of Indonesia's Mujahidin, MMI). Asep Maoshul is also an elected member of DPR from the ranks of the Islamist PPP, the largest political party in the region. He was especially hostile to Ahmadiyah and did not hesitate to encourage Muslim students and alumni from his *pesantren* to join FPI to carry out campaigns against so-called un-Islamic elements, including Ahmadis. It is in fact widely known that some teachers and leaders from this *pesantren* (and other associated *pesantrens*) were already active FPI members.[19] These religious leaders and students forged an informal coalition to coordinate actions with many other *pesantrens* and Muslim youth groups, including KAMMI (Kesatuan Aksi Mahasiswa Muslim Indonesia) and HMI (Himpunan Muhasiswa Indonesia), and to organize various demonstrations and actions in the name of defending Islam.[20] The influence of this intolerant coalition seems to have grown even more dramatically in the region after the demise of a prominent NU *kiai*, KH. Ilyas Ruhiyat, in 2007. Ruhiyat was the head of the prestigious Pesantren Cipasung, a close ally of the former president Wahid, and a founding leader of the National Awakening Party (PKB), a moderate pluralist party founded by Wahid.[21]

In Tasikmalaya regency as well FPI was readily integrated into the lowest ranks of state-sponsored religious policymaking structures, specifically MUI and FKUB, as a minor partner. These radical Islamists thus gained access to powerful positions sponsored by the state to work closely with or for prominent religious leaders to achieve their shared goals—namely to defend Islam and the Muslim community against common adversaries.[22]

Such a powerful intolerant coalition, headed by prominent religious leaders from prestigious *pesantrens* (usually identified with NU), can dominate state-sponsored religious policymaking and leave moderate religious organizations and civil society activists, especially the GP Ansor, largely powerless and weak. They are not logistically equipped to propagate and enforce their moderate and pluralistic visions for Islam and the Indonesian nation, let alone offer physical protection to minority communities, to the extent to which their NU and Ansor counterparts in other provinces and districts have.[23]

Given that the Islamist party PPP is traditionally dominant in the region and structurally embedded in local Muslim communities, endorsement and certification from prominent clerics is indispensable for political elites to win public office, leaving the secular elites beholden to the dominant religious elites.[24] Under such conditions, unsurprisingly, state security apparatuses, especially the local police force, are rather reluctant to interfere in religious conflict and to protect the minority communities targeted by the coalition of powerful religious elites and organizations as "enemies of Islam". This is true even if there was considerable pressure from Jakarta and prodemocracy human rights organizations and activists to prevent violence—until, at least and at last, the current president Joko Widodo adopted stringent policies to criminalize organizations and actions deemed "anti-Pancasila" in 2017.[25]

Garut: Tolerant Coalition, Weak Radical Islamism, and Limited Collective Intolerance

In contrast to Tasikmalaya, Garut (regency) has managed to keep collective intolerance minimal, despite its physical proximity to Tasikmalaya and other similar attributes—deep historical lineage with DI and radical Islamism and vibrant Islamic organizations and institutions. Garut also houses sizable Ahmadiyah communities and villages, with around 1500 members, both active and nominal. Tenjowaringin, a small village dominated by the Ahmadiyah community located on the hilltop bordering Garut and Tasikmalaya, could in fact have been another "Manis Lor," an Ahmadi-dominated village in Kuningan that endured the most vicious attacks and persistent harassment in the province.[26] However, the village (administratively located on the Tasik side) has mostly avoided radical attacks, keeping Garut as a "green zone" for the Ahmadiyah community. The regency is categorized as adequately safe, and they carry out regular religious and social activities without fear of violence or pressure to go underground.[27]

A close observation of Ahmadiyah activities and relations with other Muslim communities and local leaders in the region demonstrates that the Ahmadis here are peacefully integrated into the local community. Almost none of the influential MUI leaders I surveyed between 2012 and 2016 talked negatively about the Ahmadiyah. Quite surprisingly, they instead emphasized how cordial their relations were and how peacefully they settled issues, despite the doctrinal disagreement of local leaders. Nor were they unaware of controversies concerning Ahmadiyah activities in other districts.

This unexpectedly inclusive atmosphere for Ahmadi communities is in part attributed to the "integration" strategy put in place by Garut Ahmadi leaders after violence flared up elsewhere against the group in the 1990s. The Ahmadi local branch leader, Rahmat Syukur (also known as Pak Ukun), the business owner of a Muslim-friendly luxury hotel resort (Sumber Alam Resort), has regularly sponsored a range of social, welfare and cultural activities in order to cater for the welfare of Garut's population, regardless of their ethnic or religious background and affiliation. Some of the popular programs he sponsors include free medical services and organic herbal medicines, blood donation campaigns, and boxing training and tournaments for youth groups. Moreover, through his sponsorship of these religious, social, recreational, and charity activities, Pak Ukun has built close working relations and partnerships with local business and religious organizations and elites as well as with high-ranking government officials. Furthermore, in 2010 both he and his wife were invited to join the honorary board of the police force at the provincial level alongside other local leaders and notables, largely due to their social and business contributions to the local community. Pak Ukun insists that his close working relations with high-ranking police officers and the *bupati* (regent) as well as other religious leaders is the key in maintaining a safe environment for Ahmadiyah communities.[28]

For the Ahmadis to be accepted and integrated into the local community, the endorsement and protection provided by dominant religious leaders in the regency was essential. Garut's religious community and institutions, more heterogeneous than those in Tasikmalaya, comprise not only a majority of NU *pesantrens* and ulama but also sizable and influential modernist Persis and Muhammadiyah communities. These religious leaders have built a broad coalition and working relations both among the various Islamic communities and with other secular and liberal segments of civil and political society. MUI Garut is dominated by these religious leaders and has forged an alliance with secular NGOs and activists to mobilize anticorruption campaigns, leading to the resignation of the then *bupati* Agus Supriadi in 2007 (Djani 2013).[29] In contrast to Tasik's MUI elites who have actively integrated FPI and radical Islamists in their policymaking structures, Garut's MUI elites systematically excluded them from any and all positions of religious policymaking and influence.

Garut's *ulama* and religious elites commonly perceive radical Islamists, including those self-proclaimed descendants of the DI movement, as their enemies and potential agents of disturbance when it comes to the cohesion of the local community and its peaceful social order. Although these religious elites do not agree with Ahmadi doctrines (just like any other mainstream Islamic organizations and elites throughout the country), they are not interested in joining forces with vigilante radicals to launch campaigns, let alone use violence, against Ahmadiyah or any other minority or secular groups. Instead, these leaders insist, MUI Garut facilitates and mediates informal discussions and offers peaceful mediation and resolution among local ulama and Islamic groups, government officials, security forces, and Ahmadi leaders so that they can manage conflict in the regency.[30]

Under such conditions, even puritanical movements that other scholars consider doctrinally and ideologically most intolerant (e.g., Persis) are here willing to join the dominant coalition, promoting religious tolerance and communal peace. Their eagerness to be seen as moderate and tolerant has less to do with their doctrinal position or personal or organizational attitude and more with their corporate interest in maintaining their religious influence and achieving survival in a local community. As suggested above, Persis leaders want to avoid being perceived as "radicals" or "enemies of the state (*negara*) and Pancasila" which would translate into being excluded from the positions of influence and access to state powers and community resources they currently enjoy. They contend that they suffered for a long time from such perception and exclusion because of their close association with Masyumi and DI in the 1940s–50s.[31] Now, to highlight their friendly relations with other religious communities in the region, both Muslims and not, Garut MUI leaders refer proudly to their annual community event: "We, the Garut community, celebrate our 'Garut Birthday (*Hari Jadi Garut*)' together with all other religious and ethnic communities to build a community."[32] Ahmadiyah is part of this community-building enterprise.

This grand tolerant coalition forged among religious elites and organizations allows other pluralist and moderate youth groups connected to NU, especially GP Ansor, to stay active and effective in protecting minority communities, whether Ahmadi or Christian, in the name of Pancasila and the Unitary State of the Republic of Indonesia (NKRI). Moreover, GP Ansor closely coordinates and trains with the state security apparatus, especially the police force, to fight radical groups from penetrating local Muslim communities and *pesantrens* and ultimately to manage religious conflict peacefully.[33] As a result, the penetration and influence of radical Islamists remains very weak. Furthermore, in Garut, local police forces and political elites are more willing to coordinate with moderates to protect minority communities than in more intolerant regions such as Tasikmalaya and Kuningan.

Religious Pluralism and Indonesian Democracy

This chapter offers comparative case studies of religious intolerance in West Java to account for the rise of antiminority violence in a democratic Indonesia. In doing so, it seeks to gain some insight into the challenges—and possibilities—facing Muslim-majority democracies to protect a pluralistic social condition wherein various religious and secular communities can coexist and practice their respective faiths without coercion. My comparative analysis incorporates systematically selected tolerant and intolerant districts in the same province, in order to demonstrate that collective intolerance tends to rise and persist when traditional clerical elites forge a coalition with vigilante radicals to dominate the structures of religious policymaking in a given district. The West Java districts of Tasikmalaya and Kuningan confirm this proposition. Alternatively, when clerical elites build a coalition with other segments of civil society, including moderates, secular, and liberals, and actively exclude radicals from the structures of religious policymaking and influence, religious tolerance is more likely to dominate. Other districts including Garut and Cirebon served as a counterfactual case to confirm this proposition.

Moreover, my theoretical and empirical findings are equally beneficial in understanding the state's approach to religious conflict and minorities. In line with the findings of other scholars of collective violence in Indonesia (De Juan, Pierskalla and Vüllers 2015; Jaffrey 2019; Panggabean and Ali-Fauzi 2015; Tajima 2014), my study demonstrates that the function of informal institutions, especially religious institutions, are essential in both escalating and resolving religious conflict. This is because the state security and bureaucratic apparatuses as well as elected executives are mostly dependent on dominant religious elites in not only seeking popular support and compliance but also—and even more important—in maintaining social and communal order at the grassroots level. This is especially true when it comes to the question of religion. In other words, my findings suggest that it is not primarily the instrumental use of religion by secular politicians that has been the primary determinant for the escalation of religious intolerance and declining religious pluralism in a democratic Indonesia, nor is it the influence of vigilante radicals. Rather, it is the result of strategic coalitions that local religious elites have forged with vigilante radicals to dominate religious policymaking and regulate local communities according to their exclusive visions and interpretations of Islam. Additionally, the religious coalition also helps account for when and how the shared perception of threat among Muslim elites is cultivated and turned into collective action.

Without doubt, collective intolerance is detrimental to the strengthening of the state's ability and willingness to protect the fundamental constitutional rights of religious and secular populations. The consolidation of democratic rule and institutions in Muslim-majority nations such as Indonesia has been complicated by thriving religious fundamentalism, transnational jihadism and counterterrorism, and politicized religious identities on a global scale. It is against this backdrop that traditional clerical elites tend to be apprehensive and defensive about the idea of "religious pluralism." They view the idea as a political ideology and tool to undermine their authority and powers by secular and non-Muslim minority interests who, in their view, have dominated the Indonesian state, modern economy, and nation-building to the detriment of the "majority" Muslim community, a point Saba Mahmood aptly reiterates in the Middle-Eastern context (Mahmood 2012). Thus the mobilization of collective Muslim sentiment and action against what the clerical elites categorize as "enemies of Islam"—whether ideologically left or right—should be understood as their quest for authority and power in Indonesian society and democracy.

Notes

I would like to thank Ihsan Ali-Fauzi, Jacques Bertrand, Jamie Davidson, Greg Fealy, Sana Jaffrey, Alexandre Pelletier, Tom Pepinsky, and Yuhki Tajima for their critical comments and feedback. Ceng Husni Mubarak provided superb and cheerful logistical support to collect valuable data in Garut and Tasikmalaya.

1. For province-level comparative analysis of Islamist activism, see Buehler 2013, Pelletier Forthcoming.

2. Data obtained from Setara institute (http://setara-institute.org/). According to their coding, the number of acts/actions tend to be higher than incidents because in one reported incident, more than one type of act (e.g., damaging a place of worship, condoning, reporting to police, discrimination) tend to take place.

3. Confidential communications, June 21, 2012, and July 29–31, 2016.

4. Personal communications with the chairman of Muhammadiyah, Haedar Nashir, Yogyakarta, July 22, 2016; Abdul Mu'thi, secretary general, Muhammadiyah, Jakarta, July 30, 2013.

5. There are numerous official documents, personal memoirs and autobiographies, periodicals, magazines, and publications published by NU, Muhammadiyah, and associated organizations and authors to evaluate their perception of threat. Some examples are: Hamka 1970; Pimpinan Pusat Muhammadiyah 2005; Sabirin 2004; Siandes 2005.

6. Confidential communication, July 29, 2016.

7. Personal communications with the chairman of Muhammadiyah, Haedar Nashir, Yogyakarta, July 22, 2016; Abdul Mu'thi, secretary general, Muhammadiyah, Jakarta, July 30, 2013. For the NU's position, see for example "Masya Allah! 12 Yayasan ini Dituduh PBNU sebagai Salafi-Wahabi," voa-Islam.com, December 6, 2011, https://www.voa-islam.com/read/indonesiana/2011/12/06/16930/masya-allah-12-yayasan-ini-dituduh-pbnu-sebagai-salafiwahabi-penebar-teror/. Various other internal documents, discussions, and periodical publications have also been obtained by the author.

8. E.g., "Manuver Gus Dur Mengimbangi Israel," *Suara Nahdlatul Ulama*, February 10, 2017, http://www.nu.or.id/post/read/75243/manuver-gus-dur-mengimbangi-israel-.

9. "Gus Dur Proposed as National Hero," *Jakarta Post*, January 9, 2010; "Gus Dur: A Champion of Pluralism," *The Straits Times*, January 16, 2010.

10. "Ketua MUI: PDIP adalah Musuh Islam & Musuh Umat Islam," *Kabarnet.in*, June 1, 2014. https://kabarnet.wordpress.com/2014/06/01/ketua-mui-pdip-adalah-musuh-islam-musuh-umat-islam/ (accessed April 19, 2021).

11. Confidential communications with Christian organizations and leaders: Jeirry Sumampou, PGI Jakarta, August 26, 2013; Yasmin Church leaders, September 8, 2012; September 1, 2013; June 22, 2014. See also, "Ketua MUI Pusat: Partai yang Memata-matai Khotbah Jumat adalah Musuh Islam," *Beritahukum.com*, May 31, 2014, http://new.beritahukum.com/2014/05/31/ketua-mui-pusat-partai-yang-memata-matai-khotbah-jumat-adalah-musuh-islam/ (accessed April 19, 2021), or a post on MUI's Facebook page from

June 1, 2014, https://www.facebook.com/MajlisUlamaIndonesia/posts/884678928213985 (accessed on July 23, 2020).

12. Fatwa Majelis Ulama Indonesia Nomor: 11/MUSAN VII/MUI/15/2005 Tentang Aliran Ahmadiyah; Fatwa Majelis Ulama Indonesia Nomor: 7/MUNAS VII/MUI/11/2005 Tentang Pluralisme, Liberalisme Dan Sekularisme Agama.

13. Peraturan Bersama Menteri Agama dan Menteri Dalam Negeri No. 9 2006, https://ntt.kemenag.go.id/file/file/dokumen/rndz1384483132.pdf.

14. "Yudhoyono Says Indonesia Is Tolerant Nation," *Jakarta Globe*, August 16, 2011.

15. According to the Ministry of Religious Affairs, there are 758 *pesantens* in the regency and 100 in the city in Tasikmalaya.

16. The group is locally born and has no formal connection with Afghanistan's Taliban.

17. Confidential communications with Firdaus Mubarak, Ahmadiyah spokesperson, August 10, 2012; Ahmadiyah Tasikmalaya branch leaders, August 1, 2016.

18. "Muncul Spanduk Penolakan, Habib Rizieq Justru Disambut Puluhan Ribu Jamaah di Tasik," *Suara-Islam.com*, August 27, 2016, http://www.suara-islam.com/read/index/19575/Muncul-Spanduk-Penolakan--Habib-Rizieq-Justru-Disambut-Puluhan-Ribu-Jamaah-di-Tasik (last accessed on March 7, 2017, no longer available); "KH Asep Maoshul Affandy: Ahmadiyah Bukan Islam," *Kuningan Mass*, August 10, 2016, https://kuninganmass.com/government/kh-asep-maoshul-affandy-ahmadiyah-bukan-islam.

19. "Pesantren Miftahul Huda Tasikmalaya Tak Larang Santrinya Jadi Anggota FPI," *Indonesia Today*, October 13, 2013, http://archive.itoday.co.id/politik/pesantren-miftahul-huda-tasikmalaya-tak-larang-santrinya-jadi-anggota-fpi, available at https://www.kaskus.co.id/show_post/5268f617be29a05a348b4579/66/- (accessed April 19, 2021).

20. Confidential communications with KH Achef Noor Mubarok, chairman, MUI Kota Tasikmalaya, July 6, 2012; KAMMI Kota Tasikmalaya branch leaders, July 27, 2012.

21. KH. Ilyas is one of the prominent NU *kiais* who declared the founding of PKB, the party headed by Wahid. His eldest son, Acep Zam Zam, is an artist and civil society advocate for Wahid's NU lines of progressive Islam and religious pluralism together with Ansor leaders within the region. Personal communication with Acep Zam Zam, July 24, 2012.

22. Confidential communications with FKUB/MUI officials, FKUB, Singapurna, Kabupaten Tasikmalaya, August 1, 2016.

23. Confidential communications with Ketua GP Ansor, Tasikmalaya city and regency, Kota Tasikmalaya, July 5, 2012; Ketua GP Ansor, Cirebon, July 18, 2012; Ketua GP Ansor, Kuningan, September 18, 2013; Ketua GP Ansor, Garut, July 30, 2016.

24. Confidential communication with then Tasik PPP politician, Dede Sudrajat, July 3, 2012. Sudrajat was the running mate with Budi Budiman for the executive office as vice mayor during their election campaign. He left PPP to run for the mayoral position in 2017.

25. Confidential communication with Ahmadiyah leaders, August 1, 2016.

26. Around three thousand villagers belong to Ahmadiyah in this village alone.

27. Confidential communication with Ahmadiyah leaders, July 29, 2016.

28. Confidential communication with Pak Ukun, Garut, July 31, 2016.

29. Confidential communications with Luky Djani, International Corruption Watch, Jakarta, June 18, 2012; Agus Rutandi, Garut Governance Watch (GGW), June 20, 2012; Agus Sugandi, GGW, July 6, 2012.

30. Confidential communications with MUI Garut officials, June 21, 2012; July 6, 2012; July 29–30, 2016.

31. Confidential communication with a Persis leader/MUI official, Garut, July 29, 2016.

32. Confidential communication with Syamhari, vice secretary, MUI Garut, July 29, 2016. He is also a NU branch official.

33. Confidential communication with Subhan Fahmi, Ketua GP Ansor Garut, July 30, 2016.

References

Almond, Gabriel A, R Scott Appleby, and Emmanuel Sivan. 2003. *Strong Religion: The Rise of Fundamentalisms around the World*. Chicago: University of Chicago Press.

Beck, Heman L. 2005. "The Rupture of the Muhammadiyah with the Ahmadiyya." *Bijdragen tot de Taal-, Land-en Volkenkunde (BKI)* 161, no. 2/3: 1–33.

Buehler, Michael. 2008. "The Rise of Shari'a By-laws in Indonesian Districts: An Indication for Changing Patterns of Power Accumulation and Political Corruption." *South East Asia Research* 16, no. 2: 255–85.

Buehler, Michael. 2013. "Subnational Islamization through Secular Parties: Comparing *Shari'a* Politics in Two Indonesian Provinces." *Comparative Politics* 46, no. 1: 63–82. https://doi.org/10.5129/001041513807709347.

Buehler, Michael. 2016. *The Politics of Shari'a Law: Islamist Activists and the State in Democratizing Indonesia*. Cambridge: Cambridge University Press.

Burhani, Ahmad Najib. 2014. "Treating Minorities with Fatwas: A Study of the Ahmadiyya Community in Indonesia." *Contemporary Islam* 8, no. 3: 285–301. https://doi.org/10.1007/s11562-013-0278-3.

Bush, Robin. 2015. "Religious Politics and Minority Rights during the Yudhoyono Presidency." In *The Yudhoyono Presidency: Indonesia's Decade of Stability and Stagnation*, edited by Edward Aspinall, Marcus Mietzner, and Dirk Tomsa, 239–57. Singapore: Institute of Southeast Asian Studies.

Crouch, Melissa. 2014. *Law and Religion in Indonesia: Conflict and the Courts in West Java* London: Routledge.

Dahl, Robert A. 1986. *Democracy, Liberty, and Equality* Oslo: Norwegian University Press.

Dahl, Robert A. 1991. *Democracy and Its Critics*. New Haven: Yale University Press.

De Juan, Alexander, Jan H. Pierskalla, and Johannes Vüllers. 2015. "The Pacifying Effects of Local Religious Institutions: An Analysis of Communal Violence in Indonesia." *Political Research Quarterly* 68, no. 2: 211–24. https://doi.org/10.1177/1065912915578460.

Djani, Luky. 2013. "Reform Movements and Local Politics in Indonesia." PhD diss., Murdoch University.

Duncan, Christopher R. 2013. *Violence and Vengeance: Religious Conflict and Its Aftermath in Eastern Indonesia*. Ithaca, NY: Cornell University Press.

Elson, R. E. 2013. "Two Failed Attempts to Islamize the Indonesian Constitution." *SOJOURN: Journal of Social Issues in Southeast Asia* 28, no. 3: 379–437.

Fealy, Greg, and Robin Bush. 2014. "The Political Decline of Traditional Ulama in Indonesia." *Asian Journal of Social Science* 42, no. 5: 536–60. https://doi.org/10.1163/15685314-04205004.

Feillard, Andrée, and Rémy Madinier. 2011 *The End of Innocence? Indonesian Islam and the Temptations of Radicalism*. Translated by Wong Wee. Singapore NUS Press.

Fish, M Steven. 2011. *Are Muslims Distinctive? A Look at the Evidence*. Oxford: Oxford University Press.

Formichi, Chiara. 2012. *Islam and the Making of the Nation: Kartosuwiryo and Political Islam in 20th Century Indonesia*. Leiden: KITLV Press.

Grim, Brian J, and Roger Finke. 2011. *The Price of Freedom Denied: Religious Persecution and Conflict in the Twenty-first Century*. Cambridge: Cambridge University Press.

Hamayotsu, Kikue. 2011a "The End of Political Islam? A Comparative Analysis of Religious Parties in the Muslim Democracy of Indonesia" *Journal of Current Southeast Asian Affairs* 30, no. 3: 133–59.

Hamayotsu, Kikue. 2011b. "Political Rise of the Prosperous Justice Party in Post-Authoritarian Indonesia: Examining the Political Economy of Islamist Mobilization in a Muslim Democracy." *Asian Survey* 51, no. 5: 971–92.

Hamayotsu, Kikue. 2012. "A House for All Muslims?" *Inside Indonesia* 108, https://www.insideindonesia.org/a-house-for-all-muslims.

Hamayotsu, Kikue. 2013. "The Limits of Civil Society in Democratic Indonesia: Media Freedom and Religious Intolerance." *Journal of Contemporary Asia* 43, no. 4: 658–77.

Hamayotsu, Kikue. 2014. "Conservative Turn? Religion, State and Conflict in Indonesia." *Pacific Affairs* 87, no. 4: 815–25.

Hamayotsu, Kikue. 2015. "Democracy and Religious Pluralism in Southeast Asia: Indonesia and Malaysia Compared." Working paper. Religion and World Affairs Series, The Institute on Culture, Religion, and World Affairs, Boston University. http://www.bu.edu/cura/henry-luce-foundation-funding/cura-luce-seminar-series-on-key-issues-in-religion-and-world-affairs/.

Hamayotsu, Kikue, and Ronnie Nataatmadja. 2016. "Indonesia in 2015: The People's President's Rocky Road and Hazy Outlooks in Democratic Consolidation." *Asian Survey* 55, no. 6: 129–37.

Hamka. 1970. *Beberapa Tantangan Terhadap Ummat Islam Dimasa Kini: Secularisme, Syncritisme dan Ma'shiat*. Jakarta: Bulan Bintang.

Hasan, Noorhaidi. 2006. *Laskar Jihad: Islam, Militancy, and the Quest for Identity in Post-New Order Indonesia* Ithaca, NY: Cornell Southeast Asia Program.

Hasan, Noorhaidi. 2007. "The Salafi Movement in Indonesia: Transnational Dynamics and Local Development." *Comparative Studies of South Asia, Africa and the Middle East* 27, no. 1: 83–94.

Hoesterey, James Bourk. 2015. *Rebranding Islam: Piety, Prosperity, and a Self-Help Guru*. Stanford: Stanford University Press.

Horikoshi, Hiroko. 1975. "The Darul-Islam Movement in West Java (1948–62): An Experience in the Historical Process." *Indonesia* 20: 59–86. https://doi.org/10.2307/3350996.

Jaffrey, Sana. 2019. "Leveraging the Leviathan: Politics of Impunity and the Rise of Vigilantism in Democratic Indonesia." PhD diss., University of Chicago.

Juergensmeyer, Mark. 2017. *Terror in the Mind of God: The Global Rise of Religious Violence*. 4th ed. Berkeley: University of California Press.

Kloos, David, and Mirjam Künkler. 2016. "Studying Female Islamic Authority: From Top-Down to Bottom-Up Modes of Certification." *Asian Studies Review* 40, no. 4: 479–90. https://doi.org/10.1080/10357823.2016.1227300.

Kompas. 2005. *Wajah DPR dan DPD, 2004–2009*. Jakarta: Penerbit Buku Kompas.

Kompas. 2010. *Wajah DPR dan DPD, 2009–2014: Latar Belakang Pendidikan dan Karier*. Jakarta Penerbit Buku Kompas.

KontraS. 2012. *Pemantauan Pemolisian & Hak Atas Berkeyakinan, Beragama, dan Beribadah (Jemaah Ahmadiyah Indonesia di Manis Lor, Ciputat, Cikeusik & Jemaat Kristen HKBP Ciketing dan GKI Taman Yasmin)*. Jakarta: Komisi untuk Orang Hilang dan Korban Tindak Kekerasan (The Commission for the Disappearances and Victims of Violence).

Künkler, Mirjam. 2018. "Law, Legitimacy, and Equality: The Bureaucratization of Religion and Conditions of Belief in Indonesia." In *A Secular Age beyond the West: Religion, Law and the State in Asia, the Middle East and North Africa*, edited by John Madeley, Mirjam Künkler, and Shylashri Shankar, 107–27. Cambridge: Cambridge University Press.

Künkler, Mirjam, and Shylashri Shankar. 2018. "Introduction." In *A Secular Age beyond the West: Religion, Law and the State in Asia, the Middle East and North Africa*, edited by John Madeley, Mirjam Künkler, and Shylashri Shankar, 1–32. Cambridge: Cambridge University Press.

Lerner, Hanna. 2013. "Permissive Constitutions, Democracy, and Religious Freedom in India, Indonesia, Israel, and Turkey." *World Politics* 65, no. 4: 609–55.

Liddle, R. William. 2001. "Indonesia in 2000: A Shaky Start for Democracy." *Asian Survey* 41, no. 1: 208–20. https://doi.org/10.1525/as.2001.41.1.208.

Liddle, William R., and Saiful Mujani. 2007. "Leadership, Party, and Religion: Explaining Voting Behavior in Indonesia." *Comparative Politics Studies* 40, no. 7: 832–57.

Mahmood, Saba. 2012. "Religious Freedom, the Minority Question, and Geopolitics in the Middle East." *Comparative Studies in Society and History* 54, no. 2: 418–46. https://doi.org/10.1017/S0010417512000096.

Menchik, Jeremy. 2016. *Islam and Democracy in Indonesia: Tolerance without Liberalism*. Cambridge: Cambridge University Press.

Panggabean, Rizal, and Ihsan Ali-Fauzi. 2015. *Policing Religious Conflicts in Indonesia*. Jakarta Centre for the Study of Religion and Democracy (PUSAD), Paramadina Foundation.

Pelletier, Alexandre. Forthcoming. "Competition for Religious Authority and Islamist Success in Indonesia." *Comparative Politics* 53, no. 3.

Pepinsky, Thomas B., William R. Liddle, and Saiful Mujani. 2012 "Testing Political Islam's Economic Advantage: The Case of Indonesia." *American Journal of Political Science* 56, no. 3: 584–600.

Pew Research Center. 2014. *Religious Hostilities Reach Six-Year High*. Washington, D.C.: Pew Research Center.

Pimpinan Pusat Muhammadiyah. 2005. *Berita Resmi Muhammadiyah: Tahfidz Keputusan Muktamar Muhammadiyah ke-45 di Malang*. Yogyakarta: Pimpinan Pusat Muhammadiyah.

Platzdasch, Bernhard. 2011 "Religious Freedom in Indonesia: The Case of the Ahmadiyah." ISEAS Working Paper: Politics & Security No. 2. Singapore Institute of Southeast Asian Studies.

Platzdasch, Bernhard, and Johan Saravanamuttu. 2014. *Religious Diversity in Muslim-Majority States in Southeast Asia: Areas of Toleration and Conflict*. Singapore: Institute of Southeast Asian Studies.

Rahman Alamsyah, Andi, and Vedi R. Hadiz. 2017. "Three Islamist Generations, One Islamic State: The Darul Islam Movement and Indonesian Social Transformation." *Critical Asian Studies* 49, no. 1: 54–72. https://doi.org/10.1080/14672715.2016.1260887.

Sabirin, Rahiman, ed. 2004 *Muhammadiyah Melawan Radicalisme*. Jakarta: Institute for Justice and Peace.

Siandes, Sudah, ed. 2005. *Jelang Satu Abad Muhammadiyah Menuju Kebangkitan Kedua: Suplemen Keputusan Sidang Tanwir Muhammadiyah di Mataram Tahun 2004*. Jakarta Biantama Public Relations.

Soedirgo, Jessica. 2018. "Informal Networks and Religious Intolerance: How Clientelism Incentivizes the Discrimination of the Ahmadiyah in Indonesia." *Citizenship Studies* 22, no. 2: 191–207. https://doi.org/10.1080/13621025.2018.1445490.

Stepan, Alfred. 2007. "The World's Religious Systems and Democracy: Crafting the 'Twin Tolerations.'" In *Arguing Comparative Politics*, 213–53. Oxford: Oxford University Press.

Sullivan, Winnifred Fallers, Elizabeth Shakman Hurd, Saba Mahmood, and Peter G Danchin. 2015. *Politics of Religious Freedom*. Chicago: University of Chicago Press.

Tajima, Yuhki. 2008. "Explaining Ethnic Violence in Indonesia: Demilitarizing Domestic Security." *Journal of East Asian Studies* 8, no. 3: 451–72. https://doi.org/10.1017/S1598240800006500.

Tajima, Yuhki. 2014. *The Institutional Origins of Communal Violence: Indonesia's Transition from Authoritarian Rule*. New York: Cambridge University Press.

Tilly, Charles. 2003. *The Politics of Collective Violence*: Cambridge University Press.

Tilly, Charles, and Sidney Tarrow. 2007. *Contentious Politics*. Boulder Paradigm Publishers.

Toft, Monica Duffy, Daniel Philpott, and Timothy Samuel Shah. 2011. *God's Century: Resurgent Religion and Global Politics*. New York: W. W. Norton & Company.

Van Bruinessen, Martin. 2011. "What Happened to the Smiling Face of Indonesian Islam? Muslim Intellectualism and the Conservative Turn in Post-Suharto Indonesia." RSIS Working Paper Series. Singapore: S. Rajaratnam School of International Studies.

Van Bruinessen, Martin, ed. 2013. *Contemporary Developments in Indonesian Islam: Explaining the "Conservative Turn."* Singapore: Institute for Southeast Asian Studies.

Varshney, Ashutosh. 2002. *Ethnic Conflict and Civic Life: Hindus and Muslims in India*. New Haven: Yale University Press.

The Wahid Institute. 2010. *Laporan Kebebasan Beragama/ Berkeyakinan dan Toleransi 2010*. Jakarta: The Wahid Institute.

Waskito, Abu Muhammad. 2010. *Cukup 1 Gus Dur Saja!* Jakarta: Pustaka Al-Kautsar.

Wilkinson, Steven. 2004. *Votes and Violence: Electoral Competition and Ethnic Riots in India*. Cambridge: Cambridge University Press.

Wilson, Ian. 2014. "Morality Racketeering: Vigilantism and Populist Islamic Militancy in Indonesia." In *Between Dissent and Power: The Transformations of Islamic Politics in the Middle East and Asia*, edited by Boo Teik Khoo, Vedi Hadiz, and Yoshihiro Nakanishi, 248–74. London: Palgrave Macmillan

5

DEITY STATUE DISPUTED

The Politicization of Religion, Intolerance, and
Local Resistance in Tuban, East Java

Evi Lina Sutrisno

In early August 2017, people's attention was awoken when the Surabaya-based
Bhoemi Poetra Menggugat, an alliance of Muslim and nationalist groups, pro-
tested against Kwan Sing Bio, a Chinese temple in Tuban, a town on the northern coast of East Java. The temple management had built a thirty-two-meter
(105-foot) high statue of Kwan Kong (Guan Yu or Guan Di)—the highest statue
of its kind in Southeast Asia (MURI 2017).[1] Kwan Kong was a legendary general during the Three Kingdoms War (ca. 184–280 A.D.) who became a Chinese
deity worshiped by the followers of Confucianism and Chinese folk religion
(Goldman 2017). The protesters considered the huge Chinese god statue in a
Muslim-based town inappropriate, disrespectful of the faith of the majority
group and their feelings of Indonesian nationalism. To make the case worse,
false news was circulated in social media saying that the statue has been built in
the city's center park (*alun-alun*), while the actual location of the statue was in
the back of the temple. The fear of China's supremacy and more general anti-
Chinese sentiments added a complicated layer of feelings against China's and
Chinese Indonesians' growing power in the economic and political spheres.
Enraged, the protesters demanded that the statue be demolished. None, however,
expected that three years later, on April 16th, 2020, the statue would begin to fall
into ruin for an unknown reason (Rofiq 2020).[2]

In this chapter, I explore the struggles of a Chinese-Indonesian community
to express their religiosity and identity during the recent turn of Islamic conservatism and hypernationalism in post-reformation Indonesia. As the relationship between Islam as the majority religion and other minority groups entered

FIGURE 5.1. The Kwang Kong statue. © Evi Sutrisno.

FIGURE 5.2. The Kwang Kong statue covered. © Detik.com, printed with permission.

FIGURE 5.3. The Kwang Kong Statue destroyed. © Detik.com, printed with permission.[3]

turbulent and conflicting situations in 2016–17, I argue that the politicization of fear and threats by China and Chinese-Indonesians was a strategy used by Islamic conservative groups to mobilize Muslim crowds and to gain more power and domination in the political sphere. However, I also demonstrate that there is discrepancy between politics at the national and at the grassroot levels, which enables local people to resist the orchestrated violence. To examine this argument, I address three issues: the rising Islamization process and nationalism that excludes the contribution of Chinese-Indonesians; the "hate spin" mechanism that generates Sinophobia; and the social and economic network between the temple management and the local people that go against Sinophobia and negative stereotypes of Chinese-Indonesians.

The preconditions for hostility against the Chinese-Indonesians and Sinophobia have been discussed in previous scholarship, yet there is little discussion about their impact on Chinese religion and religiosity. In the postcolonial context, the scholarly discussion on Chinese religious issues has focused on the repressive nature of Soeharto's New Order (1966–98), including its role in controlling and limiting Chinese religious and cultural expressions in the public sphere and in the degradation of Confucianism into a sect, which forced its believers to adjust their theological concept in accordance to Pancasila (Coppel 1977; Suryadinata 1974). In the reformation era, scholars have concerned themselves with the reacknowledgement of Confucianism as a religion by the Indonesian government and the Confucian believers' access to the state civil administration (Abalahin 2005; Suryadinata 2015; Sutrisno 2018).

This chapter endeavors to broaden this scholarship by analyzing the recent conflict that has emerged between Chinese-Indonesians and fundamentalist Islamic and nationalistic groups. In the first two sections I contrast iconoclasm in the perspective of the Islamic conservatism and iconography in the Chinese folk religion. Then, I move on to discuss the local religious and social dynamics in Tuban where, on the one hand, the lifestyle of the *abangan*—best defined in Ricklefs's (2012, 16) words as "nominal or non-practicing Muslims"—is still dominant and, on the other hand, the regent office initiates stricter Islamic values for its community. Further, I analyze the Bhoemi Poetra Menggugat's protest by borrowing George's concept of "hate spin" mechanism. And last, this chapter analyzes the responses of the temple management and their neighbors—who were surprisingly resistant to the violent provocation—toward the protest. By analyzing the case of failed "hate spin" in Tuban, I offer a reflection on George's (2016, 4) top-down approach of "hate spin," in which he focuses on the role of political entrepreneurs in orchestrating hatred and violence, whereas there is limited discussion about the agency of the common people to reject such intrigue. I also discuss the long pattern of collaboration and inclusiveness between temple management and local people, their efforts to keep peace, and the support they received from interfaith activists. However, this discussion is not to deny that there are other irresistible and uncontrollable "hate spins." The conflict resistance in Tuban should be contextualized in current political and social dynamic, as Tuban is in transition from a moderate to a stricter Muslim town.

Statues are Idolatrous: The Politics of Islam and Selective Iconoclasm in the Post-Reformation Era

Iconoclast actions, defined as destructive actions against religious and cultural icons, have been perpetrated by religious and nonreligious groups from the Calvinists to China's Communist Party during the Cultural Revolution. Yet in more recent years iconoclasm has been connected to Islamist movements such as the Taliban destruction of the Bamiyan Buddha statue in Afghanistan and the Islamic States jihadists' demolition of ancient statues at the Mosul Museum, Iraq (Harding 2001; *Economist* 2015). However, Flood (2002) has argued that political reasons may provoke stronger motivations for the destruction of statues, visual art, and icons—what he calls "instrumental iconoclasm"—rather than the "expressive iconoclasm" conducted to express one's ambition or belief. A journalistic investigation reports that the Bamiyan destruction was an expression of outrage against the expensive plan to protect the Buddha statues while millions of Afghans suffered under the world's economic sanctions to expel Osama bin Laden, who was at the time living under the protection of the Taliban regime (Crosette 2001). However, I shall demonstrate that in the current context of Indonesia's Islamization, expressive and instrumental modes of iconoclasm are inseparable.

I was able to trace twenty-seven cases of iconoclasm in the post-reformation (*Reformasi*) period. These actions were pursued by various actors, including unidentified individuals, local governments, local communities, and religious groups. The reasons vary, ranging from concern over the potential for idolatry to perceptions of vulgarity and incompatibility with local (dominant) religious values and/or Indonesian nationalism; but there were also cases with as yet unknown reasons.[4] Among these cases, Islamic religious groups—independently or in alliance with other (nationalist) groups—have been involved twelve times. Meanwhile, there are two cases that involve a minority religious group and/or individual as protesters: a Buddhist youth organization that considered a statue of Buddha with the face of Abdurrahman Wahid (the fourth

Indonesian president, known as Gus Dur) to be offensive and inappropriate; and a Catholic youth who demolished the statues of Jesus and Mary because of an internal conflict.

But in the context of rising Islamism in post-Soeharto Indonesia (Van Bruinessen 2011, 5–6; Priamarizki 2013), iconoclasm has been largely an Islamically-defined phenomenon, targeting the statues of minority religious figures and popular artists, as seen in Purwakarta where five Javanese Hindu figures—Semar, Bima, Gatotkaca, Antareja, and Arjuna—were burned down in 2011 and 2016. The incidents demonstrate the dissatisfaction and frustration of Islamic groups toward Purwakarta's regent, Dedi Mulyadi, a cadre of Golongan Karya, the nationalist political party founded by Soeharto, who insisted on building these statues regardless of strong objections and warnings from local Islamic groups. Applying the Indonesian state's cultural policy, Mulyadi argued that these statues preserved local memory, stimulating inspiration and creating role models from local heroes vis-à-vis a concerning growing popularity of foreign superheroes (*superhero luar negeri*) like Batman and Superman. Even though none of those statues was vulgar or erotic, from the perspective of the protesters the statues were idolatrous (Abramena 2017). Thus, the demand to demolish them becomes a way to express the protesters' Islamic faith, as it was expressed by a protester: "It is very inappropriate to jam-pack Purwakarta, a *santri* [devout Muslims] town, with idols (*berhala*). Islamic teaching clearly mentions that statues are symbols of idolatry (*symbol kemusyrikan*). Therefore, they should be destroyed" (Sutisna 2011). But while they rejected fiercely the Hindu Javanese figures, none of the protesters problematized the statues of the three national heroes—Soekarno (the first president and founding father of Indonesia), Mohammad Hatta (Soekarno's vice president), and Abdurrahman Wahid (the fourth president)—in their town, thus illustrating what I call the phenomenon of "selective iconoclasm." With the exception of the closing down of the Sultan Ageng Tirtayasa statue in Serang in 2003 (followed by the statue's mutilation in 2018), Islamic groups have mostly accepted the statues of national heroes (Rifa'i 2018). Hence one might infer that "selective iconoclasm" relates to how the Indonesian state applies Pancasila and nationalism as a civil religion and exercises a repressive approach against nonconformists.

Yet there were six cases of iconoclasm in which the local governments and/or local parliaments took the initiative to remove a statue in the area. In four of these cases, their reasons were not very different from the Islamic fundamentalist groups, such as inappropriateness with local values and incitement of idolatry or vulgarity. While there is heterogeneity within the Indonesian government body itself, the increasing adoption of Sharia laws suggests that several local governments and parliaments are experiencing rapid Islamization.

The growing number of local regulations based on Sharia law becomes another notable proof of the shared values between the government and (conservative) Islamic groups. These regulations facilitate and justify the application of Islamic morality in political and governance spheres.[5] The Islamization process within the Indonesian government contributes to its inability and failures in protecting religious minority groups as in the oppressions against Ahmadiyah, Syiah, and Baha'i adherents (Menchik 2014, 593; Crouch 2011, 56–57; see also Hamayotsu in this volume). In the cases of iconoclasm against religious minority groups, to the best of my knowledge there have been no legal sanctions applied to the perpetrators.

As Kwan Kong Wishes: Iconography in the Chinese Folk Religion and Its Contestation

Exchanges and hybridization among Indian, Chinese, and Arab sojourners and local cultures in Java have taken places naturally and in relatively smooth ways under the local rulers. The history of Tuban also records a long process of pluralism mirroring that of many other port cities. Prior to the coming of Islam, Tuban was a vibrant trading port where many Indian and Chinese traders developed their business networks and settlements. It was one of the wealthiest towns in northern coastal Java, frequently mentioned in the reports of Chinese chroniclers such as the fifteenth-century traveler Ma Huan (Salmon and Siu 1997, 861). Hybrid culture and intermarriages commonly took place in the town. After Tuban was led by a Muslim ruler, it maintained neutral and friendly relationship with the Hindu Javanese ruler of Majapahit, who was considered to be an infidel from the Islamic perspective (Pigeaud and De Graaf 1976, 14). After the fall of Majapahit, Tuban was conquered by the Mataram kingdom.

The pattern, however, changed drastically during the colonial period as the Dutch practiced a policy of racial segregation. Negating the long acculturation between the three racial groups and local people, in 1814 the Dutch introduced a new racial group between the "Europeans" and the "Natives." This new racial group was the "Foreign Orientals" (*Vreemde Oosterlingen*), which included Indians, Arabs, and Chinese. In religious terms, the impact of a new strengthened Chinese identity can be seen in the growing numbers of Chinese temples starting in the second half of the eighteenth century, whereas earlier Chinese immigrants had previously tended to convert to Islam.[6] These temples host deity statues through which we can identify their religious affiliation(s)—Daoism, Buddhism, Confucianism, and/or folk religion. An extensive survey of the Chinese temples in the archipelago shows that deities such as Kwan Im (Guan Yin, Goddess of

Mercy), Makco (Mazu, Goddess of Ocean), and Hok Tek Tjing Sin (Fu De Zheng Shen, God of Earth and Riches) are worshipped widely. Many temples embrace local holy figures as their deities, among others Mbah Djugo (the guard of Kawi Mountain), Brawijaya (the King of Majapahit), Mbah Lawu (the guard of Lawu Mountain), and Dewi Sri (the Hindu-Javanese Goddess of Earth) (Salmon and Lombard 1980, lv). Common ritual practices among temple goers include venerating the deities as their patrons and developing human interaction and communication with the divine figures. While these temples celebrate the Chinese holidays such as Imlek (Chinese New Year) and King Hoo Ping (Ji Hao Peng, the Hungry Ghost Festival), they also incorporate local art and traditions as a part of their celebrations (Tjoa 1887, 14). These syncretic characteristics bring their religious affiliation closer to the Chinese folk religion than the modern religious conception of Confucianism, Buddhism, and/or Daoism, as Clammer (1983, 1) conceptualizes below.

> Folk religion in this sense is almost always an amalgam of beliefs and activities often drawn from several traditions. It is pluralistic and it includes (often with a very central role) activities such as divination, which would be thought peripheral or even "magical" in the western religious tradition.

Since the eighteenth century, Tuban has hosted two Chinese temples and several Chinese tomb complexes in the town. The temples are the Kwan Sing Bio (Guan Sheng Miao, Temple to Guan Di) and Tjoe Ling Kiong (Ciling Gong, Temple of Divine Compassion). For the purpose of this chapter, I focus mainly on the history of the Kwan Sing Bio. There are at least two versions of the foundation of the Kwan Sing Bio. While the oldest inscription found in the temple is dated 1871, it is believed that it was built in 1773 (Salmon and Siu 1997, 865). As noted above, the main deity is Kwan Kong, a military general during the Three Kingdoms War. According to the myth, he was a brave, smart, strategic general whose loyalty to his king was unquestionable until his death.[7] Many Chinese worship him, particularly traders who make business agreements in which they expect the partners to be trustful and keep their word as Kwan Kong did. They pray for Kwan Kong's protection and inspiration for smart strategies when they grow their business.

The Kwan Kong statue, as well as other statues, plays a central role in the temples. Many believe these statues possess supernatural powers whenever the spirits of the deities are willing to stay within. Thus the sacredness of a temple is associated with the power of the deities it hosts. These statues become a tangible and visible medium to communicate with the deities (Graham 1961, 172–73). According to a local tale, Kwan Kong even had agency in choosing the location of his current temple. It happened when a Chinese family who lived near Tuban planned to move the shrine of Kwan Kong to another place. They sailed the statue to the East. In the middle of its journey, the boat could not move further for an unknown reason. The family finally conducted a ritual in front of the Kwan Kong statue, asking whether he would prefer to stay at this location, and he answered "yes" (Kwan Sing Bio, n.d.). The relationship of human and nonhuman figures in the Chinese religious tradition, manifested in sacred objects, is far from unique, and similar relationships can be observed in other cultures, such as in South Asia (Gell 1998, 8).

In the early twentieth century, however, Chinese folk religion received a challenge from the modern conception of world religion when several educated Chinese *peranakans* founded the Tiong Hoa Hwee Koan (THHK, The Chinese Association) in Batavia in 1900.[8] Supporting the pan-Chinese movement, the THHK proposed to their Chinese fellows in the Dutch East-Indies that they embrace Confucianism as their "authentic" religion.[9] A Confucian reform, in the THHK's vision, would stimulate rational and modern Chinese subjects, whose pride of and loyalty to China were reliable. The THHK criticized harshly the syncretic Chinese religious practices as "irrelevant," "old fashioned," and "influenced by local cultures" (Kwee 1969, 6, 8–9). The THHK also criticized idolatry of deities in many Chinese temples as superstitious cult practices (Kwee 1969, 26–27). Despite the THHK's criticism and the spread of Confucian teaching through the THHK schools, many if not most of the Chinese temples kept their original deities and rituals.

Until present times, knowledge of the powerful Kwan Kong at the Kwan Sing Bio has been widespread among the Chinese Indonesians. The temple is a religious tourist destination for many Chinese Indonesians, even visitors from around Southeast Asia. On average there were three to five hundred visitors every day. On some big occasions such as the birthday of Kwan Kong, there can be up to ten thousand people gathered in the temple, praying for his blessings. Another acknowledgment of Kwan Kong's power and blessings can be seen from the large number of donations received by the temple management, which makes the Kwan Sing Bio one of the richest temples in Java. The temple management invests the donations into several land assets and schools. In 2015, Hindarto (Lie Suk Chen), a wealthy Chinese-Indonesian merchant of Surabaya who believed that he had received abundant blessings of Kwan Kong, planned to donate a statue of Kwan Kong. Through a ritual, he and the temple management asked whether Kwan Kong blessed the plan and how big the statue should be. In their communication with Kwan Kong they received his approval for making a statue. A longer and more complicated series of rituals was conducted to determine the size of the statue. They started with two meters (six feet) in height and increased the size gradually until the deity agreed on thirty-two meters (105 feet). Treating the size as Kwan Kong's will, the temple management never expected that it would invite controversy later, when the Bhoemi Poetra Menggugat would consider it to be a symbol of the Chinese's arrogance and the Confucian reformists would see it as syncretism and idolatry.

Re-Islamizing Tuban: *Bumi Wali* as a Disciplining Tool

In 2013, the government of Tuban region (*kabupaten*) introduced a new city brand, *Tuban Bumi Wali: The Spirit of Harmoni* (Tuban as the land of the early Islamic propagators: the spirit of harmony). The concept of *Bumi Wali* reflects three meanings and goals. First, it aims to preserve the memory of Tuban as one of the important loci of Islamic civilization in Java. Located on the northeastern coast of Java, Tuban was one of the earliest places where the spread of Islam in Java took place in the end of the fifteenth century and throughout the sixteenth. It was the birthplace of Sunan Kali Jaga, one of *Wali Songo* (the nine early Islamic propagators in Java), and several other key figures of early Islam are buried here, including the *wali* Sunan Bonang and Syekh Maulana Ibrahim Asmaraqandi, the father of the *wali* Sunan Ampel. Second, the slogan revitalizes the region's economic potential through religious tourism (Pemerintah Daerah Kabupaten Tuban 2013, 259). In 2018, the Indonesian Ministry of Tourism launched the *Pesona Wisata Ramadhan* (The attractive tour during fasting month) program and included Tuban as one of the destinations (Putra 2018). But the slogan excludes non-Islamic religious sites, such as the two Chinese temples.

Third, the slogan demonstrates the Islamization process of the current local government as the regent's office uses the brand as a disciplining tool to imagine and achieve a pious Muslim community of Tuban, trying to replace the previous brand of Tuban as *kota tuak* (the palm wine town). Although its population is predominantly Muslim and the town has a strong history of Islamization, Tuban has been notoriously known for its high production and consumption of an alcoholic beverage made from fermented palm fruit. The *kota tuak* evokes an image of the *abangan* (Red) community. Ricklefs (2006, 35) defines the *abangan* as "a category of people who were defined by their failure—in the eyes of the more pious—to behave as proper Muslims." The *abangan* are also known for their adoption of local culture. Many of them flexibly combine their Islamic belief with other spiritual and mystical practices. Hefner (2011, 72) calls these *abangan* practices "non-standard Islamic tradition," which is in accordance with Ahmed's

(2016, 124, 148) recognition of various local and native versions of Islam amid debates and efforts to apply Islam as a singular and normative category for Muslims worldwide.

In Tuban, *abangan* communities regularly host traditional religious ceremonies (collectively referred to as *selamatan*) such as *Sedekah Bumi* (offerings to the Earth), *Sedekah Laut* (offerings to the Sea), and *Manganan* (offerings to the sacred tombs) (*Rakyat Independen* 2016; Supriyatno 2017; Maswid, 2018). Celebrations might invite dancers from the *tayub* tradition, a folk Javanese artform known for its erotic styles, or masters of *wayang*, a shadow puppet show with roots in the Hindu, Islamic and Javanese traditions (Sears 1996, 34). These celebrations do not put the communities at odds with normative Islamic interpretation as they still observe conventional (normative) Islamic rituals. Some consider these *selamatans* ancestral traditions (*tradisi leluhur*) that do not compromise their Islamic faith (personal interview, November 5, 2018). As I will explain later, this type of inclusive and adaptive spirituality has played an important factor in resisting the "hate spin" of the Kwan Kong statue.

In contrast to the *abangan* tradition, the groups embracing normative forms of Islamic devotion—the *putihan* (the White)—tend to have little tolerance for alcohol consumption and *selamatan* practices, even though for some Muslims alcohol consumption does not necessarily compromise their faith (Ricklefs 2006, 35; Ahmed 2016, 3). While in Tuban several *selamatans* are still practiced as part of the local cultural and spiritual heritage, the city's branding as *Bumi Wali* has gradually altered the habits of the Tubanese *abangan*. The regent office attempted to reduce the *tuak* drinking habits by launching regulations for making, trading, and consuming alcohol in 2014. Since then, the police have regularly confiscated alcohol and illegal drugs and has closed down illegal *tuak* production houses. The chief of police expects the operation to help Tuban transform itself into the *Bumi Wali* faster (Pemerintah Kabupaten Tuban 2018). Islamic organizations support the government's disciplining efforts through their social activities, such as inviting members of the "punks" youth clubs, whose lifestyle is associated with messy appearance, alcohol, and drug consumption, to Qur'anic reading (*pengajian*) events (*Muhammadiyah* 2017).

The rise of Islamic fundamentalism, marked among other things by the emergence of groups such as the Front Pembela Islam (FPI, The Front of Islamic Defenders), has affected changes at the national and local level (see contributions by Hefner and Jones in this volume). Notably, my informants explained how the majority of Muslims in Tuban rejected the foundation of the FPI branch in their town a couple of years ago. Through Nahdlatul Ulama (NU) and Muhammadiyah representatives, they negotiated with the regent office to keep Tuban free from these "radical" groups as—they claimed—the majority of Muslims in Tuban wanted to keep their *abangan* religious traditions, including their casual habit of drinking *tuak*. While the efforts to keep the FPI away has so far worked well, unanticipated Islamization has also come from the regent's government, joined by the moderate Islamic organizations, who recently applied stricter policies and surveillance of drinkers and "punks," always with the goal in mind of achieving the image of Tuban as *Bumi Wali*. In the spiritual sphere, however, there is still no strict surveillance or limitation of the *selamatans*, unlike what has happened in Banyuwangi, East Java (*CNN Indonesia* 2018).

In the city's branding of *Tuban Bumi Wali*, however, there is no discussion about its qualification as representative of "the spirit of harmony," despite the fact that the Chinese and other minority groups have existed in the town for centuries. The regent's office (Pemerintah Daerah Kabupaten Tuban 2013, 94–98) has only been keen to acknowledge the Chinese Muslims who contributed to the spread of Islam, ignoring the non-Muslim Chinese and other religious minority groups. The exclusion of other (minority) religious groups in the city branding emerges then as another aspect of Islamization being initiated by the local government.

Bhoemi Poetra Menggugat and the Mechanism of (Failed) "Hate Spin"

On July 17, 2016, Zulkifli Hasan, the chairman of the People's Consultative Assembly and former chairman of Partai Amanat Nasional (The National Mandate Party, PAN), visited the Kwan Sing Bio temple and inaugurated the huge Kwan Kong statue I described at the beginning of this essay. The event took place several months after the massive rallies initiated by the FPI and its allies to sue Basuki Tjahaja Purnama (also known as Ahok) as a blasphemer of Islam (see Lohanda in this volume). Resulting in a two-year prison sentence, the case of Ahok evokes fear and insecurity among Chinese-Indonesians and other minority groups. So, when Zulkifli Hasan arrived at the Kwan Sing Bio and attended the event, he took to Twitter and tweeted about how harmonious the interreligious relation in Tuban was. He highlighted the good relationship with two hashtags, #Respect and #KhatamToleransi.[10] The word *khatam* refers to the complete reading of the Qur'an or a book, and in this case it meant the literacy or knowledgeability of tolerance that he attributed to Tuban's Muslims.

While Hasan may have personally appreciated harmony and tolerance, his party's alliance with the FPI during the anti-Ahok campaign required him to mitigate the harsh and hostile image of Muslims. Three weeks later, when the statue became disputed and was covered with a white cloth, Hasan did not follow up on his previous statements about tolerance and respect; meanwhile the protesters demanded that he apologize for his participation in the statue's inauguration. To the journalists' queries he simply replied, "It's a small matter" ("Itu sepele") (*TribunNews* 2017). Hasan's rhetorical attitude is one commonly practiced by Indonesian officials whenever escalating conflicts between the religious majority and minority groups take place. Their statements about democracy, harmony, unity, and tolerance resemble more spectacle politics than a real commitment to these values. The collaboration between state officials and majority groups for the sake of their political interests have left the minority groups unprotected.[11]

The statue controversy moved onto social media several days after its inauguration, spreading manufactured hoaxes and hate speech against the Chinese Indonesians. The Twitter wars disseminated the stereotypes of Chinese arrogance, disloyalty to Indonesian nationalism, and domination over the so-called Natives. Some statements on the Twitter spread the idea of worshipping (Chinese) idols, which is strictly forbidden in Islam. To exaggerate the offense, the hoax described the statue as being located on the *alun-alun* (town center park) of Tuban, which would have changed the city's image of *Bumi Wali* into a site of Chinese cultural and religious domination. Yet, in reality the statue was located in the back of the Kwan Sing Bio and invisible from the main street.

As George argues, instead of being spontaneous and impromptu, this type of hate speech is carefully manufactured using long-developed stereotypes against the Chinese (George 2016, 17–19). Much of it has existed since the Dutch colonial period and has been reproduced by the Indonesian postcolonial regimes, particularly under Soeharto (1966–98), including stereotypes about the arrogance of the rich Chinese and their inability to assimilate with Indonesia and the fear that their close connections with China's politics and economy will defeat Indonesia. For example, Nazaruddin Sjamsudin, a professor of political sciences at the University of Indonesia and the former head of the General Elections Commission, tweeted, "It's just a statue. The next will be Chinese navy bases in Pontianak, Semarang, and Palembang. Watch out!" (@Nazarsjamsuddin, July 25, 2017). Sjamsudin was not alone—many post-reformation Indonesian political elites who identify themselves as Native, Muslim, and/or nationalist share his perspective. His tweet marks the first step of politicization of fear, distrust, and suspicion against the Chinese-Indonesians, whose loyalty toward the Indonesian nation has been questionable (Setijadi 2017, 7). It uses old stereotypes to harbor a new set of suspicions and threats against the Chinese-Indonesians. Many native elites perceive a potential danger of Chinese Indonesian's supremacy when they see the freedom that Chinese Indonesians enjoy for Chinese cultural and religious expressions in the public sphere, their flourishing participation in politics, and their economic domination in the post reformation period. The closer China-Indonesia diplomatic relations, followed by China's bigger investments in Indonesia, stimulate suspicion that the Chinese-Indonesians may transfer their loyalty to China (Herlijanto 2017, 3; Setijadi 2017, 8).

Politicizing fear is a common strategy that has been applied widely in many countries. In the case of Indonesia, George (2016, 113) considers that there is an ecosystem of organizations and interest groups, consisting of political parties, militant gangs, government agencies, and the main Muslim clerical body, whose uncoordinated actions cultivate an environment that is conducive to hate. The ritualization of hate speech manifests itself in carefully tailored messages of being threatened by foreign capitalism, communism, deviant sects, and non-Islamic religions. It may include propaganda, false news, and biased facts. Another step is forming collective and persistent fear, in which the role of social media becomes crucial for it circulates the words quickly and widely. Hate speech manifests as "hate spin" when there is "manufactured vilification or indignation, used as a political strategy that exploits group identities to mobilize supporters and coerce opponents" (George 2016, 4). For the Chinese-Indonesians, hypernationalism and the exclusion of the Chinese from the imagined Indonesian community has positioned them as the "other" regardless of the fact that they are not strangers (Hui 2011, 15–17; Tsai 2008, 5–6). Even though the population of the Chinese is approximately 1.2% of the total Indonesian population or about 2.8 million in 2010 (Arifin, Hasbullah, and Pramono 2017, 316), their economic potential and the essentialized primordial connectivity with China—a newly emergent superpower—has created what Appadurai (2006, 51–59) calls "predatory identity," which potentially endangers the Indonesian nation-state.

On August 7, 2016, the Twitter war became a real protest and demonstration, initiated by the Bhoemi Poetra Menggugat, an alliance of forty-seven organizations in East Java. The political aspirations of its allies were mainly nationalistic and Islamic, with a possible blending between the two. The most interesting fact about the alliance is that none of these organizations comes from Tuban. The demonstration was initiated in front of the Dewan Perwakilan Rakyat Daerah (DPRD—the Regional House of Representatives) in Surabaya and organizers claimed that around three hundred people joined the action. Their statements echo those posted on Twitter and other social media platforms. They rejected the statue for several reasons. First, it was an icon of a Chinese general who had made no contribution to Indonesia. The expression of unfairness continued: "The statues of our national heroes are not that high. This is not racism. But, the statue offends our feelings of nationalism as the children of the nation"

("Melukai semangat nasionalisme kita sebagai anak bangsa"), said Didik Muadi, the demonstration coordinator (Hidayat and Faishal 2017). A religious sentiment occurred among the protesters who brought a banner "We are not idol worshippers" ("Kami bukan penyembah berhala") (Ardiansjah 2017). Another reason relates to the fact that the temple management did not obtain a permit from the regent's office prior to the development of the statue.[12] In the Bhoemi Poetra Menggugat's perspective, it represents the real character of the ethnic Chinese who always find unlawful ways to achieve their aims. The offended feelings of the Bhoemi Poetra Menggugat justifies a deep expression of nationalism.

George (2016, 14) differentiates anger from hate speech. While the former is more spontaneous, normally exists in social life, and can even coexist with positive feelings, the latter involves "more objective harms, such as discrimination, intimidation, oppression, violence and systematic exclusion of a vulnerable group from the full enjoyment of its democratic rights." The Bhoemi Poetra Menggugat's action should not have been considered hate speech had they invited a mediated talk with the temple management and provided opportunity for them to explain their perspective and/or find a solution. Instead, they used coercion and demanded, "We give 7 x 24 hours for the owner to demolish the statue. Otherwise, we'll demolish it!" (*Tempo* 2017). Several videos on YouTube and online news sites document their agitating oration and heroic outcries, which make the offense appear more daring and threatening (*Seruji* 2017).

Another unexpected response came from the Confucian community, as the case of the Kwan Kong statue invited a dispute that had been latent for more than a century. Kris Tan, the leader of the Confucian youth organization (Generasi Muda Khonghucu—Gemaku) represented the standpoint of the Confucian reformists and criticized the Kwan Sing Bio temple management for being submissive toward the conglomerate donors' will. He differentiated the building of the statue from the Confucian tradition and considered the equation between the two a slander (*fitnah*). He further criticized the statue as a cult of Kwan Kong and a syncretic practice. In fact, he applied a similar interpretation of idolatry to that used by the Bhoemi Poetra Menggugat.

> In the Chinese ancestral teachings, there is no doctrine to build a pretentious and absurd statue, which leads [us] into undermining practices towards the Almighty God (*praktik-praktik menduakan Tuhan Yang Maha Esa*).
>
> In the Confucian tradition, worshipping objects is not the substance of religiosity and spirituality. Instead, we should learn from and apply

the attitudes of Kwan Seng Tee Koen, who is a notable figure in upholding *Zhi, Ren* and *Yong*: Wisdom, Love and Truth.

An excessive idolatry blemishes the main Chinese ancestral teaching, which reveals "No other place to ask and pray other than to the
Almighty God." (Tan cited in Syafirdi 2017).

Tan demands that the temple management demolish the statue at the cost of
maintaining social harmony as a nation.[13] His perspective echoes the modern
approach of Confucianism endorsed by the THHK at an earlier period and the
Majelis Tinggi Agama Khonghucu Indonesia (MATAKIN, Indonesian High
Council of the Confucian Religion) and the Indonesian state today. He was also
worried that many Confucian worshipping places might become the target of
destruction, particularly after the case of Meliana, an ethnic Chinese Buddhist
woman who complained about the loud sound of *azan* (the Islamic prayer call)
from a nearby mosque in Tanjung Balai in 2016 (see Vignato, this volume). After
a "hate spin," eight temples were burned down and she was jailed for a year and
a half (*BBC News Indonesia* 2016; Arifah 2018). Tan's detachment from the folk
Chinese religion was an effort to save the Confucians from a "hate spin" situation
(Tan, personal interview, May 22, 2019).

During the agitations, the temple management did not respond to blame and
vilification. Instead, they covered the statue with white cloth within three days
after the protest. Their silence can be understood as the result of psychological
trauma and a sense of vulnerability after the long oppression during the New
Order regime and the memory of the riots against them in particular. The violence against religious minority groups increased during the post-reformation
period, while there is little commitment of the regimes to protect their religious
freedom. The closing down of a giant Buddha statue and the burning of eight
viharas and temples in Tanjung Balai, North Sumatra, in 2016 made the temple
management extremely cautious, applying self-censorship.

> What else can we do other than covering the statue with cloth? It's the
> fastest way to mitigate (*meredam*) the conflict, while waiting for a better
> solution. We are just a small minority. There is no way we can counter
> them. (Gunawan Wirawan, Personal interview, Oct 25, 2017).

The Twitter war and the real demonstration share a similar concern over
the fact that the Chinese deity's statue evoked a feeling of threat and offence
on the part of the Indonesian nationalists and Muslims, at the hand of the Chinese minority. The remaining questions to answer are: why did the majority
people of Tuban, who are Natives and Muslims, not share the same feelings and
not join the call to demolish the statue, and what factors made them resistant
to conflict? To answer these questions, I offer an analysis of inclusive practices,

applied by the temple management and the local people in building collaboration in the spiritual, economic, and social spheres.

Our Islam is Different from Theirs: Local Religiosity and the Mechanism of Resistance

The mechanism of "hate spin" depends on the role of political entrepreneurs in selectively appropriating existing hatred and negative stereotypes. The slanderous tweeting of racial and religious stereotypes against the Chinese is, in my opinion, a two-layer strategy intended to intensify insecurity and anger, both on the part of the Native Muslims (the majority of the Indonesian population) and on the part of the smaller non-Muslim Native communities whenever they focus on secular issues such as Chinese disloyalty, economic and cultural domination, and social exclusivity, as I will discuss in the following section. Concerning religious issues, the Bhoemi Poetra Menggugat proposes the conservative Islamic perspective, which considers the Kwan Kong statue potentially idolatrous. This perspective may originate from the Islamic organizations that are Bhoemi Poetra Menggugat's allies, such as the FPI, Muhammadiyah Youth, and Indonesian Muslim Association. The *abangan* Tubanese, however, do not share this faith. In contrast, their syncretic practices allow them to combine Islamic and Chinese religious traditions. During my visit to the Kwan Sing Bio temple, I observed Muslim people praying in the temple and doing the ritual in front of the Kwan Kong's statue as the Chinese believers do. They sought Kwan Kong's advice and blessing in dealing with various life problems, from business strategies to getting a divorce. These rituals provide more immediate and tangible social interaction between human and divine figures, manifested in statues or other objects. Once these objects are attributed with divine characters, they possess "intelligent immobility" with which people can consult and refer to, prior to making any decision. From the perspective of the Muslim visitors, doing the Chinese rituals does not necessarily compromise their faith, for they still observe Islamic teachings and rituals faithfully. One of the Muslim woman visitors told me that beside the five obligatory prayers (*sholat lima waktu*), she frequently conducts *tahajud* (an Islamic midnight prayer), during which she sometimes receives guidance to go to Kwan Kong, and she perceives the idea as Allah's guidance (*petunjuk*) for solving her problems. Other visitors shared with me that it was common and acceptable for the Tubanese Muslims to observe different rituals, such as *selametan* and visiting temples, as long as they keep their belief in Islam.

Syncretism has been a marker of the *abangan* communities across the archipelago. This practice invites harsh criticism and, even worse, violence from the fundamentalist groups. While in Tuban the *abangans* can still maintain their nonnormative belief, Hefner (2011, 86–87) demonstrates that the process of "*de-abanganization*" happens in many places in Java and Bali due to modern education, nationalism, and the state's favoritism toward the normative Islamic groups. However, Ricklefs (2012, 383–87) suggests a more optimistic view by providing data on smaller-scale *abangan* groups who are resilient and have survived throughout Java despite those challenges. The current nonnormative practices, manifested in *tuak* consumption, syncretism, and the rejection of fundamentalism in Tuban, seem to support Ricklefs's hypothesis. Yet the dialectic process among the *abangan* and the *putihan* continues, manifested in the protest of the local NU organization, which to the surprise of many, demanded the statue be permanently covered in favor of unity and tolerance among religious groups and the Indonesian nation and state, obedience to regulations in building worshipping places and objects, and the avoidance of Chinese arrogance (Purnomo 2017).

This unexpected demand invited internal criticism, particularly among the NU-Gusdurian members. Gus Dur was the NU national headman (1984–98) and was well known for his tolerance and advocacy toward religious minority groups. After his death in 2009, many NU members and different religious groups committed to continue Gus Dur's hard work for democracy and pluralism through the Gusdurian Network. Tasyuman (pseudonym), one of the Gusdurian activists in Tuban, shared with me his disappointment at the recommendation of the Pengurus Cabang NU (PCNU—the local branch office of the NU) and explained that it was mainly the perspective of the board, whom he called *oknum* (to refer to a misbehaving person), but it did not necessarily represent the NU members at large. He continued by relating his awkward experience meeting the head of the temple management to mitigate the conflict. Before he had an opportunity to apologize for the incident, the temple head withdrew from the conversation as he mistakenly assumed that Tasyuman as an NU activist would support the PCNU's demand. In contrary to the NU, the Muhammadiyah did not suggest the demolishing of the statue for reasons that I will discuss later. While many expect the NU will be the model of a tolerant organization in Indonesia, this phenomenon demonstrates that conservatism may take place in an unexpected path.[14]

Countering Sinophobia: The Temple as an Inclusive Religious Space

Chinese arrogance and exclusivity are stereotypes that have existed since the Dutch colonial time. The social and economic gaps between the Chinese and the Natives may create barriers for social interactions, as does the wealth of other ethnic groups, all of which contributes to the process of alienating each other. While the Bhoemi Poetra Menggugat claims this pattern to evoke Indonesian nationalism, the local Tubanese do not share the same experience. Instead, there are at least two types of inclusivity that the temple management offers to their neighbors, which relates to economic empowerment and social participation and results in social cohesion. In 1995, UNESCO defined inclusive society as "a society for all, in which every individual has an active role to play. Such a society is based on fundamental values of equity, equality, social justice, and human rights and freedoms, as well as on the principles of tolerance and embracing diversity." In its later development, the main tasks of ensuring inclusion in various sectors like education, economics, politics, and urban planning have been perceived as governmental duties (Armstrong 2010; Gidley et al. 2010; Sasaki 2010). However, civil groups and individuals can play significant roles in creating social inclusion as well; I call this the non-state's initiative of social inclusion. Gidley et al. (2010) explain that the development of social inclusion in the society depends on its degrees of inclusion. The narrowest interpretation considers social inclusion as access, while a broader one allows participation and the widest involves human empowerment. My observation shows that the temple management practices the second interpretation to the local people.

As a popular religious tourist destination, the Kwan Sing Bio has created an economic network among locals who have opened souvenir shops, restaurants, and hotels and set up as food vendors (*warung*). During my first visit in October 2017, two months after the conflict, the town was quiet since the number of the temple visitors had declined sharply. The food vendor owners nearby the temple complained desperately about smaller income beginning after the hoax and Twitter war circulated on social media and reaching its worst point when the temple management put a white cloth on the statue. For the local people, who are mostly Muslims and Natives, the sacredness of the Kwan Sing Bio influences their sources of income. During Kwan Kong's birthday anniversary, the town becomes crowded, with the number of visitors sometimes reaching more than ten thousand people. In an effort to organize the huge number of tourists, the temple management invites the local people to manage the kitchen, lodging, and security, from which they build teamwork and receive an extra stipend.

In the literature of peacebuilding, limited attention has been paid to its economic dimension. Appleby (2015, 185) proposes that humanitarian aid and development can work as peacebuilding whenever they apply inclusive participatory strategies, such as engaging the local people in planning and executing programs and providing a space to manage different values and conflicts. While it is far from the kind of long-term developmental project suggested by Appleby, religious tourism in the Kwan Sing Bio provides the same kind of participatory model of social and economic network that works as the main principle in peaceful collaboration. The collaboration between the temple management and the local people creates connectivity and a beneficial network for both sides. This model, however, may not work in a different interreligious network when the Muslim groups perceive the humanitarian network model as a proselytization strategy. In the case of Chinese religion, there is less concern about conversion since there is a common view that only the Chinese can observe Chinese religion.

Social inclusivity exists in different practices, which contributes significantly to peaceful coexistence between the Kwan Sing Bio and its neighbors. While it is most strongly affiliated with Chinese religiosity and rituals, the temple serves common people in several ways. For example, its kitchen provides free food for visitors and local people. Inclusivity has been practiced here as in addition to food with pork, the temple management also serves vegan food for Muslim and Buddhist visitors. A local fisherman shared with me his gratitude to the temple management for the free food, which helps him survive when he does not have enough income. During the Islamic fasting month, the temple management invites its Muslim neighbors to break the fasting (*buka puasa*) and to recite Qur'an together (*pengajian*) in the temple complex. They also host a podium for talent shows on which the Tubanese youth can perform their talents. The temple built a panda theme park in the back; opened to common visitors for free, this park has become a favorite place for families with young kids.

The temple management has built social connection through donation as an effort to empower other religious organizations. The leader of the local Muhammadiyah office recalled the temple management's donation when he needed to build the current office. He mentioned that the donation stimulated a sense of brotherhood (*seperti saudara sendiri*), which became a bridge between Islamic and Chinese theological differences. His harmonious experience with and good perception of the temple management are contradictive to that of the Muhammadiyah youth group of Sidoarjo, who joined the Bhoemi Poetra Menggugat to demolish the statue. Similar stories were shared by other local Islamic communities, whom the temple also provided supports and donations.

Interfaith Coalition for Peace and Pluralism: Resistance at the Regional Level

Two days after the statue was covered with a white cloth, an alliance for peace and religious pluralism gathered in the Boen Bio temple in Surabaya. Initiated by Aan Anshori, a coordinator of the Islamic Network for Anti-Discrimination (Jaringan Islam Anti-Diskriminasi) and activist of Jaringan GusDurian (the Network of Gus Dur's Supporters), and Liem Tiong Yang, a Confucian and an interfaith movement activist of Surabaya, the alliance called for respect and social harmony among the pluralistic groups in Indonesia. They condemned the "hate spin" and the efforts to discipline the ethnic minority under the names of Islam and the Natives. As an NU and Gusdurian activist, Anshori warned of the influence of ISIS radicalism in Indonesia. The rise of iconoclasm in several places was a serious warning sign of declining interfaith tolerance and respect for pluralism in Indonesia. He admitted that iconoclasm has been indispensable to the history of Islam since the time of Prophet Muhammad and had been included in several chapters (*surat*) in Qur'an and Hadiths, which nurtured "theological antipathy" against idolatry. While "theological antipathy" may have justified his Muslim fellows such as the PCNU Tuban, the Muhammadiyah youth group, and the FPI to destroy the statue, he reminded them that there are more peaceful Qur'anic verses, such as Al Hajj 39–40, to create social harmony with the minority groups (Anshori 2017; Aan Anshori, personal interview, November 24, 2018).

Liem Tiong Yang, another figure in this movement, was concerned with the return of the New Order's assimilationist policy toward Chinese-Indonesians, but this time using the politicization of Islam. While Liem is a reformist Confucian whose theological standpoint is similar to those of the THHK and Kris Tan, he called for the moderation of religious identities. As an activist in several interfaith groups, he emphasized the importance of interfaith dialogue at the grassroots level as a counter to the rise of rigid interpretations about one's religion that may lead to intolerance and radicalism. The meeting launched a statement that proposed protection for the statue and condemned the intolerant actions (Riski 2017; Liem Tiong Yan, personal interview, October 28, 2018).

The support from the interfaith community offers an analysis on the contribution of religion in peace building. Halafoff (2013) discusses the two inherent yet contradictory potentials of religion. On the one hand, all major religions have claims toward superiority and mutual supersession, which inevitably may lead into conflict. A holy duty to protect a religious moral order may legitimize violence and wars, which includes the theological justification of demonizing the opponents and the requirement for the believers to enter the divine struggles. On the other hand, there is the reflexive nature of religion. It advocates the transformation of self-centered and adversarial individualism or group dynamics into cooperative, compassionate mutuality and global responsibility. As in the case of Anshori and Liem, reflection and self-analysis require religious peace-builders to understand the theological roots of violence rather than denying them. These peace actors equip themselves with alternative interpretations and social analysis that may transform and advance peace within their community. As proponents of Gus Dur's pluralistic and inclusive approach, Anshori and Liem considered that democracy should promote diversity and equality for the minority groups. According to Gus Dur, as a faithful Muslim one should not obstruct the state in its duty to be impartial and neutral to non-Muslim citizens.

> Al Quran has declared Islam as God's chosen religion. Yet, it does not mean that the state should not treat all religions the same. In contrary, the unity of the nation can be achieved when the state treats all citizens equally before the law (Wahid 1999, 83–84).

The disputed Kwan Kong statue in Tuban and several other cases of iconoclasm represent the struggle for pluralism and bring to light the rise of Islamic conservatism in various areas of Indonesia. And a closer look shows that conservatism and radicalism might be shared by state and non-state actors, including by the members of so-called moderate organizations like NU and Muhammadiyah. The failed attempt at "hate spin" in Tuban relates to the diversity in Islamic religious identities and the discrepancy between the political elite and the people at the grassroots level. While Islamic conservative groups justify iconoclasm with Islamic doctrines and Indonesian nationalism, the local people's resistance against "hate spin" shows that Islamic identities—the *abangan, putihan,* and radical—may be in conflict with each other. Yet the Islamization process promoted by the regent's office and religious organizations may eliminate the relatively flexible and syncretic *abangan* and exclude the contribution of non-Muslims in the future.

The inclusive approach applied by the temple management has worked as an effective counteractor of Sinophobia and has built both an environment of mutual respect and a network between the Chinese community and the local people. The interfaith and peace-building movements by the NGO activists have helped mitigate the conflict and promote tolerant theological interpretations, while state actors focused more on administrative and security issues. The failed iconoclasm, however, does not dissuade conservative groups from intolerant actions. Following the disputed deity statue in Tuban, there have been at least three iconoclasm cases driven by religious motives in several places in Indonesia. These cases demonstrate the tightening contestation in politics, yet they also reflect spiritual confrontation through which the proponents of iconoclasm justify their actions as a divine struggle to keep their version of moral order in Indonesia.

Notes

1. In this chapter, Chinese names, places, and terminology follow the Fujian dialect as Chinese-Indonesians commonly use them. I provide the Mandarin in brackets whenever necessary.

2. At the time of writing, the investigation about the reason behind the statue destruction is still going on. Yet the temple management claims the statue was likely destroyed by natural causes (*faktor alam*) (Adirin 2020).

3. Figures 5.2 and 5.3 are adapted from Rofiq (2017, 2020).

4. It is worth noting that the closure of a statue may be attributed to several overlapping reasons that are not always related to religion.

5. Between 1998 and 2013, there were 443 sharia-based regulations nationwide, of which 67.5 percent were applied in the six most populous provinces, including East Java (Buehler 2016, 1–2). Muhtada (2014) categorizes these regulations into seven clusters of issues: (1) moral order, such as alcohol prohibition, antiprostitution and antigambling; (2) tax and donation; (3) education; (4) finance, such as Sharia banking; (5) women's conduct, such as wearing jilbab and time limit for outside activities; (6) treatment toward deviant sects; and (7) other issues, such as hajj and pilgrimage. The Pew's (2013) survey demonstrates that 72 percent of Indonesian Muslims supports the implementation of the Sharia law.

6. There are arguments that many of the early Chinese immigrants to the archipelago were Muslims. They participated in the Islamization of Java in the fifteenth and sixteenth century (Pigeaud, De Graaf, and Ricklefs 1984; Salmon and Lombard 1980, xvii-xxx; Lombard and Salmon, 1993).

7. Duara (1988) includes a more complete description of Guan Yu's apotheosizing process.

8. *Peranakan* means the Chinese who have been living in Indonesia for generations and developed mixed culture and identities with local people through marriage and collaboration.

9. Coppel (1981, 179–96) discusses the influence of Christianity in the newly introduced Confucianism, while I argue elsewhere that Confucianism acts as a counter against Christian proselytization by making it comparable to, even higher than, Christianity (Sutrisno 2018, 67–75).

10. His original tweets are:

> Together with the Chinese friends of the Kwan Sing Bio Temple in Tuban . . . Tolerance finds its best place in Indonesia . . . Let's take care of it together. #Respect. (@ZUL_Hasan, July 16, 2017).

> My sharing from Tuban, the *Bumi Wali*. In Tuban, tolerance is not merely a slogan, but a part of daily life. #KhatamToleransi. (@ZUL_Hasan, July 17, 2017).

> In the middle of the majority Muslim society in Tuban, the 10-hectare wide Kwan Sing Bio temple stands. [It is] Safe, peaceful and no problem. #Khatam-Toleransi. (@ZUL_Hasan, July 17, 2017)

> Those who are spreading intolerant stigmas [toward Islam], visit Tuban. See how tolerance has been a part of daily life. #KhatamToleransi. (@ZUL_Hasan, July 17, 2017)

11. This pattern also takes places in intrareligious conflicts in which the fundamentalists persecutes the "deviant" Ahmadiyyah and Syiah believers. See Menchik (2014), Sofjan (2016).

12. The legal permit to build a place of worship (Izin Mendirikan Bangunan Rumah Ibadah or IMB Rumah Ibadah) is a procedure of evaluation by the local government

to avoid conflict with local people. After conflict arose concerning several Christian churches and Ahmadiyah mosques, the local government has had a tendency to hold the IMB for the minority group's worshipping places (see Crouch 2007, 116). For the Kwan Kong statue, there was a lot of coverage in the media and on social media about the statue's no permit issue. The debate covers the issue of whether it needs a legal permit since it is an ornament built within a private worshipping place. In talks with DPRD representatives, however, the Bhoemi Poetra Menggugat was more concerned about its offended feelings and Chinese arrogance than the permit issue (*Seruji* 2017).

13. Almost two years later, Kris Tan changed his perspective, becoming more reflective and accepting the Chinese folk religion (Tan, personal interview, May 23 2019).

14. The rising pattern of intolerance within the NU has also occurred at the national level. As the NU national leader and head of the Majelis Ulama Indonesia (Indonesian Ulama Council), KH Ma'ruf Amin, the current vice president of Indonesia, has tarnished his reputation by launching controversial *fatwas* such as the banning of Ahmadiyah, the prohibition of Muslims wearing non-Muslim religious attributes, and his testimony against Ahok in the blasphemy trial.

References

Abalahin, Andrew. 2005. "A Sixth Religion?: Confucianism and the Negotiation of Indonesian-Chinese Identity Under the Pancasila State." In: *Spirited Politics: Religion and Public Life in Contemporary Southeast Asia*, edited by Andrew C. Willford and Kenneth M. George, 119–42. Ithaca, NY: Southeast Asia Program, Cornell University.

Abramena. 2017. "Filosofi di Balik Patung-Patung yang Bertebaran di Purwakarta." *Liputan 6*. July 26. https://www.liputan6.com/regional/read/3036447/filosofi-di-balik-patung-patung-yang-bertebaran-di-purwakarta.

Adirin, Ahmad. 2020. "Pihak Kelenteng Sebut Patung Dewa Perang Seharga 2,5 Miliar Roboh karena Faktor Alam." *Liputan 6*. April 16. https://today.line.me/id/pc/article/Pihak+Kelenteng+Sebut+Patung+Dewa+Perang+Seharga+Rp2+5+Miliar+Roboh+karena+Faktor+Alam-GLpyrP.

Ahmed, Shahab. 2016. *What is Islam? The Importance of Being Islamic*. Princeton, NJ: Princeton University Press.

Anshori, Aan. 2017. "Merobek Kafan Patung Tuban." *Geotimes*. August 20. https://geotimes.co.id/kolom/sosial/merobek-kafan-patung-tuban/.

Appadurai, Arjun. 2006. *Fear of Small Numbers: An Essay on the Geography of Anger*. Durham, NC: Duke University Press.

Appleby, Scott. 2015. "The New Name for Peace? Religion and Development as Partners in Strategic Peacebuilding." In *The Oxford Handbook of Religion, Conflict and Peacebuilding*, edited by Atalia Omer, Scott Appleby, and David Little, 183–211. Oxford: Oxford University Press.

Ardiansjah, Noer. 2017. "Dianggap Berhala, Massa Minta Patung Dewa Perang di Tuban Dibongkar." *Merah Putih*, August 7. https://merahputih.com/post/read/dianggap-berhala-massa-minta-perobohan-patung-dewa-perang.

Arifah, Iffah Nur. 2018. "Terdakwa Penistaan Agama di Tanjung Balai Divonis 1,5 Tahun Penjara." *ABC News*, August 24. https://www.abc.net.au/indonesian/2018-08-22/kasus-penistaan-agama-tanjung-balai/10149586.

Arifin, Evi N., M. Sairi Hasbullah, and Agus Pramono. 2017. "Chinese Indonesians: How Many, Who and Where?" *Asian Ethnicity* 18, no. 3: 310–29. https://doi.org/10.1080/14631369.2016.1227236.

Armstrong, Kenneth. 2010. *Governing Social Inclusion: Europeanization through Policy Coordination*. Oxford: Oxford University Press.

Buehler, Michael. 2016. *The Politics of Shari'a Law: Islamist Activists and the State in Democratizing Indonesia*. Cambridge: Cambridge University Press.

BBC News Indonesia. 2016. "Amuk Massa di Tanjung Balai, Vihara dan Kelenteng Dibakar." July 30. https://www.bbc.com/indonesia/ berita_indonesia/2016/07/160730_indonesia_rusuh_tanjung_balai.

Clammer, John. 1983. "Editor's Introduction." *Contribution to Southeast Asian Ethnography* 2: 1–2.

Coppel, Charles. 1977. "Contemporary Confucianism in Indonesia." *Proceedings, Seventh IAHA Conference*: 739–57.

Coppel, Charles. 1981 "The Origins of Confucianism as An Organized Religion in Java, 1900–1923." *Journal of Southeast Asian Studies* 12, no. 1: 179–96.

Crosette, Barbara. 2001. "Taliban Explains Buddha Statue Demolition." *New York Times*. March 19. https://www.nytimes.com/2001/03/19/world/taliban-explains-buddha-demolition.html.

Crouch, Melissa. 2007. "Regulating Places of Worship in Indonesia: Upholding the Freedom of Religion for Religious Minorities?" *Singapore Journal of Legal Studies*, July 2007: 96–116.

Crouch, Melissa. 2011. "Ahmadiyah in Indonesia: A History of Religious Tolerance Under Threat?" *Alternative Law Journal* 36, no. 1: 56–57.

CNN Indonesia. 2018. "Makna Sakral Tari Gandrung yang Ditolak FPI di Banyuwangi." October 20. https://www.cnnindonesia.com/hiburan/20181019202747-241-339966/makna-sakral-tari-gandrung-yang-ditolak-fpi-di-banyuwangi.

Duara, Prasenjit. 1988. "Superscribing Symbols: The Myth of Guandi, Chinese God of War." *The Journal of Asian Studies* 47, no. 4: 778–95.

Economist. 2015. "Iconoclasm and Islamic State: Destroying Historical Treasures." March 5. https://www.economist.com/middle-east-and-africa/2015/03/05/destroying-historys-treasures.

Flood, Finbarr. 2002. "Between Cult and Culture: Bamiyan, Islamic Iconoclasm, and the Museum." *Art Bulletin* 84, no. 4: 641–59.

Gell, Alfred. 1998. *Art and Agency: An Anthropological Theory*. Oxford: Clarendon Press.

George, Cherian. 2016. *Hate Spin: The Manufacture of Religious Offense and Its Threat to Democracy*. Cambridge, MA: MIT Press.

Gidley, Jennifer, Gary P. Hampson, Laurel Wheeler, and Elleni Bereded-Samuel. 2010. "Social Inclusion: Context, Theory and Practice." *Australasian Journal of University-Community Engagement* 5, no. 1: 6–36.

Goldman, Russell. 2017. "In Indonesia, Chinese Deity Is Covered in Sheet after Muslims Protest." *New York Times*, August 10. https://www.nytimes.com/2017/08/10/world/asia/indonesia-chinese-statue-islam-muslims-protest-guan-yu.html.

Graham, David. 1961. *Folk Religion in Southwest China*. Washington, DC: Smithsonian Institution.

Halafoff, Anna. 2013. "Encounter as Conflict: Interfaith Peace-Building." In *Understanding Interreligious Relations*, edited by David Cheetham, Douglas Pratt, and David Thomas, 262–80. Oxford: Oxford University Press.

Harding, Luke. 2001. "Taliban Blow Apart 2000 Years of Buddhist History." *The Guardian*, March 3, 2001. https://www.theguardian.com/world/2001/mar/03/afghanistan.lukeharding.

Hefner, Robert. 2011. "Where Have All the Abangan Gone? Religionization and the Decline of Non-Standard Islam in Indonesia." In *The Politics of Religion in*

Indonesia: Syncretism, Orthodoxy, and Religious Contention in Java and Bali, edited by Michel Picard, and Rémy Madinier, 71–91. Abingdon: Routledge.

Herlijanto, Johanes. 2017. "How the Indonesian Elite Regards Relations with China." Perspective 8. Singapore: ISEAS Yusof Ishak Institute.

Hidayat, Mohammad A. and Faishal, Nur. 2017. "Patung Dewa di Tuban Dianggap Tak Terkait dengan Sejarah RI." Viva. August 7. https://www.viva.co.id/berita/nasional/943935-patung-dewa-di-tuban-dianggap-tak-terkait-dengan-sejarah-ri.

Hui, Yew-Foong. 2011. Strangers at Home: History and Subjectivity among the Chinese Communities of West Kalimantan, Indonesia. Leiden: Brill.

Maswid. 2018. "Warga Kaligede Sugiharjo Tuban Gelar Tradisi Manganan." April 25, 2018. https://maswid.web.id/2018/04/25/warga-kaligede-sugiharjo-tuban-gelar-tradisi-manganan/. Accessed April 19, 2021.

Kwan Sing Bio. n.d. "History." Accessed November 12, 2017. http://www.kwansingbio tuban.com/en/about/kwan-sing-bio/

Kwee, Tek Hoay. 1969. The Origins of the Chinese Modern Movement in Indonesia. Translated and edited by Lea E. Williams. Ithaca, NY: Southeast Asia Program, Cornell University.

Lombard, Denys and Claudine Salmon. 1993. "Islam and Chineseness." Indonesia 57: 115–31.

Menchik, Jeremy. 2014 "Productive Intolerance: Godly Nationalism in Indonesia." Comparative Studies in Society and History 54, no. 3: 591–621. https://doi.org/10.1017/S0010417514000267.

Muhammadiyah. 2017. "Muhammadiyah Tuban Ajak Komunitas Punk Ngaji Bareng." August 21. http://m.muhammadiyah.or.id/id/news-11708-detail-muhammadiyah-tuban-ajak-komunitas-punk-ngaji-bareng.html.

Muhtada, Dani. 2014. "The Mechanisms of Policy Diffusion: A Comparative Study of Shari'a Regulations in Indonesia." PhD diss., Northern Illinois University.

MURI. 2017. "Pembuatan Patung Dewa Kwan Kong Tertinggi." July 20. http://muri.org/pembuatan-patung-dewa-kwan-kong-tertinggi/.

Pemerintah Daerah Kabupaten Tuban. 2013. Tuban Bumi Wali: The Spirit of Harmoni (sic.). Tuban: Pemerintah Daerah Kabupaten Tuban.

Pemerintah Kabupaten Tuban. 2018. "Pemusnahan Miras, Kapolres: Wujudkan Tuban Bumi Wali, Bukan Kota Arak." January 3. https://tubankab.go.id/entry/pemusnahan-miras-kapolres-wujudkan-tuban-bumi-wali-bukan-kota-arak#.

Pew Research Center. 2013. "Chapter 1: Beliefs About Sharia". The World's Muslims: Religion, Politics and Society. April 30. https://www.pewforum.org/2013/04/30/the-worlds-muslims-religion-politics-society-beliefs-about-sharia/.

Pigeaud, Theodore G. Th., and Hermanus J. De Graaf. 1976. "Islamic States in Java 1500–1700: A Summary, Bibliography and Index." Verhandelingen van het Koninklijk Instituut Voor Taal-, Land- En Volkenkunde 70. The Hague: Springer Science Business Media.

Pigeaud, Theodore G. Th., Hermanus J. De Graaf, and Merle C. Ricklefs. 1984. "Chinese Muslims in Java in the 15th and 16th Centuries: The Malay Annals of Sĕmarang and Cĕrbon." Monash Papers on Southeast Asia 12. Clayton, Victoria: Monash University.

Priamarizki, Adhi. 2013. "Indonesia's National Elections: Islamic Parties at the Crossroads." RSIS Commentaries 005: 1–2. https://www.rsis.edu.sg/wp-content/uploads/2014/07/CO13005.pdf.

Purnomo, Edy. 2017. "NU Tuban Rekomendasikan Patung Kong Cho Ditutup Permanen?" Bloktuban. August 14. http://bloktuban.com/2017/08/14/nu-tuban-rekomendasikan-patung-kong-cho-ditutup-permanen/

Putra, Yudha M.P. 2018. "Kemenpar Luncurkan Pesona Wisata Ramadhan 2018."
    Republika, May 18. https://www.republika.co.id/berita/gaya-hidup/travelling/
    18/05/18/p8xbeh284-kemenpar-luncurkan-pesona-wisata-ramadhan-2018.
Rakyat Independen (sic.). 2016. "Sedekah Bumi Klumpit, dengan Tradisi Selamatan
    dan Pagelaran Tayub Tuban." May 4. https://rakyatnesia.com/05/04/3175/
    sedekah-bumi-klumpit-dengan-tradisi-selamatan-dan-pagelaran-tayub-tuban/.
Ricklefs, Merle C. 2006. "The Birth of the Abangan." *Bijdragen tot de Taal-, Land- en
    Volkenkunde (BKI)* 162, no. 1: 35–55.
Ricklefs, Merle C. 2012. *Islamisation and Its Opponents in Java: A Political, Social, Cul-
    tural and Religious History, C. 1930 to the Present.* Singapore: NUS Press.
Rifa'i, Bahtiar. 2018. "Patung Sultan Ageng Tirtayasa Dibuang Karena Syirik?"
    DetikNews, November 10. https://news.detik.com/berita/d-4296025/
    patung-pahlawan-sultan-ageng-dibongkar-dan-dibuang-karena-syirik.
Riski, Petrus. 2017. "Masyarakat Lintas Etnis dan Agama di Jawa Timur Tolak
    Rencana Perobohan Patung di Tuban." *VOAIndonesia.* August 8. https://www.
    voaindonesia.com/a/masyarakat-lintas-etnis-dan-agama-di-jawa-timur-tolak-
    rencana-perobohan-patung-di-tuban/3978319.html?fbclid=IwAR0GQLc_
    qYf2axcfVWBzg8J69DlA3xoDoI2Xpv00ZD89XJeTc-2wY9aX_3M.
Rofiq, Ainur. 2017. "Patung Dewa Kelenteng Tuban Ditutup Kain, Jadi Bikin Orang
    Penasaran." *DetikNews*, August 6. https://news.detik.com/berita/d-3588137/
    patung-dewa-kelenteng-tuban-yang-ditutup-kain-jadi-bikin-orang-
    penasaran.
Rofiq, Ainur. 2020. "Patung Dewa Setinggi 30 Meter di Tuban Runtuh: Siapa yang
    Dirugikan?" *DetikNews*, April 17. https://news.detik.com/berita-jawa-timur/
    d-4981308/patung-dewa-setinggi-30-meter-di-tuban-runtuh-siapa-yang-
    dirugikan.
Salmon, Claudine, and Denys Lombard. 1980. *The Chinese of Jakarta: Temples and
    Communal Life.* Paris: Association Archipel.
Salmon, Claudine, and Anthony Siu, eds. 1997. *Chinese Epigraphic Materials in
    Indonesia.* Vol. 2, part 2. *Java.* Singapore: South Seas Society.
Sasaki, Masayuki. 2010. "Urban Regeneration through Cultural Creativity and Social
    Inclusion: Rethinking Creative City Theory through a Japanese Case Study."
    Cities 27 (Supplement 1): 53–59.
Sears, Laurie J. 1996. *Shadows of Empire: Colonial Discourse and Javanese Tales.*
    Durham, NC: Duke University Press.
Seruji. 2017. "Video: Orasi Heroik Aktivis Ini Menuntut Perobohan Patung Kwan
    Seng Tee Koen." August 10. https://seruji.co.id/berita-video/video-orasi-
    heroik-aktivis-boemi-poetra-menggoegat-menuntut-perobohan-patung-
    kwan-kong/.
Setijadi, Charlotte. 2017. "Chinese-Indonesians in the Eyes of the *Pribumi* Public."
    Perspective 73. Singapore: ISEAS Yusof Ishak Institute.
Sofjan, Dicky. 2016. "Religious Diversity and Politico-Religious Intolerance in Indo-
    nesia and Malaysia." *Review of Faith & International Affairs* 14, no. 4: 53–64.
    https://doi.org/10.1080/15570274.2016.1248532.
Supriyatno, Helmi. 2017. "Nelayan Kabupaten Tuban Gelar Larung Sesaji." *Harian
    Bhirawa,* May 03. https://www.harianbhirawa.co.id/nelayan-kabupaten-tuban-
    gelar-larung-sesaji/
Suryadinata, Leo. 1974. "Confucianism in Indonesia: Past and Present." *Southeast Asia:
    An International Quarterly* 3, no. 3: 881–903.
Suryadinata, Leo. 2015. "State and 'Chinese Religions' in Indonesia: Confucianism,
    Tridharma and Buddhism During the Suharto Rule and After." In *After*

Migration and Religious Affiliation: Religions, Chinese Identities and Transnational Networks, edited by Tan Chee-Beng, 20–42. Singapore: World Scientific.

Sutisna, Nanang. 2011. "Empat Patung Wayang di Purwakarta Dibakar Massa." *Tempo*, September 18. https://nasional.tempo.co/read/356852/empat-patung-wayang-di-purwakarta-dibakar-massa/full&view=ok.

Sutrisno, Evi. 2018. "Negotiating the Confucian Religion in Indonesia: Invention, Resilience and Revival (1900–2010)." PhD diss., University of Washington.

Syafirdi, Didi. 2017. "Umat Khonghucu Protes Keras Keberadaan Patung Guan Yu di Tuban." *Merdeka*, August 6. https://www.merdeka.com/peristiwa/umat-khonghucu-protes-keras-keberadaan-patung-guan-yu-di-tuban.html.

Tempo. 2017. "Pembongkaran Patung di Kelenteng Tuban, Didemo Ormas Jawa Timur." August 7. https://nasional.tempo.co/read/897807/pembongkaran-patung-di-kelenteng-tuban-didemo-ormas-jawa-timur/full&view=ok.

Tjoa, Tjoe Koan. 1887. *Hari Raja Orang Tjina*. Batavia: Bataviaasch Genootschap van Kunsten en Wetenschapen.

TribunNews. 2017. "Patung di Klenteng Tuban Ditutup, Ketua MPR: Itu Sepele." August 6. https://www.tribunnews.com/nasional/2017/08/06/patung-di-klenteng-tuban-ditutup-ketua-mpr-itu-sepele.

Tsai, Yen-Ling. 2008. "Strangers Who Are Not Foreign: Intimate Exclusion and Racialized Boundary in Urban Indonesia." PhD diss., University of California, Santa Cruz.

Van Bruinessen, Martin. 2011. "What Happened to the Smiling Face of Indonesian Islam?: Muslim Intellectualism and the Conservative Turn in Post-Suharto Indonesia." *RSIS Working Paper* 222. Singapore: Nanyang Technological University.

Wahid, Abdurrahman. 1999. *Tuhan Tidak Perlu Dibela*. Yogyakarta: LKiS

6

THE TRAGEDY OF BASUKI TJAHAJA PURNAMA

Mona Lohanda

On September 27, 2016, Basuki Tjahaja Purnama (at the time also referred to as Ahok), who had stepped in as governor after Joko Widodo vacated the position to run as president of the Republic, was campaigning for the new round of Jakarta gubernatorial elections on Pramuka Island, Kepulauan Seribu. During the one hour and forty-eight minute session, the audience listened to a speech on the Jakarta program on fish farming and *ikan kerapu* (grouper), but, unavoidably, a question about Ahok's candidacy (as a non-Muslim) for the Jakarta elections was also raised.

A key issue during the 2016 campaign was the suggestion that Muslims could not (or should not) elect a non-Muslim leader. Ahok unwisely engaged with this question by quoting from the Qur'an: "Bapak-Ibu dibohongin *pakai* Surat Al-Maidah 51 . . ." (roughly translatable as "You are being deceived *with* sura al-Maidah")[1] The word *pakai* ("with") was later cut off in a Facebook post that went viral, igniting the anger of Muslims all over the country, as it came to mean "You are being deceived *by* sura al-Maidah."[2]

Two times Ahok expressed his regret for his words being misunderstood and misquoted. On October 6, he emphasized that he never intended to misquote or stain (*menista*) the Qur'an. He also stated that he disliked politicizing holy verses, whether from the Qur'an, the Bible, or any other holy book. On October 10, he specifically asked for forgiveness from the members of the Muslim community and anyone who had been offended by this matter.

On October 24 Ahok visited the State Police Headquarters to explain and clarify his Pramuka Island speech, which by now had become well known through viral spreading on social media. He intended to clear up all the resulting political rumors in Jakarta, and those who supported him also reported the original poster to the authorities for manipulating Ahok's words.

But by October, petitions against Ahok had already flooded the Criminal Research Body of the State Police. The Pulau Seribu post had spread among the general public of Jakarta, yet heated talk occurred mainly within elite political circles, Islamic political parties in particular. Criticism of Ahok was getting louder and louder, to the point that a rally against Ahok seemed unavoidable. A rally was proposed for a Friday, the second day of November 2016.[3]

After Friday prayer at Masjid Istiqlal members and followers of Islamic organizations gathered in front of Merdeka Palace in Jakarta. On the same day, rallies also took place in Solo, Palembang, and Bandung; in all of these cases radical Islamic groups were leading the charge. At the time, Ahok did not take the matter seriously, but President Joko Widodo (also called Jokowi) took note of the broad support gathered by the organizers among other Islamic organizations. It was said that the rally was organized by the Gerakan Nasional Pembela Fatwa MUI (GNPF-MUI), joined by about thirty-five Islamic organizations and other mass associations, including Habib Rizieq Shihab and the Front Pembela Islam (FPI).

The rally had been a long time in the making, as these groups' call to impeach Ahok for blasphemy had not gotten any response from the police. The fact that police had been working on the case did not relieve any of the tension. Fifteen witnesses had been summoned, seven professionals had been consulted on the basis of their academic background, and Ahok was scheduled for interrogation the following Monday, on November 7, 2016.

Surprisingly, the big rally of November 4, 2016, ran peacefully to begin with. Prabowo gave a speech, but President Joko Widodo did not come out to meet the crowd. Dynamics changed with a speech by Habib Rizieq Shihab (HRS) as he ignited the demonstrators, calling the rally a *jihad konstitutional* and asking for the immediate killing of Ahok.[4] HRS had organized the rallies of October 10 and November 4 (and would later organize the largest one ever, on December 2, 2016), but the organizing committee remained with the GNPF-MUI.

On November 4, violence and skirmishes did not take place until the end of the rally, when some groups stayed in front of the Merdeka Palace demanding to meet president Joko Widodo, but vice-president Jusuf Kalla received them instead. After two hours, despite the efforts of security guards and the police to secure the commotion, the situation got completely out of hand. Skirmishes took place in several places in the capital city. Some moved forward to the parliament building for another rally, others went to North Jakarta, ransacking some mini markets and florists. Police offices and military buildings located around the Merdeka Palace also became targets. A seven-hour drama took place in Luar Batang, North Jakarta, where the mob occupied the area along Jalan Panjang from Friday night until Saturday morning; then a few shops were ransacked and cars burnt.[5]

President Joko Widodo suspected the involvement of political actors in the rally and regretted the conflict that occurred afterwards. The rally had taken place shortly after the Pulau Seribu affairs and it was well planned, with the participation of several Islamic mass organizations, communication with people from outside Jakarta, and well-organized accommodation and logistics, all of which indicated that the rally organizers had enjoyed substantial financial support from behind the scenes. The police were not able to find out who the sponsor behind the rally was, but allegations were made against the former president and chairman of the Democratic Party, Susilo Bambang Yudhoyono (SBY). A document dated November 2, 2016, was found containing a chronology of the reactions to Ahok's misquoting, a social media analysis relating to "blasphemy," and election maps of those supporting and those opposing Ahok. This discovery led to the conclusion that the rally was related to the upcoming Jakarta governor election. The fact that one of the candidates for governor was none other than Agus Harimurti Yudhoyono, SBY's eldest son, led to making this allegation directed to him.[6]

After the rally, many participants moved to the parliament building in Senayan where they reportedly received envelopes with single 50,000 IDR (circa 4 USD) banknotes as "transportation money," distributed by the speaker of the FPI. Two eyewitnesses mentioned receiving money after the Friday prayer at Masjid Istiqlal too. A driver at a private company in Kwitang, Central Jakarta, was asked by his friend to participate in the rally; to join the rally they had to register and wear a (provided) *baju koko* (male tunic). Inside the shirt's pocket they found an envelope with a 100,000 IDR banknote.[7]

On November 7, 2016, Ahok was summoned by the police and by November 15, 2016, the lawsuit against him started behind closed doors. Ahok accepted that he was being sued for alleged blasphemy, and in the case of the Pulau Seribu he would not retreat from his responsibility on the matter.[8] On December 2, 2016, a second big rally was joined by hundreds of thousands of people who occupied the National Monument, located in front of Merdeka Palace, and spread onto Jalan Thamrin. On this occasion, President Joko Widodo and some ministers met with the demonstrators. After December 2—the date that the anti-Ahok "2/12 movement" took for its name—rallies were held almost every day in the main boulevard.

Ahok's political career might have collapsed very rapidly, but it had been in the making—and successfully so—for over a decade.

Twelve Years of Politics

Born Zhong Wan Xe on June 29, 1966, in Gantung, a small village on the island of Belitung, Sumatra, Ahok is mostly known by his nickname (Ahok) or by his Indonesian name, Basuki Tjahaja Purnama (later collapsed into BTP), which he received in 1967. Ahok spent his early years through high school in his parents' home village, then he graduated with a major in mining engineering. After a few years spent in Jakarta, Ahok returned to Gantung when his father fell ill. There he set up a gravel pack sand company producing quartz sand and, capitalizing on his experiences in dealing with local bureaucracy, Ahok eventually entered politics.

Ahok joined PPIB (Partai Perhimpunan Indonesia Baru), becoming the chairman for its East Belitung chapter. Ahok's status as a double minority, being both Christian and of Chinese descent, created many obstacles to his ascent but also shaped his approach to politics. During his campaign for the legislative elections of 2004, this experience strengthened Ahok's idea of good leadership (Santosa 2016, 68–74). Playing on his own nickname, Ahok built his policy on "BTP": *Bersih* (clean), *Transparan* (transparent), and *Profesional* (professional).

Driven by a desire to make a broader impact on the socioeconomic conditions of his community, after only six months in the legislature, Ahok decided to run for election in the East-Belitung regency. Commenting that in their desire "to catch the destructive mice, the people of Belitung do not care about the color of the cat!," Ahok won the election, gaining 37.13 percent of the votes in East-Belitung (a 90-percent Muslim majority area) despite his Christian-Chinese background.[9]

For Ahok, the way of eliminating corruption among civil servants at any level was to start in the budgeting sector, as "clean government" was the surest way to eradicate poverty among the people. As education and public health were also key concerns, he set up programs for free education and health services.

As the new regent of East-Belitung, Ahok gained popularity for his principles of anticorruption and anticollusion in local government. In 2006, he was awarded the title of Tokoh Anti-Korupsi and *Tempo* magazine listed him as one of the *10 Tokoh Pilihan yang Mengubah Indonesia* (10 Elected Leaders Who are Changing Indonesia). In 2007 Ahok entered the electoral competition for the Bangka-Belitung governorship; as he had to rely on the support of small parties, he lost his bid.

Back in Jakarta in April 2007, Ahok was offered the position of General Secretary of the PPIB National Board, which he accepted but then quit in September of the same year. He later established the Center for Democracy and Transparency 31 (CDT 31), which focused on surveying public opinion on political matters and educating people in terms of general election and *pilkada* (pemilihan kepala daerah, regional election).[10]

Seeing that he could do more, Ahok entered the general parliamentary election of 2009 as a candidate for Golkar Party and was listed as no. 4 for the legislative body. He became the target of a smear campaign under the so-called SARA label (*suku, agama, ras dan antar golongan* [ethnicity, religion, race, and intergroup conflict]). Despite his very slim chances, his strategy of using personal contacts allowed Ahok to obtain the majority of the votes and thus secure a seat as Golkar representative of Bangka-Belitung.

Officially appointed on October 10, 2009, Ir. Basuki Tjahaja Purnama was a member of the Indonesian parliament for the 2009–14 term. As a member of the main legislative body of parliament, Ahok dealt with all legislative matters, and in particular dealt with the Ministry of Home Affairs, the Committee of General Election, the Supervision Body of General Election, the Ministry of State Apparatus, and the National Land Body. Ahok also made a point of meeting his constituencies to investigate how things worked at the local level, and he soon realized that the *rumah inspirasi* (house of inspiration) program—established to facilitate face-to-face meetings between MPs and their constituencies—was just another avenue for embezzlement.[11] Embezzlement, corruption, and abuse and disuse of authority in the legislative body took place in front of his eyes as public funds were being used for personal profit. Having shown his displeasure with this *modus operandi*, Ahok became unpopular among his peers.

Ahok was inspired by what he learnt during overseas visits. Visiting India in May 2011, Ahok was particularly impressed with the country's Labor Social Security (*Jaminan Sosial Kaum Buruh*), its border management—including the role played by local inhabitants and military defense—and its digital registration system, which Ahok thought was quite efficient in keeping people's data and which might be implemented in Indonesia.[12]

From his experiences in parliament, Ahok realized that to successfully obtain justice, protect the welfare of the common majority, and establish a "clean" government and democracy, one needed to join the executive body. Ahok first attempted to register as an independent candidate without party endorsement. This, however, required the support of 500,000 Jakarta identity card-holders (circa 4 percent of the metropole's population) and about 10 trillion rupiah in donations. People thought Ahok was too optimistic, too ambitious, and even too bold to think that a representative of a minority group could tread on political grounds. In response to this, he argued that those who objected to his joining the governorship election on the ground of "SARA" only showed their ignorance of the principles of the Pancasila.[13] Ahok ultimately failed to enter the election.

Ahok's faith was to take an unexpected turn when the alliance between Megawati Sukarnoputri (PDI-P) and Prabowo Subianto (Gerindra) for the 2009 presidential election failed. At the same time, it had become evident that whoever won the 2012 Jakarta Election would also win the 2014 presidential competition. PDI-P nominated Joko Widodo, the former mayor of Solo, for the Jakarta governorship, so Gerindra decided to approach Ahok for the vice-governorship. At the beginning, Ahok was not interested, given that at the time he was the Golkar Party representative in parliament, but when Prabowo presented him with his vision for Jakarta, Ahok was impressed. During the meeting, Prabowo talked much about the future development of Jakarta and the ideal of building the capital for the welfare and the pride of the nation. Both agreed that any development for Jakarta could be a new phase of reformation, or *Reformasi Jilid II*.[14]

Upon Ahok's acceptance of the Gerindra candidacy, Prabowo was criticized for pursuing *politik cuci tangan* (hand-cleansing politics) referring to his known involvement in the anti-Chinese riots of May 1998. Ahok contested this opinion, saying that Prabowo's political offer had nothing to do with sin-cleansing, as he was not "soap detergent," no cleaner of sins![15] Ahok left Golkar and joined Gerindra in March 2012.[16]

The transition was not as smooth as anticipated. Hashim Djojohadikusumo, Prabowo's younger brother, would not accept Ahok as the party candidate for the Jakarta election, as Gerindra had its own candidates. Prabowo reportedly said jokingly to Ahok: "Hashim, who is also a Christian like you, does not accept you, he says you are not 'saleable.'"[17] But thanks to Prabowo's persuasion, Hashim— who was the key financial supporter of Gerindra—eventually accepted Ahok's candidacy. Inside Gerinda political circles many were of the opinion that Ahok was likely to drag down Joko Widodo due to his background as a Christian of Chinese descent. Some others looked at the bright side of the election, stressing how Ahok had succeeded in the East-Belitung regency election despite its historical record of being a Masyumi region.

The PDI-P also needed to clear the way for Joko Widodo's nomination. Two days before the registration closed, Megawati Sukarnoputri obtained a unanimous endorsement to propose Joko Widodo as a candidate for the Jakarta governorship. Ahok's candidacy for vice-governorship also took time to be confirmed, as shown by the joint-meeting of PDI-P and Gerindra on 19 March 2012, the last day of registration for the Jakarta election. Joko Widodo agreed with the two parties' proposal of having Ahok as his running-mate. He did not comment on Ahok's double minority status, concerned that any political rumor might blemish the election. Joko Widodo reportedly said, "As the East-Belitung regent, Basuki showed a very good performance. For sure, we take notice that he is a representative of an ethnic minority, that the people of Jakarta are 90 percent Muslims, and that they certainly will ask about that. So, to elect him means making a very brave decision, as it is also a risky doing" (Santosa 2016, 145–47).

On the afternoon of March 19, 2012, Joko Widodo and Ahok officially registered as candidates to join the Jakarta election of 2012. On registration day, their appearance became a trademark for their followers and fans as they wore colorful checkered shirts of blue, red, and white, representing Jakarta's pluralistic community. This colorful shirt later become the identity of their supporters, bearing idea of *semangat kaum muda* (the spirit of the young generation). They arrived at the Kantor Pemilihan Umum Daerah on a *metro mini*.

On election day, on July 11, 2012, the people of Jakarta made their choice among five candidates. From the first run, the Jokowi-Ahok (Joko Widodo—Basuki Tjahaja Purnama) ticket obtained 42.60 percent while Fauzi Wibowo and Nachrowi Ramli received 34.05 percent of the vote. In preparation for the second run, Jokowi became the target of smear campaigns and was accused of being non-Muslim; Ahok was the target of "SARA" politicking.

A note came from Habib Mahdi Alatas, helping the Jokowi-Ahok campaign with his Islamic approach. A long-time friend of Ahok in East-Belitung, Habib Mahdi Alatas spoke widely about Ahok's positive performance as regent, also noting that Ahok was a good leader and there would be nothing to fear about his way of ruling Jakarta. The voting result of the second run reported that Jokowi-Ahok obtained 53.82 percent, while Wibowo-Ramli received 46.18 percent of the total votes.

Joko Widodo and Basuki Tjahaja Purnama were officially appointed governor and vice governor of the Capital Special Region of Jakarta on October 15, 2012. The official ceremony took place at the Jakarta Regional Parliament, attended by people from all walks of life. Megawati Sukarnoputri was seen in attendance, but Prabowo Subianto was not present.

Ahok for Jakarta

The first day in office started with a plenary meeting with all those involved in the Jakarta local government. After the meeting, Jokowi went *blusukan* (impromptu visit) to the Kali Ciliwung low-laying area (*bantaran*) and to Bukit Duri to check the construction of *kampung deret*, a "horizontal people housing complex." On the second day, Ahok visited all working units in the office of Jakarta City Hall, reportedly soliciting enthusiastic responses from officials at all levels. The idea of visiting every working unit was also to check on maximum utilization of working spaces at City Hall, seeing that often offices were left empty. Space efficiency meant also cutting back expenses for electricity, water, and phone bills. The main goal was ultimately to cut down unnecessary spending together with improving the process of budget drafting, as austerity should go hand-in-hand with a transparent, clean bureaucracy supported by professional staff. Ahok made his work known to the public by recording his visits and disseminating the images through official social media channels.

On November 10, 2012 the Jakarta Government launched the Kartu Jakarta Sehat (KJS) and Kartu Jakarta Pintar (KJP), key policies that were later developed for the entire country (becoming known as Kartu Indonesia Sehat and Kartu Indonesia Pintar, KIS and KIP). The first launching of KJS was directed at those dwelling in the six *kelurahan* (sub-districts) that comprise the bulk of Jakarta's slum areas. Similarly, the KJP was meant to help pupils of low-income families to continue their education. At first it was given to high school students, then to primary and junior secondary pupils (Santosa 2016, 175–76).

Another remarkable innovation brought forward by Ahok as vice governor was the opening up of City Hall as a public meeting place where the Jakarta people could come to raise their complaints or ask for help. Ahok was known for personally meeting those who wanted to express their concerns to him, and he tasked his staff with following up on any related matters.

One year after being sworn-in, Ahok was still dissatisfied with what had been done to improve Jakarta's living conditions. He was particularly concerned about traffic congestion in most places in the capital. The soaring numbers of private cars in Jakarta are in fact incompatible with any effort in infrastructure construction. Another unsolved problem concerned sidewalk vendors (or *pedagang kaki lima*), in particular in the Tanah Abang area, an unruly area at risk of becoming riotous. Ahok decided to move those vendors in Pasar Blok G in order to clear off Tanah Abang's sidewalks for pedestrian traffic. Ahok had to face the commotion and resistance raised by thugs opposing this move; they even had the support of a vice-chairman of the Jakarta Regional Parliament, representing the Partai Persatuan Pembangunan (PPP).[18]

Joko Widodo and Ahok had different working styles, but ultimately Jokowi's preference for *blusukan* matched Ahok's transparent and efficient approach, despite his outspokenness and anger. Jokowi would go straight to the field to see the problem; Ahok focused on getting the bureaucracy to solve the problem. The pair created a system of sharing, in terms of vision, burden, information, paradigm, and leadership. A Javanese from Solo, Jokowi was already known as being soft-spoken, calm, and smooth in appearance. Ahok, in contrast, fit the stereotype of Sumatra's Chinese, deemed to be open, straightforward, with a sometimes unyielding personality; yet they worked well together.

A turning point occurred in March 2014. President Susilo Bambang Yudhoyono was about to complete his second term in office. By March 14, 2014, the PDI-P decided to propose Joko Widodo as their candidate for the presidential election, breaking the political coalition between PDI-P and Gerindra, and thus splitting their followers between Jokowi and the Gerindra candidate, Prabowo.

As Jokowi accepted the mandate for the next presidency, Ahok was set to take over as governor. Pressure mounted right away, and he might have anticipated future problems, but Ahok reportedly said that *hargaku adalah nyawaku*, "death is my price" (Santosa 2016: 220, also the title of Santosa's book).

Jokowi's candidacy raised criticism from many sides. Those who could not accept the notion reminded Jokowi-Ahok to keep their promise of completing their five years in Jakarta. Others urged PDI-P to stick to the *Perjanjian Batu Tulis* of May 16, 2009, signed by Megawati and Prabowo. This alliance had been weakened, though: among other reasons, Prabowo wanted to strengthen the position of vice-president to resemble that of prime minister, and Megawati was quite reluctant to endorse such political position, arguing that such proposal was unconstitutional. The fact that PDI-P proposed Joko Widodo for presidency of the 2014 general election obviously changed the rules of the game. Jokowi and Ahok had been seen by many as nothing more than "riding horses" for Prabowo to enter the State Palace, but now he had to face one of them in the contest (Santosa 2016, 223).

Rising confidence that Jokowi would be elected also raised the likelihood that Ahok would become governor in 2014. However, within elite political circles—particularly those of the Muslim hardliners—Ahok needed to be rejected. By June 1, 2014, Jokowi officially went on leave, and Ahok became acting governor, pledging to continue executing the programs promised in their electoral platform (Santosa 2014, 38).

While Jokowi was hectically campaigning for his presidential candidacy, Ahok kept busy with his daily government works. He avoided taking sides, supporting neither Jokowi from PDI-P nor Prabowo from Gerindra. The electoral results of the 2014 general election showed that Joko Widodo-Jusuf Kalla received 53.15 percent of the total vote. Prabowo Subianto-Hatta Rajasa did not accept the results and sued the Committee of General Election for unfairness. On July 25, 2014, Prabowo-Hatta Rajasa brought their claim to the Constitutional Court. On August 21, their supporters held a big demonstration in front of the Constitutional Court building in Central Jakarta. During their plenary meetings of August 6 and 18, the nine members did not find any violation of the electoral process, and their judicial decision rejected Prabowo-Hatta Rajasa's complaint. On July 23, Jokowi returned to work as governor, and Ahok's role as acting governor terminated after fifty-two days. In October Jokowi was inaugurated as the new president.

The animosity of Islamist hardliners had been strengthening against Ahok since the beginning of the Jokowi-Ahok administration in Jakarta due to Ahok being a double minority. That a representative of a non-Muslim minority would lead a Muslim majority was the main point of contention for those who opposed Ahok. One of the vice-chairmen of the DPRD-DKI (Dewan Perwakilan Rakyat Daerah-DKI Jakarta [local parliament of Jakarta]) vehemently rejected the notion of appointing Ahok as governor, but this was also an expression of political disappointment with his party, Gerindra.

Rallies against Ahok commenced as early as September and continued in October and November, with participants rejecting him as a *musuh Islam*, "enemy of Islam." These protests were led and organized by FPI and FBR (Forum Betawi Rembug [Forum of Betawi Deliberation]) and joined by several other mass organizations. For the next few years, Ahok was the target of this hardliners' movement.[19] Amid such mayhem, Ahok was officially appointed governor of Jakarta based on Presidential Decree no. 130/P of 2014 (Santosa 2016, 253–78, 295–96). The officiating ceremony took place in the State Palace, meaning it was the president of the republic who appointed Basuki Tjahaja Purnama. Ahok's governorship only lasted for about two years (2014–16).

As his term was approaching its end, Ahok started to campaign for the coming election of Jakarta governor for 2016–21. He intended to continue his work for Jakarta. During his campaign, Ahok insistently expressed his ideal style of leadership. On one occasion, a Ketua Rukun Wilayah from a slum area asked about the advantages of their voting for him. Ahok answered, "If we build and develop this area because you people voted for us [Ahok and his running-mate, Djarot Syaiful Hidayat from PDI-P], what would happen to the next neighborhood if they had not voted for us? This would be really unfair. Being a politician is not about seeking power, but giving people a political education" (Nugroho 2018, 204–5).

Ahok actually intended to join the election as an independent candidate. *Teman Ahok* or Ahokers (as his supporters were known then) started campaigning for his candidacy, asking the Jakarta people to join and support him; they got 1,024,632 ID card-holders signed up to support his independent candidacy.[20] On Jokowi's advice, however, he later approached and obtained PDI-P's support; the other supporting parties were Partai Nasional Demokrat, Partai Hati Nurani Rakyat, and Partai Golkar.[21] Djarot Syaiful Hidayat, the former mayor of Blitar, East Java, was chosen as Ahok's partner for vice governorship. When the pair campaigned in some areas of Jakarta, most *kampung* dwellers in the four *wilayah* (districts) *Jakarta* rejected them. This happened after the Pulau Seribu post went viral within Jakarta's Muslim community.[22]

Detained

The first session of Ahok's case was opened on December 13, 2016. Based on *locus delicti*, the trial should have taken place in the Pengadilan Negeri Kepulauan Seribu, Jakarta Utara, but for security reasons and facility of access, the first session was held in the National Court in West Jakarta. The whole area was blocked by a rally.

Thirteen persecutors and five judges decided that Ahok was not to be detained, that he would not run away and would not destroy any evidence pertinent to his legal case, as he was proving very cooperative. Legal charges were brought against him based on Criminal Law article 156/a for blasphemy, but his team of defenders raised complaints and objected.[23]

Ahok had to attend twenty-one legal sessions between December 13, 2016, and May 9, 2017, each one crowded by demonstrations of those against and those supporting him. The rally on May 2, 2017, was led by GNPF-MUI, showing their role in the last session and verdict on the case, which was read on May 9, 2017.

Ahok's legal team questioned the ability and neutrality of the witnesses presented by the prosecution team, in particular the testimony of Habib Rizieq Shihab, who had offered himself to be an expert witness, and which was rejected by the defense team.[24] The defense argued that since Rizieq Shihab was the person who had actually sued Ahok for blasphemy, Rizieq Shihab could not claim himself to be an expert witness but only a fact witness. It was the investigators' decision to select expert witnesses.[25] While the *habib* was also facing a lawsuit for insulting the Sundanese in 2008 and for defamation of the late president Sukarno and the Pancasila, Rizieq Shihab himself belonged to the Formative Council of GNPF-MUI.[26]

During the seventh session, four fact witnesses stated that they never recognized a blasphemous statement in Ahok's words; two fishermen from Pulau Seribu said they neither knew nor understood "blasphemy," nor did they pay any attention to the *sura* al-Maidah.[27] The chairman of the neighborhood of Pulau Panggang, in Kepulauan Seribu regency, said that there was no protest against Ahok mentioning the *sura* al-Maidah. And a member of staff at the Mass Communication Division of the Jakarta government, who had been making a video recording of the entire time Ahok had spent in Pulau Pramuka that was then submitted to his superior and uploaded on the DKI YouTube

Channel, said there was no protest from the audience during the meeting in Pulau Pramuka; he only heard about the accusation of blasphemy after being summoned by the prosecutors.[28]

The fifteenth and sixteenth sessions centered on the testimonies of expert witnesses from the fields of linguistics, criminal law, and religion (Islam). The linguistics experts did not see any *penistaan agama* or blasphemy, stressing the use of the word *pakai* by Ahok, and they became quite decisive in this case. In their opinion, the word *pakai*, used between *dibohongi* ("deceived") and "al-Maidah," was not about the *sura* or the Qur'an, but rather it was about the person who had uttered the statement for political interests. Thus verses from *sura* al-Maidah were quoted in Ahok's speech in Pulau Pramuka just as an illustration.[29]

Beside the words *pakai* and al-Maidah, another point to be taken was the *fatwa* signed by the chairman and secretary general of MUI on October 11, 2016, which strengthened the hardliners in their attack against Ahok. In his cross-examination, Ahok maintained that the Pulau Seribu video was not uploaded in its entirely but rather it had been edited to suit the interests of the poster and to make it go viral. Based on his experiences running for elections in 2008 in Belitung, he was familiar with *sura* al-Maidah, as it was often repeated by his political rivals.[30]

The sentence recommendation read by the prosecutors during the sixteenth session held on April 20, 2017, stated that Ahok was guilty of blasphemy and should be jailed for one year plus two years of probation. The charge against him was reinforced by accusations of causing unrest leading to security problems, though none of the commotion was Ahok's responsibility. On April 25, 2017, in his 634-page defense, Ahok maintained his stance that he *tetap melayani walau difitnah* (keeps serving despite false accusation).[31]

On May 5, 2017, the GNPF-MUI held a rally in front of the Supreme Justice building, putting pressure on the council of judges working on their verdict on Ahok's case.[32] The May 9th verdict issued by the five judges used Criminal Code article 156/a to sentence Ahok to 2 years in jail. On the same day, the Minister of Home Affairs swore in Djarot Syaiful Hidayat as acting governor.[33] Responses to the charge against Ahok came from many sides and drew comments from the international media. From the beginning, the chairman of the defense team claimed that this judicial case was nothing more than a "trial by mob" and that the judges took over the prosecutors' position as they tried to prove Ahok's guilt. The prosecutors used article 156 without any proof of blasphemy, while the judges deployed article 156/a just to maintain Ahok's guilt. One lawyer on the defense team said that the verdict was understandable but unacceptable.[34]

A political scientist from the Centre for Strategic and International Studies noted that the Ahok trial could set a very bad political precedent as politics was spun into the field of religion and primordialism just to trample Ahok.[35] A state lawyer noted that given how the process had been used politically by certain groups, this would be a lesson for Indonesia's democracy. It was a political case rather than a legal one, for Ahok's case was actually an ethical infraction and should have been dealt with by administrative sanctions rather than a judicial process.[36]

A meeting of the Dutch parliament declared Ahok's sentence a direct attack on Indonesia's freedom of expression, and the majority of members agreed to forward this case to the European Union and the Indonesian government.[37] Amnesty International and Human Rights Watch noted that the sentence tarnished Indonesia's reputation of tolerance.[38] And the United Nations' Human Rights Commission called upon Indonesia to review its regulations and laws on blasphemy.[39]

Altogether, the trial took about five months and the two-year prison sentence was to be carried out in Cipinang, a notorious prison for criminals.[40] For security reasons, Ahok was later moved to Kelapa Dua, Depok, until he was released in January 2019.

On May 10, 2017, the day after Ahok was sentenced, a solemn concert took place in the Jakarta City Hall. About a thousand people dressed in red and white sang Indonesia Raya, the national anthem, and Garuda Pancasila.[41] Since his trial, sympathetic support for Ahok has been expressed with flowers left lined up in front of City Hall and all the way until Merdeka Square. *Save Ahok* was also a slogan deployed by members of the Indonesian diaspora in Sydney, California, Germany, the Netherlands, Hong Kong, Singapore, and elsewhere.

The Aftermath

The case of Ahok did not end the tumult around blasphemy cases. In fact, it opened the flood-gates, as members of various minority groups, either in terms of religion (Christians, Buddhists, Confucian, Bali-Hindu, and other traditional beliefs) or ethnicity (Chinese in particular), remain vulnerable to misuses of the law.

Shortly after Ahok's sentence, there were at least three cases that show how things had become so very sensitive for those vulnerable to the law. First was the case of a North Sumatra woman who complained about a loud call to prayer (see also Vignato in this volume). Second was the case dealing with the placement of a cross on the grave of a Catholic man in Central Java. And the third case was about political statements by the chairman of a new political party, Partai Solidaritas Indonesia.

These cases indicate how Indonesia has, in the last two decades, become more intolerant, with the government—whether central or local—managing unwisely the sociopolitical ambiguities of cultural and religious expression. Cases of intolerance have occurred not only in the realm of religion but also in relation to any individual expressions, dragging along its public consequences.

Meiliana, a mother of four, used to do her grocery shopping at a *warung* near her house. It was a Friday, on July 29, 2016, when she complained about the *azan* getting louder and louder, unlike in the old days. She complained about the volume, not about the *azan* itself. Meiliana's family lived near the mosque al-Maksum and she had hoped that the owner of the *warung* would intercede with the administrators of the mosque; but that evening the mosque council members visited Meiliana's house for a rather unpleasant exchange. Her husband later went to the mosque asking for forgiveness. But rumors about 'blasphemy' quickly spread around the neighborhood, and by 9:30pm riots had already started. Three Buddhist *viharas*, eight Chinese *klenteng* temples, two *Yayasan Tionghoa* (Chinese Foundations) buildings, one clinic, and Meiliana's own house were all ransacked and burned.[42] In March 2017, Meiliana, despite having already asked for forgiveness, was reported to the police for blasphemy. In May she was detained.

On July 24, 2018, the trial was held in Medan. She was charged with Criminal Code article 156/a against blasphemy, using two documents as legal proof: a declaration letter signed by a hundred members of the BPK (Badan Pengurus Kerukunan [Governing Body of Harmony]) at Masjid al-Maksum and a *fatwa* issued by MUI-Sumatra Utara. On August 21, 2018, Meiliana was sentenced to eighteen months' imprisonment, while the eight people who had trigged the riots in July 2016 got only one to three months in prison.[43] In response to Meiliana's verdict, a petition signed by fifty thousand netizens pleaded for her release.[44] Comments from legal practitioners said that *fatwas* are not a basis of legal enforcement and should not be used in legal cases.[45]

International organizations also noted that Criminal Code article 156/a had been used in January 1965, but during the following forty years it was only applied in eight cases. Under SBY's presidentship, however, this law was used in 89 cases victimizing 125 persons.[46] They also stressed that a complaint against noise was not a crime, and that this case was coerced to meet the persistence of a certain pressure group.[47] On October 25, 2018, Meiliana appealed to the higher court, but her request was declined. She is Buddhist-Chinese.

The following case does not relate to blasphemy, but nonetheless it similarly shows how vulnerable minorities are in Indonesia, in particular in the new millennium. On December 17, 2018, Albertus Slamet Sugihardi, an inhabitant of Purbaya, Kotagede, Yogyakarta, passed away. The family wanted him to be buried in the nearby graveyard of Jambon. It is said that members of the neighborhood gave a helping hand in preparing the burial. However, this got out of hand, as the majority of the inhabitants demanded that the cross on Albertus's grave should be cut off, leaving the tombstone in the form of a T. They also demanded that the burial ground should be located at the margins, and not in the middle, of the graveyard.[48] As news of the incident spread, one of the village leaders explained that the family agreed to this and that Albertus's wife, Maria Sutris Winarni, had signed a letter of agreement. Yet, it was later discovered that the letter had been prepared ahead of time and then brought by seven people representing the county office, local police, village security, and village administration to Maria's home. Also, it was said that to have a *requiem* at Albertus's domicile was not allowed. As he belonged to the Santo Paulus Church of Pringgolayan, the *requiem* was then held at noon in this Catholic church.[49]Learning of this unpleasant occurrence, the governor of Yogyakarta, Sultan Hamengku Buwana X, apologized for the events, promising to turn Yogyakarta into a place well known for its tolerance.[50] Two days after the Albertus affair, the Yogyakarta Vicarious Episcopacy explained that the graveyard was a common public ground, meaning that it did not belong to any specific community.[51]

The case of Ahok also allowed for the formation of a new political party in late 2014, as most members of PSI (Partai Solidaritas Indonesia [Indonesian Solidarity Party]) are in fact, former *Ahokers*. Led by Grace Natalie, a double minority—or even triple, as a young woman in Indonesian politics—the PSI made public statements against mainstream politics. Unsurprisingly, the PSI often got shafted from all sides. During a speech in late 2017, Grace Natalie stated that the party opposed applications of Perda Syariah (Peraturan Daerah Syariah [Regional Regulation Based on Shari'a]) and their Christian equivalents (Perda Injil) in Indonesia to prevent any injustice and unfairness based on religious identities; the party also opposed polygamy when implemented through local regulation.[52] As expected, shortly afterward, the chairwoman of PSI was reported for "blasphemy."[53] In November 2018, PSI again made political statements rejecting the application of Pengawasan Aliran Kepercayaan Masyarakat (Public Monitoring on Local Belief, PAKEM), which had been launched by the Jakarta District Attorney's Office. PSI noted that such application might be used to report local belief groups or mass organizations for deviation, leading to potential persecution.[54] Observing rampant, normalized intolerance, PSI issued a public statement against regulation relating to the construction of religious buildings. The party proposed removing such a decree for violation of religious freedoms as enshrined in the 1945 Indonesian constitution.[55]

Indonesian Rhapsody: Unfinished?

The Indonesian people believed that *Reformasi* meant a new phase of Indonesian politics and history, that it would make all their dreams of freedom come true— freedom of expression, freedom of belief, freedom to have a good life—and that many things would come together for a better Indonesia in the future. It is like a rhapsody, an enthusiastic and ecstatic utterance, lingering in an extended move- ment. But how far did it go?

It has been over twenty years since Indonesia's *Reformasi*. Nevertheless, for those who belong to a minority group, these years of reformation have been a time of endurance, anxiety, and vulnerability. With a long history of anti-Chinese sentiment, Indonesian minorities—not only the Chinese but also non-Muslims in general—have had to face violence of many kinds.[56] As shown above, cases against various minorities have now also entered a more sensitive phase. In the old days, both under the Old and New Order regimes, it was the Chinese minor- ity that regularly became the scapegoat of economic failure. But in *tahun refor- masi*, if you are non-Muslim or even a Muslim of different *aliran* (current) such as Shi'i or Ahmadi, you are prone to be victimized (see contributions by Hef- ner, Hamayotsu, and Jones in this volume).

Ahok was released on January 24, 2019. He had spent one year, three months, and seven days in prison at Kelapa Dua, Depok. At the eve of his release the *Ahokers* held a vigil in the front yard of Kelapa Dua, and the day of his release was marked by flowers saying *Justice for Ahok*.[57] A couple of days earlier, Ahok sent a letter to his followers asking not to welcome him at the moment of his release and also to now call him "BTP," no longer "Ahok."[58] However, as he is too famous as "Ahok," the common people and the media still call him by this nickname. By the end of January 2019, BTP joined the PDI-P, saying that he wanted "*PDI-P kembali berjaya*," great again.[59]

The case of Ahok-BTP might be over, but it does not mean that the root of this failure of tolerance and pluralism of which the Indonesian government is so proud (see Hoesterey's contribution to this volume) has been managed well. There had already been signs of emerging intolerance within Indonesian society; the Ahok-BTP case was just the opening of the Pandora box of Indonesian poli- tics. Public intolerance had been spreading widely among Indonesians at almost every level of society, even within close-knit families, and the exclusion of certain groups eventually brought along religious violence, a kind of radicalism that has become particularly strong after *Reformasi*.[60] It is also noted that the government bureaucracy is in fact far from immune to such a radical notion, which is seemingly hard to control.[61]

Under this kind of intolerance it is then easy to send someone to jail for blasphemy. Yet these things happened only to those belonging to minority groups, and particularly so to those who are double minorities. The famous essayist Goenawan Mohamad wrote, "I am not like Meiliana because, according to some convention which started I don't know when, I am not 'a minority.' I am also not like Meiliana because so far I have been included in 'the majority.'"[62]

Identity politics becomes the talk of the day, making plural harmony distorted. Petty cases occur here and there, and—unlike the Ahok-BTP case—do not enter the realm of politics.[63] Growing conservatism in politics came along with identity politics, which have marred *tahun reformasi* since 2016, peaking during the Jakarta governor's election in 2017. The 2019 anniversary of *Gerakan 2/12* (2/12 movement, a name taken from the date of the second large mass demonstration against Ahok-BTP on December 2, 2016, as noted earlier) solidified its base and gave a solid voting block to the Prabowo-Sandiaga Uno candidacy in the 2019 presidential election. It is a disturbing fact that the prominent leaders of the oldest Islamic organizations, Nahdlatul Ulama and Muhammadiyah, are seemingly losing their charisma among Muslim millennials. These younger Muslims are more attracted to the sermons of preachers who are not associated with these two organizations.[64] Islam has been treated as a quantity, assessed according to its sociopolitical position.[65]

At the same time, the fear of those who share concerns about negative sentiments against Chinese-Indonesians has not stopped members of minority groups from having political representation. Young politicians of Chinese descent have been convinced to go on to fight against discrimination. Although race-based discrimination is still strong, those young politicians will concentrate and woo voters from all groups of society. They are aware of smear campaigns, but as they want to serve the people and do not seek social status or economic power for themselves, they believe that Chinese voters will seemingly put ideology ahead of ethnicity. It is a deciding factor in their voting, and for these reasons those young Chinese politicians have so far preferred PDI-P and NasDem (Partai Nasional Demokrat [National Democrat Party]).[66]

The result of the presidential election of April 2019 showed how the country is split along political and religious lines. Jokowi-Ma'ruf Amin obtained the majority in most provinces: 4 in Sumatra, 4 in Java, Bali, Southeast Timor, 3 in Kalimantan, 2 in Sulawesi, Maluku and Papua. Prabowo-Sandiaga Uno received full support from Aceh, West Sumatra, South Sumatra, Banten, West Java, South

Kalimantan, South Sulawesi, Southeast Sulawesi and North Maluku. Thus, Jokowi-Ma'ruf got their main support from the Javanese (Muslim and non-Muslim), non-Javanese, non-Muslim, and Chinese, while Prabowo-Sandiaga Uno are much in preference among the hardliners.

The democracy process in Indonesia is like an unfinished rhapsody; it is not ended yet, and it should carry on until justice has been achieved for all.

Notes

1. The full text of his answer was "Jadi enggak usah pikiran. Ah, nanti kalau enggak kepilih pasti Ahok programnya bubar. Enggak, saya (jadi gubernur) sampai Oktober 2017. Jadi jangan percaya sama orang. Kan, bisa saja dalam hati kecil Bapak-Ibu enggak bisa pilih saya. Karena dibohongin pakai Surat Al-Maidah 51 macem-macem gitu lho (peserta pertemuan tertawa). Itu hak Bapak-Ibu, ya. Jadi kalau Bapak-Ibu perasaan enggak bisa pilih, nih saya takut masuk neraka, dibodohin itu, ya enggak apa-apa, karena ini kan panggilan pribadi Bapak-Ibu. Program ini jalan saja . . . (So, don't you worry. If he was not elected, for certain, Ahok's programs will be dismissed. No, no, I would be governor until October 2017. So, don't trust any others. You may say in your heart not to elect me; just because you're being cheated with Al-Maidah 51 letter, just like many other things [audiences laughed] That is your right. So if you feel you can't elect me, or thinking of getting into hell, you are tricked, it's all-right to me, as this is your personal calling. The program will continue)." "Dari Pulau Seribu . . .," *Tempo*, November 7–13, 2016, 36–37.

2. Buni Yani, "Penistaan terhadap Agama," Facebook, October 6, 2016. See Alsadad Rudi, "Penjelasan Buni Yani Tulis 'Penistaan Terhadap Agama?' soal Video Ahok," *Kompas.com*, April 28, 2017, https://megapolitan.kompas.com/read/2017/04/28/19355001/penjelasan.buni.yani.tulis.penistaan.terhadap.agama.soal.video.ahok.

3. For further details, see "Jam-jam yang Mencekam," *Tempo*, November 7–13, 2016, 33–35.

4. "Lima hal yang perlu diketahuui soal demonstrasi 'tangkap Ahok' 4 November," *BBC Indonesia*, November 1, 2016, https://www.bbc.com/indonesia/trensosial-37831654. "Bunuh Ahok, bunuh Ahok sekarang, sekarang juga" was a lyric accompanied by the tune of a folksong widely sung in many public gatherings. See Kampung Liputan, SCTV (Surya Citra Televisi), "Basuki Tjahaja Purnama Melecehkan al-Quran," Youtube video.

5. Administrator, "Rusuh Selepas Senja," *Tempo*, November 14, 2016, 35, https://majalah.tempo.co/read/nasional/151947/rusuh-selepas-senja

6. Administrator, "Safari Siaga Setelah unjuk Rasa," *Tempo*, November 14, 2016, 32–34, https://majalah.tempo.co/read/nasional/151946/safari-siaga-setelah-unjuk-rasa; Robertus Belarminus, "Alasan Pengacara Ahok Tanyakan Latar Belakng Saksi," *Kompas.com*, January 19, 2017, https://yogyakarta.kompas.com/read/2017/01/19/19593021/alasan.pengacara.ahok.tanyakan.latar.belakang.saksi. Three reporting eye-witnesses among the six were affiliated with Agus Harimurti Yudhoyono-Sylvana Murni.

7. Administrator, "Bagi-bagi Duit di Jum'at Siang," *Tempo*, November 14, 2016, 36–37, https://majalah.tempo.co/read/nasional/151948/bagi-bagi-uang-di-jumat-siang.

8. "Ahok: Saya Menerima, Tapi Tidak Akan Mundur," *BBC Indonesia*, November 16, 2016, bbc.com/indonesia/indonesia-37996242.

9. "Politik Akal Sehat Antarkan Basuki T. Purnama Jadi Bupati Belitung Timur," *PPIB online*, June 30, 2005, cited in Santosa 2016, 79.

10. Number 31 refers to the CDT office in Pejompongan, South Jakarta.

11. "Anggaran 15 milliar per tahun untuk setiap anggota DPR?," *Ahok.org*, June 5, 2010, cited in Santosa 2016, 125–26; "Siaran pers: menyikapi rencana pembentukan rumah aspirasi bagi anggota DPR," *Ahok.org*, August 4, 2010, http://ahok.org/tentang-ahok/dpr/suara-senayan/siaran-pers menyikapi rencana-pembentukan-rumah-aspirasi-bagi-anggota-dpr.

12. "Laporan KunKer (Kunjungan Kerja) ke India (Bagian IV)," *Ahok.org*, May 5, 2011, http://ahok.org/tentang-ahok/dpr/suara-senayan/laporan-kunker-ke-india-bagian-iv/.

13. "Ahok Pantang Mundur Maju Pilkada Jakarta," *Ahok.org*, January 16, 2012, http://ahok.org/tentang-ahok/ahok-pantang-mundur-maju-pilkada-jakarta/.

14. "Detik-detik Jelang Ahok Dipinang Prabowo," *Kompas.com*, March 22, 2012, https://megapolitan.kompas.com/read/2012/03/22/1404501/Detikdetik.Jelang.Ahok.Dipinang.Prabowo.

15. "Ahok Tukang Cuci Dosa? Emangnya Gue Diterjen?," *Ahok.org*, September 3, 2012, http://ahok.org/tentang-ahok/ahok-tukang-cuci-dosa-emangnya-gue-diterjen/.

16. "Golkar: Ahok Harus Keluar dari Golkar dan DPR," *Republika.co.id*, March 20, 2012, https://republika.co.id/berita/menuju-jakarta-1/news-menuju-jakarta-1/m15xjy/golkar-ahok-harus-keluar-dari-golkar-dan-dpr.

17. "Alasan Kenapa Ahok Ikut Gerindra dan Prabowo Subianto," cited in Santosa 2016, 312.

18. "Basuki; Saya Memang Agak Sakit Jiwa . . .," *Ahok.com*, July 26, 2013, http://ahok.org/berita/news/basuki-saya-memang-agak-sakit-jiwa/; "5 Cerita 'Perang Panas Dingin' Ahok vs. Haji Lulung," *DetikNews*, July 30, 2013, https://news.detik.com/berita/d-2318454/5-cerita-perang-panas-dingin-ahok-vs-haji-lulung; Ana Shofiana Syatiri, "Isi Perbincangan Ahok dan Haji Lulung," *Kompas*, July 31, 2013, https://nasional.kompas.com/read/2013/07/31/0841209/Isi.Perbincangan.Ahok.dan.Lulung; Santosa 2016, 187–92.

19. "M. Taufik dan H. Lulung Pun 'Berduet' Anti-Ahok," *Medcom.id*, November 10, 2014, https://m.medcom.id/nasional/metro/5b28R1eK-m-taufik-dan-h-lulung-pun-ber duet-anti-ahok.

20. "Teman Ahok dan Soal KTP," *BBC Indonesia*, June 19, 2016, https://www.bbc.com/indonesia/berita_indonesia/2016/06/160619_indonesia_ahok_1000ktp.

21. "PDIP Dukung Ahok-Djarot," *DetikNews*, September 20, 2016, https://news.detik.com/berita/d-3302368/pdip-dukung-ahok-djarot-golkar-makin-banyak-makin-bagus.

22. "Sidang Ahok dipindah ke PN Jakarta Pusat," *Kontan.co.id*, December 1, 2016, https://nasional.kontan.co.id/news/sidang-ahok-dipindah-ke-pn-jakarta-pusat.

23. "Sidang PK Ahok di Ruangan Saat Sidang Kasus Penodaan Agama," *Kompas.com*, February 26, 2018, https://megapolitan.kompas.com/read/2018/02/26/10021741/sidang-pk-ahok-di-ruangan-saat-sidang-kasus-penodaan-agama.

24. "Alasan Pengacara Ahok Tanyakan Latar Belakang Saksi," *Kompas*, January 19, 2017, https://yogyakarta.kompas.com/read/2017/01/19/19593021/alasan.pengacara.ahok.tan yakan.latar.belakang.saksi;"Rizieq Shihab Ajukan Diri Sebagai Saksi Ahli Dalam Kasus Ahok," *TribunJateng.com*, November 2, 2016, https://jateng.tribunnews.com/2016/11/02/rizieq-shihab-ajukan-diri-sebagai-saksi-ahli-dalam-kasus-ahok?page=1.

25. "Koordinator Tim Pembela Demokrasi Indonesia tentang Saksi pada Pengadilan Ahok," *Kompas.com*, November 3, 2016, https://nasional.kompas.com/read/2016/11/03/14033991/tpdi.secara.hukum.rizieq.shihab.tidak.bisa.jadi.ahli.kasus.ahok?page=all.

26. "Sidang ke 12: Rizieq Shihab Jadi Saksi, Tim Ahok Menyebutnya 'Residivis'," *BBC Indonesia*, February 28, 2017, https://www.bbc.com/indonesia/indonesia-39112013.

27. "Sidang Kesembilan Ahok: Pengacara Anggap Saksi Ahli MUI Tidak Independen," *BBC Indonesia*, February 7, 2017, https://www.bbc.com/indonesia/indonesia-38895365.

28. "Sidang Ketujuh Ahok: Saksi Fakta 'Tidak Menyadari' Ada Dugaan Penistaan Agama," *BBC Indonesia*, January 24, 2017, https://www.bbc.com/indonesia/indonesia-38734595.

29. "Sidang ke-15 Ahok: Kata 'Pakai' Sebelum Al-Maidah Amat Penting," *BBC Indonesia*, March 21, 2017, https://www.bbc.com/indonesia/indonesia-39336200.

30. "Sidang ke-17: Ahok Jelaskan Lagi Mengapa Singgung Al-Maidah," *BBC Indonesia*, April 4, 2017, https://www.bbc.com/indonesia/indonesia-39487559; "Sidang ke-16 Ahok: Tidak Ada Penistaan Agama Menurut Para Saksi Ahli," *BBC Indonesia*, March 29, 2017, https://www.bbc.com/indonesia/indonesia-39436607.

31. "Sidang 19 Al Maidah: Ahok mengaku korban fitnah," *BBC Indonesia*, April 25, 2017, https://www.bbc.com/indonesia/indonesia-39701361.

32. "Aksi 505: Massa GNPF-MUI Akan Beraksi Lagi Saat Sidang Vonis Ahok," *BBC Indonesia*, May 5, 2017, https://www.bbc.com/indonesia/indonesia-39816199; "Vonis Penjara Ahok Lewat Kaacamata Media Internasional," *BBC Indonesia*, May 9, 2017, https://www.bbc.com/indonesia/dunia-39855994.

33. "Jakarta governor Ahok found guilty of plasphemy," *BBC.com*, May 9, 2017, https://www.bbc.com/news/world-asia-39853280

34. "Pengacara 'Maklum' pada Putusan Hakim yang dalam Tekanan Massa," *BBC Indonesia*, May 9, 2017, https://www.bbc.com/indonesia/live/indonesia-39853316/page/2.

35. "Akankah Ahok 'Dikorbankan' untuk Meredakan Suhu Politik?," *BBC Indonesia*, May 9, 2017, https://www.bbc.com/indonesia/indonesia-37887952.

36. "Kasus Ahok Dinilai Dipolitisasi," *Kompas.com*, June 9, 2017, https://megapolitan.kompas.com/read/2016/12/30/06571491/kasus.ahok.dinilai.dipolitisasi.

37. "Parlemen Belanda Angkat Upaya Pembebasan Ahok dalam Debat," *BBC Indonesia*, May 10, 2017, https://www.bbc.com/indonesia/dunia-39872700.

38. "Seruan Badan Internasional atas Vonis 'Penistaan Agama' Ahok," *BBC Indonesia*, May 10, 2017, https://www.bbc.com/indonesia/indonesia-39871119.

39. "Blasphemy Law Has No Place in a Tolerant Nation Like Indonesia—UN Rights Experts," United Nations Human Rights, May 22, 2017, https://www.ohchr.org/en/News Events/Pages/DisplayNews.aspx?NewsID=21646&LangID=E.

40. "Vonis Ahok: Dua Tahun Penjara Langsung Ditahan di Cipinang," *BBC Indonesia*, May 8, 2017, https://www.bbc.com/indonesia/live/indonesia-39853316.

41. Kate Lamb, "Protests in Jakarta after Christian Governor Convicted of Blasphemy," *Guardian*, May 10, 2017, https://www.theguardian.com/world/2017/may/10/jakarta-protests-christian-governor-ahok-guilty-blasphemy.

42. "Ini Kronologi Kasus Penistaan Agama Meiliana di Tanjung Balai," *Tempo.co*, August 23, 2018, https://nasional.tempo.co/read/1119663/ini-kronologi-kasus-penistaan-agama-meiliana-di-tanjung-balai.

43. Ibid.

44. "Dibui Karena Keluhkan Volume Azan," *Detiknews*, August 23, 2018, https://news.detik.com/berita/d-4185608/dibui-karena-keluhkan-volume-azan-meliana-resmi-ajukan-banding.

45. "Surat Pernyataan dan Fatwa MUI Bukan Dasar Penegakan Hukum Apalagi Masalah Pidana," *Detiknews*, November 22, 2018, https://news.detik.com/berita/d-4312196/meliana-pengkritik-volume-azan-ajukan-kasasi-ini-6-alasannya.

46. "Keluhkan Suara Azan Perempuan Tanjung Balai Dijerat Pasal Penodaan Agama," *BBC Indonesia*, August 15, 2018, https://www.bbc.com/indonesia/indonesia-45161029.

47. "Media Internasional Ramai Beritakan Meiliana Pengeluh Volume Azan," *Detiknews*, August 28, 2018, https://news.detik.com/internasional/d-4178727/media-internasional-ramai-beritakan-meiliana-pengeluh-volume-azan.

48. "Duduk Perkara Nisan Salib di Yogyakarta," *Kompas.co*, December 22, 2018, https://regional.kompas.com/read/2018/12/22/06271311/berita-populer-nusantara-duduk-perkara-nisan-salib-di-yogyakarta-hingga-ibu.

49. "Klarifikasi Lengkap Pemotongan Nisan Salib di Makam Kotagede, DIY," *Kompas.co*, December 21, 2018, https://yogyakarta.kompas.com/read/2018/12/21/08565691/klarifikasi-lengkap-pemotongan-nisan-salib-di-makam-kotagede-yogyakarta?page=all.

50. "Yogya Dinilai Sebagai Kota Intoleran," *Indonesia.ucan.news, Tempo.com*, March 23, 2016, https://nasional.tempo.co/read/756278/yogyakarta-dinilai-sebagai-kota-intoleran.

51. "Klarifikasi Lengkap Pemotongn Nisan Salib di Makam Kotagede, DIY," *Kompas.co*, December 21, 2018, https://yogyakarta.kompas.com/read/2018/12/21/08565691/klarifikasi-lengkap-pemotongan-nisan-salib-di-makam-kotagede-yogyakarta?page=all; "Cerita di Balik Pemotongan Nisan Salib di Pemakaman Umum di Yogyakarta," *Liputan6.com*, December 18, 2018, https://www.liputan6.com/regional/read/3842236/cerita-di-balik-pemotongan-nisan-salib-di-pemakaman-umum-yogyakarta.

52. "Eggi Sudjana Laporkan Grace Natalie soal PSI Tolak PErda Syariah," *DetikNews*, November 16, 2018, https://news.detik.com/berita/d-4304986/eggi-sudjana-laporkan-grace-natalie-soal-psi-tolak-perda-syariah; "PSI: Poligami Lebih Banyak Mudarat Ketimbang Manfaat," *Tempo.co*, December 15, 2018, https://nasional.tempo.co/read/1155619/psi-poligami-lebih-banyak-mudarat-ketimbang-manfaat.

53. "Tolak Perda Syariah, Grace Natalie: Saya Tidak Anti-agama," *Tempo.co*, November 17, 2018, https://nasional.tempo.co/read/1147272/tolak-perda-syariah-grace-natalie-saya-tak-anti-agama.

54. "Setelah Tolak Perda Syariah, Kini PSI Tolak PAKEM," *Jawapos.com*, November 27, 2018, https://www.jawapos.com/nasional/politik/27/11/2018/setelah-tolak-perda-syariah-kini-psi-tolak-pakem/.

55. "PSI: SKB 3 Menteri Tempat Ibadah Diskriminasi Kebebasan Beragama," *Tempo.co*. February 12, 2019, https://nasional.tempo.co/read/1174702/psi-skb-3-menteri-tempat-ibadah-diskriminasi-kebebasan-beragama.

56. "Editorial," *Guardian*, May 9, 2017.

57. "PA 212 Tunggu Sikap Tobat Ahok Bebas dari Penjara," *Tempo.co*, January 23, 2019, https://metro.tempo.co/read/1167760/pa-212-tunggu-sikap-tobat-ahok-bebas-dari-penjara.

58. "Ahok Writes a Heartfelt Letter about How Prison has Transformed Him into a Better Man One Week Prior to Release," *Coconut Jakarta*, January 1, 2019, https://coconuts.co/jakarta/news/ahok-writes-heartfelt-letter-prison-transformed-better-man-1-week-prior-release/; "'Call Me BTP Not Ahok,'" *Jakarta Post*, January 18, 2019, https://www.thejakartapost.com/news/2019/01/18/call-me-btp-not-ahok.html.

59. "Ahok ingin PDIP kembali berjaya," *Liputan6.com*, January 30, 2019, https://www.liputan6.com/news/read/3883474/video-ahok-ingin-pdip-kembali-berjaya; "'I Have Always Been a Sympathizer; Ahok Joins PDI-P,'" *Jakarta Post*, February 8, 2019, https://www.thejakartapost.com/news/2019/02/08/i-have-always-been-a-sympathizer-ahok-joins-pdi-p.html.

60. "Paham Radikal di Kampus Kita," *Tempo*, May 28–June 3, 2018, 23, 36–47; "Internet Contributes to Radicalism among Young Indonesian Muslims; a Study," *Jakarta Post*, February 24, 2019, https://www.thejakartapost.com/news/2019/02/24/internet-contributes-to-radicalism-among-young-ri-muslims-study.html. A joint research study by UIN (Islamic State University) and UNDP in 2017 found that 88.55 percent of young Indonesian Muslims said government should ban religious minority groups.

61. "Sikap Intoleran 'Kian Meluas' di Masyarakat Indonesia," *BBC Indonesia*, February 22, 2016, https://www.bbc.com/indonesia/berita_indonesia/2016/02/160222_indonesia_intoleransi.

62. Goenawan Mohamad, "Catatan Pinggir, 'Meiliana,'" *Tempo*, September 1, 2018, https://majalah.tempo.co/read/catatan-pinggir/156073/meliana. "Saya tak akan seperti Meiliana karena, menurut konvensi yang tak jelas kapan dimulai, saya bukan warga 'minoritas.' Saya juga tak akan seperti Meiliana sebab sejauh ini saya dimasukkan ke 'golongan mayoritas.'"

63. For instance, "Going Ham; Neighbors in West Jakarta Quarrel over the Smell of Pork Being Cooked," *Coconut Jakarta*, February 15, 2019, https://coconuts.co/jakarta/news/going-ham-neighbors-west-jakarta-quarrel-smell-pork-cooked/. It took place in Cengkareng Barat when a Chinese man grilled pork at his home and was confronted by his Muslim neighbor, saying it was *haram*. As there are no rules banning this, the quarrel was settled, but the Chinese man had to sign an agreement that he would install a ventilator to prevent the smell from spreading to his neighbor.

64. Noory Okthariza, "Impact of 2018 Identity Politics," *Jakarta Post*, January 4, 2019, https://www.thejakartapost.com/news/2019/01/04/impact-2018-identity-politics.html.

65. Goenawan Mohamad, "Catatan Pinggir," *Tempo*, September 1, 2018, https://majalah.tempo.co/read/catatan-pinggir/156073/meliana.

66. "Chinese-Indonesian Politicians up against Racism," *Jakarta Post*, January 24, 2019, https://www.thejakartapost.com/news/2019/01/24/chinese-indonesian-politicians-up-against-racism.html; "Editorial: Up against Discrimination," *Jakarta Post*, January 26, 2019, https://www.thejakartapost.com/academia/2019/01/26/up-against-discrimination.html.

References

Nugroho, Wisnu, ed. 2018. *Ahok dan Hal-hal yang Belum Terungkap*. Jakarta: Gramedia Pustaka Utama, 2018.

Santosa, Agus. 2014. *The Jokowi Secrets: Bagaimana Kepemimpinan Sederhana Menyelesaikan Masalah-masalah Tak Sederhana*. Yogyakarta: Gradien Mediatama.

Santosa, Agus. 2016. *Ahok: Hargaku Adalah Nyawaku*. Jakarta: Gramedia Pustaka Utama, 2016.

7

REGULATING RELIGION AND RECOGNIZING "ANIMIST BELIEFS" IN INDONESIAN LAW AND LIFE

Lorraine V. Aragon

This volume on religious pluralism reconsiders and dignifies the concept of animism by framing it as a parallel category to Indonesia's six official religions: Buddhism, Catholicism, Confucianism, Hinduism, Islam, and Protestantism. Chiara Formichi's proposal, which includes the term "Animism" (capitalized) within a list of the nationally recognized religions, in neutral alphabetic order, was remarkable. Such an inclusive classification only became imaginable, or even possible, in late 2017 when Indonesia's Supreme Constitutional Court (Mahkamah Konstitusi or MK) ruled that the 2013 Law on Civil Administration's specification that only official religions could be listed on citizens' identity cards is discriminatory. In this chapter I begin to explore the complex background and implications of the 2017 legal decision for religious pluralism and parity in Indonesia. I show how the court ruling unsettles prior legal policies, which have been motivated by Dutch colonial, Cold War, and Muslim majoritarian interests that solidified particular categorical assumptions about religion and citizenship. More often than not, state policies and clerics have diminished and distanced ancestral cosmologies and minority ritual practices despite observed counterexamples where ordinary citizens have achieved advantages by cooperation through religious differences.

In the sections below, I use a variety of Indonesian historical, legal, ethnographic, and media examples to illustrate how state policies and actions work to control and undercut the expression of minority traditions deemed threatening to national uniformity or majoritarian precedence. The examples also highlight instances where many ordinary Indonesians, bound together through cross-cutting local ties, show ready acceptance of religious diversity, including their elders' ancestral practices. Historical analyses of indigenous cosmologies in Southeast Asia note their unified focus on continuing relations with the dead and their ever-evolving protection of localism against imperial control (O'Connor 2003, 290–97). Analyzing Indonesia's state of religious pluralism requires recognition of the archipelago's historically intertwined religious and political practices of state and regional rule as well as of local understandings of precedence, everyday ecumenicalism, and conviviality across difference.

Indonesia's national ideology of Pancasila, which obliges "belief in a Supreme God," is potentially challenged by the 2017 decision's implication that traditional and other minority sect beliefs—rarely deemed monotheistic—should be legally recognized on national identity cards along with Indonesia's six official religions, all of foreign origin.[1] Examining Indonesia's history of religious and legal policies illuminates three basic points. First, Indonesia's colonial-driven, modernist preference to rank imported scriptural religions above indigenous cosmologies makes it logically and politically challenging to reclassify regional "beliefs" (*kepercayaan*) as "religion" (*agama*). Second, the Indonesian state prefers to deny the extent to which the nation's official religions and ancestral traditions already are interlaced within both communities and individuals. Third, Indonesian laws and state actions evidence a polarized ambivalence about whether Indonesia guarantees religious freedom—as the 1945 constitution asserts—or instead prioritizes state control and security when facing threats of religious protests and disorder by spokespersons for the majority.

The classificatory challenge of the 2017 ruling that envisions ancestral beliefs as equivalent to the six official religions has prompted resistance that is comparable to that seen in prior attempts to gain equal legal protections for all peripheral faiths. Hardline Muslim clerics have alleged that various minority religious practices—whether indigenous, Christian, or unorthodox Muslim (Ahmadi or Shi'a)—cause unacceptable insult to the Sunni Muslim majority and thereby threaten national stability. Recent trends in Islamic majoritarianism (see chapters here by Robert Hefner and Sidney Jones) have led to demands for differentiated national citizenship rights. Groups such as the Salafi-influenced Wahdah Islamiyah (WI), for example, only agree to political leadership by Muslims and even argue that basic citizenship rights should only apply to members of Indonesia's other official religions who submit to the practices and political precedence of the Sunni Islam majority (Chaplin 2017).[2] For WI and the other hardline groups, "belief practitioners" (*penghayat kepercayaan*) do not qualify.

The Constitutional Court's ruling implying that native faith traditions or "beliefs" be entered on national identity cards as a new category of religion opens a new legal avenue for democratic pluralism. At the same time, the decision irritates public narratives that view Indonesia as a "Muslim country" or otherwise rigidly separate orthodox adherents of Indonesia's official religions from all others. The routine coexistence or even widespread complementarity of official religions and ancestral cosmologies generally is ignored or denied. To better expose the moral logic and global history of these state simplifications, I examine data about Indonesia's religious laws on blasphemy and the construction of houses of worship. I also discuss the genealogy of animism as an historic political and academic category. The European origins of "animism" as a generic term to describe "pagans" anticipate how the Indonesian term "beliefs" (*kepercayaan*) is used by many clerics and officials who apply it with derision to those not following the official religions. Categories of religion are prescriptive, not analytic, terms.

The Constitutional Court's 2017 ruling raises both conceptual and political questions that few dared to ask before but that we can now broach. The ruling bears on citizens' constitutional rights—the legal basis of the decision—as well as religious recognition, national record keeping, and group monitoring. The ruling may influence a range of identity-based relationships, including perceptions of the indigenous revivalism arising among some Indonesian ethnic minorities in the post-Suharto period (Davidson and Henley 2007). The ruling also meshes with the creation of a new agency, the High Council for Beliefs (Majelis Luhur Kepercayaan Indonesia or MLKI), and its subsequent efforts. MLKI began with a 2012 national congress convened to anchor ancestral belief followers within Indonesia's Pancasila and scriptural religion framework (MLKI n.d.). Beyond national politics, the 2017 Constitutional Court decision resonates with scholarship on discriminatory religious laws and recent global studies of indigenous animism as an ontology. This line of research, described below, shows how animist cosmologies offer thought-provoking philosophical correctives to imperial Enlightenment assumptions about personhood, agency, and developmental modernism's often unthinking relationship with earth's other beings and resources.

The 2017 Court Decision in Identity Card Options for "Belief Practitioners"

On November 7, 2017, Indonesia's Constitutional Court ruled that the prior 2013 Civil Administration Law caused legal uncertainty and violated principles of equal justice for all citizens (McBeth 2017; Sapiie 2017a). Article 64 of the 2013 law requires those who do not claim state-recognized religions, including indigenous "belief practitioners," to leave the religion column of their national identity or residency cards (Kartu Tanda Penduduk or KTP) blank (Republik Indonesia 2013). The 2013 law states that "blank box citizens" without a religion should still be served by government officials. The 2017 Constitutional Court ruling, however, admitted the real-world difficulties and inequities that indigenous faith followers encounter when they visit civil service offices to register their marriages, births, divorces, and deaths. In fact, minority "belief practitioners" face routine discrimination when they seek licenses, education, employment, or even access to burial without a religion listed on their national ID cards (Budijanto 2016). The 2017 ruling seeks religious parity in citizenship through a straightforward civil rights decision.

Almost tangentially, the 2017 ruling inspired the creation of a new official religious category of "beliefs" (*kepercayaan*). Clearly, though, the category of "beliefs," which does not represent any single organization or previously unified set of faith tradition, appears as an "orange" among the "apples" of the nation's scriptural religions: Islam, Protestantism, Catholicism, Hinduism, Buddhism, and Confucianism. This seismic shift in Indonesia's religious classification system quickly upset some leaders of the powerful, established religious groups even as others remained stoic. Muhammadiyah and Nadlatul Ulama (NU) leaders publicly said that they agreed with the ruling and did not fear its impact. By contrast, Ma'ruf Amin, head of the Indonesian Ulama Council (Majelis Ulama Indonesia or MUI) and vice president to President Joko Widodo (Jokowi) following the April 2019 elections, strongly objected. Amin argued that "beliefs" (*kepercayaan*) "are not religions" (*bukan agama*) and therefore cannot be listed as religions on KTP cards (Chairunnisa 2017; Sapiie 2017b). Amin proposed that followers of belief sects (*aliran kepercayaan*) receive separate identity cards, with their affairs overseen by the Ministry of Education and Culture, not the Ministry of Religion (*Jakarta Post* 2017).

The numbers of minority faith groups and adherents affected by the 2017 Constitutional Court ruling is uncertain. Most estimates, including from the Ministry of Education and Culture (Kementerian Pendidikan dan Kebudayaan or Kemendikbud), range from 180 to 500 groups with a total of ten to fifteen million adherents across the archipelago (Kurniawan 2017; McBeth 2017; Sapiie 2017a). As with all unofficial and disfavored groups, the categories' boundaries are somewhat arbitrary. The numbers of individuals within each group are even more difficult to assess accurately. Hoping to avoid discrimination, most Indonesians would be tempted to simply list an official religion on all government documents. Being a member of any religious organization is about group identity, personal interactions, ritual experiences, and community benefits as well as theological "belief."[3]

No matter what the exact numbers, the 2017 ruling pursues an equitable civil rights solution for Indonesia's indigenous faith groups as a remedy for past discrimination based on the 2013 law. At the same time, the ruling does not question the prevailing assumption that indigenous cosmological ideas and ritual practices are inevitably discrete from adherence to scriptural religions. Indonesian state laws as well as common parlance suggest that the state-approved religious practices and ancestral beliefs or localized ancestral practices are fully compartmentalized and inevitably practiced by different individuals and groups. Both my own ethnographic observations of Protestants in Central Sulawesi (Aragon 2000) and countless case studies of other Indonesian ethnic groups affiliated with all six of Indonesia's official religions refute these platitudes.

Indonesia's 2017 ruling thereby prompts questions about the classification of indigenous and ethnic minority faith traditions more generally. A genealogy of how the dichotomy between "world religions" and "animism" arose in the West illuminates how it endures unredeemed within Indonesia's twenty-first century category of "beliefs." These concepts were co-constructed in ways that now require cognitive erasures to serve state simplifications and limit Indonesian communal tensions between exclusivist branches of the Muslim majority and all they consider religious others. Recent collaborative research with marginal and self-defined indigenous peoples has pushed scholars working in anthropology and religious studies to further "decolonize" theoretical assessments about what people that others call animists think and do. Obsolete social evolutionary views undergirded Dutch colonial policies and subsequent Indonesian religious laws, making harmonious religious pluralism in Indonesia difficult to achieve. As Chiara Formichi (2014) and Michael Peletz (2009) assert, twenty-first century democratic pluralism requires not just bare tolerance of diversity but a legitimization of difference.[4]

Given the efforts by majority religious and political figures to again bureaucratically separate indigenous belief practitioners from other card-carrying citizens, the thrust of the 2017 ruling may be undone, ignored by regional officials, or even become a liability for those it aims to benefit. The NU leadership opined that Indonesians are now "mature enough" to legally accept indigenous belief practitioners (Sapiie 2017b). Yet databases that may accrue as a result of the legal incorporation of native faiths could be used to target those who dare to choose "beliefs" rather than the prior official religions. In the early 2000s, when regions including Central Sulawesi and Maluku became roiled with violence between Christians and Muslims, travelers who carried KTP residency cards that listed a religion other than the majority religion of the neighborhood where the card was inspected often found the cards to be a dangerous liability, not an aid to government access (Aragon 2001, 2005). Democracy advocates need to monitor whether the new classification leads to future religious litmus tests instead of cheerful civil service.

Nevertheless, the Supreme Constitutional Court's decision is transformational from both conceptual and political standpoints. Changes to the national religious classification system—and its open discussion—invite shifts in public views about Indonesia's religious pluralism that are likely to reverberate far beyond a small blank box on the KTP identity card, a box which many Indonesians already find unnecessarily constraining. A humorous 2016 video called "KTP," which I discuss below, illustrates the disconnect between the religious tolerance often seen in everyday village life and the religious gate-keeping of politicians. To grasp how the 2017 legal change may move forward, it is critical to see public reactions to the ruling not only in terms of "tolerant" and "intolerant" but also in terms of the parallel tension between two historically competing legal priorities in Indonesia: religious freedom and state security. Whereas the "KTP" video exemplifies the tolerance for religious free choice at the grassroots village level, the intolerant side defended by the priority of state order is illustrated by Indonesian prosecutions of the laws on blasphemy (or defamation) and the construction of houses of worship, considered in later sections. But first, I review historical perspectives on animists in the archipelago.

Connecting Colonial to Postcolonial Views of the Archipelago's Regional "Beliefs"

Before plumbing the depths of Indonesia's religious classification system, I offer a quick reminder of how followers of indigenous cosmologies—known as "animists," "unbelievers," or "infidels" (*kafir*)—have been viewed by both Muslim and Christian authorities. Under Dutch colonial rule, Netherlands Indies animists were described as innocent sheep to be gathered and enlightened for gradual entry into the Christian flock (Aragon 2000, 116–29). Christian missions seeking converts in the outer island and upland peripheries served multiple goals: to save pagan souls, jump-start European models of civilization and economics, and foster colonial alliances with local leaders. The Netherland Indies government expected that the new coreligionists, largely outside Muslim majority Java, would support their goals and form a buffer against any uncooperative indigenous rulers, especially Muslim ones.

In the mid-1980s when I began fieldwork in Central Sulawesi, ethnic minority communities who did not yet claim affiliation with one of the official religions were classified not with dispassionate terms such as "native faith followers" or indigenous "belief practitioners" (*penghayat kepercayaan*), or even the 1990s term "isolated traditional communities" (*kommunitas adat terpencil*). Rather, they were called *suku terasing*. Glossed in English variously as "isolated," "estranged," or "foreign" ethnic groups, the derogatory label cast them as backward tribes "who did not yet have a religion" (*yang belum beragama*). They were considered alien to the civilized nation and suspect in terms of their citizenship. Moreover, the Cold War in Indonesia outlasted the Berlin Wall, spanning the entire Suharto regime (1966–98). Pagans and atheists—potential communists all—were to be converted and socialized for the safety of the state and benefit of the nation. "Ordinary traditions" (*adat biasa*) that did not trouble the state were allowed, but superstitious "tribal" or traditional beliefs (*kepercayaan suku* or *adat kepercayaan*) were to be replaced as soon as possible with scriptural religion (*agama*).

I saw Indonesia's late-stage religious conversion process underway in Central Sulawesi during 1987 when I visited an upland group of Da'a Kaili who were forced by the government to move to a lower elevation for "socialization." The Da'a population recruited for relocation (termed local transmigration or *transmigrasi setempat*) invited ministers from the oldest Dutch Protestant church in Palu (Gereja Protestan Injil Donggala or GPID) to help their newly moved community solve its governmental problems and discriminatory treatment. According to the Palu-based European missionaries asked to oversee the villagers' mass conversion, the Da'a had chosen Protestantism because becoming Muslims (the other obvious choice in the region) would require them to give up pig husbandry and forswear pork as their customary feast food (Aragon 2000, 284, 303). Although the ministers did not sense any deep spiritual desire for religious conversion on the part of the villagers, they hoped the Da'a would learn to love and obey God once they organized a church and heard the gospel. Visiting the Da'a Kaili region half a dozen years earlier, Greg Acciaioli reports how villagers practicing indigenous traditions were told that they must "cease to live as monkeys," and follow state guidance to transform their ancestral ritual practices into ethnic art performances (Acciaioli [1985] 2016, 146). Ancestral ritual ceremonies were to be secularized and transformed into folkloric arts—regionally distinctive folk songs and dances—as communities accepted state-recognized religions.

Denigration of, or discrimination against, ethnic minorities who remain unaffiliated with their state's official religions is not particular to Indonesia, as Christopher Duncan's (2004) edited volume on marginal Southeast Asian citizenship shows. National approaches to governance that use religion and its institutions as a primary pathway to define morality and direct economic development are widespread across Southeast Asia. They are legacies of European law-making and a colonial discourse that utilized scriptural religions as part and parcel of modernist rule. In sum, Indonesia's classification of religions began as a colonial state effect, endured as a litmus test for Cold War communist threats, and then continued to deny or grant legitimacy and equal citizenship rights to millions of people, primarily ethnic minorities and non-Muslims.

State Simplification Separating Religious Categories from Everyday Realities

Discrepancies between Indonesia's formal religious classification scheme and citizens' practices generally are erased in public discourse. As James Scott notes, legibility is "a central problem in statecraft" (Scott 1998, 2). States classify their citizens for the purposes of legal processing and monitoring, and this results in "state simplifications" (Scott 1998, 80). Indonesia's religious classification system, like most state simplifications, works discretely, like a digital on-off switch. Users have before them a set of Aristotelian choices: "A" or "not A." Either one is a Muslim or not; a Protestant or not; a Catholic, a Hindu, a Buddhist, a Confucian, or not. Where none of the above applied, Indonesians prior to the 2017 ruling received a blank—meaning "no religion"—on their national identity cards. Having a blank likely indicated that they lived on Indonesia's periphery with minimal government notice, without strong pressures to register an official religion.

As noted, people "without religion" were politically suspect in the Cold War era of the 1960s, '70s, and '80s. With the 2017 ruling, such individuals and communities might emerge from the shadows. Still, if the reported figures are anywhere near accurate, these people would be a relatively small percentage of Indonesia's roughly 275 million citizens (as of 2020). Taking the estimate of fifteen million native faith followers at face value for a moment: if these citizens now can "fill in the blank" and gain access to register their births, marriages, and deaths if they can obtain licenses, schooling, and jobs, we may ask why this should be threatening to leaders of other religious groups, or to the state.

One answer, already suggested, involves the politically self-serving intolerance of some officially recognized religious leaders. Another answer rests not only in the definition of what constitutes a "real religion" but also in the implicit and problematic link between religious classification ideals and actual practices. If we examine Indonesians' everyday discourse and behavior carefully, most of the Indonesian citizens who enact ancestral practices at some moments in their lives are not just the approximately fifteen million targeted by the 2017 ruling. They will also be found among the roughly 260 million *other* citizens: those registered (as of the 2010 census) as Muslims (roughly 87 percent), Protestants

(7 percent), Catholics (3 percent), Hindus (2 percent), Buddhists (1 percent), or Confucians (.5 percent). Virtually all of the ordinary Indonesians in dozens of provinces whom I have heard mention presenting ritual offerings to ancestral or guardian beings on ceremonial occasions have been Protestants, Catholics, Muslims, Hindus, Buddhists, or Confucians. Indonesian regional arts producers who discuss how unseen beings come to them in dreams or enter their dances or masks to make their textiles or performances potent generally are Catholics, Muslims, or Hindus (Aragon and Leach 2008; Aragon 2018; Harnish and Rasmussen 2011; Sutton 2002; Ross 2016). Some Javanese performers I have met insist that their ancient performance genres (for instance the *topeng* mask dances) were created by one of the nine Muslim saints (*wali songo*) for Islamic proselytization. Such appropriation of ancestral practices does not necessarily vitiate scriptural religion piety. Yet the widespread incorporation of ancestral practices into long-converted communities may be more difficult to ignore if "beliefs" is formalized as a distinct new religious choice.

The rich cosmological heritage of Austronesian and other Southeast Asian people is steeped with relational connections to ancestors and other earthly beings. The numinous presence of these beings is invoked in performance and graphic arts as enduring authorities, enlivening spirits, and mnemonic devices. They remind humans how to interact with each other and the world around them in ways that, for the most part, require no recourse to state laws, police, courts, or jails. Although relegated officially to superstition or touristic folklore since Dutch colonial times, indigenous cosmological knowledge and customs still serve a range of community purposes from heritage education and hierarchy maintenance to economic livelihoods. Although this is rarely acknowledged, the Indonesian nation also benefits from the ability of local communities to draw on ancestral traditions as well as scriptural religious teachings to manage and repair social conflicts autonomously without heavy state administrative costs and policing. Nevertheless, the layering of indigenous and imported religious guidelines for living presents potential cognitive dissonance and heritage identity challenges. The 2017 court ruling particularly unsettles the way Indonesia's official religious sects have seen themselves as the standard bearers for Pancasila's precept of monotheism.

Pancasila as a National Guide and Guarantor of Rights for Religious Adherents

During my field research among Protestants in Central Sulawesi from 1986 to 1989, Pancasila precepts were strategically raised or overlooked in public and private discourse as a way to justify or critique state development policies (Aragon 2000, 312). At its most regressive, the first Pancasila precept of "belief in a Supreme God" (*ketuhanan yang Maha Esa*) was invoked by government agents to justify interventions among ethnic minorities deemed less developed, such as the highland Da'a Kaili discussed earlier. Pancasila's precept about a just and civilized humanity similarly supported disregard for and reformation of minority groups' cultural behaviors and local economies. The Pancasila precepts invoking national unity (*persatuan*) and deliberative political consensus (*permusyawaratan*) were sometimes used by government leaders to stifle local objections to New Order economic and social development projects (*proyek pembangunan*), from decorative red and white-washed picket fences at town centers to "Two Is Enough" birth control programs.

By contrast, at its most progressive, Pancasila's precept of belief in a Supreme God was invoked by non-Muslim groups of other official religions to advance their equal claims to citizenship rights and opportunities. Central Sulawesi Protestants I knew sometimes noticed that their villages were overlooked for desired schools, clinics, or roads. Some Christians encountered barriers, including elevated fees, to enter higher education classes or civil service internship jobs. They reacted by framing what they considered ethnoreligious discrimination as a violation of their Pancasila rights, given their status as citizens with an official religion (*yang beragama*). In short, Pancasila precepts, including belief in God, were understood and deployed not just as a means for the government to keep atheistic communism at bay or for Muslim clerics to keep their constituents preeminent in lieu of the Islamic state some demanded at Independence but also as a means for non-Muslim minorities to expect equal rights in law across the official religious denominations. Native faith practitioners were formerly denied any expectations of equal rights, but making "beliefs" an official religion would extend them.

Arguably, Indonesian religious pluralism and toleration has resided not in the limited array and multiple choice format of the state's official religion categories but rather in the vision (although not always the reality) that the government would not micromanage ritual observances within its official religious categories. The constitution leaves the choice and specific tenets of religious practices to individuals, families, and their clerics. In theory, given the legal possibility of choice among congregations, clerics should gain by being somewhat lenient or flexible in order to maintain the loyalty of their constituencies. But local practicalities are not so clear cut and simple. Individuals, starting with children, may find themselves with few or no religious choices in their home region. The state generally defers to clerical leaders in many policy areas although the government oversees religious education, funding for the religion councils (Majelis Agama), the *haj*, and family law (Bagir 2013, 6, n.15).

To the extent that the government remains agnostic to the particularities of citizens' religious practices beyond official affiliations, indigenous cultural practices are often adapted to coexist with scriptural religions drawn from other cultural milieus. Indonesians are known as masters of selective importation and indigenization. As a Javanese phrased it to me bluntly, "I am a Muslim, but I am not an Arab" (*saya orang Muslim tapi saya bukan Arab*). Such a statement now might be traced to an older Indonesian Muslim who grew up before the Wahabi Reformist trends tracked by scholars such as James Peacock (1978), Bob Hefner (2000), and Nancy Smith-Hefner (2019). Orthodoxy valences have shifted, and state law now may reinforce a new and less tolerant Sunni Muslim status quo.

Some exclusivist Muslim and Protestant Christian groups criticize other religious communities on the grounds that only their own religion is truly monotheistic. But, with Hinduism, Buddhism, and Confucianism legally recognized as national religions, there are little grounds for invoking a Pancasila-based monotheism litmus test to exclude native faith traditions. As noted, Hinduism was used as an umbrella religious category for well-organized ethnic minority groups in Kalimantan who managed to legitimize their ancestral cosmologies. Buddhism and Confucianism were made official religions to accommodate ethnic Chinese who, like native faith worshippers, lived in the archipelago prior to when the Pancasila doctrine was negotiated at independence. Although my assessment originates from conversations with more lay people than clerics, most Indonesians I have encountered tend not to scrutinize the "belief in a Supreme God" precept that they avow. This leaves its precise meaning (Is there only a Supreme God, or does the Supreme God coexist in a cosmos with other lesser deities?) both questionable and largely unquestioned.[5] Not only do most Indonesians not spill much intellectual ink on the question of what belief in a Supreme God means, they—like people in plural societies everywhere—often value and prioritize local ethnic and personal alliances in their communities over technical theological differences among neighboring religious sects (*aliran*).

Problems with Counting and Classifying Ancestral Beliefs and Believers

Given Indonesia's strained history of religious classification, the Constitutional Court's 2017 decision feels decidedly postcolonial and twenty-first century in its advocacy of equal human rights before the law. It offers the promise of a seventh umbrella category for the estimated several hundred "traditional faiths" practiced by millions of followers. The numbers of ancestral belief practitioners reported by various agencies likely underrepresent practitioners of ancestral faiths in two ways: first, because they only count self-appointed native faith followers—people who took the considerable risk to eschew affiliation with Indonesia's legally recognized, imported religions; and second, because the figures imagine locally named spiritual traditions—for instance, *Aluk to Dolo* ("ways of the ancestors") of South Sulawesi Toraja, *Wiwikan* of western Java Badui, or indigenous beliefs more generally—as discrete and systematized bundles of ideas and practices that exist apart from, but analogous to, the six official religions. In other words, individuals who list a world religion on their documents are no longer counted as practitioners of their regional traditions, whether they still practice some or not. Even when communities have resisted formal conversion, Indonesian governments have encouraged efforts to reformulate and present ancestral regional traditions as more like the nation's official religions (Atkinson 1983). Similarly, the professional website of the High Council on Indonesian Beliefs (MLKI), which only began with a national congress in 2012, clearly shows that the group is working hard to fit in with Indonesia's national model for religion. Many of its threads invoke Pancasila and belief in a Supreme God. The council sports an iconic symbol and issues statements of creed and activities that precisely mirror those of Indonesia's other official religions.

Beyond the challenges of how to assess, accurately count, and positively promote native faith followers, the 2017 ruling raised uncertainties about exactly what terms would be allowable to denote local belief traditions on KTP identity cards. As directed by President Widodo, Central Java's director general of population and national records ministry (*Direktur Jenderal Kependudukan dan Catatan Sipil Kementerian Dalam Negeri*) Zudan Arif Fakrullah reported to the press that as of July 1, 2018, those who did not adhere to an official religion could insert "beliefs" (*kepercayaan*) in the religion column of their identity cards but not a specific local sect or organization name. The example he gave of what would not be allowed to be named was *Sapta Darma*, literally "Seven Obligations," a small New Religion or spirituality group created during the twentieth century in East Java (Permana 2018). The example illustrates how disparate minority traditions—from ancient regional ancestral practices to New Religions—are being lumped together into the new outlier category of "beliefs."

Indonesia made similar Procrustian efforts in the past to bundle diverse kinds of regional cosmologies and practices into generic categories suitable for state management. Prior to the 2017 ruling, the only recourse for Indonesians wishing to claim an indigenous tradition as a religion was to register it as a form of Hinduism. This was done in 1969 by a small percentage of Sa'dan Toraja people in South Sulawesi (Volkman 1990), and then later in 1980 by Ngaju Dayak of Central Kalimantan for their *Karharingan* tradition (Schiller 1997, 9). As with Balinese after independence (see Picard in this volume), the Ngaju in Indonesian Borneo were instructed on Indian Hinduism by the Ministry of Religion and they formulated descriptions of *Karharingan* to make it qualify as Indonesian Hinduism.

The 2017 ruling would make such tortured efforts to legitimize ethnic minority religions as Hinduism unnecessary. It would expand toleration and parity under Indonesia's already diffuse Pancasila framework. Yet adding a generic category of "beliefs" to the national list of legal religions is still unthinkable to some, including the Indonesian Ulama Council and the Islamic Defenders Front (Fron Pembela Islam or FPI). The leaders of these groups seek to purge what they see as dangerous forms of deviance, blasphemy, defamation, syncretism, or even ecumenicalism. They are invested in maintaining "hardscape" boundaries among Indonesia's religious groups with Islam at the top. The resulting religious isolation helps maintain the current political hierarchy of religions. Religious group isolation also supports religious leaders' community gate-keeping and the state's strategic erasures.

While the state is concerned with the security and management of religious affiliations and clerics are concerned with obedience and support, millions of ordinary Indonesians are networked with each other along multiple dimensions, with religious affiliation and precise orthodox practice being only two. Hope for a tolerant and democratic religious pluralism may reside as much or more in the neighborhood or village as in state management whose bureaucratic straight-jackets are satirized in the 2017 short comedy video called "KTP."

The "KTP" Video: State Bureaucracy and Religious Cosmopolitanism in the Village

In 2016, two Yogyakarta filmmakers, Shinta Oktania Retnani and Bobby Prasetyo, made a humorous fifteen-minute video that cleverly satirizes the gap between Indonesian religious record-keeping and local reality (Morrow 2019). The Indonesian language video "KTP," which went viral on YouTube, illustrates the procedures for—and questions the validity of—recording religion on national identity cards. The plot opens with a Javanese government worker named Darno riding his motorcycle on a dirt road through a hilly forest. He is looking for remote villagers who still need to file KTP data in order to enlist in a health outreach program. When Darno stops at the simple rural house of an elderly man, he finds that Grandpa Karsono (Mbah Karsono) does not know his age, his exact birthdate, or even how to respond appropriately to the Muslim greeting, "Assalamu 'Alaikum."

When asked to name his religion, the frail old man says he follows *Kejawen*, the tradition of his ancestors. Darno shakes his head and points out that there is no option on his government form for Kejawen. To meet the demands of his job, Darno is perfectly willing to concoct an imaginary birthdate for Grandpa Karsono, and he suggests that the elderly man simply list himself as Muslim. When Karsono rebuffs the idea, explaining that he has never done Muslim prayers (*sholat*), the civil servant Darno sheepishly admits that he has never done the prayers either. This is an audience laugh line.

The jape illustrates the familiar term "Muslim KTP." The label refers to the millions of Indonesians, including the demographically dominant Javanese, who dutifully enlist as Muslims on their identity cards but whose practices are less orthodox and more melded with ancestral mystic practices (Geertz 1960; Ricklefs 2006, 6–8, 2012). These Muslims may fast in public and attend Ramadan celebrations with family, but their knowledge of Islamic scriptures and prayers remains limited and layered with other cultural traditions such as Kejawan or its regional equivalents. Some Indonesian Muslims even jokingly call themselves "Muslim Semangka," or "Watermelon Muslims," meaning that they are green (Muslim) on the outside, but are red (holding more egalitarian or communist sympathies) on the inside.

Regionalization of official religions takes various forms. On Sulawesi I met Kaili, who said that, as Muslims, they never ate pork but only ate "the deer with short legs" (*rusa kaki pendek*.) They meant that they ate wild pigs or boar, animals that their ancestors hunted and ate since time immemorial. I met Protestants for whom wearing closed shoes to church services and keeping a Bible in their granary bin were important aspects of their Christian devotion. Localization invariably influences official religious practices, just as many "indigenous" spiritual traditions have been influenced by historical contacts with followers of world religions. Although the various forms of hybridity that get termed syncretism often are repressed in the name of either political purification (Stewart and Shaw 1994) or categorical simplification, many endure, at least in part, whether passing unnoticed or delineated for reformist extirpation.

In daily life, as in the video, KTP categories become the subject of jokes because, unlike the formulaic choices presented, religious faith and practices vary along a spectrum. Individuals of every faith must negotiate with real-world subsistence constraints dependent upon complicated relationships with kin, spouses, neighbors, and trading partners. At least until it became dangerous to do so during the regional religious conflicts that flared between 1998 and 2007, I observed mixed ethnic couples in Central Sulawesi (and elsewhere) who raised some of their children as Muslim and some as Christian. I noticed girls being raised in their mother's religion while boys were raised in their father's, each attending their respective gender-segregated houses of worship. In the past, such pluralistic identities within a family (or even within a single individual over the course of a life) made it possible to connect positively across male and female kin branches of extended families and communities through space and time. Devout practice of any nationally recognized world religion was considered good by most Indonesians until the end of the New Order in 1998.

In principle, Pancasila and the Indonesian Constitution should guarantee the legitimacy and safety of marital choices across two official religions. But the 1974 Marriage Law (article 2, clause 1) leaves a gray area when it says, "A marriage is valid if conducted according to laws of religion and belief of both sides." In practice then, the possibilities for interfaith marriage depend on supportive decisions by regional leaders: for example, Muslim clerics who note that the Qur'an says that Muslims may marry any "people of the book." In the absence of ecumenical communities, a union may depend on the willingness of one partner to change his or her official religion status upon marriage. During conflict periods, in places such as Poso, Central Sulawesi, between 1998 and 2007, mixed religion couples suddenly became at risk for violence. Many clerical pronouncements aimed to purify and divide religious communities. Some mixed religion couples, or the minority religion spouse, fled. Some spouses converted under duress.

The ending of the "KTP" video offers a more peaceful vision of Pancasila to solve the contradiction between state categories and everyday practices of religious pluralism. As Darno wrestles with the coding problem raised by the Kejawen elder's refusal to enlist as Muslim—or Christian, or any of the other choices on his form—first Karsono's adult daughter, then the hamlet leader (RT or Kepala Rukun Tetangga), and then other neighbors enter the house and join the discussion, one by one. By the end of the video, the room is filled with a motley mix of local men and women, young and old, traditional and modern. Some are dressed in headscarves or *songko* hats, some in Javanese batik and *kebaya*, others in the sassy modern outfits worn by many Indonesian youths. They all seem to get along, even as some comically try to swipe another's full glass of tea or a nice new pair of sandals left outside the front door. They tease each other with humorous nicknames, showing the kind of intimate affection that arises in small, close knit communities. After tossing out many suggestions, the large crowd inside Grandpa Karsono's tiny sitting room overrules Darno with a hamlet consensus about what their elder should do. They defend Karsono's decision not to lie on the government form. They declare that Karsono won't need the KTP after all. Instead, they publicly vow to Darno that they, his neighbors and family, will help Grandpa Karsono whenever he needs financial or medical aid. The religiously plural group depicted is the soul of tolerance and conviviality amidst diversity. Notice that the people portrayed are stereotypically rural; not the urban Asian cosmopolitans who analysts generally expect to be more tolerant and willing to live together under conditions of pluralism (Mayaram 2009).

The utopian punchline of the video invokes the Javanese tradition of *gotong-royong* or mutual aid for the benefit of the community. The hamlet group's solution is not like the demand for *courvée* labor or the top-down "community service" required under the Suharto regime's deployment of the same lexicon of *gotong-royong* under Pancasila. Rather, the villagers' aid is pledged and offered willingly to Grandpa Karsono's household on the basis of cherished relationships and likely obligations of delayed reciprocity. These kindnesses and socially indebted forms of help require no laws or categories of religion on a national ID card. They are born of place-based rural relations that in many parts of Indonesia are still enmeshed in and remembered through past and present material exchanges. Much of the usefulness of those exchanges is premised on human differences, including occupational or geographic ones linked to religious affiliations that make the transactions of material goods or services desirable.

With a final tongue-in-cheek twist, after listing the cast, the "KTP" video credits thank "Tuhan Maha Esa," the Supreme God. This surely is a reminder that God or Allah is not the authority requiring that official religions be listed on Indonesian ID cards. The popularity of the "KTP" video on social media, its willingness to satirize the infelicities of Indonesia's religious classification, and especially the Kejawen character's unwillingness to assent to the KTP form's bureaucratic straightjacket resonate with the epilogue vignette in Ken George's 1996 ethnography about Mambi, South Sulawesi. George returns to his fieldwork area and tentatively inquires of a Mambi friend whether he converted to Christianity since his prior visit. The man gives the following answer to explain why he did not convert and why, as the man puts it, "there is no need to make problems over religion." The Mambi man says, "I have God inside of me. I am Muslim. I am Protestant. I am Catholic. I am Hindu. This is Pancasila. I have Pancasila inside of me. What is wrong if I am *mappurondo* [the ancestral tradition] too?" (George 1996, 272). The Mambi man exemplifies a classic Southeast Asian perspective that if one source of spiritual knowledge is good, the accumulation of more sources of religious knowledge can only be better.

If the government, in accordance with Pancasila, recognizes each official religion equally, why shouldn't a citizen respect them all? (Aragon 2000, 313). The "KTP" video's humorous plot and the Mambi man's bold words herald the implications of the 2017 Constitutional Court's ruling to disrupt the state's ID card rules. We again see the state's use of Aristotle's Law of the Excluded Middle as it pertains to scriptural religions since at least the time of European colonial conquests: what is "A" cannot also be "B." Whereas the Mambi man in the 1990s suggested that ecumenicalism would help avoid problems over religion, the prospect of allowing indigenous faiths to be listed on KTP card opens up what can only be an exclusivist Muslim's (or Protestant's) worst nightmare. It is essentially what Mary Douglas (1966) framed as dangerous pollution or "matter out of place" in the body politic. The cognitive dissonance of placing ancestral beliefs into the esteemed category that holds Abrahamic and other scriptural religions draws us back to consider the conceptual dichotomy and hierarchy established by Europeans between "civilized" religion and their colonized natives' "uncivilized" animism.

Animism and Religion as Co-constructed Concepts

The Indonesian controversies on religious categories unveil a broader, global truth: that animism hovers everywhere around scriptural religions' orthodoxy. Although clerics of Christianity and Islam work tirelessly to deny, suppress, and extirpate the "small gods" of indigenous cosmologies, lay people's experience of accessible and directly encountered local deities and spirits refuses extinction (Aragon 2018; Ostling 2018). Ideas about spirits of the dead or local beings with energetic powers seem to haunt all long-lived branches of scriptural religions. The *Nats* and *Phi* spirits of Theravada Buddhism; the *Jinns* of Islam; the saints, satans, and ghosts of Christianity; these are only a few examples of how animism enters—through debate, purification discourses, even appropriation—into orthodoxies that generally would prefer they did not. Local relations with unseen beings, welling from human history and often defending "ancestral values," are negotiable and flexible enough to serve both old and new purposes. Many of these beings, however transformed, resist erasure, even when the modern states and clerical institutions that usurped their preeminence insist they must be.

What is now understood as only a problem of orthodox theological politics descends from the formulation of "religion" as a semantic umbrella category. By the end of the twentieth century, religious studies scholars came to the shocking conclusion that "appearances to the contrary notwithstanding, religion is a *modern Western invention*" (Taylor 1998; italics original). What Mark Taylor means by the term "invention" is the definitional category of scriptural religion—*agama* in Indonesian parlance—not the component ritual acts, everyday practices, institutions, material culture, or ideas related to unseen powers. Religious ideas and practices preceded the formal concept. Once we acknowledge that religion as an umbrella category is a relatively recent invention with a knowable history that became formulated unevenly across the globe, animism can be seen more clearly to be its mistreated stepchild.

Originally and still mostly an exonym, the category of "animists"—or its present Indonesian equivalent, *penhayat kepercayaan* (practitioners of beliefs)—is the epitome of what Geertz (1973) calls an "experience far" category. Few people say, "I am an animist" or "I am a belief practitioner," although implementing the 2017 ruling could lead to more such professions of identity. The exonym status of *kepercayaan* (which many translate pejoratively into English as "superstition") makes it a different kind of religious category from Indonesia's other official options of Islam, Protestant Christianity, Catholicism, Hinduism, Buddhism, and Confucianism. Yet, the names of many scriptural religions also began as exonyms formulated by culturally dominant groups before they became widely adopted and internalized as personal experience (Sharf 1998).

On the invention of religion, Jonathan Z. Smith writes, "'Religion' is not a native term," or at least wasn't in the 1500s at the start of the colonial encounter" (Smith 1998, 269). Smith focuses on the development of the category by Europeans who saw it as having potential universal application. Talal Asad counters that any universal definition of religion is impossible because it hides European Christianity's linkage with power (Asad 1993, 27–29). The powerful—now generally each nation-state—decide what criteria turn a "cult" into a religion. After World War II and postcolonial independence movements, scriptural religions became taught and naturalized, with affiliation made a national requirement in many states around the world. Scriptural religion's unregulated and most "wild" (*liar*) others, to be persecuted by leaders of state-affiliated orthodoxies, were local "beliefs" and rituals or animism.

Edward B. Tylor's 1871 book on *Primitive Culture* famously defined animism as "belief in spirits" and cast animism as the earliest stage of religion (Tylor 1871). Tylor provided us with animism as a scholarly euphemism for paganism. His book is its early encyclopedia. Tylor's comparative vision was strong, but his social evolutionist analysis became less and less acceptable over time. Recent cross-cultural research on indigenous lifeworlds abandons Tylor to view animist cosmologies anew through a positive lens: as a much-needed epistemological corrective to modernism's misguided dichotomies between mind and body, nature and culture, civilized and savage. Contemporary psychology, epigenetics, climate crises, and antiracist movements all demand reconsideration of other ontological perspectives.

Looking back to Irving Hallowell's discussion of "other-than-human-persons" among Ojibwa Indians (Hallowell 1960), anthropologists have reframed animism as a cosmology of subject-to-subject relations with all beings beyond the human (Harvey 2006, 2013, 1–12). This relational definition of animism is theoretically capacious enough to encompass monotheistic religions including the Abrahamic God or Allah. But scholarship on what is termed the "New Animism" focuses specifically on cosmologies where humans maintain ecological relationships with non-human beings, animate and inanimate, conceived as subjects with agency (Descola 1992, 2013; Harvey 2006, 2013; Vivieros de Castro 2004). Arturo Escobar coins the term "pluriverse" for the way different people on our planet live with diverse ontologies of relationality and coexistence (Escobar 2017). He seeks an open form of pluralism.

"New Animism" scholarship, much of it centered on Latin America, concentrates on the perspectives of small-scale groups for whom the classical Western distinction or boundary between nature and society becomes meaningless (Bird-David 1999; de la Cadena 2015; Descola 2013, 78; Harvey 2006, 2013; Ingold 2000; Vivieros de Castro 2004). Courtney Work makes a further religious connection to modern capitalist dysfunction. She argues that scriptural religions facilitate uneven economic development in states by downgrading all non-humans into the category of exploitable resources. She contrasts this perspective to animists' careful relationships with land guardians, which foster more ecological awareness and dwelling habits (Work 2019).

World religion scriptures and postcolonial modernism (what Descola 2013 calls "naturalism") combine to divide the entirety of non-human "nature" from humanity. This conceptual divide reduces empathy and allows the former to be considered as mere fodder to grow the economies of the latter. The model of a combined scriptural religion and utilitarian or neoliberal economic system is now institutionally predominant in most states worldwide. Against this backdrop, animism's continued low-level hum in communities large and small, urban and rural, represents a tiny seed bank of human ecological history, interdependent relationality, and ontological diversity.

The significant features of animism (or "beliefs") within the Indonesian context include: permeability among energetic forms and beings as a caution against wanton habitat destruction, a model for human tolerance of diversity and inclusiveness, attention to temporal and ethical continuity with predecessors and, finally, the use of ancestral customs for negotiating local conflict or asserting autonomy in the face of unwarranted state interventions (Aragon 2018; Aragon and Leach 2008). Indonesian and other followers of indigenous cosmologies generally posit a symbiosis and cautious permeability between humans and "wild nature," among living humans, ancestors, deities, and other non-human beings. These challenging ideas break down religious walls exactly where scriptural religions, long entrenched in political structures, tend to build them up. Recent investigations of animism across Southeast Asia note both its cosmological diversity and its ability to coexist "below, or besides, or within the seemingly dominant world religions in place" (Sprenger 2016, 32). The 2017 ruling pulls that latent diversity and coexistence into the open.

The pragmatic question then becomes how the 2017 ruling and various clerics' reactions to it will transform the way animist and other subaltern religious sects, officially labelled as "beliefs," are further elevated, incorporated, or repressed by the Indonesian state. Indonesia's categorical framing of animism as "beliefs" actually is a remarkable approach to the conceptually challenging problem of placing animist practices beside varieties of scriptural religion. Unlike Confucianism, the most recently added official religion, "beliefs"—just like "animism"—is a catch-all category with potentially global reach. The term can aggregate cosmological worldviews that bear no necessary genealogical relation to one another beyond their possibly deep time horizon and original basis in small-scale societies. It is apparent that native faith leaders in Indonesia will reorganize and publicize what these faiths are in nationalistic and Pancasila-friendly terms invoking a single Supreme God (Tuhan Maha Esa), rather than allowing their harshest critics to decry what they are not (MLKI n.d.). The difficulty such groups face, however, is that Indonesia's use of discriminatory religious laws and prosecutions and the political leverage of intolerant Islamist groups is rising rather than falling.

Indonesia's Constitution on Religious Freedom Versus Laws Supporting Intolerance

The early twenty-first century has been a risky period for Indonesian religious minorities. The 2016–17 blasphemy accusation, hardline Islamist demonstrations, and the jailing of the former Jakarta governor Basuki Tjahaja Purnama (BTP, also known as Ahok; see Monika Lohanda's chapter in this volume) indicate that new forms of legalized intolerance have arisen in Indonesia. Legal records back up this claim. BTP's experience was only the most politically prominent example. There were almost five times more blasphemy prosecutions in Indonesia between 1998 and 2012 (N=47 cases) than there were between 1966 and 1998—that is, during the entire New Order regime (N=10 cases; Crouch 2012, 11).

Indonesia's blasphemy prosecutions originate with a 1965 presidential decree that was enshrined in law in 1969 by President Suharto (UU No.5/1969). The decree's trajectory aligns with contemporary resistance to the legitimization of "beliefs." In 1954, an interdepartmental committee was established to monitor "beliefs" (*kepercayaan*) as a matter of surveillance and social control of communists (Crouch 2012, 6). In a nutshell, the blasphemy policies deployed by intolerant

Muslim organizations that now raise serious concerns among democracy and human rights advocates seem to have originated with Cold War fears of rising communism, not with intolerance of religious diversity per se.

Indonesia's prior guarantee of religious freedom goes back to Article 29(2) of the 1945 constitution, which promises all citizens freedom of worship according to their own beliefs. A post-Suharto constitutional amendment solidified the freedom of individuals to profess religions and worship according to their conscience (Crouch 2012, 18–19). Attacks on houses of worship (*tempat ibadah*)—specifically three church buildings that were located in Aceh, Makassar, and Jakarta, respectively—started to occur only in the late 1960s (Crouch 2010). Based on these three particular attacks and threats of religious disorder, Suharto's Ministry of Religion and Home Affairs issued Joint Decree 1/1969 to regulate all religious activities and construction of houses of worship in the archipelago. This brief, vague decree gives regents and local ministries of religion the responsibility and discretion to issue religious building permits in ways that should not disturb peace and order among local communities. Denigration of other religions is forbidden, but primarily with the aim of preventing any disharmony that could become a threat to state control.

In 2006, a revised Joint Ministerial Decree (No. 1/2006) on the Construction of Houses of Worship added exacting implementation regulations that has since made it difficult for churches—or any minority religious structure—to be built or renovated in Indonesia. The 2006 decree stipulates that congregations who have more than ninety members may establish a legal house of worship, but only after receiving supportive signatures from a minimum of sixty local people *from other religions*. Then a religious panel based proportionally on the neighborhood's current sectarian statistics must also agree to the petition. If the requirements above—demographically more difficult for Christians and other religious minorities than for the Muslim majority—are not met, police or Muslim paramilitary groups such as those linked with the Islamic Defenders Front can terminate worship services by force. Ironically, these Indonesian regulations governing houses of worship are known as "Religious Harmony Laws."

Since the original decree in 1969, thousands of existing and proposed Christian church buildings have been shut down under semilegal pressures, threats, or violent attacks. Melissa Crouch (2010, 404) argues that, especially in former Darul Islam strongholds such as West Java, local governments have bowed to pressures from Islamic militants in the post-Suharto era of decentralization and electoral popularity politics. These laws, often built upon MUI fatwas that increasingly are amplified by social media, work to silo or insulate Indonesia's religious communities from personal knowledge of and communion with each other. Whereas Indonesians once were divided primarily by island geography, they now often are cloistered by religion-specific communications and routines. Effectively amplified by electoral politics and social media platforms, this closed religious network messaging foments new threats to state order.

In 2009, a diverse group of NGOs sought a Constitutional Court Judicial Review of the 1969 Blasphemy Law. They argued that the law unconstitutionally violates religious freedom, creates uncertainty, and discriminates against minorities who are targeted as deviant or upsetting religious order in complaints by hardline Muslim clerics. Note that the Indonesian legal phrase routinely translated as "blasphemy" (*penyalahgunaan dan/atau penodaan agama*, literally, "to misuse and/or despoil a religion") actually covers many behaviors considered heresy, insult, or deviance as defined by clerics of recognized religions. Zainal Abidin Bagir notes that "defamation of religion" is a more apt term for what the "blasphemy" law targets. Bagir describes how it has been applied most recently and harshly to Ahmadis and Shi'a and that its vagueness allows clerics to turn theological "differences or disagreements into crimes" (Bagir 2013, 5). Despite arguments from several human rights NGOs in 2009, the Constitutional Court upheld the 1969 Blasphemy Law, which was adamantly supported by the Ministry of Religion, the Ministry of Law and Human Rights, the directors general of Islam, Protestantism, and Catholicism, the MUI, Muhammadiyah, the Dewan Dakwah Islamiyah Indonesia, the FPI, and Hizbut Tahrir. The government and clerics from scriptural religions united and won against the less powerful human rights activists and groups advocating for minority religion practitioners.

Although the Indonesian constitution promises freedom of religious worship, the state has limited that promise by weighing it against public security concerns. In recent years, the disruptions have been generated by Muslim demonstrations and street protests where hardline clerics speak for the entire religion of Islam. They consider their majoritarian argument to be a valid democratic consideration. More to the point, their vocal protests are an existential concern for Indonesian political leaders who see dissent and "diversity without unity" as a source of national weakness, not laudable democratic pluralism.

The laws concerning the construction of houses of worship and blasphemy discriminate against religious minorities and limit their religious freedom. They permit violent attacks on "deviants" and then blame the victims for upsetting religious peace (Bagir 2013). They violate the constitution's promises of the right to recognition, security, protections, and certainty of just laws and equal treatment before the law (Crouch 2012, 21). These laws fail the constitution's democratic goals of protecting all citizens equally under law.

How then, after the 2017 Constitutional Court ruling, will "belief practitioners" be allowed to build temples or practice freely when followers of both regional traditions and non-majority official religions such as Christians have been labeled deviant threats since the 1960s? Moreover, even if some or all of the "belief" sects are brought under the national wing, who will oversee the orthodoxy of their clerics or "ulama," as the Ministry of Religion expects of each official religious group? The 2017 ruling's challenge to Indonesia's identity card rules opens up these kinds of long-range practical questions along with the more fundamental question of what is to be accepted as legitimate religion in an ethnically diverse archipelago nation.

A genie escaped from the bottle with the Indonesian Constitutional Court's ruling in November 2017. It is a civil rights decision that arguably was long overdue, ever since independence, when many Indonesians might have noticed that their official religions were all foreign born. What stopped Indonesians, freed from foreign rule, from being able to follow their indigenous cosmologies and spiritual practices? The answer, which I have explored here from a variety of angles, begins as follows. Scriptural religions and ancestral traditions in Southeast Asia have at various times worked with or against ruling states that pursued regional centralization and with or against localized communities that pursued autonomy to manage their own livelihoods (O'Connor 2003, 280–97). Indonesians inherited a set of religious categories, criteria, and laws from Dutch colonial rulers and from the Muslim clerics and institutions who stood in opposition to colonial power. Indonesian nationalism was built around concepts of developmental modernism, including scriptural orthodoxies, plus an anticommunist agenda that favored religious oversight by a state prepared to use military force to ensure order. Ancestral cosmologies and ritual practices were largely on the losing end of these twentieth-century battles. Nevertheless, because they are irrepressibly adaptable to serve local purposes, they evolved to endure both within and around the peripheries of missionary zeal. Pan-archipelago evidence shows that many Indonesian ancestral cosmologies and practices were adjusted to fit, at least partially, within imported scriptural religions. South Sulawesi's ancient La Galigo epic coexists as a behavioral model with scriptural Islam for many ethnic Bugis. Ancestral ideas and norms for the authorized use of land coexist in highland Central Sulawesi with a Protestantism largely agnostic on such matters. Bali's distinctively productive division and schedule of village, rice, and death temple rituals coexists readily with Hinduism. The examples are legion, even though ancestral practices' ecological and societal services remain little recognized. Now, following the 2017 court decision elevating "beliefs" as a separate religious category on national identity cards, Indonesians must face, or continue to ignore, the unequal statuses and interpenetration of majority religions and minority beliefs.

The legal option to claim indigenous beliefs on Indonesian identity cards aims to improve the basic civil rights of tens of millions of Indonesian citizens. This is no small accomplishment when many vulnerable citizens previously lacked the right to register or obtain birth certificates, education, employment, marriage certificates, burials, and death certificates. Only future research can show how implementation of the 2017 legal ruling will transpire in islands, provinces, and districts that vary dramatically with respect to demographic ratios and institutions that support democratic religious pluralism. Ideally, the legal shift might encourage people to see the complex realities of Indonesian religious practices in light of historical continuities. These suggest that citizens across the islands, while diverse in specific traditions, have much in common. As Chiara Formichi suggests in her overview of pan-Asian examples, the gold standard for pluralism is to have both a strong legitimization of diversity in law and normative paradigms for conviviality that are dispersed across regions, sects, and social classes (Formichi 2014, 1–4).

Postcolonial Indonesia's historic framework of religious pluralism denied the political legitimacy and cosmological challenges of indigenous faiths during the "Long Cold War." Exclusivist religious leaders continue to do so when they oppose allowing the legitimization of minority and ancestral belief practitioners. Given incidents such as the 2016–17 blasphemy accusations and subsequent jailing of former Jakarta governor BTP and the other legal prosecutions described here, we might expect a rocky road ahead for many native faith followers. Legitimacy across sects is not yet accepted as a national constitutional principle by all Indonesian political and clerical leaders. Yet the relatively small membership of native faith groups may not garner widespread concern as long as they are not deemed threatening to national stability and the hegemony of the politically powerful. Indonesian minorities often survive through quietude. The 2017 ruling may be denounced periodically by intolerant Muslim organizations and perhaps some Christian groups until the day comes when their partisan objections are deemed inappropriate by an engaged and broadly vocal public. Then, inequitable religious laws like those on blasphemy and houses of worship construction may be revised. Someday even the religion column on Indonesia's national ID card may be removed as unnecessary.

Notes

I am grateful to fellow participants of the 2019 Cornell SEAP Conference and especially to Chiara Formichi for inviting me to join this project, offering smart critique, and shepherding the volume to completion. I am also indebted to the reviewers for pushing me harder, and to Liz Coville and Greg Acciaioli for generous correspondence that improved my initial formulation of the topic.

1. As most readers will know, Hinduism and Buddhism reached Southeast Asia in the first millennium C.E. from its early centers in South Asia. Islam originated in Arabia in that period but reached the Indonesian archipelago centuries later after contact with Middle Eastern and South Asian Muslim traders. Christianity originated in the

Mediterranean region but arrived after the 1500s with Protestant and Roman Catholic missionaries from Europe. Confucianism originated in ancient China and arrived periodically over the centuries with migrants.

2. Although this essay's scope is bound to Indonesia, historical evidence shows that, at various time periods and locations, the laws and policies of other nations, including electoral democracies such as the US, also have granted full citizenship rights only to members of those particular religious, ethnic, or racial groups in the ruling majority.

3. Also beyond the scope of this chapter are philosophical debates about exactly what the term "belief" means, a topic of focus for Rodney Needham (1972).

4. World history indicates that legitimization may entail asymmetrical hierarchy rather than symmetrical equivalence. Asymmetrical legitimization can involve a hierarchy based on a single value such as purity, as in Indian caste (Dumont 1970), or individual autonomy (Keeler 2017). By contrast, Austronesian systems of precedence often rank people asymmetrically according to multiple, overlapping priorities such as age, gender, or kinship lines linked to village founders (Fox 2006, 134–35). Formichi (2014, 1–4) and Peletz (2009), however, advocate legitimization with equal citizenship rights.

5. It is possible that foreign scholars misguidedly focus on English or other European linguistic glosses, which are strict about the singular-plural distinction, rather than recognizing Austronesian languages' ambiguity and context dependence in this regard. For example, a Central Sulawesi vernacular term for indigenous owner god(s) or guardian being(s) (*pue'*, Uma), was adopted in the singular form and capitalized by European missionaries for the Christian God (*Pue'*, Uma) although the Uma language term is, like most Indonesian nominatives, either singular or plural, depending on context (Aragon 2000, 168–69).

References

Acciaioli, Greg [1985] 2016. "Culture as Art: From Practice to Spectacle in Indonesia" (republished with postscript). In *Punks, Monks, and Politics: Authenticity in Thailand, Indonesia, and Malaysia*, edited by Julian CH Lee and Marco Ferrarese, 145–63. London: Rowman & Littlefield.

Aragon, Lorraine V. 2000. *Fields of the Lord: Animism, Christian Minorities, and State Development in Indonesia*. Honolulu: University of Hawai'i Press.

Aragon, Lorraine V. 2001. "Communal Violence in Central Sulawesi: Where People Eat Fish and Fish Eat People." *Indonesia* 72 (October): 45–79.

Aragon, Lorraine V. 2005. "Mass Media Fragmentation and Narratives of Violent Action in Sulawesi's Poso Conflict." *Indonesia* 79 (April): 1–55.

Aragon, Lorraine V. 2018. "Who Owns the World? Recognizing the Repressed Small Gods of Southeast Asia." In *Fairies, Demons, and Nature Spirits: 'Small Gods' at the Margins of Christendom*, edited by Michael Ostling, 277–99. London: Palgrave Macmillan.

Aragon, Lorraine V., and James Leach. 2008. "Arts and Owners: Intellectual Property Law and the Politics of Scale in Indonesian Arts." *American Ethnologist* 35, no. 4 (November): 607–31.

Asad, Talal. 1993. *Genealogies of Religion: Discipline and Reasons of Power in Christianity and Islam*. Baltimore: Johns Hopkins University Press.

Atkinson, Jane Monnig. 1983. "Religions in Dialogue: Construction of an Indonesian Minority Religion." *American Ethnologist* 10: 684–96.

Bagir, Zainal Abidin. 2013. "Defamation of Religion Law in Post-*Reformasi* Indonesia: Is Revision Possible?" *Australian Journal of Asian Law* 13, no. 2: 1–16.

Bird-David, Nurit. 1999. "'Animism' Revisited: Personhood, Environment, and Relational Epistemology." *Current Anthropology* 40: S67–S91.

Budijanto, Oki Wahju. 2016. "Penghormatan Hak Asasi Manusia bagi Penghayat Kepercayaan di Kota Bandung." *Jurnal Hak Asasi Manusia* 7, no. 1: 35–44.

Chairunnisa, Ninis, ed. 2017. "Putusan MK Soal KTP, Ketua MUI: Aliran Kepercayaan Bukan Agama." *Tempo.com*, November 15. https://nasional.tempo.co/read/1034049/putusan-mk-soal-ktp-ketua-mui-aliran-kepercayaan-bukan-agama.

Chaplin, Chris. 2017. "Islam and Citizenship." *Inside Indonesia* 129, July–September. https://www.insideindonesia.org/islam-and-citizenship-3.

Crouch, Melissa. 2010. "Implementing the Regulations on Places of Worship in Indonesia: New Problems, Local Politics and Court Action." *Asian Studies Review* 34: 403–19.

Crouch, Melissa A. 2012. "Law and Religion in Indonesia: The Constitutional Court and the Blasphemy Law." *Asian Journal of Comparative Law* 7, no. 1: 1–46.

Davidson, Jamie S., and David Henley, eds. 2007 *The Revival of Tradition in Indonesian Politics: The Deployment of Adat from Colonialism to Indigenism*. London: Routledge.

De la Cadena, Marisol. 2015. *Earth Beings: Ecologies of Practice across Andean Worlds*. Durham, NC: Duke University Press.

Descola, Philippe. 1992. "Societies of Nature and the Nature of Society." In *Conceptualizing Society*, edited by Adam Kuper, 107–26. London: Routledge.

Descola, Philippe. 2013. "Beyond Nature and Culture." In *The Handbook of Contemporary Animism*, edited by Graham Harvey, 77–91. Durham: Acumen.

Douglas, Mary. 1966. *Purity and Danger: An Analysis of Concepts of Pollution and Taboo*. New York: Praeger.

Dumont, Louis. 1970. *Homo Hierarchicus: The Caste System and Its Implications*. Translated by Mark Sainsbury. Chicago: University of Chicago Press.

Duncan, Christopher R., ed. 2004. *Civilizing the Margins: Southeast Asian Government Policies for the Development of Minorities*. Ithaca, NY: Cornell University Press.

Escobar, Arturo. 2017. *Designs for the Pluriverse*. Durham, NC: Duke University Press.

Formichi, Chiara. 2014. "Religious Pluralism, State, and Society in Asia." In *Religious Pluralism, State, and Society in Asia*, edited by Chiara Formichi, 1–9. London: Routledge.

Fox, James J. 2006. "The Transformation of Progenitor Lines of Origin: Patterns of Precedence in Eastern Indonesia." In *Origins, Ancestry and Alliance: Explorations in Austronesian Ethnography*, edited by James J. Fox and Clifford Sather, 133–56. Canberra: ANU Press.

Geertz, Clifford. 1960. *The Religion of Java*. Chicago: University of Chicago Press.

Geertz, Clifford. 1973. *The Interpretation of Cultures*. New York: Basic Books.

George, Kenneth M. 1996. *Showing Signs of Violence: The Cultural Politics of a Twentieth-Century Headhunting Ritual*. Berkeley: University of California Press.

Hallowell, A. Irving. 1960. "Ojibwa Ontology, Behavior, and Worldview." In *Culture in History: Essays in Honor of Paul Radin*, edited by Stanley Diamond, 19–52. New York: Columbia University Press.

Harnish, David D., and Anne K. Rasmussen, eds. 2011. *Divine Inspirations: Music and Islam in Indonesia*. Oxford: Oxford University Press.

Harvey, Graham. 2006. *Animism: Respecting the Living World*. New York: Columbia University Press.

Harvey, Graham, ed. 2013. *The Handbook of Contemporary Animism*. Durham: Routledge.

Hefner, Robert W. 2000. *Civil Islam: Muslims and Democratization in Indonesia*. Princeton, NJ: Princeton University Press.

Ingold, Timothy. 2000. *The Perception of the Environment: Essays in Livelihood, Dwelling and Skill*. London: Routledge.

Jakarta Post. 2017. "MUI Suggests Special ID Cards for Native Faith Followers." *Jakarta Post*, November 30. https://www.thejakartapost.com/news/2017/11/30/mui-suggests-special-id-cards-for-native-faith-folowers.html.

Keeler, Ward. 2017. *The Traffic in Hierarchy: Masculinity and Its Others in Buddhist Burma*. Honolulu: University of Hawai'i Press.

Kurniawan, Frendy. 2017. "Seberapa Banyak Jumlah Penghayat Kepercayaan di Indonesia?" *Tirto News Online*, November 14. https://tirto.id/seberapa-banyak-jumlah-penghayat-kepercayaan-di-indonesia-cz2y.

Mayaram, Shail. 2009. "Introduction: Rereading Global Cities: Topographies of an Alternative Cosmopolitanism in Asia." In *The Other Global City*, edited by Shail Mayaram, 1–34. London: Routledge.

MLKI. n.d. "Majelis Luhur Kepercayaan Indonesia (MLKI)". Accessed July 10, 2020. https://www.mlki.or.id/.

Morrow, Avery. 2019. "Review: Short Film 'KTP'" *Inside Indonesia* 135, January–March. https://www.insideindonesia.org/review-short-film-ktp.

McBeth, John. 2017. "A Leap for Faith in Indonesia." *Asia Times*. November 22. http://www.atimes.com/article/leap-faith-Indonesia/.

Needham, Rodney. 1972. *Belief, Language and Experience*. Chicago: University of Chicago Press.

O'Connor, Richard A. 2003. "Founders' Cults in Regional and Historical Perspective." In *Founders' Cults in Southeast Asia: Ancestors, Polity, and Identity*, edited by Nicola Tannenbaum and Cornelia Ann Kammerer, 269–311. New Haven: Yale University Press.

Ostling, Michael, ed. 2018. *Fairies, Demons, and Nature Spirits: 'Small Gods' at the Margins of Christendom*. London: Palgrave Macmillan.

Peacock, James L. 1978. *Muslim Puritans: Reformist Psychology in Southeast Asian Islam*. Berkeley: University of California Press.

Peletz, Michael G. 2009. *Gender Pluralism: Southeast Asia since Early Modern Times*. New York: Routledge.

Permana, Dian Ade. 2018. "Mulai 1 Juli 2018, Kolom Agama di KTP Bisa Diisi Aliran Kepercayaan." *Merdeka.com*, April 12. Accessed April 15, 2021. https://www.merdeka.com/peristiwa/mulai-1-juli-2018-kolom-agama-di-ktp-diisi-aliran-kepercayaan.html.

Republik Indonesia, 2013. "Undang-Undang (UU) No. 24/2013 Perubahan UU 2006 Tentang Administrasi Pendudukan." Accessed April 19, 2021. https://pih.kemlu.go.id/files/19.%20%20UU_%20No%2024%20Th%202013.pdf.

Ricklefs, Merle C. 2006. *Mystic Synthesis in Java: A History of Islamicization from the Fourteenth to the Early Nineteenth Centuries*. Norwalk, CT: EastBridge.

Ricklefs, Merle C. 2012. *Islamicization and Its Opponents in Java c.1930 to the Present*. Singapore: Singapore University Press.

Ross, Laurie Margot. 2016. *The Encoded Mask: Materiality, Flow, and Meaning along Java's Islamic Northwest Coast*. Leiden: Brill.

Sapiie, Marguerite Afra. 2017a. "Constitutional Court Rules Indigenous Faiths 'Acknowledged' by State." *Jakarta Post*, November 7. http://www.thejakartapost.com/news/2017/11/07/constitutional-court-rules-indigenous-faiths-acknowledged-by-state.html/.

Sapiie, Marguerite Afra. 2017b. "NU, Muhammadiyah Welcome Wider Rights for Native-Faith Followers." *Jakarta Post*, November 10. http://www.thejakartapost.com/news/2017/11/10/nu-muhammadiyah-welcome-wider-rights-for-native-faith-followers.html.

Scott, James 1998. *Seeing Like a State: How Certain Schemes to Improve the Human Condition Have Failed*. New Haven: Yale University Press.

Schiller, Anne. 1997. *Small Sacrifices: Religious Change and Cultural Identity among the Ngaju of Indonesia*. New York: Oxford University Press.

Sharf, Robert H. 1998. "Experience." In *Critical Terms for Religious Studies*, edited by Mark C. Taylor, 94–116. Chicago: University of Chicago Press.

Smith, Jonathan Z. 1998. "Religion, Religions, Religious." In *Critical Terms for Religious Studies*, edited by Mark C. Taylor, 269–24. Chicago: University of Chicago Press.

Smith-Hefner, Nancy J. 2019. *Islamizing Intimacies: Youth, Sexuality and Gender in Contemporary Indonesia*. Honolulu: University of Hawaii Press.

Sprenger, Guido. 2016. "Dimensions of Animism in Southeast Asia." In *Animism in Southeast Asia*, edited by Kaj Århem and Guido Sprenger, 31–51. London: Routledge.

Stewart, Charles, and Rosalind Shaw, ed. 1994. *Syncretism/Anti-Syncretism: The Politics of Religious Synthesis*. London: Routledge.

Sutton, R. Anderson. 2002. *Calling Back the Spirit: Music, Dance, and Cultural Politics in Lowland South Sulawesi*. Oxford: Oxford University Press.

Taylor, Mark C. 1998. "Introduction." In *Critical Terms for Religious Studies*, edited by Mark C. Taylor, 1–19. Chicago: University of Chicago Press.

Tylor, Edward B. 1871. *Primitive Culture: Researches into the Development of Mythology, Philosophy, Religion, Art, and Custom*. London: Murray.

Vivieros de Castro, Eduardo B. 2004. "Exchanging Perspectives: The Transformation of Objects into Subjects in Amerindian Ontologies." *Common Knowledge* 10, no. 3: 463–84.

Volkman, Toby Alice. 1990. "Visions and Revisions: Toraja Culture and the Tourist Gaze." *American Ethnologist* 17, no. 1: 91–110.

Work, Courtney. 2019. "Chthonic Sovereigns? 'Neak Ta' in a Cambodian Village." *Asia Pacific Journal of Anthropology* 20, no. 1: 74–95.

8

FROM IMPOSED ORDER TO CONFLICTING SUPERDIVERSITY

The Tamil Hindu and Their Neighbors in Medan

Silvia Vignato

Mixed religion environments have defined Medan since its early history as a sultanate (founded in 1632) and a colonial hub.[1] In the early 1990s when I started my research, a smooth religious and ethnic pluralism—that is, an ideal pacific coexistence of different systems of social and spiritual belonging—was locally acknowledged as one of the characteristics of the city and as a Medanese and Indonesian way to be a citizen. Things have evolved since, both in daily practice and in ideological discourse. This chapter tries to capture some elements of this transformation when observed through the prism of a neighborhood with a meaningful "Indian" Hindu presence.[2] This implies considering the changing position of Indian Hinduism within a local and national religion-scape as well as the symbolic role played by overlapping and contrasting symbolic areas in a shared living space.

In order to underline the historical change in practiced religious tolerance here I shall compare the same Tamil Hindu ritual carried out in the same mixed neighborhood of Medan and largely by the same families in 1995, 1999, and 2011, with special attention to the non-Hindu neighbors' standpoint. The ceremony revolves around a blood sacrifice with a divination session that can be carried out for different occasions—calendar dates, personal vows, achievement celebrations, and so on.

The physical structure of the urban environment and its radical transformation is the background of my analysis. Appadurai (1995, 209) has long claimed the value of using the neighborhood as an analytical unit as it underlines the interplay of spatialized and embodied ideas and values as opposed to a more politically designed "locality." This is particularly true for multiethnic, migration-based growing cities like Medan where ethnicity is constantly challenged and reformulated through shifts in constructed space and changes in materials, ownership, and regulations. Taking a neighborhood as a standpoint seems then particularly appropriate when looking into religious plurality as lived day-by-day experience, what Formichi has defined as an "ordinary religious pluralism" (2013, 53).

My reading of the neighborhood's dynamics is partly informed by Bourdieu's notion of a "religious field" as the intimate construction of lived levels of submission through the manipulation of "salvation goods": moral integrity, after-life salvation, self-improvement, health and general welfare (Bourdieu 1971). Bourdieu's vision does not specifically account for religious plurality, though, and I suggest that the "religious field," the constant exchange between moral and material gains, is made to correspond not to one religion but rather to the entire social dynamics related to immaterial powers.

Enacted pluralism in a neighborhood also requires a specific analysis of moral values. Robbins (2013) grounds it in the hierarchical opposition between monistic and pluralistic values that, he suggests, is structural to any society. Our goal as researchers should be to document "which kinds of configurations of monist and pluralist relations we tend to find" (2013, 99). This includes what our interlocutors think about their neighbor as well as what the state entitles them to aspire to through their religious belonging. The case examined here—of Indonesian Tamil Hindus living in a mixed neighborhood during the change of a political regime—offers great insight into how different state ideologies empower different and evolving visions of religious alterity.

The Indonesian case also highlights how the elaboration of ideologies of religious pluralism is an open question worldwide. Casanova and Eck underline that it is tempting for researchers to see egalitarian pluralism—that is, the peaceful coexistence and identical entitlement of different faiths and groups of adepts within the same society—as intrinsically good. "Pluralism," writes Casanova, looks "progressive, tolerant, liberal and modern" (2018, 66). Both the secularization of European societies and the development of laicism as the base for a policy of religious freedom have pointed to individual pluralism as the ideal pattern of religious coexistence and plurality (Champion 1999; Bender and Klassen 2010). Such an attitude, though, blurs the boundary between what researchers aspire to and what they actually see (Eck 2007; Casanova 2018, 66). This was certainly the case for me in the first years of my fieldwork: I believed that the Medanese lived in mutual acceptance of diversity. In this chapter, I shall underline that for the Indonesians, a discourse on "perfect pluralism" was not the result of a sort of traditional tendency toward democratic tolerance but rather the outcome of Indonesian nationalism coupled with New Order repression.

Throughout the chapter, I shall consider pluralism in both its descriptive and prescriptive meaning (Bender and Klassen 2010) and underline the interplay between the two levels. This is reminiscent of Vertovec's idea of superdiversity (2007), adapted by Burchardt and Becci (2016) as *religious* superdiversity, which considers contemporary migrant societies as animated by a contested hierarchy rather than an egalitarian pluralism.

Religion as a Contested Field of Personal and National Development

When I carried out my main ethnographic research about the invention of a Medan-based, Tamil-Karo-Balinese Hinduism (1991–97), the developmentalist and autocratic regime enforced by Suharto had defined what a cult must feature in order to be accepted as a "religion" (*agama*) and granted protection by the constitution: a name, a sacred book, and the belief in *Tuhan Yang Maha Esa*, an Only God. The state encouraged all actions fostering the transformation of "not-yet" religious people (*belum beragama*) into members of one of the five official religions as a positive evolution and as a part of development (Howell 1982; Hefner 2005; Picard 2005, 2011; Schiller 1996; Vignato 2000, 2005). Bourdieu's idea of a "religious field" as an ensemble of habitus where internalized oppression is achieved through embodied religious symbols seems to describe the Indonesian national situation quite to the letter, although in the Indonesian case the state plays the role that Bourdieu gave to religious institutions. The process of "religionization" of complex symbolic universes (Hefner 2011) that started during Suharto's "New Order" (*Orde Baru*, 1967–98) really was as strongly personal as it was national.

Hinduism was made to fit into the national framework through debates and specific policies mostly but not exclusively rooted in Bali (Picard 2005; Ramstedt 2005). The elaboration of an Indonesian Hinduism also concerned Indonesians of Indian descent, however, and particularly their largest group, second- to fourth-generation Tamil migrants who lived in North Sumatra. The quasi-natural match between their being "ethnically" Indian and "religiously" Hindu did not exclude or shelter them from questioning their devotional practices. On the one hand, as ethnic Indians they were engaged in diaspora-informed, intra-communal conflicts where the struggle to perform a "better" religion, a "right" ritual was common and meaningful in the transformation from migrant to set-tler (Vignato 2006). On the other hand, as Indonesian citizens, they wanted and needed to be rightfully affiliated to the state through a "religion" and believed that a national Hinduism could (and in fact should) represent them and their aspirations. Religion was felt as a deep source of modern citizenship that needed improving for the sake of a better life. Unlike in Bourdieu's definition, the "sal-vation goods" to be desired and capitalized concerned this life rather than the afterlife, as the example of the Karo converts in North Sumatra illustrated below exemplifies.

In North Sumatra, the Tamils shared Hinduism with the Balinese migrants and transmigrants and, most remarkably, with a small group of Karo converts. The Karo conversion to Hinduism tells much about the status of religion and religiousness during the New Order. Between 1970 and 1990, in North Suma-tra, affiliation to a world religion indicated non-atheism in a region deeply scarred by post-1965 violence. Becoming Hindu was thus a strategic conver-sion for the Karo who aimed to erase all suspicions of their being involved in the 1965 alleged communist coup and in Indonesia's Communist Party (Partai Komunis Indonesia, PKI) (Steedly 1993). It also suited those who didn't want to be included in far larger and more powerful groups (such as Christians or Muslims) for fear of losing important established traditions; Hinduism seemed to work well for them, giving national dignity to domestic or communal rit-uals that risked otherwise being dismissed and despised as "animist" (*animis* in Indonesian), ghost worshipping, or even satanic. But in that context, and whatever the mixed reasons for it, converting in itself—albeit to an unclear religion such as Indonesian Hinduism in the making also meant acquiring access to national and international networks, both in a merely utilitarian understanding and in a symbolic, intellectual one. The Karo people engaged in a serious cognitive and creative effort in order to design specific ceremo-nies that would fuse Karo traditions with Balinese and Indian ritual frames (Vignato 2000).

The mixture of personal drives and political elaboration that pushed some Karo to study Indian Hindu *puja* (a basic ritual in Sivaist devotion) at a Tamil Hindu temple animated many people from other religious horizons as well. In Medan, at the time, it was fairly common to meet multireligious families and serial converts—that is, people who repeatedly changed religion in the course of their life. *Pindah agama*—"conversion," or rather, "moving from one religion to a new one"—was seen not necessarily as a betrayal of former belongings but rather as an aspect of a serious engagement with one's life through religious practice. This is to say that people took it really to heart to define what their religion was and what it would help them become.

As Bowen (1993) has described well for the Gayo in an Islamic context, the idea of "not getting it wrong" went alongside the "making it better" that characterizes modern religions and particularly Islam (see also Feener 2013 and Kloos 2017 for the Acehnese context). In Medanese neighborhoods active engagement in religious amelioration under the sign of modernity concerned most groups, far beyond the minority of Indian-descent communities, but in very different forms and involving different vital issues. The opposition between "before" and "now" constantly came up in discourses and actions and involved different planes of contention. Geertz (1957) and Hefner (2011) report that for the (now disappearing) *abangan* in Java all that concerned death was handled within a more orthodox Islamic frame. On the contrary, my research with the Karo showed that the traditional rituals concerning death and the dead's soul were a key factor of resistance to conversion to monotheistic religions and, for some, a strong reason to convert to Hinduism, as it allowed them to retain preconversion practices. In yet a different attitude, the Tamils' dispute about funerals focused on customary practices as it concerned the abolition of caste duties—such as the obligation for the low castes to play funerary drums—and the transformation of funerals into a private rather than a communitarian performance.

Reformasi and the ensuing lightning-fast liberalization and globalization of Indonesian multireligious environments have established a more specific idea of what divinity and its consequent morality are and should be in each separate religion (Howell 2005; Feillard 2008; Hefner 2011; Picard 2011; Formichi 2014; Hasan 2017). Today, unlike during the New Order, the supposed backwardness of "animism" is no longer felt as a menace to acknowledged cults, but worshiping "the One God" (*Tuhan Yang Maha Esa*) no longer seems a large, inclusive, and safe path to modernity, political integration, and interreligious respect. The following analysis of a Hindu ceremony shows how much, during the New Order, the political landscape framed that path, both from within and from outside people and communities.

A Hindu Tamil Ceremony in the City

Between 1994 and 1995, I lived in intense frequentation of the Medan Tamil Hindu community and attended a series of rituals in small domestic shrines elevated, often for that sole day or week, to the dignity of "temple" (*koil*). Because everyone insisted on the authenticity of his or her own ritual deployment and because I befriended a specific group of ritual experts who kept debating the subject, I became obsessed with the quest for what was considered essential in the ritual performance and what was acknowledged as acceptable variation due to personal ignorance, village origins, caste, or any other reason. Not only did I attend rituals, I was also constantly involved in the debate that surrounded them.

Segren, fifty-three years old in 1995, was a goat butcher, son of an India-born goat butcher. Although he never directly named his caste to me, because of his father's job and what others said about him, I knew that he ranked low even among the *paraiyar* ("funerary drummers," a group of service castes whose ritual duty was to play at funerals). He was a committed devotee of a form of the Hindu female divinity Singamakali, which he himself had re-named "*Kali kampung*" (or "village Kali"); he claimed that this female demon, which takes the form of a lion, had also possessed him.[3] He was a well-known medium. People consulted him at his domestic temple for all sorts of reasons: misfortune, sickness, suspected sorcery, amulet fabrication, and general advice. He had learned his skills through a specific initiation but had also served as an ordinary help-priest in a couple of plantation temples in North Sumatra. This means that he had no literate Brahmanical knowledge but had worked to achieve and consolidate his position in the Medan Tamil community beyond what had been passed on to him by his father and his teacher. He lived in the North part of Medan, on land that had originally belonged to the (now state-owned) plantation where his grandfather and father, like so many other Tamils, had been employed. Once a year he held a big celebration that showed the essential structure of the larger temple's yearly cults: spread over five days, it began with a smaller sacrifice (a chicken) and the raising of the ceremonial flag; on the third day, always scheduled on a Sunday to allow people to attend, the ritual featured larger sacrifices of goats. The final day involved a more intimate closing, which included further small sacrifices.

Its attendees and the other ritual specialists thought that Segren's ceremony was reliable and well-structured and that it held a great deal of "power" (*sakti*). It taught me the structure of most South Indian Hindu rituals addressing familiar salvation divinities in Indonesia and Malaysia, with particular regard to the Goddess. It also taught me the importance of devotion for the Tamils and the weight and the multiple aspects that devotional practice, as "a religion," had in the non-Tamil neighbors' eyes.

Public Secrets and Mutual Dependence among Tamil Settlers

While I had established myself as a peculiar kind of devotee of ceremonies featuring blood sacrifices, I was quite friendly, too, with the ethnic Indian officials appointed to represent the Parisada Hindu Dharma Indonesia, PHDI (Indonesian Board for the Hindu Religion). Mine was an ambiguous position, as the people running the PHDI had succeeded in having blood sacrifices officially banned from North Sumatra if perpetrated by Tamil Hindus in the name of Hinduism as a religion: sacrifices and self-sacrifice practices were discarded as wrong (*salah*) Tamil customs and an insult to the true Hindu religion under the 1965 blasphemy law. The police had been called on a few occasions and some devotees, including Segren, had spent a few nights in jail for violating the ban and slaughtering a goat. As a result, the sacrifice rituals that took place in full view of Segren's neighbors were kept secret from the Tamil Hindu religious leaders, for fear they alert the police.

At first, I considered being informed of the forbidden ceremony a demonstration of trust—as if devotees honored me by believing that I wouldn't tell on them to the PHDI authorities I had also befriended. I then discovered that in the Tamil community, everyone, including the officers of the PHDI and the few Indian-ethnic policemen they relied upon, knew about Segren's sacrifices, but that as long as nobody reported and complained, tolerance would be practiced. This understanding did not keep the ban from generating great anger among devotees, as Tamil Hindu celebrations need to be seen and lived in the communal social space, not merely tolerated. Moreover, the fact that a group of people— the rich lobby also controlling the PHDI—had manipulated political power to repress a sacred act was felt as an abuse (Vignato 2018).

While in the field, though, I could not fathom to what extent anger and hypocrisy were part of a general culture of forced silence over well-known abuses that reigned in Medan during those years, and I did not really understand what allowed this culture of silence to be so strong, extending far beyond the Hindu ritual case. Indeed, as I learned later, seeing and not saying was a common attitude: "public secrets" (*rahasia umum*) were, as a Medanese Tamil friend said in 2002, "a Medanese way of life."

Certainly, it was a Tamil way of life. Within the Tamil group, swallowing abuses and sticking to the community was a question of material and symbolic survival. People lived in a very strong patron-client network imbued with different ideas of both traditional and modern Hinduism, a network that depended on former modes of migration and their actualization. *Mandur* families—that is, descendants of the migration brokers—still exercised a moral authority over those whose parents and grandparents had been helped to migrate from India. Similarly, newly enriched families held a growing "Indonesian" control, with access to many levels of the Indonesian state (requests of documents, authorizations, trading permits, tenders . . .) as well as to jobs and economic possibilities. On the practical level, most Indonesian Indians I knew worked for other

Indians, borrowed money from other Indians, and married inside the community, possibly within their own caste. They obtained commercial licenses, passports, and diplomas from fellow Indians working in the administration, they worked as unskilled labor for the large Indian corporation Texmaco Jaya, or gained subcontracts under its protection.

Religious independence was no more thinkable than social autonomy, as there was no discontinuity between religious and mundane positions. There was a strong awareness that the community could not afford to break into smaller competing groups if any Tamil consciousness or culture were to be preserved at all; if any religious Tamilness, any Tamil Hinduism, or any Indonesian Hinduism was to be practiced at all, so small was the group and so meaningful the possibility to accomplish communal ceremonies (Vignato 2000) that required unity. In Pierre Bourdieu's terms, the Tamil group featured an asymmetric homology between its dominant classes and its religious symbology and practices. The Tamils could not "think outside" of it.

But the Indian patronage system did not float in a vacuum. Building a migrant ethnic network implied playing out the Hindu Tamil religious field within a new social organization and in an evolving state, what I named the Indonesian religious field. I arrived on my field-site in 1991, at a time of stillness when "things" had already happened; Medan was a thriving city, but the scars of 1965 were far from being healed. Harsh violence had made Medanese citizens of foreign origin vulnerable. The main target had been the Chinese, but they had not been the only victims.

Suharto's ban on education in non-Indonesian languages had made the Tamils illiterate in their own language, excluding them from all kind of religious literature. But the fear of abuses perpetrated in the name of authority that many Tamil devotees felt primarily in terms of the restrictions imposed on their ceremonies was characteristic of the New Order regime, with its ad hoc regulations reaching far beyond "the religious." In fact, the prohibition on sacrifice rituals could exist only because the law now stated that religious heterodoxy must be prosecuted and because those who held the authority in the Indian local society and had gained control of the Medan branch of the Jakarta-lead Parisada Hindu Dharma Indonesia were also connected to the political regime and its methods, most notably through the police. While Indians could be jailed for slaughtering a chicken, the Balinese migrants at their local temple celebrated *Odalan* biting heads off chicks in the presence of PHDI Indian authorities. Practicing Indian Hinduism in Medan meant embodying a relationship of citizenship based on symbolic and material violence and ethnic discrimination, although I did not believe that was really the case at that time.

The Friendly Neighborhood: Universalism and Intercommunal Relationships

Like most Medanese Tamils, Segren too lived in a mixed neighborhood. His direct neighbors were Javanese, Karo, Nias, and mixed Malay-Minangkabau. One of the Javanese families and the mixed one were Muslim; the other Javanese and the only Indians close by were Catholic, like Segren's own grandfather had been; the Karo and Nias were Protestant, although from different churches. It was an ordinary urban neighborhood as one could find in Medan in the '90s: everyone was a migrant to the city, and the Indians were not amongst the most recent migrants. On the contrary, most of them were Medan-born and actually felt they belonged as *orang Medan*.

In the area, with a few wealthy exceptions, the houses were built in wood with some upgraded parts in brick or concrete, surrounded by small courtyards. Most people kept chickens. Households did not have telephones, and nobody owned a car but, on the whole, it was not a poor environment, just what could be defined as "very ordinary" (*biasa saja*). The relentless effort to upgrade and enlarge homes and gardens made the space more and more crowded and unorganized. Although ownership was clear as far as buildings were concerned, very few people owned land. Circulation in the courtyards and narrow streets (*lorong*) was ceaseless and quarrels on fences, wells, and paths constantly renewed.

When Segren held his ritual, the neighborhood was necessarily involved, almost in its entirety. Closing up a street and using the common space for a party is a widespread habit in Indonesia, whether it is for a marriage or for a funeral; so in this case, too, the disturbance that a large crowd created was tolerated as part of what happens in turns to all residents. A certain degree of participation in Segren's ritual was even expected on the neighbors' side, on grounds of "good manners" (*kesopanan*), and so they would pay their respects in different ways and at different moments. They said that they appreciated that a date was chosen for the main ceremony that would not clash with other religions' important celebrations. "We respect each other" (*saling menghormati*), they would add. When they compared their neighbor's religion and theirs, they often exclaimed, "*sama!*" ("it's the same!"), assuming that they all worshiped the Only God, in an attitude that Julia Howell calls, using an Indonesian formulation, "universalism": "all the major religions have a broadly similar message," and God is God for all (2005, 475).

This affirmation of identity in belief contrasted with a very refined apprehension and knowledge of differences that characterized all of Segren's neighbors and Segren himself. When the main ceremonial day arrived, whatever their religion and their ethnic origin, the neighbors observed the events with competence and commented in a mixture of awe and disdainful amusement. They knew the ceremony inside out and were good spectators. They expected the staging of ethnicity, as there would be in any other family's celebration, and true to their expectations Tamils would dress up "as Tamils." Women wore makeup and a *sari* or a *salwar kamesh*, men a white *vesti* and a shirt or went bare chest. The neighbors in their ordinary clothes commented on such display of Indianness, especially as far as girls' attire was concerned.

They also expected religious ethnicity—that is, the Indian version of what happened in all ethnic groups and was related to their tradition—possession by immaterial beings. In Segren's case, it was people screaming and trembling in possession, devotees prostrating at the medium's feet, and the goat or the goats (people often gave their own contribution to the sacrifice for a vow or a wish), once bathed and anointed, publicly slaughtered with a big knife in a deadly silence. Amulets and rings were sanctified in the victim's blood. Neighbors looked for parallelisms with similar situations that they had experienced. Comparison of each other's habits was a striking feature in multiethnic Medan. The language of *kemasukan*, "possession," in particular, was a common idiom, although many took some distance through irony from others' ethnic modes of possession. Imitations of each other's possession habits sometimes made me laugh, so true they were to the original. What possessed a human being might differ, but the fact that it happened did not raise any doubts, as it happened everywhere.[4]

Hence tolerance appeared as rooted in a feeling of sameness, or identity, in some fundamental aspects of the person's relationship to their material and immaterial world. Segren and his neighbors shared a vision of an immanent and immaterial world that had not been forced until recently to be divided between orthodox religious aspects (*agama*) and (in the eyes of legislators) superstitious "beliefs" (*kepercayaan*). Sharing the same attitude toward the immaterial potencies did not imply sharing the same symbolic contents. A mountain spirit, a *jin*, and an ancestor were clearly not the same immaterial agents—nobody would mistake one for another—and the cultural setting of possession or divine epiphany was deemed important. This practical attitude toward immaterial powers had more self-evidence than the ideas about the Only God, most likely for its relational and not essentialist dimension.

Only in one case did I witness ritual acknowledgment of a common spiritual being. Segren and the other celebrants alike always prepared an altar for the *datuk*, a local spirit who liked smoking tobacco. "Who is it?" I asked over and over. "Just the *datuk*," I was told (*cuman datuk*). Segren said that the *datuk* was a Karo spirit, or a demon (*dewata*), rather. Segren would add that the offerings that he received were "just" cigarettes (*cuman rokok*)—implying that the minimal offering that any divinity receives in a Hindu environment includes food, and the *datuk* didn't qualify for that. Still, the *datuk* had a place. The Christian Karo neighbors who smiled at seeing the cigarette put by the Tamils on the *datuk* shrine and declared that it was "just a belief" also had their small shrine in a corner, which had been included in an otherwise Christian environment. The Muslim Javanese lady was greatly pleased to see a "Medan custom" (*adat* Medan) being respected and acknowledged the *datuk*'s presence as a sort of true Muslim spirit, although it was "just" the *datuk* for her too. In the Karo tradition, *datuk* (or *datu*) is both a very knowledgeable person or sorcerer and the place where it dwells. The Karo highlands are quite close to the city and the Karo people are very present in the parts of the town where the Tamils also lived, not to mention the plantation where their fathers or grandparents had lived. The Tamils said that the *datuk* was "Karo" as an overall ethnonym that encompassed a very close "otherness," but they were also familiar with the actual Karo cults from their neighbors and their outings to the highlands.

The *datuk* was not a human, not the Only God mentioned in the Pancasila, and not even a deity for those whose religion included multiple forms of the divine, like the Hindus. It was "just" a neutral reminder of something common to the whole neighborhood, a possibility of divinity. It deserved attention but had no power in itself: it represented well the attention to each other's possibilities of the divine that one has to pay in a multicultural living space. In many ways, it contained the possibility of "thinking beyond" ethnic and religious *habitus* and even beyond the nationally framed religious field, the one relating to the Only God.

Fear: The Political Enforcement of Controlled Tolerance

In Indonesia, and particularly so during the New Order, social control over residents was not only a matter of good manners but also a structured micropolitical institution. In a city, each *lorong* has its own chief who reports to the chief of the next level, the *lurah*, and so on. Segren's celebrations were negotiated with the official representatives of the neighborhood and authorized by them. The police would be informed, but also—so claimed Segren—duly "lubricated" (*pakai pelicin*) so that no official report would be made to the PHDI.

This is to underline that the reciprocal tolerance shown in the neighborhood was not, or not exclusively, a matter of being "good natured" Medanese people and sharing a ritual, but also the consequence of a specific national policy. It included entitlement and duty to religion as a personal, family, or community matter at the same time as a strong repression of any ethnic grassroot organization outside the domain of "culture." Ethnicity had to be "culture" (*budaya*) and confined to clothes and typical food and dances; alternatively, it was *adat*, lay customary laws. The Tamils, *orang India*, staged Indianness as their culture and worshiped the "Hindu God" as their religion. They had an ethnic belonging (*suku*), a culture (*budaya*, coupled with *adat*, customs), and a religion. The Indians would wear *sari* and slaughter a goat to their goddess, just as, for example, the Karo would wear folded cloths on their heads and go to church at Christmas or pray to Allah, depending on family traditions and recent choices. Or the Javanese would wear *kebaya* and pray to Allah, too. This was the basic rule of Suharto's version of a centralized state with no localized ethnic power, no religious hierarchy, and no atheists (that is, possible communists)—a version that he imposed on his citizens.

What I have so far described as a sort of "good-natured" historically grounded respect for otherness was also a politically constructed and enforced cohabitation, which did not necessarily mean good-heartedness. At first, when they met me and my insistent questions, Segren's neighbors thought that I was an Indian spy from the official powers and served me with nice, well behaved, and respectful discourse on reciprocal tolerance. But then a certain malignancy and disdain surfaced, which was framed in interesting terms. The Muslim Javanese and the Christian Karo neighbors qualified the Tamils as backward by saying that they "still worshiped spirits" (*masih menyembah hantu*). The Catholic Indians and Javanese both said that Segren was using black magic (*main ilmu*), dealing with dead people's bodies, and giving out unclean amulets. Segren and his wife, on their part, said that the Indian Muslim next door was often drunk, but he ("the hypocrite") denied ever touching any alcohol, and they added that when someone died the Christian Karo convened more ghosts in one evening than Segren had seen in his whole life. As we see, the language of the New Order was completely internalized. In spite of all tolerance, any religion was felt as more civilized than "no religion (yet)," like a village with electricity is seen as more evolved than a village lit by gaslight and fire. Similarly, people expressed a clear appraisal of religions dealing with the "right" supernatural power—the Only God—as morally superior to those eliciting supposedly negative powers like Hinduism. Segren hated his Indian Muslim neighbor, Mamagal, because, so he said, he was a recent Muslim convert out of sheer convenience, not a "true Indian Muslim," one of those Mama who were Muslims before migration. Segren thus proved that he resented Muslims more than he would admit.

These opinions were expressed and denied, said and not said, as hierarchy among religions was repressed. The Tamils debated and fought among themselves about what was *budaya*, *adat*, or *agama*; so did the Christians; not to mention the wide world of Islamic schools and "streams" (*aliran*). But whatever the intracommunal conflicts both on a local and a national scale, in the specific neighborhood one was not to mention certain matters publicly, as Segren explained to me. Endless stories about neighborhood fights between Segren and Mamagal, the Muslim Tamil neighbor, were told, but none in which Segren or Mamagal used ethnicity or religion as a public ground for litigation. It was a very common affirmation that SARA—*suku, agama, ras dan antar golongan* (ethnicity, religion, race and intergroup [conflict])—constituted the four "forbidden" topics.

I am not implying that the public behavior of pluralist acceptance in Segren's neighborhood was solely dependent on the impositions of the New Order through a deep-rooted culture of social control and denunciation, but what I am suggesting is that such culture played an important role in neighborhood relations. The idea that citizens should hold their tongues and keep the police or any authority as far from their homes as possible made more sense when one paid attention to veiled references to people who had disappeared or had been forced to move in the 1970s. In the 1990s, I was unable to catch such references. After *Reformasi*, I was told that a part of Segren's neighborhood had formerly been inhabited by Sino-Indonesian Christian families who were forced to flee for fear of prosecution. It was hard to learn that some denunciations had also come from people I knew.

The End of the Order: Religions Unleashed

When I went back to Medan in 1999, during the rough times following the 1997 economic crisis and the end of the New Order (1998), I found a very different city from what I had previously known. A high degree of insecurity characterized most neighborhoods I had been familiar with. It was not only due to increased poverty, unemployment, and ill-employment. In 1994 and 1995 I had moved freely in the middle of the night on a scooter to attend the beginning of ceremonies, taken public transportation, and knocked on people's doors to see if anyone was home. Now, my friends insisted on accompanying me home and didn't want me to take minibuses or to turn up unexpected. Checkpoints of the main political organizations controlled the space, and at the entrance of my old neighborhood a group of men in Ikatan Pemuda Karya (IPK) uniform asked me in a threatening way what my business was there. On top of that, a thick smoky haze made breathing difficult and children were often told to play inside out of safety concerns.[5] Many of those with whom I had shared the ritual activity were in harsher economic difficulty. Segren, for example, sometimes went to work as a daily laborer at the market.

In this critical time, a sort of religious craze had seized the Tamil Hindu devotees. Although not officially, the Pancasila obligation to follow a specific religion and the possibility of being prosecuted if performing "deviant" rituals was de facto gone for the Tamil Hindus of the Medan region because the system of patronage that had upheld it for decades had been abruptly uprooted. Marimuthu, the man who had asserted his authority in the community through his religious positioning (despite his "low" caste within the "higher" group of the migrants) and who had been accused of all the ill intentions behind the ban on sacrificial and other "indecent" rituals, had been deeply affected by the fall of Suharto's regime. His textile and engineering enterprise, Texmaco Jaya, had been swept away when corruption cases started being investigated. According to Mani (2008), 40 percent of the Medanese Tamils worked for Marimuthu, directly or in outsource; beyond that, "he"—or the group of people he dealt with—held credits to nearly all families I knew. Marimuthu's fall was, for many, the end of a way to see and handle the world, a true change of power.

The intracommunal tension over blood sacrifices had been released at a generational and epochal all-Indonesia turn. Information started flowing at high speed. The migration of Indonesian Indians to and from Malaysia increased, technologies allowed images to circulate more freely than ever before, and the youngest men and women could autonomously learn a religious task without participating in a generational transmission of knowledge by watching videos online or attending rituals in Malaysia. The definition of the "right tradition" and the acceptable variations was very rapidly, much more rapidly than before, trending toward a standardized Indian Hinduism. The Medanese Hindu Tamils wanted to be *Indians*, diaspora Indians, and they had the technologies for that.

The ritual of sacrifice that I am discussing here was suddenly inflated with massive imports from Malaysia and India, and the divination part was even more dramatized than it used to be. Segren loved it and he expressed a specific religious fulfilment that I often met among the Hindu Tamils—*puas*, "satisfaction." Besides, his *kali kampung* had looked old fashioned to him: he had made a good ceremony to upgrade her to *Kaliyamman*, her sanskritized higher form, and decorated her with paraphernalia imported from India via Malaysia.[6] Even more remarkable, some people had brought drums to Segren's ceremony and played them to accompany the possessions. Drums, like sacrifices, had been banned in 1978 because of what they meant: *paraiyar* caste members being compelled to play them at funerals, on the one hand, and, on the other hand, the instigation to perform "indecent" behaviors when frenzied devotees followed an icon in a procession at the rhythm of ecstatic music. Now, as had already happened in Malaysia, the young men who played were from all kind of caste backgrounds. They played because they liked it, they felt it was a devotional act connected to their Indianness more than to their specific premigration social and symbolic position, which some of them ignored or feigned to ignore (*"Aku enggak tahu kasta!"*—"I don't know anything about caste!"—said one of them whose father, a few years before, had explained to me in detail about his own high rank). The *datuk* altar received the usual attention and a cigarette was put there on a stick as an offering, but its status was dubious: a young man was even possessed by it and, as Segren's wife jokingly pointed out, he was not possessed in the Karo way. She laughed at such "ignorant youngsters" (*anak mudah kurang tahu*).

When the celebration took place, at least a couple of the non-Hindu neighbors told their children to get inside because the place was full of devils (*seytan*). The Javanese lady invited me into her house to offer me a drink, but would not come back outside in the crowd. James Siegel writes that during the unstable years following the end of the New Order, the feeling of uncertainty produced the creation of witches—that is, the accusation addressed to some Muslim-inspired cults of being a manifestation of satanic powers. While the Indians experienced the joy of nonregulated devotion, they also estranged themselves in the eyes of their neighbors. Their divinities became devils and the *datuk* was really "just" an old habit.

The Ethnicization of the Hindu Tamil

In 2011, the ritual was no longer celebrated within the neighborhood but rather by a nearby river, where a small wooden temple had been built. Segren's neighborhood had changed even more. It was no longer an even working class habitat but instead included some well-off houses, building sites, and vagrant fields. Segren's old neighbor, the Javanese lady, told me that everyone feared eviction as, like many people in Medan, they owned the house but not the land on which it stood and could not afford to buy it.

Such sudden uncertainty did not bring the dwellers together. When I enquired about the actual reasons that had pushed Segren to shift his ceremony to an outside site, I found out that the performers' discourse on the suitability of an urban neighborhood for these rituals had changed. A few years earlier, "reciprocal respect" was the usual formulation. Now, Segren said that he didn't want to face his neighbors' judgment because he would be despised (*dihina*) as Indian, which was "unfair and un-Indonesian," but what to do, they were ultimately *keling* (the historical disparaging name for the Tamils in the Malay world), and besides, he could not claim that he never drank (one of the ethnic stereotypes cast upon the Medanese Tamil Indonesians is that they drink and worship gods while dancing in an alcoholic haze). "Men should drink" said a fellow devotee, thus establishing a clear distance from non-drinking Muslims. *"Kami sudah minori-tas etnis"* (now we are an ethnic minority), affirmed a younger devotee, which was surprising: on my first ritual trip from Medan to Malaysia, in 1993, "we" (the Medanese Indians) took the ferry to Penang to celebrate Tai Pusam grandly, with a twenty-four-hour-long procession of the chariot that carried the god Murugan, the *kavati* self-sacrifices, the drums, and the dances—all that in Medan was for-bidden. Upon learning about the Indonesian ban, a group of Malaysian Indians asked the Medanese Tamils if the rituals had been forbidden because the "bloody Melayu" discriminated against them as Indians. The Medanese were astonished. Why should they be discriminated against? Disturbance came from inside the community itself; "in Indonesia we are all equally Indonesians" (*kami orang Indonesia semua anak bangsa*), said a friend proudly, "poor Malaysian Indians." Now the *anak bangsa* (literally "equal members of a larger group") had become an ethnic minority.

But in 2011 Medan, ethnicity was everywhere (Aspinall et al. 2011). There was, quite naturally given the size and variety of the Medanese Sino-Indonesian population, a great deployment of Chinese ethnicity, ranging from religious ceremonies to language schools and origin-based associations: what had been repressed and hidden for decades could finally be done publicly. Beyond the Sino-Indonesian world, ethnic indicators that had until then been disguised in restaurants' names or confined to churches had suddenly come into the open as such: one could see tens of different associations, organizations, and cultural circles featuring Karo, Toba, Dairi, Melayu, Jawa, Minang, and all the other eth-nic denominations one could find in Medan. Besides, I was rapidly informed that an Indonesia Tamil Sangam ("Association of the Indonesian Tamils"; "sangam" is the word for "association" in Sanskrit/Tamil) had been created with the aim of strengthening the community of Indians (*membangun komunitas India*), includ-ing the Catholic and Muslim Tamils and the Sikh. This was also quite striking when compared to my first trip to Medan, in 1991, as back then most people of the higher castes would very clearly exclude lower caste members from Tamil affiliation, let alone the Catholics. The rare Muslim Tamils in Medan were not even taken into consideration, except when they had been Hindu before, like Segren's neighbor Mamagal.

In 2011 the surfacing of ethnicity had appeared alongside a shift in the urban presence of religions. Islam, which so far in most Medanese central his-torical areas had been quite discreet, became much more visible, similar to other parts of Indonesia: both in women's attire (girls flocked to school in a uniform featuring a long skirt and *jilbab* and women wore long plain dresses and *jilbab*) and in specific sites, as new mosques, Quranic schools, and prayer houses (*mush-ollah*) were built everywhere. In this new symbolic everyday urban environment, a Hindu Indian domestic ceremony was more conspicuous, on both the ethnic and the religious plane.

The new ritual performance held by the river, in an uninhabited place, no longer included an offering for the *datuk*—someone said that the *datuk* was not Indian—and featured instead a few new, rather fancy elements such as electrified decorations for the divinities and portable loudspeakers to diffuse Indian sacred music. Segren, who was less in charge of the ceremony than when it took place in his home temple, said that the people who had set up the place simply no longer knew about the "village ways." He himself had given up his "village Kali" with pride for the sake of modern times (*zaman modern*), but was not sure of what turn things would take for him now. He feared eviction. What would he do with his domestic temple? He'd better move it somewhere safe, he said. While claiming that it was good that the rituals could now be complete and "the bastard" (*binatang*, literally "the animal," a very insulting qualification) was no longer able to stop them, he seemed to be renouncing his emplaced, domestic, relational ritual habits.

Monistic Tendencies in Religious Superdiversity

The example of a marginal ritual performance such as the Tamil Hindu acknowledgment of the *datuk* within city-based sacrifice ceremonies opens a window onto the relationship between development, the "religious" as a political field, a story of migration, and the construction of present interethnic frictions in an exceptionally multiethnic urban environment such as Medan.

In her brilliant essay about the creation of the supernatural in Indonesia, Lorrain Aragon argues that before colonization and campaigns of conversion, no opposition was seen between a natural (then explainable) world and a supernatural (holy, intangible, unexplainable) dimension (Aragon 2003). Things, spaces, and houses as well as human beings were always connected to the material and the immaterial in varying degrees of intensity and following diverse narrations. In Segren's neighborhood, as we have seen, such connection was generally acknowledged, as was the difference in its symbolic and iconic manifestations. The forms of the divinity could be entirely different and differently perceived, in all sorts of relationships with *adat*, but the neutral form was like a quality admitted by all and objectifiable, as in a shrine for a *datuk*.

In the case that I considered, the respect for the *datuk* allowed both ethnic and religious plurality to go beyond the imposition of a totalitarian regime, speaking to the need to come to terms with everyday differences in a growing city of migrants like Medan on a more symbolic plane than regulated and heterodirected "good manners." I am not, just like Aragon was not, implying the existence of a sort of enchanted world that first the colonial state and then the Indonesian Republic erased through a sharp definition of divinity and the compulsory separation between the natural and the supernatural. Colonial and national state building certainly played important roles, but global interconnections and the transformation of local societies as well as the fast technologization of domestic and public environments are inseparable from the political form. At the time of my study, the Indonesian religious field was a place of contention and competition for this-world-oriented salvation goods. Safety from suspicion and prosecution was one of these goods; connection with powerful networks was another; achievement of modern consumption goals was a third.

The *datuk* was peripheral to core religious ideas and feelings, non-human but hardly religious at all, and that's why it could be included and respected at the margin of otherwise quite different cults. This implies that religions themselves were not solely determined by doctrinal guidelines but kept unchecked margins that dealt with outside major trends and sometimes pushed back against them. An urban neighborhood processed different religious issues through daily interactions. "The religious" itself was plural out of recognition of an immanent, common immaterial "thing." On a daily basis, people crossed spaces that were full of "other" entities, heard different chanting but also quarreled over a displaced fence, a stolen chicken, or another random offence, all while acknowledging a common spiritual ground. A material morality granted immaterial diversity. It is this shared precarious materiality that came undone as the city grew.

While the general process of definition of margins concerned all religions, the Medanese Tamils had a peculiar task, immersed as they were in a complicated transnational ethnic religious identity (Tamil Hinduism) rather than in a globalized and purified ideal devotion, like the religions of the book. For them, the *datuk* lost sense and meaning; it was never banned. On the contrary, "Hindu," "Indian," and "Tamil" suddenly became difficult labels that urgently needed to be disentangled from devotional practices. In the late 2000s, when in Malaysia an ethnic Indian political movement called Hindraf was constituting a political grassroots opposition fighting against positive discrimination on ethnic grounds, the Medanese felt concerned. As a measure of this new sense of identity, one of my priest friends went to Kuala Lumpur to participate in a rally, Bersih, in which Hindraf was quite well represented.

Vertovec (2007) speaks of "superdiversity" as a necessary grid to read contemporary British society without falling in past colonial and developmentalist categories of citizenship. The same can be said of the emplaced practice of religious pluralism in a city like Medan: ethnicity, past and present immigration and emigration, class, and access to local resources as well as international networks are all elements that determine how religious differences can coexist (or not) in the same neighborhood. It is a specific religious superdiversity (Burchardt and Becci 2016).

A Closing Remark on the Blasphemy Law

I conclude by connecting my fieldwork experience to the contemporary interpretation of the so-called Indonesian "law on blasphemy" as a means to repress non-Muslim citizens, whatever the reason behind the repression. The 1969 law (originally a 1965 presidential decree, Hasan 2017) originally aimed to strengthen centralized religious structures and erase any source of local power: "Anyone who publicly insults . . . an Indonesian social group . . . can be sentenced up to a maximum of 4 years imprisonment." Much has been written on several famous cases (Crouch 2012; Hasan 2017; Telle 2018; see also Aragon's and Lohanda's contributions to this volume), but I was impressed by something that happened in an environment very close to Segren's and a place close by to Medan and that flashed back on my former fieldwork experience. Meiliana, a woman of Chinese descent, was sentenced to eighteen months in jail for saying to a neighbor that the mosque's loudspeakers were giving her a headache as they were louder than usual. In the reports, she was always qualified by her ethnicity and not directly by her religious belonging, thus implying that she was "a Buddhist."[7]

Upon the request of a delegation from the mosque, Meiliana's husband hurried to apologize, but apparently she was heard screaming offensive words by a group of angry men who had erupted into her house. After she was reported for "blasphemy" (*penistaan agama*) and consequently arrested, ten Chinese temples were attacked in the surrounding area, near Medan. Her lawyer pleaded that it was not a matter of religion but of loudspeakers and therefore ought to be resolved by a common resolution (*musyawarat*) of the microlocal authorities (the *Rukun Tetangga*, "council of the neighbors," the chief of the *lorong* and the religious authorities of the mosque). But it wasn't. Her lawyer declared that she was the "victim of collective verbal [violence]" (*korban verbal massa*) as there was no proof of the blasphemy, but in 2019 her request for an appeal was turned down because she had refused to plead guilty to blasphemy.

The newspapers reported Meiliana's and her husband's comings and goings to the mosque and the rage that instantly caught in the neighborhood. They neatly reported the dynamics of the event: Meiliana had made a comment to her neighbor and had been heard by the latter's brother, who commented to a friend, who sparked the fire of the *verbal massa*. The culture of repressive silence and both forced and (so-to-speak) good hearted local interaction that had reigned in

Segren's now vanished neighborhood no longer permeates ordinary pluralism in the region. Local practices of power, such as the entitlement of local groups of moral guardians to anticipate proper justice, are imbibed less with centralized orders than with mainstream mediatized trends.

On the whole, if we compare with the first years of my fieldwork during the New Order, it has become less meaningful and useful to practice *any* religion and more meaningful to be part of a *specific* majority—a national majority like Islam or a neighborhood majority like Christianity in Medan (for Islam at the national level, see Kikue Hamayotsu in this volume). In Robbins' terms, monistic values are hierarchically superior to pluralistic ones. While the belief in immanent spirits stays unchanged and does not necessarily collide with "mainstream Islam" and the variety of Christian groups present in Medan, the idea that a neutral immanent world and a neutral transcendent power coincide to create the modern Indonesian attitude toward religion and spirits seems to have receded in everyday life.

Notes

1. What is now Medan territory includes two sultanates, Deli and Serdang, both closely dependent on the sultanate of Aceh, which was, during the seventeenth century, very powerful (Ricklefs 2008, 236).

2. I use the Indonesian ethnic category of "Indian" (*orang India*), which includes Indonesian citizens of Tamil, Malayalee, Sikh, and Sindhi descent. In my case study, they were Hindu for the majority but also, especially the Tamils, Christian and Muslim.

3. In Tamil, Segren used to call her *gramatakkali*, which quite literally means "village Kali," too. All Tamil terms mentioned here are provided in their Indonesian transliteration, as I mainly spoke Indonesian with my interlocutors.

4. However, spirit possession did raise doubts (as it always does, in my experience) with the Tamils in a Karo and Malay-Acehnese environment. Many people maintain a skeptical attitude toward both the reliability of the possessed and the whole act of being inhabited by a spirit, which does not prevent them from participating in or contributing to the event—and even, at times, falling into trance and enacting the spirit.

5. In 1997–98, forest fires were for the first time a devastating problem for Sumatra and Kalimantan. At the time of this follow up fieldwork, the Medan Polonia airport, right in the middle of the city, was regularly shut down for poor visibility after in 1997 a plane crashed into some houses.

6. "Sanskritization"—that is, the process of upgrading local divinities to their Brahmanic equivalent—is a fundamental feature of Hinduism, as first described and conceptualized by Srinivas in 1956.

7. The same process of religionization undergone by those who embraced Hinduism also happened with Buddhism, which included all traditional Chinese temples.

References

Appadurai, Arjun. 1995. "The Production of Locality." In *Counterworks: Managing the Diversity of Knowledge*, edited by Richard Fardon, 204–25. London: Routledge.

Aragon, Lorraine V. 2003. "Missions and Omissions of the Supernatural: Indigenous Cosmologies and the Legitimisation of 'Religion' in Indonesia." *Anthropological Forum* 13, no. 2: 131–40.

Aspinall, Edward, Sebastian Dettman, and Eve Warburton. 2011. "When Religion Trumps Ethnicity: A Regional Election Case Study." *South East Asia Research* 19, no. 1: 28–40.

Bender, Courtney, and Pamela Edith Klassen, eds. 2010. *After Pluralism: Reimagining Religious Engagement*. New York: Columbia University Press.

Bourdieu, Pierre. 1971. "Genèse et structure du champ religieux." *Revue française de sociologie* 12, no. 3: 295–334.

Bowen, John. R. 1993. *Muslims through Discourse: Religion and Ritual in Gayo Society*. Princeton, NJ: Princeton University Press.

Burchardt, Marian, and Irene Becci. 2016. "Religion and Superdiversity: An Introduction." *New Diversities* 18, no. 1: 1–7.

Casanova, José. 2018. "The Karel Dobbelaere Lecture: Divergent Global Roads to Secularization and Religious Pluralism." *Social Compass* 65, no. 2: 187–98.

Champion, Françoise. 1999. "De la Diversité des Pluralismes Religieux." *International Journal on Multicultural Societies (IJMS)* 1, no. 2: 40–54.

Crouch, Melissa. 2012. "The Indonesian Blasphemy Case: Affirming the Legality of the Blasphemy Law." *Oxford Journal of Law and Religion* 1, no. 2: 514–18.

Eck, Diana L. 2007. "Prospects for Pluralism: Voice and Vision in the Study of Religion." *Journal of the American Academy of Religion* 75, no. 4 (December): 743–76.

Feener, R. Michael. 2013. *Shari'a and Social Engineering: The Implementation of Islamic Law in Contemporary Aceh, Indonesia*. Oxford: Oxford University Press.

Feillard, Andrée. 2008. "Du Messianisme au Dépassement de la 'Religion': La Voie de Salamullah dans l'Indonésie du XXIe Siècle." *Archipel* 76, no. 1: 65–98.

Formichi, Chiara. 2013. "Religious Pluralism, State and Society in Asia." In *Religious Pluralism, State and Society in Asia*, edited by Chiara Formichi, 13–22. Abingdon: Routledge.

Formichi, Chiara. 2014. "Violence, Sectarianism, and the Politics of Religion: Articulations of Anti-Shi'a Discourses in Indonesia." *Indonesia* 98: 1–27.

Geertz, Clifford. 1957. "Ritual and Social Change: A Javanese Example." *American Anthropologist* 59, no.1: 32–54.

Hasan, Noorhaidi. 2017. "Religious Diversity and Blasphemy Law: Understanding Growing Religious Conflict and Intolerance in Post-Suharto Indonesia." *Al-Jami'ah: Journal of Islamic Studies* 55, no. 1: 105–26.

Hefner, Robert W. 2005. "Hindu Reform in an Islamizing Java: Pluralism and Peril." In *Hinduism in Modern Indonesia*, edited by Martin Ramstedt, 105–20. London: Routledge.

Hefner, Robert W. 2011. "Where Have All the Abangan Gone? Religionization and the Decline of Non-standard Islam in Contemporary Indonesia." In *The Politics of Religion in Indonesia*, edited by Robert W. Hefner, 86–106. London: Routledge.

Howell, Julia D. 1982. "Indonesia: Searching for Consensus." In *Religions and Societies: Asia and the Middle East*, edited by Carlo Calderola, 497–547. Berlin: Mouton.

Howell, Julia D. 2005. "Muslims, the New Age and Marginal Religions in Indonesia: Changing Meanings of Religious Pluralism." *Social Compass* 52, no. 4: 473–93.

Kloos, David. 2017. *Becoming Better Muslims: Religious Authority and Ethical Improvement in Aceh, Indonesia*. Princeton, NJ: Princeton University Press.

Mani, A. 2008. "Indians in a Rapidly Transforming Indonesia." In *Rising India and Indian Communities in East Asia*, edited by Kesavapany K, Mani A. and Ramasamy P., 227–52. Singapore: ISEAS—Yusof Ishak Institute.

Picard, Michel. 2005. "What's in a Name? Agama Hindu Bali in the Making." In *Hinduism in Modern Indonesia*, edited by Martin Ramstedt, 68–87. London: Routledge.

Picard, Michel. 2011. "Balinese Religion in Search of Recognition: From Agama Hindu Bali to Agama Hindu (1945–1965)." *Bijdragen tot de taal-, land-en volkenkunde/ Journal of the Humanities and Social Sciences of Southeast Asia* 167, no. 4: 482–510.

Ramstedt, Martin. 2005. *Hinduism in Modern Indonesia*. London: Routledge.

Ricklefs, Merle C. 2008. *A History of Modern Indonesia since c. 1200*. London: Macmillan International Higher Education.

Robbins, Joel. 2013. "Monism, Pluralism, and the Structure of Value Relations: A Dumontian Contribution to the Contemporary Study of Value." *HAU: Journal of Ethnographic Theory* 3, no. 1: 99–115

Schiller, Anne. 1996. "An 'Old' Religion in 'New Order' Indonesia: Notes on Ethnicity and Religious Affiliation." *Sociology of Religion* 57, no. 4: 409–17.

Srinivas, Mysore Narasimhachar. 1956. "A Note on Sanskritization and Westernization." *Journal of Asian Studies* 15, no. 4: 481–96.

Steedly, Mary Margaret. 1993. *Hanging without a Rope: Narrative Experience in Colonial and Postcolonial Karoland*. Princeton, NJ: Princeton University Press.

Telle, Karin. 2018. "Faith on Trial: Blasphemy and 'Lawfare' in Indonesia." *Ethnos* 83, no. 2: 371–91.

Vertovec, Stephen. 2007. "Super-diversity and Its Implications." *Ethnic and Racial Studies*, 30, no. 6: 1024–54. https://doi.org/10.1080/01419870701599465.

Vignato, Silvia. 2000. *Au Nom de l'hindouisme: Reconfigurations Ethniques chez les Tamouls et les Karo en Indonésie*. Paris: Editions L'Harmattan.

Vignato, Silvia. 2005. "Old Gods for the New World: the Ritual Struggle of the Tamil and the Karo within Hinduism in North Sumatra." In *Hinduism in Modern Indonesia*, edited by Martin Ramstedt, 254–66. London: Routledge.

Vignato, Silvia. 2006. "Sakti Karagam en Indonésie et en Malaysia: l'évolution de deux Fêtes à la Déesse dans la Diaspora Tamoule." *Rites Hindous: Transferts et Trans-formations*, edited by Gérard Colas, and Gilles Tarabout, 97–251. Paris: Éditions de l'EHESS, coll. Purusartha. *Archives de sciences sociales des religions*.

Vignato, Silvia. 2018. "Feeling Hindu. The Devotional Sivaist Esthetic Matrix and the Creation of a Diasporic Hinduism in North Sumatra." In *Asian Migrants and Religious Experience: From Missionary Journeys to Labor Mobility*, edited by Bernardo E. Brown and Brenda S. A. Yeoh, 271–303. Amsterdam: Amsterdam University Press.

9

SAINTS, SCHOLARS, AND DIPLOMATS

Religious Statecraft and the Problem of "Moderate Islam" in Indonesia

James B. Hoesterey

In this chapter, I examine Indonesia's public diplomacy efforts that link global positioning abroad with religious statecraft at home. Over the last two decades, Indonesian presidents, diplomats, and religious leaders have tried to brand the country as an exemplar of the compatibility of Islam and democracy and the home of "moderate Islam." For Western governments that approach Islam through a security paradigm, Indonesia's story from authoritarian regime to consolidating democracy was an important one. During his homecoming visit in 2010, Barack Obama waxed nostalgically about growing up in Jakarta, fondly remembering the call to prayers reverberating across the city at dusk (Obama 2010). The former US secretary of state Madeline Albright has praised Indonesia's transition to democracy and interreligious harmony. Further still, as Indonesian diplomats have proudly related countless times, another former US secretary of state, Hillary Clinton, even remarked, "If you want to know whether Islam, democracy, modernity, and human rights can coexist, go to Indonesia." But while diplomats abroad have offered these words of praise, some prominent activists and scholars of Indonesian history and culture have adamantly challenged such claims to moderation and interreligious tolerance (Harsono 2012; Menchik 2014; see also Hamayotsu in this volume). While I do not seek to adjudicate whether Indonesia's vastly diverse Muslim population fits the flawed dialectic of supposedly "good Muslims" or "bad Muslims" (Mamdani 2004), I am instead interested in how Indonesian diplomats and religious leaders conceive of, promote, and even challenge the idea of an inherently moderate, Indonesian Islam.

Indonesia is at play in a geopolitical game in which diplomats and religious leaders use the language of an exceptional Indonesian version of "moderate Islam" that resonates with Western fears and desires yet occasionally is at odds (if not open conflict) with the version of Islam espoused by coreligionists in the Middle East, perhaps most notably Saudi Arabia. In what follows, I examine Indonesia's religious statecraft—at home and abroad—to contribute to this volume's conversation about religion, pluralism, and the state. In the case of Indonesia, it is important to also attend to how intrareligious politics of piety can lend insight into the potential for (and limits of) tolerance at home and the marketing of an Indonesian "moderate" Islam abroad.

This chapter bridges anthropological analyses of the politics of piety with conversations in political science and international relations about soft power, public diplomacy, and foreign policy. Indonesia has undergone what could aptly be called an "Islamic turn" in its foreign policy agenda over the last couple of decades. I engage and build on the work of Peter Mandaville and Shadi Hamid (2018) who note that while political Islam has been the focus of abundant scholarship in recent decades, "much less attention . . . has been paid to the ways in which a number of governments—including some that are frequently the focus or target of Islamic activism—have opted to deploy Islam as a component of their own foreign policy conduct" (2). Indonesia's foreign policy abroad is also closely connected with its religious statecraft at home. Mandaville and Hamid (2018, 3) note that, at least in the cases of other Muslim-majority countries such as Jordan, Morocco, and Egypt, "the transnational projection of religion—far from representing a monolithic and deliberate expression of foreign policy intent—often tells us a lot about the balance of power between competing social and political forces *within* the country from which it emanates." Likewise, in Indonesia the search for (and articulations of) an authentic "Indonesian" Islam has also become a cornerstone of its foreign policy abroad—albeit not without domestic contestation.

Going beyond the "soft power" slogans of moderation and religious tolerance, this chapter examines how the Islamic turn in Indonesia's foreign policy has refigured long-standing domestic concerns about political Islam as well as the ideological and theological fault lines (and occasional animosity) between Indonesian traditionalists and their Wahhabi detractors both at home and abroad in countries like Saudi Arabia, whose reformist visions of Islam are often referred to colloquially (and somewhat pejoratively) as "transnational Islam." In this chapter, I offer an ethnography of "moderate Islam" that bridges domestic concerns with foreign policy agendas, lofty diplomatic goals with their unintended consequences on the ground.

Total Diplomacy, Soft Power, and the "Islamic Turn" in Indonesia's Foreign Policy

As a political project in Indonesia, "moderate Islam" has only recently been considered one of Indonesia's assets on the global stage. Sukarno's global popularity was due to his anti-imperialist swagger, not any allegiance to Islam as a political ideology, much less the global Muslim community as a political community. During the New Order, Suharto was famously adept at co-opting cultural forms of Islam while also preventing expressions of political Islam. The political scientist-turned-ambassador Rizal Sukma puts it succinctly (2012, 85):

> Before 1998 Islam was never a determining factor in Indonesia's foreign policy, because neither Sukarno nor Suharto would allow foreign policy to be dictated by Islamic considerations. Islam became part of the national identity only after reformasi, when the rise of several Islamic-based political parties placed political Islam at the centre of national politics. The effect on foreign policy has been most evident in the attempts to shape Indonesia's image as a moderate Muslim country.

After the fall of Suharto, Indonesian foreign policy aimed to project an alternative national narrative that went beyond Western concerns with the possible "Balkanization" of Indonesia in the aftermath of authoritarian rule. Part of this story, especially in the wake of 9/11 and the Bali bombings in 2002, was to brand Indonesia in terms of the compatibility of Islam and democracy and the exceptionally "moderate" nature of Indonesian Islam. Since there is no space for a thorough history in this chapter, suffice it to say that Hassan Wirajuda, who served as foreign minister under both Megawati Sukarnoputri and Susilo Bambang Yudhoyono (SBY), was one of the key architects of this new direction in foreign policy. With degrees from Harvard, University of Virginia, and Tufts's Fletcher School of Law and Diplomacy, Wirajuda was a career diplomat who held several important posts and, between 2001 and 2009, served as minister of foreign affairs. In 2002, Wirajuda created the directorate of information and public diplomacy in order to craft and implement a new soft-power strategy—an approach he referred to as "total diplomacy." Perhaps most notably on the domestic front of foreign policy, Wirajuda began to craft a religious diplomacy by forging new relationships with religious leaders (especially from Nahdlatul Ulama and Muhammadiyah), NGO activists, and journalists. Through weekly breakfast gatherings, these constituents began to chart new possibilities to forge state-society connections as part of mutual interests to project a particular image of Indonesian Islam abroad.

Wirajuda summarized his Islamic soft power vision in a 2009 speech at the Carnegie Endowment for International Peace in Washington DC:

> A few days ago in Cairo, President Obama invited the Muslim world to a partnership to address an array of critical issues: violent extremism, the Middle East situation, nuclear disarmament, democracy, religious freedom, women's rights, and economic development and opportunity. I am here to tell you that Indonesia, the country with the world's largest Muslim population, has long prepared itself to answer President Obama's call for partnership. (Wirajuda 2009)

This eagerness to project a "Soft Islam" (Hoesterey 2014) was a key component of SBY's foreign policy and broader "great power aspirations" (Fealy and White 2016). SBY, Wirajuda, and others in their administration wanted to showcase Indonesia's new profile as a Muslim-majority democracy through innovative diplomatic initiatives such as the "Bali Democracy Forum" (BDF), a high-level convention of diplomats from Asia and Africa who gathered, ostensibly, to "share lessons" about democratization, economic development, and civic pluralism. In fact, the BDF signified Indonesia's own increasing confidence on the global stage, formed just a couple years after then-President SBY (in the same diplomatic spirit) convened leaders of Africa and Asia in Bandung to commemorate the fiftieth anniversary of the original Asia-Africa conference.

When Joko Widodo (commonly referred to as Jokowi) assumed the presidency, he was reportedly less enthusiastic about showcasing the Bali Democracy Forum, something that appeared to him and his inner circle as a diplomatic leftover from the SBY years and did not resonate with the national populism of the first year of his presidency. Soon after bombs struck in central Jakarta in early 2016, however, Jokowi began to take religious statecraft and public diplomacy more seriously. As part of that shift, Jokowi opted to deliver the keynote address for the 2016 Bali Democracy Forum.

The BDF theme that year, "Religion, Democracy, and Pluralism," provided another forum to showcase Indonesia's form of "moderate Islam." At the time Jokowi gave the BDF opening address, he was contending with Islamic State–inspired terror at home, a contentious blasphemy trial of Jakarta's Chinese-Christian governor (see Lohanda in this volume), and frequent mass rallies to "defend Islam" (see both Jones and Hefner in this volume)—one of which was held at the doorstep of the state palace. The looming question at the parallel BDF media and civil society forum was whether Indonesia could still tout itself as the shining example of "moderate Islam," and the consensus was not particularly optimistic.

Domestic challenges to religious tolerance and pluralism notwithstanding, Indonesia's foreign ministry promoted the image of Indonesia as the home of religious pluralism and moderate Islam. Consider these excerpts from Jokowi's opening address at the BDF:

> Distinguished delegates,
>
> [welcoming]
>   . . . I believe that the theme for this year's Bali Democracy Forum, "Religion, Democracy, and Pluralism" is very relevant with the current regional and global situation because we are convinced that religion is Allah's blessing for all mankind or Rahmatan Lil Alamin because we are optimistic that democracy embodies the will of the people and brings greater good to the human race, because we realize that tolerance is needed since we all are different . . .
>   . . . We, in Indonesia, are fortunate. Indonesia has a very long history of pluralism. Indonesia is a home to pluralism with more than 1,300 ethnic groups living in Indonesia. Indonesia is a country with the largest Muslim population in the world. Around 85% of more than 252 million population of Indonesia are Muslims. Islam spread to Indonesia approximately in the 7th century. The history of Indonesia teaches us that Islam spread to Indonesia through peaceful means. And it is this value of peace that continues to be upheld to this day by the Islamic Ummah of Indonesia. In addition to Islam, Indonesia is also home to the adherents of Protestantism, Catholicism, Hinduism, Buddhism, and Confucianism. The adherents of all faiths in Indonesia also uphold the values of peace.
>   I have been informed that there will be a visit tomorrow to an Islamic Boarding School, the Bali Bina Insani, in Tabanan. You can only imagine how, without the value of high tolerance, an Islamic Boarding School can possibly live securely and serenely in the midst of a society that predominantly consists of Hindu adherents. All of these values have promoted a natural synergy between religion, democracy, and pluralism in Indonesia.
>
> Thank you,
Wassalamualaikum warahmatullahi wabarakatuh,
Om Santhi Om[1]

Beyond these flowery words, slick slogans, and multireligious greetings, religious diplomacy these days is about much more than speeches, joint communiques, and interfaith affirmation. On the second day of the BDF, Indonesia's foreign minister, Retno Marsudi, escorted representatives from nearly a hundred countries to the Bina Insani Islamic school located in the heart of the Hindu-majority

island of Bali. As delegates descended from luxury tour buses, they were welcomed by an ensemble of Balinese music and dance, and they took their seats
of honor in the front rows of an outdoor covered stage with a huge red banner
welcoming BDF delegates.

A young female student began the program with a Qur'anic verse, recited in
eloquent Arabic, about ethnic and religious pluralism. After government officials
welcomed BDF delegates, a Hindu woman who taught at the school shared her
personal testimony about feeling welcomed into this community. Next, school-
girls recited moving poems about tolerance and pluralism—one in English, the
other in Arabic: a linguistic showcase of an Indonesian Muslim cosmopolitanism at ease with both the West and the Arab world. (At the most esteemed
Islamic schools in Indonesia students must learn both Arabic and English.)
Finally, the school's director shared stories about his childhood in Bali, his education at the state Islamic school in Jakarta, and his return to found this school
as one way to promote Indonesia's national motto, *Bhinneka Tunggal Ika*, "unity
in diversity."

As the program concluded, the Saudi Arabian ambassador to Indonesia at
that time, Osama Mohammad Abdullah Alshuaibi, leapt to his feet and loudly
proclaimed how impressed he was that this Islamic school reflected the Qur'anic
notion that Islam came as a "blessing and mercy to all the worlds."[2] With no small
dose of national pride, the Saudi ambassador pledged his kingdom's donation of
$50,000 to the school. For decades, Saudi Arabia's cash diplomacy in Indonesia—
often connected to the state's mission to promote conservative Wahhabi
interpretations that are often at odds with traditionalist Islam in Indonesia—has
offered free hajj pilgrimages, funded the teaching of Arabic in Indonesia, and
provided scholarships for religious study in Saudi Arabia.

Scanning the diverse audience of government officials, Islamic school teachers, and foreign diplomats, I observed reactions ranging from awestruck jubila-
tion to horror and disappointment. One phrase from the cacophony of voices
was especially memorable: "*Duit boleh, asal jangan guru*," or "Your money is OK,
as long as it's not your religion teachers [i.e., Wahhabi interpretations of Islam]."
Following the festive announcement, the school director gave the delegates a personal tour of the campus, with Indonesia's director of public diplomacy walking
side-by-side with the Saudi ambassador. A couple of diplomats from Western
Europe trailed behind, murmuring about the audacity and excessiveness of Saudi
diplomacy.

This combination of awe and horror is perhaps the best way to characterize
Indonesia's complex diplomatic ties, religious lineages, and cultural fascina-
tion with Saudi Arabia. Despite Indonesia's rich heritage of globally-learned
religious scholars, Indonesians have shown little interest in exporting these

scholars (van Bruinessen 2012). Whereas the works of Arab scholars are often translated into Indonesian, the reverse has seldom been the case in the twentieth and twenty-first centuries. Saudi Arabia thus enjoys an aura of religious authenticity in some sectors of Indonesia's popular imagination. As suggested by the 2017 visit of King Salman bin Abdulaziz al-Saud, some Indonesian politicians and religious leaders jockey for Saudi praise while others bemoan Saudi Arabia as a kingdom that has gone astray from Islam's true religious principles, whose exported Wahhabi theology threatens Indonesian national integrity, and whose wealthy citizens have been accused of torturing their Indonesian housemaids. Whereas some seek to emulate versions of Islam espoused as "Arab," others fear the Arabization of Indonesian Islam. Indonesians returning from pilgrimage often recount stories of gruff, impolite, and unrefined Saudis who sharply contrast with the refinement they associate with Indonesian Muslims. Jakarta taxi drivers relish stories about Arab tourists who venture to Indonesia for sin-ridden excursions.

The machinations of "total diplomacy" become ever more complicated in light of King Salman's announcement during his trip to Indonesia that Saudi Arabia planned to partner with Indonesia to combat the Islamic State and to promote "moderate Islam."[3] Indonesian foreign policy finds itself at a crossroads. Whereas the promotion of "moderate Islam" plays well with Western parties, it can further complicate bilateral relations between Indonesia and, for example, Turkey, Egypt, and Saudi Arabia. Partnerships to promote "moderate Islam" do not necessarily imply that each country perceives the other's practice of Islam as authentic or rooted in authoritative tradition.

On the bus back to the BDF, I sat next to the Saudi ambassador and asked him whether he took issue with the ceremony at the Islamic school. He lamented the use of music and mixing of genders at the Islamic school, explaining to me that Indonesians had yet to practice "authentic" Islam. "But," he proceeded, "it would be rude to publicly declare such things. We must realize that this is their culture and how they understand Islam. Remember, Islam has only been here for a few centuries." His remark combined the linguistic finesse of a diplomat with the inexorable scorn of a colonial officer. Despite the rhetoric of cultural variety within Islam, it would seem unthinkable for the Saudi king to visit the Indonesian state palace and laud the concept of *Islam Nusantara*—the "Islam of the Archipelago"—that has served as a mantra of the authentic yet regionally distinct Islam for which Indonesians are meant to feel a sense of pride, not inferiority, vis-a-vis Arab articulations of Islam.

The Saudi ambassador who attended the Bali Democracy Forum, Al-Shuaibi, has taken special delight in criticizing NU, especially its chairman, KH Dr. Said Aqil Siraj, who in turn has also taken a particular pleasure in refuting Wahhabi theology after earning undergraduate and doctoral degrees in Saudi Arabia. Indeed, Siraj's own abhorrence of Wahhabi thought (and those Saudi diplomats trying to spread its message) is the result of a long, complex relationship with Saudi soft power, educational institutions, and political maneuvering. This became especially clear during his welcoming address to religious scholars from over thirty countries who had gathered in Jakarta for NU's "International Summit of Moderate Islamic Leaders."

International Summit of Moderate Islamic Leaders (ISOMIL)

In May 2016, NU leaders convened an international summit to which they invited international Muslim scholars from over thirty countries in order to showcase Indonesian Islam. The national PBNU leader Gus Yahya Staquf was especially important in the organizing of this event. The son of one of the founders of the political party PKB (Partai Kebangkitan Bangsa, or National Awakening Party), Staquf genuinely feels that Indonesia's "moderate Islam" is under threat from external forces—often dubbed "transnational Islam"—encroaching on traditionalist understandings of Islam that value local traditions. Indeed, the opening ceremony featured Javanese martial arts that culminated in a martial arts chop to a coconut that, upon opening, revealed the Indonesian national flag. Honorees included former President Megawati Sukarnoputri and Vice President Yusuf Kalla, who officially opened the ceremony.

The theme of Indonesia's tolerant Islam, juxtaposed against the purportedly dangerous, radical Islam of the Middle East, was underscored once again during the opening address by NU's chairman KH Said Aqil Siraj. As one who earned his undergraduate and doctoral degrees in Saudi Arabia and speaks fluent Arabic, Siraj took clear pleasure in describing the (historically nostalgic) peaceful spread of Islam across the archipelago, the key influence of KH Hashim Asy'ari in providing theological cover for nationalism, and how Pancasila and *Islam Nusantara* provide lessons for an Arab world that was still reeling from the postcolonial tensions between secular Arab nationalism and Islamist visions of nationhood. With a certain revisionist history and dubious accounting of the roots of the "conservative turn" in Indonesia, Siraj argued that recent terrorism and intrareligious conflict in Indonesia began only when "transnational" Wahhabi discourses entered Indonesian religious and political life. Considering that Siraj was welcoming dozens of *ulama* from many of the countries singled out, his nearly one-hour speech seems worth quoting in some length.[4] Here I include only those segments related to the public diplomacy and international dimension. Siraj addressed the audience in grand performative style and fluent Arabic:[5]

> Respected guests, the President of Indonesia Bapak Joko Widodo [who did not attend, but was represented by Jusuf Kalla and Megawati Sukarnoputri] . . . Esteemed guests, allow me to take this opportunity to welcome our international guest *ulamas* to your "second home." We hope that our international guests will feel comfortable and happy and that you will enjoy your time in Indonesia. *Hadirin yang terhortmat* [Indonesian: "respected guests"], religion and nationalism represent two principle factors that have brought the nation of Indonesia together. Together, they are important pillars that nurtured along the existence of Indonesia and nourished the continuity of the history and civilization of the Indonesian people. . . . Colonialism used every means and device possible to separate Islam and nationalism. Even to this moment, the strength of aggressors still takes the form of fracturing the people into conflicting ethnic groups. . . . Today our people [Indonesians] are experiencing several ominous crises, political, economic, social, and environmental crises that threaten the existence of our people and their future. Even more, this backdrop of crises has been taken advantage of by false voices here and there with various propaganda to split religion from nationalism, with the potential of dividing the people. This propaganda is supported by foreign powers that continuously strive to separate the two [religion and nationalism]. We greatly need to rethink [matters] and return to strengthening the pillars of religion and nationalism. . . . On account of this, in this address I will attempt to focus on the thinking of a leader who has already poured his strength to safeguard religion and nationalism on account of his deep awareness of the urgency of them both. . . . This was one of the pioneers of reform in Indonesia, KH Muhammad Hasyim Asy'ari, who played an important role in safeguarding the relationship between religion and nationalism.

Siraj next told the story of Asy'ari's life and role in the founding of NU and, more important, building the theological understanding to make possible a space for the state somewhere between secular and religious. Indeed, Siraj carefully crafted his message to use the model of Indonesian history (and exceptionalism) to provide an alternative vision for a Middle East that continues to suffer under regimes that occupy either secular or religious extremes. Siraj continued:

> KH Hasyim Asy'ari serves as an exemplary model of one who sensed the poisons of colonialism in this context [separating religion and

nationalism] and [the necessity of] confronting this before it became a dangerous and growing threat. In the majority of Muslim and Arab countries, for example, there has already been a polarization between religion and nationalism such that we see religious experts who typically have a weak nationalist spirit and nationalists who frequently do not have a strong commitment to religion. For example, Michael Aflaq, . . . who successfully produced the young cadre that would later become leaders in the Middle East, such as Abdul Karim Qasim and Hafez al-Asad in Syria, Hasan al-Bakr and Saddam Hussein in Iraq, Habib Burghibah in Tunisia, Jamal Abdun Nasser of Egypt, Muhammad Qadafi in Libya, and others. All of them are leaders who succeeded in freeing their countries from colonial powers, even though they felt religion was not important for confronting colonial powers. . . . KH Hasyim Asy'ari invited the Indonesian people to be resolutely committed to Islam as a way to safeguard the people and homeland. In this way Islam contributes to sustaining feelings of togetherness among the Indonesian people. . . . Let us compare the realities between Indonesia and the Middle East, where the differences of opinion concerning religion and nationalism drove Egyptian president Jamal Abdun Nasser to execute *ulama*s of the Muslim Brotherhood in the city center of Cairo. . . . *Alhamdulillah* such events did not occur in Indonesia, on account of presence of NU, founded by KH Hasyim Asy'ari, who proved/showed that religious leaders can simultaneously be those who struggle for the nation, as was also the case with other *ulama* leaders such as KH Ahmad Dahlan, KH Agus Salim, Abdul Halim, Abdurrahman Baswedan, and others who were both religious and nationalist leaders.[6] *This* is the characteristic of Islam in Indonesia (*Inilah karakteristik Islam di Indonesia*) that we call "Islam Nusantara"—Islam with an ironclad positive interaction with nationalism. Concerning this, KH Hasyim Asy'ari held the viewpoint that whoever was killed defending their homeland would die a martyr, and vice versa that the blood of whoever defended the colonists would be *halal* [permissible], even though they are not a *kafir* [unbeliever]. . . . the time has come to transfer these principles and concepts to the wider Muslim world so that the causes of conflict and division can be wiped out. We see in Afghanistan, for example, the spirit of nationalism has vanished among Muslims, and so too in Somalia, Iraq, and Syria. . . . With the rise of ISIS in some of our nations we can still see that the ranks of Muslims and Muslim nations in the Middle East is still fragile and weak on account of the failure of Muslims to understand their religion in one respect, and their nationalism in the other. My respected guests, allow me to take advantage of this opportunity to speak briefly about Indonesia's experience integrating religion and nationalism.

Siraj reviewed the principles of Pancasila and then shared a story about Abdurrahman Wahid's meeting with a Saudi delegation led by Abdullah bin Abdul Aziz bin Baz. Upon being asked about Pancasila, Wahid explained that NU gladly accepted this philosophy, which, rather than marginalizing Islam, "actually fertilized the people with Islamic values. This was not based on political force, rather according to NU is rooted in a comprehensive understanding of *kemaslahatan* [an Arabic-derived word meaning 'benefit,' 'value,' 'goodness']."

Much like Wirajuda's "sharing lessons" (but with a bit more flare and provocative language), Siraj used this occasion to shame the leaders of the Middle East and to extol the virtues of Indonesian Islam. I have now met with several of these *ulama* at NU-sponsored events between 2014 and 2019. Not surprisingly, most share the same traditionalist framework and Sufi inclinations as NU. Siraj certainly enjoyed the stage, but his opening address also speaks to the occasional tensions that structure Indonesia's relationship with the Middle East and claims to religious authority within the wider *umma*. Similar to the public diplomacy efforts by Indonesia's foreign ministry, Siraj's aim was to stake Indonesia's claim as not just a country of authentic Muslims but arguably the only Muslim-majority country in the world that has managed to strike the right balance between religion and nationalism, and to demonstrate the compatibility between democracy and *Islam Nusantara*.

In terms of the theological basis for *Islam Nusantara*, Siraj and others point to the influence of Sufism in Indonesia (Affan 2015; Sahal and Aziz 2015). Echoing some of the Western geopolitical rhetoric of the twenty-first century, Siraj and other traditionalist Muslims often identify Sufism as the foundation for tolerance and moderation. Indeed, ISOMIL's closing ceremonies included whirling dervishes in the red and white (*merah-putih*) of Indonesia's flag. Whereas this praise of Sufism as key to moderation affirms Western biases of the twenty-first century (see Laffan 2011 for a different story in the early twentieth century), it does little to assuage Arab countries such as Saudi Arabia, for whom Sufism itself is considered deviant. This geostrategic positioning reflects a wider understanding within Indonesia's own antiterror efforts. NU national religious leaders like Nasaruddin Umar, former vice minister of religious affairs and current grand imam of *Istiqlal* mosque, have even served in an advisory capacity for Indonesia's National Agency for Combating Terrorism.

ISOMIL was by no means an independent NU event. In terms of funding, among the most generous donors was Indonesia's National Agency for

Combating Terrorism, which reportedly covered all of the travel expenses for the international *ulama*s. Seen from this perspective, it is perhaps most useful to consider NU's efforts to promote "moderate Islam" not in terms of civil society but rather in terms of the nexus of civil society and state, brought together in part through the public diplomacy efforts that began in the early 2000s. Over the last several years, whether related to Qur'anic recitation in a Javanese dialect or convening the *Islam Wasatiyyah* (moderate Islam) conference in Bogor with the grand mufti of Al-Azhar, Jokowi has shifted his foreign policy in part away from the populist nationalist bravado of the ship-sinking and fire squad that characterized his first year of office and toward a more concerted effort to promote Indonesia as the model for "moderate Islam," especially the notion of Indonesian exceptionalism emerging in concepts like *Islam Nusantara*.

Islam Nusantara: Global Solution or Theological Problem?

Despite the self-assured enthusiasm of its NU proponents, *Islam Nusantara* was not exactly embraced universally among Indonesian Muslims, especially once it became the official slogan for NU's 2015 congress. The popular talk-show host Mama Dedeh angrily eschewed the concept, demanding to know where such an idea appears in the textual sources (she would later publicly reconcile with NU). On social media, provocative memes began to spread that cast *Islam Nusantara* in a negative light, including the derisive phrase "Jaringan Islam Nusantara" (Islam Nusantara Network), framed with the acronym JIN—which is meant to invoke jinn, the otherworldly beings and spirits described in the Qur'an. One popular television preacher from Cirebon with an ostensibly traditionalist NU background reportedly described *Islam Nusantara* as *"daging babi dikemas kambing"* ("pig meat wrapped in/disguised as goat meat"). What appears *halal* (permissible), this preacher implies, is actually *haram* (forbidden).

Even some conservative NU *ulama*s in East Java, calling themselves *NU Garis Lurus* (NU's Straight Path), challenged the theological basis of *Islam Nusantara*. In response, liberal-leaning online activists founded *NU Garis Lucu* (NU's Funny Brigade), poking fun at their internal nemesis through clever memes and cartoons. Not surprisingly, the modernist Muhammadiyah movement did not sign onto the concept of *Islam Nusantara*, instead championing their own aspirational and less controversial slogan of *Islam Berkemajuan* (Progressive Islam).[7] Although the theological differences have not been settled, the social media uproar settled down within a few months after the congress season passed, and over the last five years since NU has continued to promote *Islam Nusantara* as Indonesia's gift to the Muslim world. During this time, *Islam Nusantara* has acquired a certain political capital as politicians and bureaucrats have sought to operationalize the concept as a way to curb domestic terrorism and as diplomats have deployed the concept in their efforts to manage Indonesia's brand abroad.

As Jokowi has become increasingly aware of his susceptibility to attacks by Islamist hardliners, he has tried to gain his Islamic credentials by bringing senior NU figures into his political orbit (Fealy 2018). Jokowi schedules frequent visits across Indonesia (especially Java and Lombok) to develop relationships with senior NU *kyais*. Especially as the "defend Islam" (or 212) movement was gaining momentum, Jokowi summoned leaders of NU and Muhammadiyah to the palace for dialogue and photo ops. Jokowi (and indeed many observers of Indonesia) have seemed at a loss to really understand and respond to the culmination of political and religious ambitions from increasingly influential circles beyond the patronage networks of NU and Muhammadiyah. With the 2014 electoral smear campaign (that Jokowi was anti-Islam and perhaps even secretly a Christian communist) resurfacing in the run-up to the 2019 election, Jokowi was increasingly aware that he could not run a secular populist campaign in 2019. He needed religiopolitical cover, and found it in NU and *Islam Nusantara*.

To give but one indication of this, on May 24, 2017 Jokowi traveled with his entourage to attend KH Ma'aruf Amin's ceremony at UIN-Maulana Malik Ibrahim in Malang. Greg Fealy observed that Jokowi has carefully cultivated this alliance, even showing deference by escorting Amin to his seat at state events (2018). During this time, Jokowi was reportedly also quietly courting several Muslim public figures as possible vice presidential running mates, reportedly including among others the former vice minister of religious affairs and current grand *imam* of Istiqlal, Nazaruddin Umar. Over a year later, on the eve of Jokowi's decision on his running mate, it appeared he would choose the respected Muslim scholar and former chief judge of the Constitutional Court, Mahfud M.D. In a dramatic turn of events, after deliberations that one presidential advisor described as a shouting match, Jokowi announced he would be running with Ma'aruf Amin, arguably the most powerful *ulama* and also one of the major voices whose testimony and political maneuvering sent Jokowi's protégé to jail for blasphemy (on the Ahok case and the 212 movement, see Lohanda in this volume).

For many liberal-leaning observers of Indonesia, there is an unfortunate irony—perhaps even contradiction—in Ma'aruf Amin touting the tolerance and peaceful pluralism of Indonesian Islam. As Robin Bush (2015) and others have noted, Amin played an influential role as presidential advisor during the SBY administration when anti-Shi'a and anti-Ahmadiyyah violence displaced thousands of Indonesian Muslims. At that time in 2012, even the minister of religion Suryadarma Ali ruminated on the possibility of mass conversions to Sunni Islam as the only solution to the violence.[8] In retrospect, what some suspected was SBY's hesitation to advocate on behalf of Shi'a and Ahmadiyyah communities actually reflects a conscious program to criminalize and marginalize Muslim minorities (see Hamayotsu in this volume). This unification through demonization of intra-Muslim others is part of a longer historical legacy, what Jeremy Menchik has referred to as "Godly Nationalism" (2014). Indeed, in his capacity as head of MUI, Amin was among those *ulama* leading the blasphemy charge against Jakarta's former governor Ahok, and he appeared as a key witness for the prosecution (Fealy 2018). Thus, Siraj and NU's broad claims to being the exemplary bastion of moderation run into considerable resistance when one considers Amin's hardliner approach to blasphemy and so-called "deviant" sects.

Given Amin's questionable dedication to ensuring rights for religious and sexual minorities, many human rights activists and liberal-leaning NU members expressed disappointment in Jokowi's choice for vice president.[9] "Amin has been central to some of the most intolerant elements of Indonesian contemporary religious and political culture, so fear of the negative impact he could have on the rights and safety of religious and gender minorities is well founded," said Phelim Kine, deputy director of the Asia Division at Human Rights Watch.[10] Further still, during the moral panic of early 2016, Amin played important roles in both the MUI and NU declarations about the supposed danger of encroaching LGBTQ culture. It becomes even more difficult to sustain the narrative of NU as safeguard of the nation when we consider its wider historical role in Indonesian politics, especially its quasi-militant wings of Banser and Ansor and its participation in anticommunist violence in Central and East Java during the 1960s. Such historical nuance notwithstanding, Jokowi's political calculus was embarrassingly clear and, if we look at how he fared in the Muslim vote alongside the backing of the majority of Javanese, the strategy seemed to work remarkably well.

By attending to "moderate Islam" and *Islam Nusantara* as ideas always in the making and peculiar for their political and theological malleability, we are also able to connect domestic politics to foreign diplomacy. After the 2017 passing of K.H. Hasyim Muzadi, who had served on the presidential advisory council, Jokowi replaced him with Gus Yahya Staquf, secretary general of NU who has played a major role in promoting *Islam Nusantara* and traveled globally conducting public diplomacy on behalf of NU. Perhaps in part due to the backlash against NU's slogan of *Islam Nusantara* from modernists, Islamists, and even some within the NU ranks (Buya Yahya, NU Garis Lurus, and others), in 2017 Gus Yahya Staquf and other NU elite launched another slogan-based approach to Islamic moderation. This time, however, they favored a more neutral phrase—"Humanitarian Islam," written in English and Indonesianized Arabic, *al-Islam li al-Insaniyyah*—one that they hoped more Indonesians, especially reformist figures in Muhammadiyah, might be able to get behind. Stacuf told me that he regretted the perceived distancing between NU and Muhammadiyah as a result of the competing congress themes of *Islam Nusantara* and *Islam Berkemajuan*.

Stacuf and Ansor (led at that time by Stacuf's younger brother, Yaqut Cholil Qoumas) launched "Humanitarian Islam" in Jombang, East Java—at the very pesantren where NU was founded. In an effort to claim both great saints and Sufi roots, the special guests included the American Sufi shaykh and prolific author Kabir Helminski. Notable political figures also in attendance (besides the Ansor crowd) included a special panel with the Jombang native and PKB chair Muhaimin Iskandar (Cak Imin) and then-MPR speaker and PAN (Partai Amanat Nasional) politician Zulkifli Hasan. Prior to serving as minister of forestry, in 2016 Hasan in particular was especially vocal against LGBTQ communities on campuses. As Indonesian observers have noted, though never formally indicted, Hasan has been under great scrutiny for possible corruption links during his tenure as forestry minister.

At the launch of "Humanitarian Islam," as Muhaimin and Hasan were waxing nostalgic about moderation and sincerity in doing the work of the people, a group of women in the front table next to the elevated stage were talking loudly, clearly engaged in their own conversation, and occasionally breaking into laughter. Two of the women even had their backs to Muhaimin and Hasan. Although public events in Indonesia often have multiple spheres of attention and conversation, this seemed peculiarly so. When I asked one of the women during the lunch break what the conversation was about, she replied that the women are tired of the nonsense spouted by insincere politicians who publicly profess their piety. Their chatter was a form of moral protest. My purpose in pointing this out is not simply to police the borders of who can speak about, much less on behalf of, "moderate Islam." Rather, I am interested in these local articulations of moderation, in which Zulkifli Hasan seemingly feels no dissonance between anti-LGBTQ policies and the concept of religious moderation. At the same time, the example with the women makes clear the skepticism that even women in NU can occasionally feel about the self-professed exemplars of moderation and national morality. Without the space to go into too much detail, I would simply note that, yet again, public figures whose moral integrity has been questioned in the past are held up as spokespeople for Islamic moderation and Indonesian exceptionalism. This ostensibly political calculus, however, runs the risk of domestic leaders and foreign diplomats calling into question both the supposed moderation of such figures and the validity of Indonesia's Islamic exceptionalism.

In the couple of years since this event, Staquf has been especially active in bringing *Islam Nusantara* and "Humanitarian Islam" (as two faces of one NU coin) to wider audiences in Europe and North America, including sometimes controversial meetings with figures like the former US vice president Mike Pence and the Israeli prime minister Benjamin Netanyahu. In 2018, Staquf and his American colleague Holland Taylor even hired a British personal assistant to work from London and arrange his international appearances, events, and partnerships across parts of the Middle East, Europe, and the United States.[11]

Whereas these slogans play well in the West, leading with theological claims of Sufism as the root of moderation does not play out so well in either historical terms or among coreligionists and diplomats in the Middle East—especially Saudi Arabia—who are often held up as counterexamples by NU leaders during their diplomatic visits to the West (and thus part of the "Good Muslim, Bad Muslim" divide critiqued in Mamdani 2004). In the next section, I explore the ways in which the global promotion of Indonesian Islam challenges the authority and authenticity of Wahhabism more broadly and Saudi Arabia in particular. Attending to these diplomatic divides provides an interesting lens through which to understand strategies of religious diplomacy and fractures in foreign policy between Indonesia and Saudi Arabia.

Twitter Diplomacy: Saudi Critiques of NU and *Islam Nusantara*

Peter Mandaville and Shadi Hamid (2018) have described Saudi Arabia's soft power diplomacy abroad. To be sure, Saudi diplomats in Indonesia have also pursued these efforts. For decades they offered scholarships for Indonesians to study in Saudi Arabia, and more recently Saudi diplomats have tried to capitalize on Indonesian popular culture and viral stories as a way to hand out free *'umra* and *hajj* pilgrimages. Despite Saudi contempt for Sufism and traditionalist understandings and practices of Islam, Saudi diplomats have still tried to maintain relations with NU. King Salman's visit in 2017 was marked by Saudi outreach to help strengthen so-called "moderate Islam." Although Saudi ideas of moderation most likely do not map onto those of NU, their public diplomacy campaign was in full swing. Consider the Saudi ambassador Alshuaibi's visit to NU headquarters in November 2017. Siraj's tweet of this occasion includes a photo of both of them and their entourage smiling gregariously, yet also offers a semiveiled critique of Saudi Arabia's ban on Iranians performing pilgrimage. Siraj stated that Saudi Arabia's "commitment to develop/cultivate moderate Islam can begin by granting a promise, regardless of *madhab* [school of Islamic Law], to the entire global Muslim community who carries out the *Hajj* and *'umra* pilgrimages in the Holy Land" (@nahdlatululama, November 14, 2017).[12] Thus, even smiling photo-ops between Alshuaibi and Siraj can exhibit this underlying tension. One senior NU member noted that Alshuaibi intentionally excluded Siraj from King Salman's welcoming reception at the airport and state palace several months prior to this photo op. Notwithstanding the veracity of this specific claim, subsequent tensions between Siraj and Alshuaibi would lay bare the underlying tensions between Saudi Arabia and Indonesia.

In late 2018, Ansor burned a flag that was believed to belong to the now-banned Hizbut Tahrir Indonesia, but was later speculated by critics of NU to be the flag of *tawhid* (oneness of God). Ambassador Alshuaibi was quick to criticize. In a tweet that was later erased and revised, Alshuaibi laments that the actions were carried out by a "deviant organization" (later translated on social media in Indonesian as *sesat*; *menyamping*). Although the tweet would later be revised, the original had already gone viral among NU members, leading some to demand that the Saudi ambassador be sent, deported, even chased home (the more restrained replies used words like *dipulangkan* ["to be sent home"]; those in the Ansor ranks preferred *diusir*, "chased"). PBNU and Siraj in particular were quick to respond, issuing a televised press conference and formal statement showing the original tweet and stating that "Indonesia's good relations with Saudi Arabia have been tarnished by Alshuaibi's statement that spreads false information about deviant groups."[13] When the news broke, Ambassador Alshuaibi was already in Saudi Arabia, supposedly with plans for a new assignment. As a conciliatory gesture, he tweeted that he had already phoned Yenny Wahid (a well-known religious and civic activist and the daughter of the former president and chair of NU Abdurrahman Wahid) to express his regret and his respect for NU. Occasionally the slick slogans and grand aspirations of public diplomacy fall apart, laying bare the very real theological and political divides between NU and the Wahhabism of Saudi Arabia.

The predicaments of Saudi's cash diplomacy and Indonesia's "moderate Islam" have implications for how we understand issues of authority, identity, and community in relation to multiple visions of Muslim modernity. Equally important, this case also sheds light on the predicaments, possibilities, and pitfalls of public diplomacy and religious tolerance *within* the *umma*. Whereas public proclamations of an inspired and divine allegiance to a global Islamic *umma* play well in certain circles, persistent questions about religious authority and political legitimacy, informed by the moral messiness of actual bilateral relations, have strained these countries' bonds of religious solidarity. Viral stories about the abuse and torture of Indonesian domestic workers in Saudi Arabia, among other examples, have left Indonesians feeling like second-class

Muslim citizens and wondering about the limits of Muslim brotherhood.[14] The pleasantries of public diplomacy are not always compatible with the realities of realpolitik.

Ultimately, the Indonesian state's most important task will be to successfully ensure merciful and compassionate Islam at home, not just "moderate Islam" abroad. Despite Saudi overtures to help spread "moderate Islam" throughout the archipelago, Indonesia's government and council of *ulama* have moved forward with socialization and deradicalization programs of their own. As Marcel Mauss has observed, gifts are always given in relations of power, and there are no unencumbered gifts among friends. President Jokowi has already displayed a willingness to depart from Yudhoyono's foreign policy of "a million friends, zero enemies."[15] One need not make enemies in order to keep some friends at a safer distance. Yet, despite pledges for a moratorium on sending Indonesians to Saudi Arabia as housemaids, King Salman's 2017 visit seemed to indicate that Jokowi is much more interested in soliciting foreign direct investment than publicly rebuking Saudi Arabia's Wahhabist propaganda.

Indonesia's revamped image of "moderate Islam" plays much better with Western governments worried about terror than with the anxious monarchs and authoritarian rulers of the Middle East. As the 2017 visit of Saudi Arabia's King Salman to Indonesia suggests, the ruling class of Middle East monarchies are more interested in Balinese beaches than Indonesia's Sufi-inflected Islam. As Rizal Sukma cautions, "It is not immediately clear how attractive Indonesia's brand of Islam is to its coreligionist partners in the Arab Muslim world" (2012: 87). Martin van Bruinessen puts it more forcefully: "The Arab world has shown a remarkable lack of interest in Asia in general, let alone in the social and cultural forms of Islam in Southeast Asia" (2012: 117). It seems unfathomable that the king of Saudi Arabia would ever embrace *Islam Nusantara*.

Given this lack of authority in the Middle East, and despite their multiple offers to broker a peace deal for Palestinians, Indonesia has struggled to assume any significant role as a peace broker on the global stage. Azyumardi Azra laments that "despite renewed Indonesian activism in Middle Eastern affairs, the hopes that Indonesia can be a bridging and mediating force among the conflicting parties in the Middle East seem to be very difficult to realize" (2015: 151). This is certainly not due to any lack of effort. In March 2016, Indonesia hosted an extraordinary summit by the Organization of Islamic Cooperation (OIC) Palestine, yet the much-heralded "Jakarta Declaration" that came out of that summit has certainly not brought about any real political change. Despite the grandest of aspirations, Indonesia has yet to project any serious power or influence that might mitigate conflict in the Middle East.

Soft power is also expensive. If recent budget cuts are any indication, Indonesia has not seriously invested in the institutions, training, and expertise necessary to become an effective diplomatic player (Sukma 2011). Noting that Indonesia's Ministry of Foreign Affairs has only a handful of China specialists and not a single diplomat who speaks Hindi, Fealy and White conclude that the "[Ministry of] Foreign Affairs shows little signs of being able to rise to the challenges posed by Indonesia's growing diplomatic prominence" (2016: 97–98). Without a significant budget and adequate human resources, public diplomacy and soft power can go only so far.

Indonesia's ability to promote itself as a home of "moderate Islam"—at least in the West—will depend more on its own record than diplomatic stunts. When it comes to safeguarding the rights of Shi'a, Ahmadiyyah, and LGBTQ citizens, many of Indonesia's politicians and religious leaders nowadays do not exactly embody the sort of liberal-secular "moderate Islam" applauded by the West (Harsono 2012; Mahmood 2006).[16] As Dewi Fortuna Anwar has astutely observed,

> Indonesia's efforts to promote a new face for Indonesia which is moderate, democratic and progressive will be meaningless and futile if the international news on Indonesia is dominated by stories about the burning of churches, attacks against groups accused of deviating from Islam, such as Ahmadiyyah, women being forced to wear the jilbab [headscarf] and other non-democratic and non-progressive acts . . . Indonesia's public diplomacy would be received with a degree of cynicism by the international community (2008: 11; cited in Sukma 2012: 87).

This is not to mandate some liberal-secular litmus test of who can legitimately claim to be a "moderate." It is to underscore, however, that the future success of Indonesia's soft power strategies (at least in the West) will rest on the veracity of the claim that Indonesia is indeed the home of "moderate Islam." Viewed from a comparative and historical perspective, Muslims have offered a range of understandings of moderation—*wasatiyyah*. As scholars such as Yasmin Moll have observed (2017), the real struggle is not about who is moderate but rather about whose version of "moderate Islam" has political power and religious authority. Will Indonesia continue to successfully leverage its reputation as a "moderate" Muslim country? How will Indonesia maneuver within multilateral organizations such as the Organization for Islamic Cooperation? On what grounds and in which social, religious, and political spaces can Indonesia successfully export a model of "moderate Islam" to the Middle East? For Indonesia, the struggle goes on and traditional alliances and patronage networks appear to be shifting. What seems clear, however, is that Indonesia's public diplomacy abroad will be closely linked with religious statecraft at home.

Notes

This research has been generously funded by a Fulbright Senior Scholar award and a research grant with the Indonesia Research Group for the initiative "Contending Modernities." I am grateful to these organizations for making this research possible and to project collaborators for their critical reflections along the way.

1. Transcription of speech, my translation. The written speech in Indonesian can also be accessed through the website of the Ministry of Foreign Affairs, https://setkab.go.id/sambutan-presiden-joko-widodo-pada-pembukaan-forum-demokrasi-bali-ix-8-desember-2016-di-bali-international-convention-center/, accessed March 24, 2019.

2. With this phrase, the Saudi ambassador summoned in Arabic, and then translated, the Qur'anic passage from al-Anbiya 21: 107. These observations based on fieldnotes and audio recordings, December 9, 2016.

3. Eveline Danubrata and John Chalmers, "Saudi King to Work with Indonesia to Combat Islamic State—Ambassador," *Reuters*, February 28, 2017, https://uk.reuters.com/article/uk-saudi-asia-indonesia-idUKKBN1670I4; Ankit Panda, "What King Salman seeks in Asia," *Aljazeera*, March 1, 2017, https://www.aljazeera.com/indepth/opinion/2017/02/saudi-king-salman-seeks-asia-170228095334605.html.

4. My translation from written Indonesian version published in the event handout. The event had simultaneous translation in both Arabic and English and several international news outlets reported on site.

5. My translation based on a written version of the speech (in Indonesian and Arabic) that was distributed to attendees, May 9, 2016.

6. Siraj once again espouses a curious revisionist history that ignores the role of Darul Islam during the anticolonial struggle and their Islamist vision at that time (and, for some, still to this day) for a future, independent Indonesia. Although below Siraj mentions the Muhammadiyah founder Ahmad Dahlan among the national heroes, his origin story of Indonesia's purported exceptionalism, told to an audience of foreign religious scholars, is decidedly a story about NU exceptionalism.

7. I do not have the space here to adequately address Muhammadiyah's vision of *Islam Berkemajuan* or the internal contestations about authority and authenticity. Suffice it to say, PP Muhammadiyah leaders such as Haedar Nashir and Abdul Mu'ti have also embarked on public diplomacy tours to articulate this vision. I will elaborate on Muhammadiyah's public diplomacy efforts in a future publication.

8. Margareth Aritonang, "Shia Conversion is the Solution: Minister," *Jakarta Post*, September 6, 2012, https://www.thejakartapost.com/news/2012/09/06/shia-conversion-solution-minister.html.

9. While it is tempting to view Amin's choice in terms of his leadership in PBNU, one NU member I interviewed wondered to what extent Jokowi's choice might instead have been guided by Amin's sway within the conservative circles of MUI.

10. Elijas Ariffin, "Why did Jokowi pick cleric Ma'aruf Amin?," *Asean Post*, August 14, 2018, https://theaseanpost.com/article/why-did-jokowi-pick-cleric-maruf-amin.

11. Without the space to expand here, Taylor had been a friend of Gus Dur and, since his death, has continued to cultivate an especially close relationship with Gus Yahya Staquf and Gus Mus of Rembang, even going on '*umra* pilgrimage together. Whereas Taylor is viewed with suspicion by some NU members, he has become an important advisor to Staquf. In his own attempt to promote *Islam Nusantara*, Taylor directed and produced the documentary "The Divine Grace of Islam Nusantara," a film that juxtaposes images of a supposedly peaceful traditionalist, Sufi-inflected Islam with gruesome videos of terror committed by ISIS. Taylor developed a connection with the *New York Times* Jakarta correspondent Joe Cochrane, who penned a fluff piece endorsing NU's fight against the

violent extremism of the Islamic State. Cochrane, "For Indonesia, a Muslim Challenge to the Ideology of the Islamic State," *New York Times*, November 26, 2015. https://www.nytimes.com/2015/11/27/world/asia/indonesia-islam-nahdlatul-ulama.html?_r=0.

12. My translation of original tweet in Indonesian.

13. My translation of original statement in Indonesian. The statement including the original Saudi tweet can be seen here: https://arrahmahnews.com/2018/12/03/sebut-ansor-ormas-menyimpang-pbnu-usir-dubes-saudi/, accessed February 28, 2019. The original press conference can be viewed here: "PBNU: Usir Dubes Arab Saudi Dari Indonesia," streamed live on YouTube by NU Channel, https://www.youtube.com/watch?v=u-p8FHZzu34, December 3, 2018.

14. *Al Arabiya*, 2010, "Indonesians Outraged by Maid's Torture in Saudi Arabia," November 21, 2010, translated into English by Sonia Farid, https://www.alarabiya.net/articles/2010/11/21/126841.html.

15. Ted Piccone and Bimo Yusman, "Indonesian Foreign Policy: 'A Million Friends and Zero Enemies,'" *Diplomat*, February 14, 2014, https://thediplomat.com/2014/02/indonesian-foreign-policy-a-million-friends-and-zero-enemies/.

16. As mentioned earlier, I would stress that scholars of Islam must begin to better understand emic and local articulations and idioms of moderation that allow the concept to go well beyond its liberal-secular confines, in Indonesia and elsewhere.

References

Affan, Hayder. 2015. "Polemik di Balik Istilah Islam Nusantara [The Polemics behind the concept of Islam Nusantara]." *BBC Indonesia*, June 15, 2015. http://www.bbc.com/indonesia/berita_indonesia/2015/06/150614_indonesia_islam_nusantara.

Anwar, Dewi Fortuna. 2008. "Peran Diplomasi Publik dalam Kebijakan Luar Negeri Republik Indonesia [The Role of Public Diplomacy in Indonesia's Foreign Policy]." Paper presented at the Syarif Hidayatullah State Islamic University, Jakarta, December 5.

Azra, Azyumardi. 2015. "Indonesia's Middle Power Public Diplomacy: Asia and Beyond." In *Understanding Public Diplomacy in East Asia: Middle Powers in a Troubled Region*, edited by Jan Melissen and Yul Sohn, 131–54. New York: Palgrave Macmillan.

Bond, Christopher S., and Lewis M. Simons. 2009. *The Next Front: Southeast Asia and the Road to Global Peace with Islam*. Hoboken, NJ: John Wiley & Sons.

Bush, Robin. 2015. "Religious Politics and Minority Rights during the Yudhoyono Presidency." In *The Yudhoyono Presidency: A Decade of Stability and Stagnation*, edited by Edward Aspinall, 239–57. Singapore: ISEAS.

Emmerson, Donald K. 2012. "Is Indonesia Rising? It Depends." In *Indonesia Rising: The Repositioning of Asia's Third Giant*, edited by Anthony Reid, 49–76. Singapore: ISEAS.

Fealy, Greg. 2018. "Ma'aruf Amin: Jokowi's Islamic Defender or Dead Weight?" *New Mandala*, August 28, 2018. https://www.newmandala.org/maruf-amin-jokowis-islamic-defender-deadweight/.

Fealy, Greg, and Hugh White. 2016. "Indonesia's 'Great Power' Aspirations: A Critical View." *Asia and the Pacific Policy Studies* 3, no. 1: 92–100.

Harsono, Andreas. 2012. "No Model for Muslim Democracy." *New York Times*, May 21, 2012. http://www.nytimes.com/2012/05/22/opinion/no-model-for-muslim-democracy.html. Accessed March 12, 2017.

Haynes, Jeffrey, ed. 2011. *Religion, Politics, and International Relations: Selected Essays.* New York: Routledge.

Hoesterey, James B. 2014. "Soft Islam: Indonesia's Interfaith Mission for Peace in the Middle East." *Middle East Institute*, November 12, 2014. https://www.mei.edu/publications/soft-islam-indonesias-interfaith-mission-peace-middle-east.

Laffan, Michael. 2011. *The Makings of Indonesian Islam: Orientalism and the Narration of a Sufi Past.* Princeton, NJ: Princeton University Press.

Mahmood, Saba. 2006. "Secularism, Hermeneutics, Empire: The Politics of Islamic Reformation." *Public Culture* 18, no. 2: 323–47.

Mamdani, Mahmood. 2004. *Good Muslim, Bad Muslim: America, The Cold War, and the Roots of Terror.* New York: Three Leaves Press.

Mandaville, Peter and Shadi Hamid. 2018. "Islam as Statecraft: How Governments use Religion in Foreign Policy." *The New Geopolitics: Middle East.* Washington, DC: The Brookings Institutions.

Menchik, Jeremy. 2014. "Productive Intolerance: Godly Nationalism in Indonesia." *Comparative Studies in Society and History* 56, no. 3: 591–621.

Moll, Yasmin. 2017. "The Moral Economy of Islamic Television: Panic and its Perils." In *George Washington University. Project on Middle East Studies (23), Islamic in a Changing Middle East: New Islamic Media*, 18–21. https://pomeps.org/wp-content/uploads/2017/02/POMEPS_Studies_23_Media_Web-rev.pdf.

Obama, Barack. 2010. "Speech Given at University of Indonesia," November 10, 2010. https://obamawhitehouse.archives.gov/the-press-office/2010/11/10/remarks-president-university-indonesia-jakarta-indonesia.

Sahal, Akhmad, and Munawir Aziz, eds. 2015. *Islam Nusantara: Dari Ushul Fiqh Hingga Paham Kebangsaan.* Bandung: Mizan.

Sukma, Rizal. 2011. "Soft Power and Public Diplomacy: The Case of Indonesia," In *Public Diplomacy and Soft Power in East Asia*, edited by Sook Jong Lee and Jam Melissen, 91–116. New York: Palgrave Macmillan.

Sukma, Rizal. 2012. "Domestic Politics and International Posture: Constraints and Possibilities." In *Indonesia Rising: The Repositioning of Asia's Third Giant*, edited by Anthony Reid, 77–92. Singapore: ISEAS.

Van Bruinessen, Martin. 2012. "Indonesian Muslims and Their Place in the Larger World of Islam." In *Indonesia Rising: The Repositioning of Asia's Third Giant*, edited by Anthony Reid, 117–40. Singapore: ISEAS.

Wirajuda, Hassan J. 2009. "Speech at the Carnegie Endowment for International Peace," June 8, 2009. http://carnegieendowment.org/2009/06/08/indonesian-foreign-minister-wirajuda-on-u.s.-indonesian-comprehensive-partnership/mds.

10

AGAMA HINDU UNDER PRESSURE FROM MUSLIM AND CHRISTIAN PROSELYTIZING

Michel Picard

Once their island became part of the Republic of Indonesia, the Balinese people were told that they "did not yet have a religion" (*belum beragama*). This implied that they were expected to convert to either Islam or Christianity, the only "religions" (*agama*) then recognized by the Ministry of Religion (Kementerian Agama Republik Indonesia, KAGRI). While the word *agama* is commonly glossed as "religion" in contemporary Indonesia, it is actually the peculiar combination in Sanskrit guise of a Christian view of what counts as a world religion with a restrictive and prescriptive Islamic understanding of what defines a "true" religion—that is, divine revelation recorded by a prophet in a holy scripture, a codified system of law for the faithful, congregational worship not confined to a sole ethnic group, and a belief in the One Almighty God. Even if Islam failed to establish itself as the official religion of Indonesia, its proponents succeeded in imposing their own conception of the relationship between religion and the state by framing and shaping all debates about religion.

Faced with the KAGRI's rebuff, Balinese leaders struggled to have their religion acknowledged as a proper *agama*. After a successful lobbying campaign, the Balinese religion was duly accepted as "Hinduism"—or *agama Hindu* in official parlance.

In any case, this is the story being told in Bali today. What this story does not tell is that, before they began pressing the KAGRI to recognize their religion, Balinese social and intellectual elites had to invent for themselves the very idea of a "Balinese religion." Indeed, they had formerly no notion of a system of beliefs and practices that could be demarcated from other aspects of their life to be labeled "religion" and to which one could "convert"—let alone that this religion was "Hinduism." This required constructing the separate existence of "religion" as an encompassing frame of reference for the interpretation of practices that were then formulated as enactments of "Hinduism." This process was an outcome of the colonial encounter that introduced to Bali the alien categories of both "religion" and "Hinduism."

More specifically, before being compelled by Indonesian authorities to define their identity in religious terms, the Balinese had already been confronted with European orientalists, colonial administrators, Muslim schoolteachers, Christian missionaries, and Indian gurus—not to mention artists, anthropologists, and tourists. That is to say that Balinese religious identity has been dialogically constructed by means of iterative processes of assertions and ascriptions constrained by power relations through which the Balinese people appropriated the views of influential outsiders with whom they had to engage.

Before considering how Balinese opinion leaders managed to have their religion recognized by the KAGRI, I will investigate how the construction of Balinese religion has been framed by Islam and Christianity. This requires elucidating how *agama* became "religion" for the Balinese, and how *agama Bali* became *agama Hindu*. After briefly relating the trajectory of religion in Bali and describing its present predicament, I shall focus on the contemporary struggle of the Balinese people to ward off the pressure of Muslim and Christian proselytizing.

Agama: From *Dharma* to "Religion"

Agama has not always meant "religion" in Indonesia (Picard 2017). In Sanskrit, *āgama* signifies "that which has come down to the present" and it applies to "anything handed down as fixed by tradition" (Gonda [1952] 1973, 499). In particular, the term *āgama* refers to the canonical texts of the Śaiva-Siddhānta order, which had a prominent influence in Java and Bali.

Although it is difficult to establish when exactly the word *agama* came to mean religion in Indonesia, we know that in Javanese and Balinese textual traditions from the twelfth century onward, it applied to law codes related to the Indian *Dharmaśāstra*, the treatises on *dharma*, in which legal and religious features are not distinguished.[1] We also know that in Malay chronicles dating back to the fourteenth century, the term *agama* is associated with Islam and used in a sense equivalent to that of *dīn*.[2] Therefore, one has to conclude that for centuries the word *agama* in Indonesia had two distinct denotations, that of *dharma* as well as that of *dīn*, according to the context and language of its occurrence.

By appropriating that term, Indonesian Muslims endowed it with new meaning, namely, the exclusive worship of the one and only God and the requirement of conversion to a foreign doctrine whose teachings are contained in a holy book revealed by a prophet. Later on, through its adoption by Christian missionaries, *agama* became associated with an ideal of social progress, while "pagan" beliefs were scorned as outmoded superstitions and viewed as a cause for shame.

By taking on the meaning of "religion," *agama* was being dissociated not only from "law" but also from "tradition," which in Indonesia is rendered by the Arabic loanword *adat*. In the same fashion as *dharma*, the term *adat* refers to the cosmic order and to social life in agreement with that order. This comprehensive scope of *adat* was fragmented by Islam and Christianity, which confined its significance to the customs that do not have an explicit religious legitimation. In particular, the word *adat* entered the language of Islamized populations to refer to indigenous "customary law" as opposed to Islamic "religious law" (*hukum*). Subsequently, Dutch jurists codified the indigenous customary laws (*adatrecht*) of the various peoples on whom they had imposed their colonial empire. By thus attributing to each ethnic group its own *adatrecht*, Dutch colonial policy widened the divide between "tradition" and "religion."

This dissociation between *agama* and *adat* entailed certain consequences. Whereas in *adat*, practices are followed much as they have been handed down from generation to generation, in *agama*, they are held to be motivated on the basis of prior belief. And while different *agama* make exclusive claims about being the true revelation, attributing the predicates "true" and "false" to *adat* would be a category mistake. Moreover, *adat* as a specific set of practices inherited from one's ancestors is tied to a particular ethnic group that it differentiates from others, contrary to *agama* whose intrinsic proselytizing drive explicitly aims at transcending ethnic boundaries.

However, in contrast to Islamized or Christianized areas of Indonesia, in Bali the word *agama* has retained its original polysemy, as we find in Balinese-Indonesian dictionaries, which translate *agama* as (1) *agama*, (2) *hukum*, and (3) *adat*.

The Emergence of a Balinese Religion

Launched in 1846, the Dutch conquest of Bali was only completed in 1908. The colonial takeover put an end to Balinese kingship, whose power was manifested through rituals that comprised political, social, and religious features closely interwoven with each other. In order to govern the island efficiently, Dutch colonial officials imposed a uniform administrative structure throughout Balinese society. They established a new type of village, the "administrative village" (*gou-vernementsdesa*, later renamed *desa dinas*), consisting of several "customary villages" (*adatdesa*, which became known as *desa adat*). By instigating a dichotomy between customary matters, which they left to the Balinese, and administrative authority, which they appropriated, the Dutch initiated an unprecedented distinction between religious tradition and political power.

In the 1920s, the first generation of Balinese educated in colonial schools set up modern organizations and started publishing periodicals, a complete novelty for Bali. Devoted chiefly to social and religious issues, these publications were written not in Balinese but in Malay, the language of Islam as well as of colonial modernity. Thus, the same process that led the Balinese to question their identity was depriving them of their own words, by making them think about themselves in a language that was not their own but rather that used by their fellow countrymen as well as by their colonial rulers.

In these publications, the Balinese began viewing themselves as both an ethnic group, characterized by their own customs, and a religious community, threatened by the expansion of Islam and Christianity. They construed their identity—which they called their "Balineseness" (*Kebalian*)—as being based on *agama* and on *adat*. Far from expressing a primordial essence, as they claimed, these conceptual categories were alien and had to be appropriated by the Balinese according to their own references and concerns (Picard 1999).

Introduced to Bali by the Dutch, the word *adat* replaced diverse terms for locally variable customs that governed the relationships between social groups and infused the villages with a sense of communal solidarity. The incorporation of miscellaneous local customs into this generic term altered their meaning for the Balinese: what had been until then an interplay of significant differences deliberately fostered between villages became the locus of Balinese ethnic identity, in the sense of a customary body of inherited values, norms, and institutions governing the lives of the Balinese people.

As such, in Bali *adat* was not distinguished from *agama*. Indeed, Balinese ritual life is localized, connecting specific groups of people to one another, their ancestors, and their territory. It consists of a series of transactions with immaterial entities from the invisible world (*niskala*), in which human beings present offerings and worship in exchange for blessings of holy water (*tirta*) that ensure the renewal of life and the regeneration of nature.[3] Participation in these rites is a customary obligation for the Balinese, which sanctions membership in a village community, a kinship group, and a temple congregation. Rather than something to be believed in, Balinese ritual life is something to be carried out. Such evidence led the Indologist Frits Staal to conclude that "Balinese ritual is a classic case of ritual without religion" (Staal 1995, 31).

We don't know precisely when Balinese started using the word *agama* in the sense of "religion"—nor when they actually chose to designate their own *agama* as "Hindu." However, we know that long before they defined themselves as Hindus, the Balinese had already been "Hinduized" by orientalists, at a time when they had yet to learn the word "Hinduism." And it is through the works of Dutch orientalists that Balinese elites acquired their first information on Hinduism in the twentieth century. As it happened, before Dutch administrators set about dealing with Balinese society, it had been imagined by orientalists as a "living museum" of Indo-Javanese civilization, the one and only surviving heir to the Hindu heritage of Majapahit swept away from Java by the coming of Islam. Holding Hinduism to be the core of Balinese identity, colonial officials set out to turn Bali into a Hindu stronghold to counter the expansion of Islam throughout the archipelago. By thus looking for the singularity of Bali in its Hindu heritage and construing Balinese identity as formed through an opposition to Islam, the Dutch established the frame of reference within which the Balinese would later on define themselves.

We know further that *agama* still retained the meaning of *dharma* in Bali throughout the colonial period. It is significant, for example, that in the catalogue established by Balinese scholars for the library set up in 1928 by the Dutch administration to preserve Balinese manuscripts, the entry *agama* refers not to "religion" but to law codes related to the Indian *Dharmaśāstra*. There is no entry corresponding to the category "religion"—nor is there one for *adat* or for *hukum* (Kadjeng 1929). At the same time, when the first generation of Dutch-educated Balinese were assessing their identity, they used the word *agama* in the sense of "religion," as they were attempting to promote their own religion on a par with Islam and Christianity in an attempt to resist their proselytism. The fact is that *agama* could not become a boundary marker for the Balinese people until they began to view Islam and Christianity as a threat.

In that respect, Christianity appears to have posed a different challenge to the Balinese from that of Islam. The Muslim communities that had been living on the island for generations had long been integrated within the indigenous sociocosmic order, to the point that they were perceived as being as Balinese as anyone else. On the contrary, when Christian missionaries—first Protestants in the early 1930s, followed a few years later by Catholics—began to make inroads into Balinese villages, the new converts were expelled from their *desa adat* as they refused to discharge their ritual obligations to the village deities. Subsequently, in order to enable Christian families to stay in their village of origin, it became necessary to distinguish between domains of interaction in which "religion" was relevant and others where it was not, thus bringing about a conceptual differentiation between ritual and social spheres.

For the Balinese, however, Islam and Christianity were seen not only as a threat but also as a model of what a true religion should be. Confronted with Muslim schoolteachers and Christian missionaries, they were challenged to formulate what exactly their religion was about. This proved to be a highly contentious issue that triggered a protracted conflict between those Balinese who wished to retain their local traditions and those who wanted to reform them in accordance with what they assumed to be Hinduism. The conflict arose in the 1920s, when the rising elite of educated commoners opposed the conservative nobility in their attempt to hold sway over the religious life of the Balinese people. While the nobility were determined to strengthen both tradition and religion, the commoners wanted to reform *agama* while cleansing *adat* of all the customs they deemed obsolete. Thus for the nobility Balinese religion was based on tradition from which it could not be separated, whereas for the commoners religion should be dissociated from a traditional order seen as an impediment to progress. Yet they proved unable to differentiate between that which belonged to *agama* and that which pertained to *adat* (Picard 2004).

From *Agama Hindu Bali* to *Agama Hindu* and Back

Once they had become Indonesian citizens, the Balinese were compelled to distinguish explicitly between religion and tradition. In order for their rites to accede to the status of *agama*, they had to be detached from what was considered to belong to the domain of *adat*. This process amounted to a twofold invention: in the first place, that of a "Balinese religion" (*agama Bali*), and in the second, that of the Balinese religion as "Hinduism" (*agama Hindu*).

The Balinese had formerly no generic name to designate that which would later on become their "religion." Once they had adopted the word *agama* for this purpose, they referred to their religion simply as *agama Bali*. Afterwards, Balinese started using a variety of names for their religion, such as *agama Tirta*, *agama Siwa*, *agama Buda*, *agama Siwa-Buda*, *Kasewasogatan*, *agama Hindu Bali*, *agama Bali Hindu*, and *agama Hindu*.[4] Thus, the first question to be settled was for the Balinese leaders to agree on the name of their religion. After lengthy debates, they resolved in 1952 to call the Balinese religion *agama Hindu Bali*. At the same time, they adopted the name Sang Hyang Widi to designate the one and only God of the *agama Hindu Bali*. It appears that it was only after Balinese had started to convert to Islam as well as to Christianity that the name *agama Hindu Bali* became customary, in order to distinguish *Hindu Bali* from *Islam Bali* or *Kristen Bali*.

However, even if the Balinese had finally reached an agreement among themselves, they still had to convince the KAGRI of the legitimacy of the *agama Hindu Bali*. Consequently, during the following years, they kept pressing for the recognition of their religion. While some religious leaders were looking for the seeds of regeneration in their own indigenous traditions, young Balinese who were studying in India urged their coreligionists to return to the fold of Hinduism, which they presented as the source of their rites. Stressing the theological import as well as the ethical purport of religion, they attempted to restrain the Balinese ritualistic leanings while construing their Hindu heritage in accordance with Islam and Christianity.

In 1958, a *Hindu Bali* section was finally established within the KAGRI, a few weeks after Bali had become a full-fledged province of the Republic of Indonesia (Picard 2011a). The next step was to decide who should be in charge of the *agama Hindu Bali*, now that the former kings, who had previously been the patrons of the main rituals on the island, had been replaced by the republican government. For that purpose, a council was set up in 1959 to coordinate the religious activities of the Hindu Balinese—the Parisada Dharma Hindu Bali (Bakker 1993, 225–91).

The Parisada's strategy was to promote internal homogeneity in the practice of Balinese religion in order to present a united front as a Hindu minority in a predominantly Muslim nation. With the backing and subsidies of the provincial government, the Parisada undertook to translate Indic sacred scriptures, compile a theological canon (*Panca Çraddha*) (Punyatmadja 1970), publish a Hindu catechism (*Upadeśa*) (Mantra et al. 1967), devise a Hindu prayer (*Tri Sandya*) as an equivalent of daily Islamic prayers, standardize rituals, formalize the priesthood, and provide religious education to the population. This endeavor amounted to a "scripturalization" of Balinese religion, a shift in focus from ritual to text and from a collective to a personal experience of religion. Unlike the kings and the priests of yore who merely interceded on behalf of their subjects and clients, the Parisada was now instructing the Balinese on what to believe and how to practice their religion.

Such a Hinduization of indigenous ritual practices rested on a democratization of religious knowledge that constituted a drastic break with traditional ideas of forbidden knowledge, as the Balinese had to understand their religion in order to be able to defend it from the questioning of followers of other religions.[5] Thus, for the first time, Balinese individuals other than priests and literati were enjoined to find in their religion a logically coherent set of moral values and theological tenets. Furthermore, the newly instituted monotheism implied that, instead of transactions with multiple entities from the *niskala* world, Balinese Hindus were expected to establish a personal relationship of faith and devotion with their one and exclusive God—Sang Hyang Widi. This in turn entailed a two-fold differentiation, between "gods" (*dewa-dewi*) and "ancestors" (*leluhur*) as well as between the "divine" and the "demonic." While there were formerly no clear lines of demarcation between ancestors and gods but instead hierarchical ideas of less and more purified ancestors who eventually became merged with divinities, now there had to be an absolute dichotomy between human ancestors and a transcendent God. Besides, whereas *niskala* entities were inherently ambivalent, potentially benevolent as well as malevolent, Sang Hyang Widi had become an entirely positive figure.

During the 1960s, the growing presence of Balinese communities outside their own island enabled the Parisada to extend its influence across the archipelago. Cut off from their temple networks as well as from their deified ancestors, these Balinese migrants needed a delocalized and scriptural religion that they could carry with them. In these circumstances, the Parisada leaders who had studied in India advocated giving up the exclusive label *Hindu Bali* in favor of the inclusive *Hindu Dharma*, in order to strengthen the position of their religion vis-à-vis Islam and Christianity. As a result, during its first congress, in 1964, the Parisada Dharma Hindu Bali changed its name to Parisada Hindu Dharma, forsaking any reference to its Balinese origins.

Thus it is that, through their struggle to obtain the recognition of their religion, the Balinese came to define their ethnic identity in terms of *agama Hindu*. This official version of the Balinese religion—deterritorialized and individualized, where the focus is on orthodoxy to the detriment of orthopraxy—bears little resemblance to everyday rites in house and village temples. Yet it appears that the gap between actual ritual practices and the normative definition of the Balinese religion has been progressively narrowing down. This is the result of the increasing organizational efficiency of the Parisada, which allowed its instructions, endorsed by the state apparatus—in particular by the education system—and conveyed by the media, to penetrate Balinese society at village level. Accordingly, generations of Balinese children have been taught that they are Hindus and they came to believe that *agama Hindu* has always been their religious tradition, that which distinguishes the Balinese people as a non-Muslim and non-Christian minority within the Indonesian multireligious nation.

However, it is precisely from the moment the Balinese began to identify themselves as a Hindu island in a Muslim archipelago that one can date the premises of a disjunction between their religious and ethnic identities. This is because their identification of ethnicity and religion would soon be foiled by a twofold process of Indonesianization-*cum*-Indianization: on the one hand, the affiliation of other Indonesian ethnic groups with *agama Hindu* dissociated it from the Balinese, while on the other hand, the growing influence of Indian neo-Hinduism on *agama Hindu* rendered the link between religion and ethnicity ever more problematic for the Balinese.

Once detached from any ethnic reference, *agama Hindu* was no longer the sole property of the Balinese people, who had to open it up to other ethnic groups. Its official recognition brought new recruits in the wake of the anticommunist massacres of 1965–66, which provoked the "conversion" to *agama Hindu* of Javanese nominal Muslims (*abangan*) for fear of being branded "atheists," an accusation synonymous with "communists" in Indonesia. In the following years, several ethnic minorities took refuge in the Hindu fold hoping to be allowed to conserve their ancestral rites, *agama Hindu* being reputedly more accommodating in this respect than Islam or Christianity (Ramstedt 2004).

The diffusion of *agama Hindu* outside Bali continued to such an extent that the Balinese began to fear a loss of control over the religion that they had themselves established.[6] But what appeared to some Balinese as the dispossession of their own religion was perceived by other Indonesian Hindus as a Balinese "colonization." Hence the rising of a twofold tension between the Balinization of the religious practices of various ethnic groups affiliated with *agama Hindu* and the Indonesianization of the Balinese religion aimed at detaching it from its ethnic origins.

It did not take long for this tension to affect the Parisada itself, with a growing presence in its leadership of both non-Balinese Hindus and Balinese living outside of their island. After having established branches in every province of the country, at the time of its fifth congress in 1986, the Parisada Hindu Dharma became the Parisada Hindu Dharma Indonesia. As a consequence, a regional branch was opened in Bali, the Parisada Hindu Dharma Indonesia Provinsi Bali. Eventually, in 1996, at the time of the seventh congress and despite opposition from Balinese delegates, the Parisada headquarters were relocated from Bali to Jakarta, leaving only the Balinese branch on the island.

In the 1990s, the Islamic resurgence in Indonesia aroused Balinese apprehension and triggered in mimetic fashion a "Hindu revival" (*Kebangkitan Hindu*) (Setia 1993). This revival was marked by an extension of the Parisada's reach throughout the whole of Indonesia. As an example, starting in 1990, the national celebration of Nyepi, the Saka new year, was held in the ancient Hindu temple of Prambanan in Central Java with government officials in attendance. Another development was the consecration in 1992 of a new Hindu sanctuary, the Pura Mandara Giri Semeru Agung, on the slopes of mount Semeru in East Java, regarded as a replica of the mythical mount Mahameru in India. This new temple was meant to be a *pura kahyangan jagat* ("world sanctuary"), implying that it was destined for the whole of the Hindu community in Indonesia. Thereafter, on the Parisada's initiative, other *pura kahyangan jagat* were erected in various regions populated by significant Hindu minorities.

While the Parisada was thus building up its national credentials, the Balinese religious identity was becoming ever more fragmented. From then on, neither the traditional religion, attached to the correct execution of rites, nor its official version, concerned with ethics and theology, were able to meet the aspirations of a growing Balinese middle class, in quest of religious devotion and personal conviction as well as universalism. No longer satisfied with a nationally recognized religion, Balinese reformers undertook to universalize their religious identity by fully embracing Hinduism as a world religion. They initiated a renewed turn toward India, marked by the promotion of Indic concepts and practices such as vegetarianism or the performance of the revived Vedic ritual *Agnihotra*. Pilgrimages (*tirta yatra*) were organized to the holy sites of India where Indonesian Hindus were urged to look for their religious sources in the manner of Muslims going on the *hajj* to Mecca. Most of all, this rapprochement with India was marked by the establishment in Indonesia of neo-Hindu devotional movements (*sampradaya*), the most popular of which are Sai Baba and Hare Krishna. The propagation of these movements was met with some opposition from the KAGRI as well as from the Parisada, who feared the rise of conflicts between rival sects that could undermine the Hindu community.

The fall of President Suharto in 1998 unleashed a spate of ethnic and religious identity politics that led to strife within the Parisada on the occasion of its eighth national congress in September 2001. The Balinese branch of the Parisada objected to some of the decisions adopted by the congress, namely the nomination of a layman to the Parisada's chairmanship, which had until then been monopolized by *brahmana* high priests (*pedanda*), not to mention the massive presence in its direction of commoners and non-Balinese as well as prominent members of *sampradaya*. In November of the same year, the Balinese Parisada convened its own congress at Campuan, near Ubud. Accusing the national leadership of undermining Balinese identity by unduly Indianizing *agama Hindu*, the Campuan congress refused the admission of *sampradaya* into the Parisada and demanded the nomination of a *pedanda* as chairman.

Soon afterward, the central Parisada disowned the Parisada Campuan and convened a competing regional congress in March 2002 at Besakih, the main sanctuary on the island. After the Besakih congress had duly ratified the decisions of the eighth national congress, the Parisada Besakih was acknowledged as the official Balinese branch of the Parisada. During the following years, each of the two Balinese Parisada claimed to be the legitimate representative of the Balinese Hindu community. While the Parisada Besakih had the support of the middle-class urban intelligentsia and those Balinese living outside of the island, the Parisada Campuan appeared to be more aligned with the village population.

In 2007, the Parisada Campuan convened its own congress, which decided to return to the "true self" (*jati diri*) of the Balinese religion—that is, to *agama Hindu Bali*. At the same time, the congress resolved to revert to the name originally chosen by their founding fathers, Parisada Dharma Hindu Bali, thus reversing the globalization of the Balinese religion by relocalizing it. This return to *agama Hindu Bali* reveals itself to be much more than a withdrawal into Balinese parochialism on the part of a group of die-hard reactionaries, as contended by their opponents. The split in the Balinese Parisada illustrates a divide centered on two interrelated issues: the desire of preserving *brahmana*'s priestly authority on the one hand and the challenge to Balinese control over *agama Hindu* in Indonesia on the other. Its promoters attempted to put an end to the dispossession of their religion by winning back the direction of the Parisada, which had been lost to them since the 1990s, as demonstrated by the displacement of the Parisada's center from Bali to Jakarta, the increasing ascendancy of non-Balinese and non-*brahmana* within its leadership, and its inclusion of the *sampradaya* aimed at "purifying" traditional Balinese ritual practices (Picard 2011b).

In recent years, the conflict between the two Balinese factions appears to have faded somewhat, although the reasons for the initial outbreak have yet to be properly addressed. Be that as it may, the comeback of *agama Hindu Bali* might be understood as a return to a meaning of *agama* untainted by its Islamic and Christian interpretations, when *agama* had not yet been separated from *adat*. One could say that the Parisada Dharma Hindu Bali reclaimed the power to identify as *agama* that which pertained to *adat* for the Parisada Hindu Dharma Indonesia, just as the latter had claimed the power to designate as *agama* that which the KAGRI had classified as *adat*. Indeed, with *agama Hindu* construed as a world religion, it is not surprising that the Balinese would seek refuge in their *adat*, seen as the core of their Balineseness (*Kebalian*). Thus, a two-way process has been taking place: concurrently to the normative universalization of *agama Hindu*, there has been a revival of *adat Bali* with its associated ritual practices.

From *Kebalian* to *Ajeg Bali*

The return to *agama Hindu Bali* attests to a tension over Balinese identity, noticeable since the 1990s. This tension is due in particular to the increasing heterogeneity of the island's population since the development of tourism prompted a massive influx of labor migrants in search of a better livelihood—Muslims from Java, Madura, and Lombok for the most part, referred to as "outsiders" (*pendatang*). The growing presence of Muslims on Bali has created resentment among Balinese Hindus. While they had long been aware of being an ethnic and religious minority in Indonesia, now they were beginning to fear that they might become a minority on their own island. This Balinese predicament has been further compounded by the politicization of Islam sparked by the demise of the New Order, which fueled a series of confrontations between Hindu Balinese and Muslim hardliners.

It is thus in the context of an already tense situation that a series of bomb blasts shook the beach resort of Kuta in 2002. The attack was seen by the Balinese as a punishment from their gods. Too busy chasing the tourist dollars, they had disregarded their moral values and neglected their religious duties. Accordingly, they responded to the bombing with intensified religious fervor. A series of public rituals and prayers were convened, culminating with a highly mediatized purification ceremony intended to cleanse the site of the bloodbath from all trace of pollution and to restore the cosmic order by liberating the souls of the dead victims from their earthly bonds. As a result, the Balinese managed to appropriate the traumatic event by accommodating it within their own frame of reference.

Given the tensions on the island, one could have expected a backlash by Hindu Balinese against Muslim communities when it transpired that the bombing had been committed in the name of Islam. That this did not happen is mostly due to the calls for restraint from provincial authorities and tourism stakeholders, aware that any intercommunal strife might destroy the island's prospect of getting tourists back. Nevertheless, besides some rather ineffective attempts at closing the island to outsiders, the feeling of insecurity caused by the bombing brought about an exclusionary assertion of Balineseness. During the ensuing months, a party of journalists, academics, and politicians launched the slogan *Ajeg Bali*, which translates as "Bali Erect" (Satria Naradha 2004).

According to its promoters, the aim of the *Ajeg Bali* campaign was about preserving Balinese culture, so that Bali would not lose its *Kebalian*. The critical situation of Bali was due not only to the bombing but also to the fact that the Balinese people had lost control of their island, which was exploited by foreign investors, invaded by immigrant workers, and threatened by Islam and Christianity (Burhanuddin 2008). The Balinese authorities were urged to take advantage of the laws on regional autonomy to fight for a special autonomy (*otonomi khusus*) status for the province. If Aceh had been able to obtain a special autonomy on account of Islam, Bali should get it as well, since it is an island of Hinduism surrounded by a sea of Islam. Yet, despite lobbying on the part of Balinese parliamentary representatives in Jakarta, the request for a special autonomy status has not been granted to Bali thus far.

Ajeg Bali differed markedly from previous articulations of Balinese identity. On the one hand, since the bombing the Balinese have felt under siege and their plea has had a stronger sense of urgency than ever before, thus reacting by fostering an exclusive ethnic and religious identification that reflected a sense of disenfranchisement and a desire for self-empowerment. On the other hand, far from inducing the Balinese people to close ranks in the face of external threats, *Ajeg Bali* gave rise to criticism from various quarters on the island.

Progressive public intellectuals reproached *Ajeg Bali* for freezing Balinese society by preserving outdated customs and values that buttressed abusive privileges of traditional elites whose power had been jeopardized by the reforms of the post-Suharto period. They denounced a xenophobic ideology that fostered primordial ethnic and religious identification by erecting boundaries between Balinese and non-Balinese and by sparking Hindu fundamentalism as a response to Islamic pressure.

Whereas progressive intellectuals associated *Ajeg Bali* with the rise of Hindu fundamentalism, Hindu religious leaders accused its promoters of fostering Balinese cultural and ethnic identity to the detriment of the Hindu religion. According to them, if the purpose of *Ajeg Bali* was to preserve Balinese culture, then it concerned Muslim and Christian Balinese as much as it did Hindu Balinese. If this were the case, Bali was doomed to meet with the same fate as Java after the coming of Islam, when the Javanese discarded their religion while holding to their culture. Conversely, if the aim was to defend the Balinese religion against the intrusion of Islam and Christianity, *Ajeg Hindu* should be promoted instead (Picard 2009).

The slogan *Ajeg Bali* is now mostly a thing of the past. However, the problems it was meant to address have not disappeared, as the encroachment of Islam and Christianity on Bali is more noticeable than ever. Hence, in recent years, Balinese religious leaders have taken new initiatives to defend *agama Hindu* against Muslim and Christian proselytism.

Hinduism under Siege

The fact is that *agama Hindu* is threatened not only by the settling of Muslim immigrants in Bali but also by the conversion of Balinese to Islam and Christianity. Over the past decades the proportion of Balinese Hindus has been decreasing sharply. While in 1990, 93.1 percent of the population of Bali declared themselves Hindus and 5.2 percent Muslims, in 2010, the figures were respectively 83.5 and 13.6 percent (with some 2 percent Christians of various denominations).[7] As assessed by the first Dutch census, in 1920 the breakdown was estimated to be 97.84 percent Bali Hindu, 1.38 percent Bali Islam, and 0.78 percent Indonesians from elsewhere (Swellengrebel 1960, 6).

Whatever the validity of such figures, it is clear that Hindu Balinese see them-selves as being in decline on their own island. Some religious leaders even go so far as to accuse the KAGRI of deliberately weakening the position of *agama Hindu* in Bali, for the reason that its subsidies are allocated according to the national breakdown of adherents to each of the recognized religions. Thus, the largest portion of the budget of the Balinese Regional Office for Religion (Kanwil Kementerian Agama Provinsi Bali) is granted to Muslims, while Hindus, Prot-estants, Catholics, and Buddhists have to share the remainder. Similarly, crit-ics denounce the KAGRI for appointing more Muslim religious teachers than Hindu instructors and for opening more Muslim schools than Hindu schools in the province. Furthermore, they take issue with the fact that other religions are allowed to establish numerous places of worship in Bali, whereas Hindus are hindered from doing the same outside of the island. As a matter of fact, since the 1990s there has been a sharp increase in funding by the KAGRI for the construc-tion of mosques in Bali, where they have multiplied.

Along with the growing Islamization of Indonesia, the Balinese people have recently faced repeated Islamic interference in their own affairs. Thus in 2011 Balinese media expressed concern over the popularity among Indonesian Mus-lims of pilgrimages to graves said to be the resting places of seven Muslim saints in Bali—the *Walipitu*. These were seen as "sacred sites" (*keramat*) from which Bali was due to be Islamized, in the same way that Java had been Islamized by nine legendary saints—the *Walisongo*. According to Muslim activists, the history of Islam in Java, when Hinduism had to yield to Islam after the fall of Majapahit, was going to repeat itself in Bali. Indeed, most Indonesian Muslim organizations support a policy of conversion of the Balinese people, and one observes a disturb-ing progression of radical Islamist movements on the island.

Then, in 2014, the government promulgated the Law on Halal Product Cer-tification, which asserted that all products traded in Indonesia must be *halal*-certified (permissible according to Islamic law). Thereafter, numerous food stalls appeared on the island bearing the sign *Warung Halal*. Some Balinese reacted by putting up the sign *Warung 100% Haram* (prohibited according to Islamic law) on their food stalls. Then a prominent Balinese Hindu activist launched the so-called Sukla Satyagraha movement. He wanted to certify Balinese food stalls with the label *sukla* ("ritually pure") in order to persuade the Balinese people to patronize the *Warung Sukla* instead of the *Warung Halal*. His initiative gave rise to heated public debate, with Balinese religious figures claiming that *sukla* food should be offered only to deities or ancestors rather than being sold to human consumers.

The latest Islamic slight to Balinese identity dates back to February 2019, when Sandiaga Uno, the running mate to the presidential candidate Prabowo

Subianto, declared that Bali should become a *halal* tourism destination. This declaration generated an uproar on the island, whose officials, from the governor to the head of tourism, abruptly refused to develop *halal* tourism, arguing that Bali was a Hindu island, known the world over as a destination of cultural tourism (*Pariwisata Budaya*).

Yet, despite increasing Islamic pressure, the Balinese appear to aim their denunciations more willingly at the proselytism of Christian Churches than at Islamic *dakwah* (attempt to improve public behavior in line with Islamic standards). No doubt it might be less risky for Hindus to lash out at another minority religion rather than at Islam. In any event, the fact is that the debates on the evangelization of the Balinese people have multiplied in the last two decades. The contention is particularly acute regarding the appropriation of symbols and references that the Balinese Hindus consider to be legitimately theirs. While initially Christian missionaries demanded that the new converts destroy their family shrines and cut off any link with Balinese customary activities, in the 1970s Balinese Christians sought a religious practice more in tune with their ethnic culture. They opted for using music and dance and for wearing traditional Balinese costumes in church contexts, and they started building their churches in the Balinese architectural style. Such a "Balinization" of Christianity has aroused the hostility of Hindu Balinese, who accuse it of blurring the boundaries between Christians and Hindus in order to facilitate conversions. The problem is that what Christian Balinese regard as being part of culture (*budaya*), and in this respect as belonging to all Balinese, is deemed by Hindu Balinese to pertain to religion (*agama*) and therefore their exclusive property (Surpi Aryadharma 2011).

In order to prevent conversions as well as to bring back the victims of conversion to the fold of *agama Hindu*, a group of Balinese Hindu activists, priests, and academics founded in June 2018 the Forum for the Advocacy of Hinduism (Forum Advokasi Hindu Dharma). They were intent on protecting the rights of Hindus and defending them against "insults" (*pelecehan*) and "attacks" (*serangan*) perpetrated by followers of other religions. They demanded that the heads of all government bodies in Bali be bona fide Hindus. And they announced their aim to build up solidarity and unity among Hindus worshipers all over Indonesia, very much along the lines of majoritarian Muslims (see contributions by Hefner and Jones in this volume). But they do not appear to have been particularly active so far.

Then, in December 2018, an international conference was held in Denpasar on the theme "Hinduism is under Siege" (*Hindu Dalam Kepungan*). The speakers denounced both Muslim and Christian proselytizing while deploring the fact that Balinese have no qualms about converting to either Islam or Christianity.

They willingly acknowledged that such conversions are due not only to the zeal of missionary religions but also to the shortcomings of Balinese religious practices. They blamed the excessive complexity of traditional rituals and their exorbitant cost, to the extent that their religion has become a burden for the Balinese people. This, they said, is because Balinese just go about blindly practicing their rites without trying to understand their meaning, an accusation already made by religious reformers in the 1920s. In order to prevent further conversions, they urged the Parisada to simplify rituals while providing a religious education that stresses ethics and theology in order to strengthen the faith of Balinese Hindus. By learning what Hinduism truly is, they would become proud of their own religion and would then be able to defend it against the proselytism of Abrahamic religions.

Be that as it may, it appears that so far such admonitions have had only a very limited effect on Balinese religious practices.

Bali as the World Center of Hinduism

A very ambitious initiative was taken a few years ago to strengthen the position of *agama Hindu* in Indonesia. After the Balinese had successfully managed to convince the KAGRI to acknowledge *agama Hindu* as a proper monotheistic religion, they sought to persuade Indian Hindus that they truly represented a local branch of Hinduism. To this end, the Parisada affiliated itself with the World Hindu Federation, an umbrella organization established in 1981 in Nepal under the patronage of King Birendra to coordinate the activities of Hindu-based movements all over the world.

The World Hindu Federation was seriously compromised by the abolition of the Nepalese monarchy in 2008. Its leaders have been trying to revive their organization ever since, and the Parisada's chairman, following the tenth national congress in 2011, seized the opportunity to meet with the World Hindu Federation's leadership in India. They decided to launch a new organization with a view to uniting Hindus throughout the world, equivalent to the Organization of Islamic Cooperation. For this purpose, a World Hindu Summit was convened by the Parisada in 2012 on Bali, attended by delegates from wide-ranging Hindu organizations. They issued the Bali Charter, which resolved to set up a World Hindu Centre in Denpasar, in charge of implementing a World Hindu Parisad, "an organization to unify Hindus, coordinate activities and propagate Hindu Dharma globally" (*The Bali Charter*, June 9, 2012). A working committee was set up to implement the resolutions of the Bali Charter, assisted by a board of advisors, manned mostly by Balinese, with a handful of Indians representing various institutions, ashrams, and *sampradaya*, such as the Vishva Hindu Parishad, the

Arya Samaj, the International Society for Krishna Consciousness, Sri Sathya Sai Baba, Brahma Kumaris, the Sri Aurobindo Centre, the Art of Living, etc. All Hindu organizations were welcome to become members of the World Hindu Parisad, with no restrictions whatsoever.

A second World Hindu Summit was convened in 2013, which officialized the foundation of both the World Hindu Centre and the World Hindu Parisad, with the head of the Parisada named president. It was decided to organize annual meetings in Bali, oddly named "World Hindu Wisdom Meet," to discuss problems and challenges facing Hindus around the world and to provide the required solutions to address them.[8] Besides the publication of the proceedings of these meetings, the World Hindu Centre has launched a wide-ranging publishing program in both Indonesian and English.

It was initially planned to establish the World Hindu Centre on land belonging to the provincial government. Until that day, which is not foreseen in the near future, the World Hindu Parisad is accommodated in the Provincial Office for Culture (Dinas Kebudayaan Provinsi Bali) in Denpasar. Its funding is shouldered by the provincial budget until hypothetical subventions from the relevant Hindu stakeholders can take over. In the meantime, its Balinese initiators have been forced to admit that their human and financial resources are extremely limited. One may have an idea of their difficulties when one consults the World Hindu Parisad's website, which is seldom updated.

According to its leaders, the launching of the World Hindu Parisad was aimed at providing the Balinese with international backing against the growing pressure of Islam in Indonesia by securing institutional ties with powerful global Hindu networks. However, it is rather doubtful whether the Balinese are up to the task, as the discrepancy between the World Hindu Parisad's stated objectives and its available means is glaring. Not only are the Balinese riddled by division and beset by poor managing skills but some of the island's religious leaders are openly dismissive of the whole enterprise. They point out that the Parisada is not even able to properly manage *agama Hindu* in Balinese villages—how then can it hope to champion Hinduism worldwide?

Religionization

Since the colonial takeover of their island, the Balinese have increasingly been subjected to the perspectives of powerful outsiders, with whom they had to engage. Not only did they have to face the disruption of the references that ordered their lives but in addition they were confronted with alien discourses telling them who they were and how they should conduct themselves. Thus while the upheaval inflicted by the colonial occupation of their island was compelling the Balinese to question the foundations of their identity, the inquisitive gaze of foreigners in their midst impelled them to explicitly account for the definition of what it meant to be Balinese in terms comprehensible to non-Balinese.

Confronted with such intrusive interferences, Balinese opinion leaders, ashamed of how some of their customs were perceived by outsiders, became defensive. By internalizing outside points of view, they were forced to reflect on their ritual practices, which they eventually came to formulate as enactments of "Hinduism." Defence of particular practices became conflated with a defensiveness toward "Balinese religion" (Johnsen 2007)—as we saw when the Balinese construed various moves by Muslims or Christians as an "insult" against *agama Hindu.*

As the dominant religion in Indonesia, Islam has served as a model for the definition of "Balinese religion" as *agama Hindu.* Indeed, long before the KAGRI imposed its requirements for the recognition of their religion, Balinese reformers had already appropriated the Islamic conception of what a true religion should be. One could refer to the KAGRI's requirements as "religion-making from above," whereas the Balinese construction of their own religion could be qualified as "religion-making from below" (Mandair and Dressler 2011, 21–22). In that respect, Indonesian religious politics can be labelled "religionization" (*agamasasi*) (Hefner 2011, 72–73), implying that followers of local traditions are "not yet religious" and must therefore be "*agama*-ized"—meaning that they could, and should, be a target of proselytizing.

Accordingly, one should distinguish between, on the one hand, the enforcement of certain religious policies by state institutions and, on the other hand, the determination of a particular ethnic group to legitimate its religious identity. While there are negative incentives for people to affiliate with a world religion— such as the Balinese decision to embrace Hinduism in order to counter the threat of Islamic proselytizing—there are also positive motivations, since the claim that one represents a local branch of a world religion can bring access to influential global networks—which is what happened with the Balinese creation of the World Hindu Parisad. Yet there are potentially negative consequences as well, since the compulsion to define their identity in religious terms compels peoples to determine what is acknowledged as a legitimate exercise of religion and what is not. This is likely to provoke a tension between proponents of indigenous ritual practices, who consider these practices to be self-sufficient and deserving of the label "religion" in their own right, and advocates of a world religion, who deny such local traditions the qualification of "religion." In fact, this tension may coexist within the same actors, who are faced with the predicament of having to integrate both their own indigenous traditions and their newly adopted world religion into the same sociocosmic order. What constitutes "religion" is thus ideologically contested, as this category is subject to power struggles, deployed by competing sets of actors to particular ends within specific social and political contexts.

Notes

1. In the *Dharmaśāstra*, the word *dharma* refers specifically to the *varnāśramadharma*, the duties and qualifications of an individual according to his social class (*varna*) and stage of life (*āśrama*).

2. Before being glossed as "religion" in Islam, the word *dīn*—which signifies "practice, custom, law"—referred to the body of obligatory prescriptions to which one must submit.

3. Rather than conceiving an explicit polarity between the sacred and the profane, Balinese differentiate two complementary fields of experience—the manifest world (*sakala*, "what lies within the bounds of human sensorial perception") and the unmanifest world (*niskala*, "that which lies beyond the realm of the senses") (Rubinstein 2000, 49).

4. *Agama Tirta* refers to the holy water required for most rituals. *Agama Siwa* and *agama Buda* pertain to the two categories of *brahmana* priests—the *pedanda Siwa* and the *pedanda Buda*—while *agama Siwa-Buda* and *Kasewasogatan* point more specifically to the Tantric combination of Shaivism and Buddhism that originated in East Java in the thirteenth century. Lastly, one finds *agama Hindu Bali*, *agama Bali Hindu*, and *agama Hindu*.

5. Traditionally in Bali, knowledge was perceived as dangerous, inasmuch as it was dealing with the mysterious powers of the world beyond the senses (*niskala*). Hence manuscripts treating religious matters were shrouded in secrecy and protected by prohibitions. Their access was restricted to those persons who had been duly purified and had acquired the appropriate skills to study them, thereby becoming immune to hazardous forces from the *niskala* world.

6. It is rather difficult to know the number of adherents to *agama Hindu* in Indonesia, inasmuch as the religious composition of the population is a politically contentious matter. According to the census of 2010, there were around four million Hindus in Indonesia, a figure disputed by the Directorate of Hinduism at the KAGRI, which puts the number at roughly ten million, while the Parisada claims that they are eighteen million. As stated by the census, Hindus composed 1.69 percent of the Indonesian population and 83.5 percent of the population of Bali. However, in the opinion of most Balinese religious leaders, the proportion of Hindus is deliberately underestimated at the national level, whereas it is overestimated for Bali so as to prevent the Balinese people from knowing the true weight of the Muslim population on their island.

7. The majority of the Balinese Christians belong to the Gereja Kristen Protestan di Bali. A significant proportion of the Roman Catholic community (Gereja Katolik) in Bali consists of immigrants from other islands, particularly Flores.

8. The following themes have been chosen for these yearly meetings: *Hinduism Based Education* (2014), *Hindu Dharma Based Education* (2015), *Hindu Dharma Contributions to the World Civilization and Science* (2016), *Para and Apara Vidya as the Basic Hindu Body of Knowledge* (2017), *Hindu for Better Life* (2018).

References

Bakker, Frederik Lambertus. 1993. *The Struggle of the Hindu Balinese Intellectuals: Developments in Modern Hindu Thinking in Independent Indonesia.* Amsterdam: VU University Press.

Burhanuddin, Yudhis M. 2008. *Bali Yang Hilang: Pendatang, Islam dan Ethnisitas di Bali.* Yogyakarta: Penerbit Kanisius.

Gonda, Jan. (1952) 1973. *Sanskrit in Indonesia.* New Delhi: International Academy of Indian Culture.

Hefner, Robert W. 2011. "Where Have All the *Abangan* Gone? Religionization and the Decline of Non-standard Islam in Contemporary Indonesia." In *The Politics of Religion in Indonesia: Syncretism, Orthodoxy, and Religious Contention in Java and Bali*, edited by Michel Picard and Rémy Madinier, 71–91. London: Routledge.

Johnsen, Scott A. 2007. "From Royal House to Nation: The Construction of Hinduism and Balinese Ethnicity in Indonesia." PhD diss., Department of Anthropology, University of Virginia.

Kadjeng, I Njoman. 1929. "Voorloopig overzicht der op Bali aanwezige literatuurschat." *Mededeelingen van de Kirtya Liefrinck—van der Tuuk* 1: 19–40.

Mandair, Arvind-Pal S., and Markus Dressler. 2011. "Introduction: Modernity, Religion-Making, and the Postsecular." In *Secularism and Religion-Making*, edited by Markus Dressler and Arvind-Pal S. Mandair, 3–36. Oxford: Oxford University Press.

Picard, Michel. 1999. "Making Sense of Modernity in Colonial Bali: The Polemic Between *Bali Adnjana* and *Surya Kanta* (1920s)." *Dinamika Kebudayaan* 1, no. 3: 73–91.

Picard, Michel. 2004. "What's in a Name? *Agama Hindu Bali* in the Making." In *Hinduism in Modern Indonesia: A Minority Religion between Local, National, and Global Interests*, edited by Martin Ramstedt, 56–75. London: RoutledgeCurzon— IIAS Asian Studies Series.

Picard, Michel. 2009. "From *Kebalian* to *Ajeg Bali*: Tourism and Balinese Identity in the Aftermath of the Kuta Bombing." In *Tourism in Southeast Asia: New Perspectives*, edited by Michael Hitchcock, Victor T. King, and Michael J.G. Parnwell, 99–131. Copenhagen: Nias Press and Honolulu: University of Hawai'i Press.

Picard, Michel. 2011a. "Balinese Religion in Search of Recognition: From *agama Hindu Bali* to *agama Hindu* (1945-1965)." *Bijdragen tot de Taal-, Land- en Volkenkunde* 167, no. 4: 482–510.

Picard, Michel. 2011b. "From *agama Hindu Bali* to *agama Hindu* and back: Toward a Relocalization of the Balinese Religion?" In *The Politics of Religion in Indonesia: Syncretism, Orthodoxy, and Religious Contention in Java and Bali*, edited by Michel Picard and Rémy Madinier, 117–41. London: Routledge.

Picard, Michel. 2017. "Balinese Religion in the Making: An Enquiry about the Interpretation of Balinese Religion as 'Hinduism.'" In *Local Traditions and World Religions: The Appropriation of "Religion" in Southeast Asia and Beyond*, edited by Michel Picard, 123–52. New York: Palgrave Macmillan.

Punyatmadja, Ida Bagus Oka. 1970. *Panca Çraddha.* Denpasar: Parisada Hindu Dharma Pusat.

Ramstedt, Martin. 2004. "Introduction: Negotiating Identities—Indonesian 'Hindus' between Local, National, and Global Interests." In *Hinduism in Modern*

Indonesia: *A Minority Religion between Local, National, and Global Interests*, edited by Martin Ramstedt, 1–34. London: RoutledgeCurzon—IIAS Asian Studies Series.

Rubinstein, Raechelle. 2000. *Beyond the Realm of the Senses: The Balinese Ritual of Kekawin Composition.* Leiden: KITLV Press.

Satria Naradha, ABG, ed. 2004. *Ajeg Bali: Sebuah Cita-cita.* Denpasar: Pustaka Bali Post.

Setia, Putu. 1993. *Kebangkitan Hindu Menyongsong Abad ke-21.* Jakarta: Pustaka Manikgeni.

Staal, J. Frits. 1995. *Mantras between Fire and Water: Reflections on a Balinese Rite.* Amsterdam: Koningklijke Nederlandse Akademie van Wetenschappen.

Sudharta, Tjokorda Rai, and Ida Bagus Oka Punia Atmadja. 1967. *Upadeśa Tentang Adjaran-Adjaran Agama Hindu.* Denpasar: Parisada Hindu Dharma.

Surpi Aryadharma, Ni Kadek. 2011. *Membedah Kasus Konversi Agama di Bali.* Surabaya: Paramita.

Swellengrebel, Jan Lodewijk. 1960. "Introduction." In *Bali: Studies in Life, Thought, and Ritual,* edited by Jan Lodewijk Swellengrebel, 1–76. The Hague: W. van Hoeve.

11

DISPELLING MYTHS OF RELIGIOUS PLURALISM

A Critical Look at Maluku and North Maluku

Christopher R. Duncan

On January 5, 2016, the Ministry of Religion announced that it would be recognizing the district of North Halmahera in North Maluku as "an example of religious harmony" (*percontohan kerukunan beragama*) (*Antara* 2016). They based their decision largely on the perception that the Tobelo *adat* practice of *hibualamo* had allowed the people of North Halmahera to overcome enmity and to live in "harmony, peace, [and] mutual respect."[1] Sixteen years before this announcement, North Halmahera had been the site of some of the bloodiest incidents of religious conflict in post-Suharto Indonesia, leaving hundreds of people dead and tens of thousands displaced.[2] Then, in January 2019, the Ministry of Religion selected the city of Ambon (in Maluku), the site of the most prolonged religious conflict in post-Suharto Indonesia and the most violent postconflict province (Barron 2019, 64), as a winner of the Harmony Award. This award was given to Ambon for being one of the cities "with the highest levels of religious harmony" in Indonesia (Kantor Wilayah Kementerian Agama Provinsi Maluku 2019). It would appear, according to the Ministry of Religion at least, that the two provinces of Maluku and North Maluku have started to regain their preconflict reputations as exemplars of religious pluralism and harmony in Indonesia.

The Ministry of Religion's declarations were not unique; North Halmahera has often been lauded as an example of successful peace and reconciliation by the Indonesian media (Saeni 2012; *Sinar Harapan* 2012), Indonesian academics (Thalib et al. 2012), and outside observers (Barron et al. 2009, 328; Braithwaite et al. 2010, 216–21). Even more attention has been paid to the large number of peace building initiatives in Ambon and elsewhere in Maluku aimed at improving interfaith relations and facilitating reconciliation.[3] A large amount of this focus in Maluku has been on cultural approaches to reconciliation such as the revitalization of *pela gandong,* a practice that some analysts argue has been an integral aspect of peace-building.[4]

Due in part to these efforts, regional government officials frequently make public declarations about the positive state of interfaith relations or hold large public festivals celebrating religious harmony. Unfortunately, this rhetoric does not necessarily provide insight into the state of interfaith relations in the region. Can Maluku and North Maluku truly be held up as examples of religious harmony and pluralism? Have the people of these two provinces overcome the animosity and distrust that pervaded the region in the aftermath of the violence in such a short time to become models of religious pluralism for Indonesia? Or is it more a state of religious tolerance, or simple ambivalence, or even passive religious intolerance that pervades the region? To explore these questions this chapter will examine the state of religious pluralism and tolerance in North Maluku and, to a lesser degree, in Maluku. I will look at both interfaith relationships between Muslims, Christians, and followers of indigenous religions and intrafaith relations between Christian denominations and between followers of different forms of Islam.

As most discussions on religious pluralism note, it is important to distinguish between the presence of religious diversity and a deeper religious pluralism that entails mutual respect and positive relationships between communities. To state the obvious, religious pluralism is a concept that needs to be looked at along a continuum. At the minimalist end there is a vision of pluralism as something similar to a simple tolerance of the religious other. In contrast, at the maximalist end are models of pluralism, often coming out of Western contexts, that focus on an active engagement with diversity or that see pluralism as an ethic, rather than a state of affairs (cf. Eck 2007; Patel 2019). In what follows, I will base my discussion on the understanding of pluralism used by Chiara Formichi in the introduction to her volume on pluralism in Asia where she defines religious pluralism as "the transformation of a mere condition of heterogeneity, into a reality where groups representative of this diversity are accepted and integrated as equals" (Formichi 2014, 2). Formichi's conception of pluralism falls somewhere in the middle of the pluralism continuum. It is more than simple tolerance in that she requires communities to move beyond just acknowledging the existence of the religious other and requires integrating them as equals in the community. It does not, however, call to mind more normative understandings of religious pluralism focused on interfaith dialogue or theological understanding of the religious other, which makes it a bit more useful for examining the Indonesian context where such normative ideals are arguably less prevalent in the public sphere. Based on this notion of pluralism, I will argue that despite some positive developments and extraordinary efforts by numerous individuals and organizations, we simply cannot square the reality on the ground with the Pollyannaish proclamations of government officials or the optimistic or hopeful sound bites from the same set of elites and activists frequently interviewed by scholars and journalists looking at issues of pluralism and reconciliation in this part of Indonesia.

A Brief History of Interfaith Relationships in Maluku and North Maluku

Accounts of the communal violence that swept the region at the turn of the century and its aftermath are occasionally prefaced with clichéd statements about earlier periods of religious pluralism. On the ground one is often confronted with nostalgic references to an idealized vision of the preconflict period as a time when religious harmony was the norm. These descriptions, however, do not stand up to historical or ethnographic scrutiny. Although there were numerous genuine examples of inclusivist tendencies, I would argue these were the exceptions rather than the norm. Instead, what many saw as the large-scale acceptance of pluralism was more a mixture of religious tolerance and a significant amount of passive religious intolerance. Scholars of the region who have examined the *longue durée* of interfaith relations in Maluku and North Maluku have noted that religion has long been a point of contention. Although they never reached the levels of the 1999–2002 violence during the postcolonial period, tensions between communities of different faiths, whether based on fears of the religious other, economic concerns, or cultural disputes, had long been prevalent in the region.[5]

Religion has long been an integral part of life in the region in a variety of ways too numerous to explore here, and social and cultural life in both provinces were often organized around religious differences. Furthermore, for a variety of reasons, Christians were concerned for their future due to what they perceived to be the increasing Islamization of Indonesia. Similarly, some Muslims had fears about Christianization. Despite these tensions and the religiously segregated nature of social life, one could find numerous examples of positive interfaith relations. Muslim communities often assisted in the construction of churches, while Christians would do the same with mosque building. Historically, some communities would take part in each other's religious celebrations. Christians would march through the streets of Ternate in North Maluku waking up their Muslim neighbors for *sahur* (a pre-dawn meal that precedes fasting) during Ramadan and would visit them during Idul Fitri. Some Muslims would attend Christmas celebrations or take part in the more extended New Year's festivities associated with that time of year on Halmahera and Morotai. There were also examples of strong *adat* relations between some Christian and Muslim communities, such as among the indigenous people of Kao on Halmahera or various *pela gandong* relationships in central Maluku. Thus there was a certain degree of religious pluralism or tolerance that could be found in the region. This inclusivism, however, had its limits. For example, followers of indigenous religions had long faced religious discrimination, if not outright persecution, from the state and neighboring communities. Furthermore, the rise of exclusivist forms of Islam and Christianity in the latter part of the twentieth century had chipped away at what little religious pluralism existed and had a deleterious effect on religious tolerance.

The violence of 1999–2002 shattered most remaining illusions about widespread religious pluralism in Maluku and North Maluku. This violence began in the city of Ambon on January 19, 1999, when a fight between a Christian bus driver and a Muslim passenger escalated into widespread violence throughout the city. Although initially a conflict between local Christian Ambonese and Muslim migrants, it quickly took on religious overtones pitting Muslim "white" forces against Christian "red" forces.[6] The violence eventually spread throughout Ambon Island and then to other parts of central Maluku. Along similar lines, and linked to events in Ambon, violence erupted on the island of Halmahera in August 1999 in an ethnic dispute between Makianese transmigrants and indigenous groups over a government redistricting plan. This conflict eventually took on a religious character as well, pitting Muslim "white" forces against Christian "red" forces. When the dust settled (in July 2000 in North Maluku, much later in Maluku), thousands of people had been killed and approximately 750,000 more had been displaced from their homes.

Rhetoric vs. Reality: Interfaith Relations in Maluku and North Maluku

In the aftermath of these conflicts, the primary concern with interfaith relations has been on peace, reconciliation, and conflict prevention. Preventing future outbreaks of violence is the primary reason that government authorities and others promote what might be considered a very weak form of religious pluralism, one focused on peaceful coexistence rather than integration as equals, often referred to as religious harmony. Thus, it is difficult to discuss religious pluralism in the region without reference to conflict prevention efforts and issues of reconciliation. These issues are intrinsically linked in the eyes of many Moluccans, particularly religious leaders and activists who have led the struggle for expanding religious pluralism.

North Maluku was one of the first parts of Indonesia to establish what have come to be known as Religious Harmony Forums (Forum Kerukunan Umat Bergama, FKUB) at the provincial and district level. The District of North Halmahera was the first to set up one of these forums. In 2003 the local government established the Communication and Consultation Forum for Religious Communities (Forum Komunikasi dan Konsultasi Umat Beragama) aimed at maintaining religious harmony and mediating disputes that were perceived to involve religion (As'ad 2006, 92). The provincial government in North Maluku followed suit in 2004 with the establishment of a Forum for Interfaith Communication (Forum Komunikasi Antara Umat Beragama) at the provincial level and subsequently at the district level. Similar organizations were set up across Maluku. These forums are aimed primarily at resolving disputes between religious groups, approving (or not approving) the construction of places of worship, and promoting regional stability.[7] These forums have not always been proponents of expanding religious pluralism. For example, in Ternate the FKUB refused to allow a Buddhist community to build a place of worship as they did not meet the threshold of ninety members required by the law (Crouch 2016, 105; see Aragon's contribution to this volume for more on these regulations).

In the last fifteen years local governments at various levels have made numerous efforts, both formal and informal, to promote inclusivism in the region. Some of these proposals have been rather aspirational. In Ambon, the government has made the creation of religiously integrated settlements a priority in its development plans for the future. The goal is to make the towns of Poka and Paso into "plural and multicultural settlement areas" aimed at religious desegregation and to encourage interfaith relationships (NVMS and The Habibie Center 2014, 42). In 2017, the FKUB North Maluku announced similar plans (pending funding) to build Religious Harmony Villages (Kampung Kerukunan Agama) in every district. These villages would sponsor activities that taught community members the value of ensuring religious harmony and tolerance on a daily basis (*Antara* 2017). There have also been efforts to promote pluralism through the educational curriculum in both provinces (cf. Amirrachman 2014; Sapsuha 2013). The Department of Social Affairs has funded Social Harmony Programs (Program Keserasian Sosial) in both provinces since 2006 aimed at promoting inclusivism in part through the construction of shared infrastructure.[8]

Efforts have also been undertaken to revitalize *adat* in order to (re)create social relationships aimed at preventing outbreaks of violence in the future between Muslim and Christian communities. The most well-known example of these have been attempts to reestablish the institution of *pela gandong* throughout central

Maluku. *Pela gandong* refers to traditional alliances between one or more villages, often on different islands and of different faiths. One aspect of these relationships is that villages in these alliances are pledged to assist each other in times of need, such as disaster or war. Proponents argue that the existence of these relationships played a significant role in preventing religious conflict in the past. Many Moluccans now see the revival of *pela gandong* as an integral part of recreating Muslim-Christian unity in central Maluku. Another well-known example is the Tobelo *adat* practice of *hibualamo*. *Hibualamo* refers to the traditional meeting houses that used to be the center of Tobelo villages in North Maluku. These meeting houses supposedly served as spaces for the mediation of conflict and integrated different segments of Tobelo society. In post-conflict Tobelo, some see the revitalization of this tradition and a shift in focus to cultural identity as a path away from future religious conflict (Duncan 2009). These cultural approaches to peace and reconciliation have had some success in improving interfaith relations, but they have been focused primarily on peace building rather than inculcating a sense of pluralism into Moluccan communities.

In Maluku, and particularly in Ambon, there have been numerous civil society initiatives aimed at building interfaith relationships and helping prevent violence. Space does not permit an in-depth analysis of these efforts, which have been analyzed in great detail elsewhere (Al Qurtuby 2016; Fitriyah 2015). Some of these have focused directly on relationships between Islamic clerics and Protestant ministers. Lailatul Fitriyah, who studied Muslim peacebuilders in Ambon, found that some Muslim and Christian leaders were interested in learning more about each other's faith and were willing to attend religious services and discuss religion with their counterparts. She sees this as "the opening of a genuine process of interfaith dialogue" (Fitriyah 2015, 44). She notes that it is unlikely, however, that this opening will expand to include lay people as "there is no systematic effort" to include wider Muslim and Christian society in these sorts of dialogues. In North Maluku, other than the religious elite making the standard calls for religious harmony around the time of major religious holidays, elections, or major cultural events, these sorts of activities appear to be absent.

If we step outside of state institutions and activist and elite circles, this interest in building interfaith relationships or trying to develop an understanding of the faith of the religious other seems to disappear. Despite all of these activities and the associated rhetoric about religious harmony in the region, both official and informal, the state of interfaith relationships still seems more emblematic of a passive tolerance, or even a passive intolerance. In North Maluku, more than a decade since the end of the violence, interfaith relations remain limited. Religion continues to be a defining aspect in most people's lives and continues to shape intergroup dynamics accordingly. Furthermore, issues of distrust still permeate certain segments of the community. Some Christians in Tobelo store their important documents in plastic bags in readily accessible locations in case they have to flee. People still often send their children to university based on the religious demographics of the town where the campus is located. Christians still fear that religious tensions that arise in Jakarta or elsewhere could have an impact on them in Halmahera. On the Muslim side, there are still persistent fears about the intentions of Christians in the region and fears of Christianization. Furthermore, there has not been an upsurge in the embrace of religious pluralism or in the acceptance of the religious other. This should not be surprising—interfaith relations were limited prior to the conflict, so there is no reason to expect their proliferation now. As I have discussed elsewhere (Duncan 2016), many North Moluccans have little desire to expand their interaction with people of other religious faiths. They are content to tolerate their continued presence but have little interest in integrating their lives with them.

Researchers working in Maluku have noted a similar situation. Fitriyah noted that the enthusiasm for religious pluralism is rather limited in Ambon. The Muslims she spoke with were interested in "a formal peace treaty with the Christians, but not in a deeper engagement at the interpersonal level, which is basically the main foundation to achieve a sustainable peace" (Fitriyah 2015, 6). They had little interest in gaining a deeper understanding of their Christian neighbors or increasing their interactions with them. An additional complication documented by Fitriyah (2015, 54–57), at least in Ambon, is the continuing presence of some radical Muslim organizations and individuals in Maluku. One impact of these organizations is the increase in the number of *pesantren* (traditional Islamic boarding school) "with a distinct and clear religious fervor" that are focused on teaching Salafism (Fitriyah 2015, 57).[9] Fitriyah (2015, 57) also notes that these groups encourage the spread of "radical ideas" that "are not conducive for interreligious reconciliation" from several mosques in Ambon and that they pose one of the more significant obstacles to peacebuilders and proponents of religious pluralism in the city. Along similar lines, the anthropologist Sumanto Al Qurtuby (2016, 170) notes that, despite the multiple efforts at peace building and conflict resolution in Ambon and across Maluku province, interfaith relations are "still tense and fragile" and that "ordinary Christians and Muslims still feel insecure and uncomfortable in interaction with opposing religious groups." He goes on to note rather pessimistically that "what has emerged in today's Maluku is a sort of 'pseudo peace'" (Al Qurtuby 2016, 171–73). One wonders how Ambon can be held up as an example of religious harmony or religious pluralism, as many of its leaders have claimed, if communities still fear each other and social life is still largely segregated by choice.

One of the more obvious examples of this juxtaposition between rhetoric and reality happened in Ternate in December 2018 and January 2019. To celebrate the

768th Birthday of Ternate City, the city government organized what they called the Ternate Harmony Parade. The parade, which took place on December 19, was billed as a celebration of diversity and harmony in Ternate. The parade route included stops at several historically important places of worship on the island including the Catholic Church, the Protestant Church of Maluku, the Ibu Suri Agung Chinese temple, and several important mosques. Organizers had chosen the route specifically to highlight the history of religious pluralism in Ternate. Based on an interview with the mayor, the region's largest newspaper concluded that there was a larger "moral message" in the parade that "since ancient times Ternate has lived with many religions and many ethnic groups, but was still peaceful and safe. This history of harmony in Ternate must be maintained and protected for future generations in North Maluku, and especially in Ternate" (*Malut Post* 2018b). Press accounts noted that the parade was welcomed enthusiastically by the community and that thousands of people took to the streets to take part. The mayor hoped the festival would become "a new tourism icon in Ternate" and "improve harmony and togetherness in order to unite all the people of the diverse city of Ternate" (*Malut Post* 2018b).

A few weeks after the Ternate Harmony Parade that had celebrated pluralism, a front-page article in the same paper announced that the Christmas Harmony Celebration (Perayaan Natal Harmoni) that had been scheduled for January 12 in the largely Muslim neighborhood of Bastiong had been cancelled by its organizers after numerous complaints (*Malut Post* 2019). Some Muslims living in Bastiong and Muslim activists from elsewhere in the city had complained that the event should take place in a part of the city that was more representative of the participants and not in "the middle of a Muslim community . . . next to a mosque." These complaints from locals led Muslim organizations to ask the police to move the event to the neighboring island of Halmahera where there were more Christians. In a subsequent letter to the District Chief of Police, MUI (Majelis Ulama Indonesia) Kota Ternate explained they were concerned with the event because they considered it to be a worship service and Muslims should not be included. They did not object to it taking place, simply that it was being staged near a Muslim community. Despite asking for the event to be moved entirely to another island, MUI Kota Ternate noted that as Muslims they strongly believed in religious tolerance, but also noted that "misunderstandings about tolerance can also disturb religious harmony." The juxtaposition of these two events exemplifies that the normative pluralism espoused by the government and the elite does not necessarily reflect how interfaith relations play out in the daily lives of Moluccans.

Thus at the interfaith level it appears that religious pluralism is rather weak. Mistrust still pervades relationships between the two largest religious communities and continues to have an impact on interfaith relations in daily life. At the most one could argue that religious tolerance has returned to the region, but only if we accept a rather minimal definition of religious tolerance that simply requires a lack of open conflict. Locals, for the most part, continue to be far more interested in preventing outbreaks of new violence than embracing any sort of religious pluralism that requires acceptance of the religious other or integration as equals. Outside of elite and activist circles there is little effort, or interest, to understand religious others or to gain new perspectives on their place in the religious diversity of Maluku and North Maluku.

Where Pluralism Goes to Die: Intrafaith Relations in Maluku and North Maluku

Although there have been some positive developments in interfaith relationships between Muslims and Christians, the same cannot be said for intrafaith relations. While the state and its institutions support religious pluralism, that support is limited to a subset of the diversity that actually exists in the region. It extends to the six officially recognized religions, and only certain forms of those. Thus, some of the very same proponents of inclusivism are at the same time active proponents of exclusivism when it comes to other aspects of religious diversity, such as variations in Islamic practice. This paradox is mirrored in society at large, where intrafaith tensions can run high.

As elsewhere in Indonesia, Muslims in the region have long argued over what exactly constitutes the proper practice of Islam. Historically these debates have focused on differences between a reformed moderate Islam and a more traditionalist Islam infused with local practices (Al Qurtuby 2016, 103–4; Kiem 1995; Probojo 2010). In North Maluku these disagreements have long centered on the role of traditional healers or the appropriateness of interaction with various spirits in the region. A more recent development, mirrored elsewhere in Indonesia, has been concerns with the growth of heretical sects (*aliran sesat*) that local communities or authorities see as threats to peace or as heresies that must be stamped out. These anxieties and related violence about heretical sects began at least as far back as 2007 with fears about the presence of Ahmadiyah in the region (Human Rights Working Group 2011). These concerns have led the government and Islamic organizations to play an increasingly active role in monitoring differences within the Islamic community. In the last decade regional authorities have declared that a number of groups, including Gerakan Fajar Nusantara (Gafatar), certain Shia groups, the Gorontalo based Himpunan Ukhuwah Islamiyah Ilomata, and more localized movements, such as Aliran Amanah and Aliran Guru

Bais, are threats to regional stability that need to be eradicated.[10] In some cases, the followers are forced to repent in front of authorities and promise to stop following incorrect teachings and return to the "true path." In more extreme cases, regional branches of the MUI have issued fatwas declaring these groups to be heretical sects. A few cases have seen physical violence between members of these groups and mainstream Muslims, mirroring developments in other areas of the archipelago.

One of the better documented cases concerns a group referred to as Syi'ah Ja'fariyah Ajaran Nawawi Husni.[11] In approximately 2004, a Ternatese man named Nawawi Husni started teaching some of his neighbors about what he said were the teachings of Syi'ah Ja'fariyah (Twelver Shi'is). Starting with five followers, he eventually claimed more than two hundred spread across numerous neighborhoods in Ternate and possibly in the subdistrict of Jailolo on the neighboring island of Halmahera. Community members and the government initially ignored the group since Husni had no formal theological training and neighbors thought it was simply a discussion group. People started to complain when they noticed that his followers were not joining Friday prayers and had become less social. Eventually community members asked him to stop preaching and recruiting new followers. He refused to do so and his house was destroyed by some of his neighbors. In other neighborhoods there were confrontations between his followers and those who opposed his teaching. The negative reaction to the Husni sect at one point led a group of youth to create what they called the Organization of Shia Hunters (Organisasi Pemburu Syi'ah). One observer described them as a large group of rather militant youth who were fervent in their desire to expel Husni's followers from the region and willing "to take any risk [to do so], including imprisonment or death" (Muchtar 2018, 268). The head of the Ternate National and Political Unity Office (Kesatuan Bangsa dan Politik) also noted that followers of Syi'ah Ja'fariyah Ajaran Nawawi Husni had been threatened with violence by their neighbors, including death if they did not repent (*Malut Post* 2016b). In response to these disturbances regional authorities banned further activities in certain locales to prevent violence.

After these initial steps by government officials, MUI Maluku Utara issued a fatwa banning the group as a threat to public safety on August 11, 2015. The fatwa also declared the group to be "heretical and misleading" (*sesat dan menyesatkan*). MUI Maluku Utara warned Muslims to avoid Husni's influence and to avoid conflict with his followers. The final section of the fatwa stressed that their ruling was not an attack on freedom of religion but rather about combating blasphemy. In explaining the fatwa to the public, the head of MUI Maluku Utara noted that it was aimed at this particular group of Shia led by Nawawi Husni, not at Shias as a whole (*Madina* 2015). MUI Tidore Kepulauan issued a similar, albeit broader statement (*pernyataan sikap*) the following year in anticipation of the possible arrival of followers of Syi'ah Ja'fariyah on Tidore. MUI Tidore Kepulauan declared Syi'ah Ja'fariyah to be a heretical sect "because it contradicts Islam" (*Malut Post* 2016a). In this case it seems, at least according to news reports, that all forms of Syi'ah Ja'fariyah were banned, not just followers of Nawawi Husni (*Malut Post* 2016a).

Rather than taking the lead, MUI often appears to be acting in response to complaints from local communities or civil servants. Members of the security apparatus routinely voice concerns about heretical sects in public speeches and presentations. For example, during a speech to a local agricultural college in the district of West Halmahera, the district chief of operations felt it necessary to note that his mission was focused on "the prevention of terrorism, separatism, radicalism and heretical sects and [activities that were] anti-Pancasila" (Polres Halbar 2017). In the Husni case, MUI Maluku Utara acted after the regional government had intervened and after conflict had already occurred on the island of Ternate. In some cases, people have taken matters into their own hands. In January 2015, a crowd of people in West Halmahera ransacked local Gafatar offices after MUI issued a fatwa declaring the group a heretical sect (Okezone.com 2015). On August 25, 2016, just weeks after MUI Maluku Utara had issued a fatwa banning Syi'ah Ja'fariyah Ajaran Nawawi, a group of between eighty and a hundred people stoned the home of a follower of Husni Nawawi in Ternate who continued to hold Syi'ah Ja'fariyah prayer services. As they stoned the house the crowd was heard to yell, "Kill the Shia. The Shia are infidels." In this case, the police, with the assistance of the army, were able to restore order (Nusantaratimur.com 2016). In November 2018, police had to rescue seventeen people accused of being in a new, as yet unnamed heretical sect who were attacked by locals intent on carrying out vigilante justice (*Malut Post* 2018a). Members of the larger Muslim community across the region seem to see these groups as threats to community harmony.

Although intrareligious tensions within the Christian community do not make the headlines in the same way that efforts to combat diversity within Islam do, they are no less evident. These tensions are focused primarily on the rise of charismatic and Pentecostal churches in the region and their impact on the two major mainstream Protestant Churches, the Protestant Church of Maluku (GPM) and the Evangelical Protestant Church of Halmahera (GMIH). Conflicts over the establishment of these new denominations and doctrinal differences have a long history but have become more common in recent years as charismatic and Pentecostal churches have gained popularity. Dutch colonial policy had kept diversity within the Christian community to a minimum. Each part of the colony that was open to proselytization was given to a particular missionary organization. Much of what now constitutes the central part of Maluku was given to the Protestant

Church in the Netherlands Indies. North Maluku was given to the Utrecht Missionary Society. These Protestant missions enjoyed a near monopoly on Christianity and were able to block most efforts by other Protestant churches to work in the region (Haire 1981, 68). The dominance of mainstream Protestantism in Maluku was first challenged in 1921 with the arrival of the Seventh Day Adventist Church (Nainggolan 1984, 39), followed by the Pentecostal Assemblies of God in 1938 (Wiyono 2016). The first Protestant challengers to GMIH's hegemony in North Maluku arrived in 1949 when the Pentecostal Church of God in America, which later became the Pentecostal Mission Church in Halmahera, began work on the islands of Ternate, Bacan, and Halmahera (Wiyono 2005, 309). Gani Wiyono, a historian of Pentecostalism in Indonesia, notes that, in the case of Pentecostals, these missionaries were zealous in their desire for converts and "generally disregarded the traditional boundaries of comity long established by mission agencies in Europe . . . this meant they were not reluctant to start a Pentecostal congregation even in places where other Protestant denominations had already established churches" (2005, 310). In contrast, GMIH and GPM had arisen "in the tradition of the prevention of the 'double mission' and considered these new denominations as intruders in 'their territory'" (Steenbrink and Tapilatu 2008, 399).

The diversity within Protestantism has increased dramatically in the last seventy years. Multiple new denominations have been established, including Jehovah's Witnesses and Baptists as well numerous Pentecostal and charismatic churches. In some cases, the local growth in diversity has been quite overwhelming. For example, the town of Tobelo in northern Halmahera was home to only one Protestant denomination in 1949: GMIH, the successor to the Dutch missionaries who had worked in the region. By 2020 there were approximately two dozen different denominations competing for adherents in the same town. Across North Maluku there were thirty-one Protestant denominations competing for followers in 2020, albeit some with only one congregation. This increase in diversity has not always been welcomed by the Christian community. These new churches compete with mainstream churches for adherents. The resulting tension, often focused on the poaching of congregants, creates rifts within villages, particularly smaller ones, and within families. The FKUB in North Halmahera, set up in the aftermath of the Muslim-Christian conflict to prevent future outbreaks of interfaith violence, now spends a significant percentage of its time defusing tensions between followers of GMIH and newer churches. At times these rifts have led to violence and newer churches have been destroyed and their followers expelled from the community, or in a few rare cases actual fist fights between competing ministers.

One example comes from the Modole village of Soamaetek in western Kao in northern Halmahera. Soamaetek is an entirely Christian village that until 2000 was home to a single GMIH congregation. The son of the village head returned in 2000 after several years working in another part of Halmahera. During his time away, he had joined a Pentecostal church and decided to establish a branch in his natal village. He started preaching to his immediate family, and eventually several other villagers began to attend his Sunday services and Bible study rather than take part in GMIH services. He also began to build a small chapel next to his father's house that he hoped to expand into a full-size church. Not all of his neighbors were happy with these developments. The GMIH preacher expressed concern that a reduced congregation would hurt his ability to raise funds, particularly important as they were in the midst of building a new church. Some villagers were worried that divisions might arise in the community; they had just weathered a period of communal violence and did not welcome anything that might cause rifts within the village. Others were concerned with the appropriateness of this new church and its mode of worship (they used North Moluccan Malay rather than standard Indonesian). These concerns and others eventually led to an altercation when a large crowd confronted the young man and demanded he stop preaching. When he refused, he was assaulted by some of his neighbors, his church was destroyed, and he and his followers, including the village head, were expelled from the village. They eventually built a small settlement on the outskirts of Soamaetek with a small church. Similar examples can be found across Maluku and North Maluku.

When these denominational splits occur, they are first and foremost seen as a tear in the social fabric of the community. In much of the region (outside of large cities), community and church membership are seen as one and the same. To remove oneself from the church congregation is often equated with removing oneself from the community. Doctrinal differences can also cause problems. Some of the major points of contention have been on proper modes of worship, the appropriate language for church services, methods of baptism, and the importance of the holy spirit. The newer Protestant denominations also tend to be less tolerant of religious pluralism and *adat* (Al Qurtuby 2016, 181). Dieter Bartels noted this development in Christian communities in Ambon in the 1970s, as new migrants to the region brought with them new forms of Christianity. Over forty years ago Bartels (1977, 324–25) warned,

> Extremists among [these migrants] demand the "purification" of religion from beliefs which are not in line with pan-Islamic or pan-Protestant beliefs. Thus, they have launched attacks on beliefs that God is one and the same for Christians and Muslims, and they have demanded the discontinuance of ancestor veneration and most of *adat* (tradition), all of which would lead to the further weakening of interfaith ties.

Qurtuby confirms Bartel's predictions when he writes in 2016 that Pentecostal and charismatic leaders "strongly criticize GPM for having practiced and amalgamated two contrasting traditions: pure Christian faith and impure *adat* belief" (Al Qurtuby 2016, 181). The same could be said for North Maluku where some of the more conservative Christian denominations have little tolerance for *adat* traditions and are often openly dismissive of them, if not outright hostile to their continued practice.

Proselytization not Pluralism: Animism in North Maluku and Maluku

The few remaining followers of indigenous religions in Maluku and North Maluku have rarely received any support to maintain their indigenous belief systems and ritual practices. In most cases they have faced outright persecution. These groups are very small in number as many coastal communities converted to either Islam or Christianity, at least nominally, by the end of the colonial period. Those groups that had not often did so in the decade after the events of 1965, either by choice or by government fiat. For the most part the only groups that avoided these situations were those that lived in the interior of the larger islands in the region. Most of these forest-dwelling groups have, however, been subject to proselytization for decades. These efforts first began, albeit sporadically, under the Dutch and continued after independence. These efforts have been rather successful in the destruction of animist communities. Roy Ellen (2012, 3) notes that "where animist groups still exist [in Maluku], demographic decline has led to the severe erosion and disarticulation of ritual cycles." He argues that, with the exception of the Nuaulu on Seram, there are few if any viable animist communities remaining.

Since the New Order period, efforts to convert these populations have taken one of two paths. The most common has been the (often forced) resettlement of these communities to more accessible locations either near new transmigration sites in the interior of larger islands or on the coast. These relocations have often been done under the auspices of the government's program aimed at developing indigenous minorities deemed to be "backwards." The aim of this government program has been to turn these indigenous groups into modern citizens through sedentarization, incorporation into the local economy, and the introduction of public education. Another aspect of these resettlement programs has been the introduction of either Islam or Protestantism to these groups as the government argues that the adoption of a recognized religion is a sign of modernization (for a comparative reflection from Sumatra, see Aragon in this volume).

A second strategy for eradicating indigenous religion that has often gone hand in hand with resettlement programs has been the support or encouragement of proselytization activities focused on these groups. In North Maluku, GMIH has long made sporadic efforts to convert newly resettled Forest Tobelo to Christianity. In the 1980s, the New Tribes Mission, a nondenominational Evangelical Protestant missionary organization based in the United States, established mission stations throughout Maluku. They worked in the interior of Buru, Seram, Halmahera, and Taliabu. In northeastern Halmahera the New Tribes Mission had significant success convincing the Forest Tobelo living along several river valleys to convert to Christianity (Duncan 2003). Some of these converts subsequently took on the role of evangelist themselves and have opened at least five new mission fields aimed at converting the few remaining non-Christian Forest Tobelo. Beginning in 2016, the Muslim group Lembaga Amil Zakat Nasional Baitul Maal Hidayatullah (BMH) began *dakwah* (Islamic missionary activity) work among the Forest Tobelo in at least two parts of Halmahera and has claimed to have had some success (Baitul Maal Hidayatullah 2018).[12]

These proselytization efforts have often been supported by neighboring communities of Muslims and Christians who see the eradication of indigenous ritual practices as the best way to bring "civilization" to these groups. Allowing them to continue practicing their indigenous cosmology is largely seen as a nonstarter. In North Maluku, there are virtually no individuals or organizations that voice support for the religious freedoms of the few remaining animist Forest Tobelo communities. The North Maluku branch of the Alliance of Indigenous Peoples of the Archipelago (Aliansi Masyarakat Adat Nusantara, AMAN) has focused on natural resource extraction and indigenous land claims in response to the massive influx of timber, mining, and plantations over the last two decades. It has expressed no interest in protecting the religious freedom of indigenous peoples. The situation in Maluku is slightly different. The Maluku branch of AMAN has actively called on the provincial government to respect the indigenous religion of the Nuaulu (and by implication others) in its "Haruku Resolution" released in 2017, demanding more respect for the rights of *masyarakat adat* in Maluku (Aliansi Masyarakat Adat Nusantara 2016).

Conclusion: Religious Pluralism and Problems of Scale

As the previous discussion has shown, religious pluralism, if not religious tolerance, remains more of an ideal in the region than a reality. Not everyone would agree, however, with this conclusion. A common rebuttal to views of religious

intolerance in Maluku and North Maluku is to point to examples of positive relationships between religious communities. These examples often include stories
of Christians helping Muslims build mosques, Muslims helping Christians build
new churches, the participation of Christians in various aspects of Ramadan,
or examples of particular villages or family ties. There is no denying that there
are many such ties across religious boundaries in Maluku and North Maluku.
Throughout both provinces one can find innumerable examples of religious
pluralism at the microlevel, including interfaith relationships within families,
between neighboring communities, and between *pela gandong* partners in central Maluku. Interviews and discussions about interfaith relations are filled with
examples of trust and mutual cooperation when the discussion is focused on the
near religious other. These are the examples often highlighted in media accounts
or writings on peace and reconciliation. I would argue this should not lead one
to the conclusion that an acceptance of religious pluralism exists in any serious
sense across the broad spectrum of North Moluccan or Moluccan society.

These localized interfaith relations were also the case prior to the outbreak
of violence in 1999 and, in most cases, they failed to prevent conflict. These ties
were visible when individuals or communities went to great lengths to protect
their Muslim or Christian neighbors. Yet oftentimes the same people who res-
cued their neighbors also took part in religious violence elsewhere. The most
obvious example would be the people of Kao in northern Halmahera. The indigenous people of Kao have a very strong notion of unity based on *adat* relationships that link four indigenous groups in the region, the Modole, the Pagu, the
Tobelo Boeng, and the Towiliko.[13] The first three groups are virtually 100 percent
Christian, while the last includes a small number of Muslims often referred to
as the Kao Islam. Throughout the conflict the Kao Islam were never attacked or
bothered by their Christian neighbors—in fact, the Kao Islam fought alongside
Christians against other Muslims throughout the conflict. Even during the height
of the religious tensions in the region their *adat* identity took precedent over
their religious faith. These close ties with the Kao Islam did not, however, prevent
Christians in Kao from taking part in horrific violence against other Muslim
communities throughout northern Halmahera.

I would argue that when talking about pluralism or tolerance in the region we
must consider the issue of scale. In this case we need to distinguish between a
localized acceptance of religious difference (at the micro-level or even the meso-
level) within particular neighborhoods, villages, or families or between *pela
gandong* partners and a larger, more general acceptance of religious pluralism
(at the macro-level) across the region. Individuals and communities are able to
recognize the possibility of positive interfaith relationships between them and
their immediate neighbors, but this recognition loses purchase as they zoom

out. In other words, people are often happy to maintain interfaith relations with their neighbors or *adat* partners, but they do not extend this receptivity to the religious other as a whole. As we zoom out, the acceptance or tolerance that can be found within these particular relationships gets replaced or suppressed by the phantasmic image of antipluralist Muslims or proselytizing Christians as the agents of Western imperialism. The positive nature of the relationships they have with those in their immediate circle is often considered an exception to the norm rather than a norm that should be, or could be, expanded. Ironically, these positive relationships do not demonstrate the possibility of a wider religious pluralism, but rather argue against it. Instead they prove that people are capable of accepting difference and being decent if only they can look beyond their Islamic and Christian identities.

Based on this examination of interfaith and intrafaith relations in Maluku and North Maluku, one would be hard pressed to make an argument that either province supports a culture of religious pluralism. As noted earlier, Formichi (2014, 2) defines religious pluralism as "the transformation of a mere condition of heterogeneity, into a reality where groups representative of this diversity are accepted and integrated as equals." Neither province would appear to meet this definition of religious pluralism. Religious diversity is not accepted in Maluku or North Maluku so much as a certain subset of religious diversity is, at most, tolerated. Muslims and Christians are resigned to tolerating the presence of Muslims or Christians, not because they accept their presence but because the government requires them to do so. Furthermore, recent history has shown them that the alternative can lead to violence and bloodshed. Many on either side of the Muslim-Christian divide do not see the other as an equal; instead they argue that religious minorities should be aware of their place in society and act accordingly. Acceptance and integration simply do not apply to minority Muslim sects or to followers of indigenous religions in either province. It would seem that despite the vast amount of effort that has been put into cultivating a sense of religious pluralism in the region, there remains much work to be done.

Notes

1. *Hibualamo*, which translates as big house in English, is a Tobelo *adat* practice that focuses on unity, conflict prevention, and conflict resolution within Tobelo communities in eastern Indonesia. Big house is a reference to the traditional meeting houses (Tobelo, *o hibualamo*) that used to be the center of Tobelo villages in North Maluku and were supposedly places of mediation in the community. See Duncan (2009) for a discussion of the practice of *hibualamo*.

2. See Duncan (2013) for an in-depth examination of the conflict.

3. The list of publications discussing peace and reconciliation in the province of Maluku is vast and includes Al Qurtuby's (2016) work on religion and conciliation, Fitri-yah's (2015) work on Muslim peacebuilders in Ambon, and Kusumaningrum (2015) and Manupully et al. (2017) on reconciliation and interfaith relations in Maluku.

4. *Pela gandong* refers to traditional alliances between one or more villages in central Maluku, often on different islands and of different faiths. The number of publications on *pela gandong* is extensive, but see Bräuchler's (2015) research on the cultural aspects of peace making in Maluku.

5. Al Qurtuby (2016, 35–44) provides a detailed examination of these tensions in the province of Maluku and Duncan (2013, 22–46) does the same for North Maluku.

6. Muslim troops wore white headbands since Muslims in Maluku associate that color with Islam and purity. Christians wore red bands to distinguish themselves and also because Moluccans often associate the color red with war and masculinity.

7. These religious harmony forums were eventually standardized across Indonesia by the central government. Human Rights Watch (2013) notes that these forums have not been without their problems, nor do they always side with proponents of religious pluralism.

8. Research by the Habibie Center (NVMS and The Habibie Center 2014) notes some of the limitations of this program in Ambon.

9. Salafism is a movement within Sunni Islam that seeks to purify the religion by returning it to the earliest forms of Islam as practiced by the first three generations of Muslims, which is seen as the purest and most correct form of Islam.

10. Local community members reported the Aliran Amanah group to the police in Ter-nate in June 2008 (Okezone.com 2008a, 2008b). MUI Halmahera Selatan declared Aliran Guru Bais a heretical sect in a fatwa released in February 2019 (Kabarmalut.com 2019).

11. Much of my description of the Husni case comes from Muchtar (2018), supple-mented by local media accounts.

12. BMH appears to have developed a focus on *dakwah* aimed at groups that still prac-tice their indigenous religion and have efforts aimed at converting the Wana in Central Sulawesi and the Badui in Banten as well as the Forest Tobelo in North Maluku.

13. There is some disagreement in the literature and on the ground over what con-stitutes the four ethnic groups of Kao. According to a recent local publication in Halma-hera, the four ethnic groups in Kao are the Modole, the Pagu, the Tobelo Boeng, and the Towiliko (also referred to as Toliliko or Tololiku) (Banari 2014, 14–15). Fraassen's (1980, 134–38) analysis of the Dutch literature lists the four ethnic groups (which he refers to as "domains") as the Modole, the Pagu, the Tobelo Boeng, and the Kao, with the Tololiku being included among the Kao, along with the Kao Islam. According to Manan (2014, 20), some Muslims in Kao see themselves as a completely distinct ethnic group, rather than part of the Towiliko. Retnowati and Manan (2014) provide an in-depth discussion of the Kao, while Handoko et al. (2018) examine the archaeological evidence for the establish-ment of Islam in the Kao region.

References

Al Qurtuby, Sumanto. 2016. *Religious Violence and Conciliation in Indonesia: Chris-tians and Muslims in the Moluccas.* London: Routledge.

Aliansi Masyarakat Adat Nusantara. 2016. "Muswil II PW AMAN Maluku Serukan 'Resolusi Haruku.'" http://www.aman.or.id/muswil-ii-pw-aman-maluku-serukan-resolusi-haruku/.

Amirrachman, R. Alpha. 2014. "Education in the Conflict-Affected Moluccas: Local Tradition, Identity Politics and School Principal Leadership." *South East Asia Research* 22, no. 4 (December): 561–78. https://doi.org/10.5367/sear.2014.0235.

Antara. 2016. "Kemenag Jadikan Halmahera Utara Percontohan Kerukunan Beragama," January 5. https://www.antaranews.com/berita/538296/kemenag-jadikan-halmahera-utara-percontohan-kerukunan-beragama.

Antara. 2017. "FKUB Programkan Pembentukan Kampung Kerukunan Umat Beragama," September 12. https://ambon.antaranews.com/berita/40524/fkub-programkan-pembentukan-kampung-kerukunan-umat-beragama.

As'ad, Muhammad. 2006. "Forum Komunikasi Antar Umat Beragama (FKAUB) Maluku Utara (Sebuah Harapan dalam Pemeliharaan Hidup Rukun dan Damai)." *Jurnal "Al-Qalam"* 12, no. 18: 85–100. http://dx.doi.org/10.31969/alq.v12i2.561.

Baitul Maal Hidayatullah. 2018. "Mari Muliakan Saudara Muallaf Kita." https://www.bmh.or.id/mari-muliakan-saudara-muallaf-kita/.

Banari, Jesaya R. 2014. *Mencari yang Pernah Ada.* Tobelo: Pustaka Dabiloha.

Barron, Patrick. 2019. *When Violence Works: Postconflict Violence and Peace in Indonesia.* Ithaca, NY: Cornell University Press.

Barron, Patrick, Sri Kusumastuti Rahayu, Sunita Varada, and Vita Febriany. 2009. "Disturbing the Equilibrium: Movements out of Poverty in Conflict-Affected Areas of Indonesia." In *Moving out of Poverty: Rising from the Ashes of Conflict*, edited by Deepa Narayan and Patti Petesch, 290–337. London: Palgrave Macmillan UK.

Bartels, Dieter. 1977. "Guarding the Invisible Mountain: Intervillage Alliances, Religious Syncretism and Ethnic Identity among Ambonese Christians and Moslems in the Moluccas." PhD diss., Cornell University.

Braithwaite, John, Valerie Braithwaite, Michael Cookson, and Leah Dunn. 2010. *Anomie and Violence: Non-Truth and Reconciliation in Indonesian Peacebuilding.* Canberra: Australian National University E-Press.

Bräuchler, Birgit. 2015. *The Cultural Dimension of Peace: Decentralization and Reconciliation in Indonesia.* London: Palgrave Macmillan.

Crouch, Melissa. 2016. "Legislating Inter-Religious Harmony: Attempts at Reform in Indonesia." In *Religion, Law and Intolerance in Indonesia*, edited by Helen Pausacker and Tim Lindsey, 95–112. New York: Routledge.

Duncan, Christopher R. 2003. "Untangling Conversion: Religious Change and Identity among the Forest Tobelo of Halmahera, Indonesia." *Ethnology* 42, no. 4 (Fall): 307–22. https://doi.org/10.2307/3773831.

Duncan, Christopher R. 2009. "Reconciliation and Reinvention: The Resurgence of Tradition in Postconflict Tobelo, North Maluku, Eastern Indonesia." *Journal of Asian Studies* 68, no. 4 (November): 1077–1104. https://doi.org/10.1017/S002191180999074X.

Duncan, Christopher R. 2013. *Violence and Vengeance: Religious Conflict and Its Aftermath in Eastern Indonesia.* Ithaca, NY: Cornell University Press.

Duncan, Christopher R. 2016. "Coexistence Not Reconciliation: From Communal Violence to Non-Violence in North Maluku, Eastern Indonesia." *Asia-Pacific Journal of Anthropology* 17, no. 5: 460–74. https://doi.org/10.1080/14442213.2016.1206615.

Eck, Diana L. 2007. "American Religious Pluralism: Civic and Theological Discourse." In *Democracy and the New Religious Pluralism*, edited by Thomas Banchoff, 243–70. Oxford: Oxford University Press.

Ellen, Roy. 2012. *Nuaulu Religious Practices: The Frequency and Reproduction of Rituals in a Moluccan Society.* Leiden: KITLV.

Fitriyah, Lailatul. 2015. "Muslim Peacebuilders of Ambon: A Story of Building Peace after Interreligious Violence." MA thesis, University of Notre Dame.

Formichi, Chiara. 2014. "Religious Pluralism, State and Society in Asia." In *Religious Pluralism, State and Society in Asia,* edited by Chiara Formichi, 1–9. London: Routledge.

Haire, James. 1981. *The Character and Theological Struggle of the Church in Halmahera, Indonesia, 1941–1979.* Bern: Peter D. Lang.

Handoko, Wuri, Muhammad Al Mujabuddawat, and Joss Whitaker. 2018. " Islamicization Strategies in Kao Ancient Village, North Halmahera." *Kapata Arkeologi* 14, no. 1: 49–62. https://doi.org/10.24832/kapata.v14i1.507.

Human Rights Watch. 2013. *In Relgion's Name: Abuses against Religious Minorities in Indonesia.* New York: Human Rights Watch.

Human Rights Working Group. 2011. *Crimes against Humanity towards the Ahmadiyya Community in Indonesia.* Jakarta: Human Rights Working Group.

Kabarmalut.com. 2019. "MUI Halsel: Aliran Guru Bais di Desa Jiko Sesat dan Menyesatkan." https://kabarmalut.co.id/2019/02/15/mui-halsel-aliran-guru-bais-di-desa-jiko-sesat-dan-menyesatkan/.

Kantor Wilayah Kementerian Agama Provinsi Maluku. 2019. "Warga Ambon Tumpah Ruah Sambut Harmony Award 2019." https://maluku.kemenag.go.id/berita/warga-ambon-tumpah-ruah-sambut-harmony-award-2019.

Kiem, Christian G. 1995. "Re-Islamization among Muslim Youth in Ternate Town, Eastern Indonesia." *Sojourn* 8, no. 1 (February): 92–127.

Kusumaningrum, Diah. 2016. "Interdependence Versus Truth and Justice: Lessons from Reconciliation Processes in Maluku." *Jurnal Ilmu Sosial dan Ilmu Politik* 20, no. 1 (July): 34–49. https://doi.org/10.22146/jsp.17998.

Madina. 2015. "Kembali Menerbitkan Fatwa Sesat, MUI Diminta Lebih Arif." http://www.madinaonline.id/s5-review/kembali-menerbitkan-fatwa-sesat-mui-diminta-lebih-arif/.

Malut Post. 2016a. "MUI Larang Syiah Jafariah Masuk Tidore: Bentengi Warga dari Ajaran Sesat," September 20.

Malut Post. 2016b. "Pemkot Warning Pengikut Syiah Jafariah: Petinggi Syiah Minta Pengikutnya Tidak Terprovokasi," August 11.

Malut Post. 2018a. "17 Jamaah Diamankan dari Kepungan Warga," November 2.

Malut Post. 2018b. "Ternate Harmoni, Satu Keragaman: Parade Karnival, Eratkan Silaturahmi antar Agama," December 18.

Malut Post. 2019. "Perayaan Natal Harmoni Dibatalkan," January 11.

Manan, Mohammad Azzam. 2014. "Ritual Tagi Jere dalam Komunitas Etnik Kao: Peran Lembaga Dewan Adat dan Badan Syara' dan Perkembangannya." *Jurnal Masyarakat & Budaya* 16, no. 1: 27–50.

Manuputty, Jacky, Zairin Salampessy, Ihsan Ali-Fauzi, and Irsyad Rafsadi, eds. 2017. *Basudara Stories of Peace from Maluku: Working Together for Reconciliation.* Clayton, Victoria: Monash University Publishing.

Muchtar, Ibnu Hasan. 2018. "Dinamika Lahirnya Fatwa MUI Provinsi Maluku Utara tentang Sesatnya Syi'ah Ja'fariyah Ajaran Nawawi Husni (Ong)." *Harmoni* 17, no. 2 (July–December): 256–71.

Nainggolan, Rajoaman. 1984. "Indonesia Union College: A Historical Study of a Seventh-Day Adventist Institution." PhD diss., Andrews University.

Nusantaratimur.com. 2016. "Warga Marikurubu Lempari Rumah Penganut Aliran Syiah Jafariah." https://www.nusantaratimur.com/2016/08/warga-marikurubu-lempari-rumah-penganut.html.

NVMS and The Habibie Center. 2014. *Post-Conflict Segregation, Violence, and Recon-struction Policy in Ambon*. Jakarta: National Violence Monitoring System Program and the Habibie Center.

Okezone.com. 2008a. "Sebarkan Aliran Amanah, 12 Penganut Bertobat," June 26. https://news.okezone.com/read/2008/06/26/1/122249/sebarkan-aliran-amanah-12-penganut-bertobat.

Okezone.com. 2008b. "Sumber Ajaran Amanah, Wangsit dari Mimpi," June 26. https://news.okezone.com/read/2008/06/26/ 1/122251/ sumber-ajaran- amanah-wangsit-dari-mimpi.

Okezone.com. 2015. "Kantor Gafatar Halmahera Barat Diobrak-Abrik Massa," January 29. https://news.okezone.com/read/2015/01/29/340/1098720/ kantor-gafatar-halmahera-barat-diobrak-abrik-massa.

Patel, Eboo. 2019. *Out of Many Faiths: Religious Diversity and the American Promise*. Princeton: Princeton University Press.

Polres Halbar. 2017. "Pelaksanaan Kegiatan Pembukaan Diklat Dasar Anggota Korps Sukarela (KSR) PMI Halbar Angkatan II Thn 2017." http://halbar.malut.polri. go.id/pelaksanaan-kegiatan-pembukaan-diklat-dasar-anggota-korps-sukarela-ksr-pmi-halbar-angkatan-ii-thn-2017/.

Probojo, Lany. 2010. "Ritual Guardians versus Civil Servants as Cultural Brokers in the New Order Era: Local Islam in Tidore, North Maluku." *Indonesia and the Malay World* 38, no. 110: 95–107. https://doi.org/10.1080/13639811003665421.

Retnowati, Endang, and M. Azzam Manan, eds. 2014. *Identifikasi Bahasa dan Kebu-dayaan Etnik Minoritas Kao*. Jakarta: LIPI Press.

Sapsuha, M. Tahir. 2013. *Pendidikan Pasca Konflik: Pendidikan Multikultural Berbasis Konseling Budaya Masyarakat Maluku Utara*. Yogyakarta: LKiS.

Sinar Harapan. 2012. "Mempersatukan Rakyat Lewat Adat." May 10, 2012.

Steenbrink, Karel A., and Mesakh Tapilatu. 2008. "Moluccan Christianity in the 19th and 20th Century between Agama Ambon and Islam." In *A History of Christi-anity in Indonesia*, edited by Jan S. Aritonang and Karel Steenbrink, 383–428. Leiden: Brill.

Saeni, Eni. 2012. "Harmony and Tradition in Tobelo." *Tempo*, May 23. http://magz. tempo.co/konten/2012/05/23/OUT/24772/Harmony-and-Tradition-in-Tobelo/39/12.

Thalib, Usman, Tontje Soumokil, John Pattiasina, and Rabiyatul Uzda. 2012. *Hibua Lamo dalam Kehidupan Masyarakat Adat Tobelo di Halmahera Utara*. Ambon: Balai Pelestarian Nilai Budaya Ambon, Kementerian Pendidikan dan Kebudayaan.

Van Fraassen, Ch. F. 1980. "Types of Sociopolitical Structure in North Halmaheran History." In *Halmahera dan Raja Ampat: Konsep dan Strategi Penelitian*, edited by E. K. M. Masinambow, 87–150. Jakarta: LEKNAS- LIPI.

Wiyono, Gani. 2005. "Pentecosalism in Indonesia." In *Asian and Pentecostal: The Charismatic Face of Christianity in Asia*, edited by Allan Anderson and Edmund Tang, 307–28. Costa Mesa, CA: Regnum Books International.

Wiyono, Gani. 2016. "The Beginning of the Assemblies of God of Indonesia (1936–1951)." https://pentecost.asia/articles/the-beginning-of-the-assemblies-of-god-of-indonesia-1936-1951/.

Glossary

212 Movement a coalition of Islamist groups involved in the campaign to bring down the Jakarta governor Ahok

abangan non-normative Muslims

adat customary law

adat biasa ordinary or secular custom(s)

agama glossed as "religion" in contemporary Indonesia; a combination of a Christian view of what counts as a world religion with an Islamic understanding of what defines a "true" religion.

agama Hindu Bali Hindu Balinese religion; official name of the Balinese religion between 1952 and 1964.

agama Hindu Hindu religion; official name of the Balinese religion since 1964.

āgama Sanskrit term signifying "that which has come down to the present" and applying to anything handed down as fixed by tradition.

Agamanisasi "religionization"; Indonesian religious politics implying that followers of indigenous traditions are "not yet religious" and should be a target of proselytizing.

Ahmadiyah Islamic movement established by Mirza Ghulam Ahmad (1835–1908) in India, considered heretical by many Sunni Muslims due to its supposed belief that Ahmad was a prophet

Ajeg Bali "Bali Erect"; slogan launched after the Islamic bombing at Kuta in 2002.

al-Islam li-l-Insaniyyah Humanitarian Islam

alun-alun city center park

aurat Islamic term referring to parts of the body that must be hidden from all but spouses or immediate family members.

azan Islamic prayer call

berhala idol(s)

brahmana highest of the four Balinese *wangsa*, from which the consecrated high priests (*pedanda*) are drawn.

buka puasa breaking the fasting at the sunset

Bumi Wali land of the (Islamic) Saints

bupati regent

dakwah Islamic outreach such as proselytizing and preaching

datuk/datu local spirit

dharma that which upholds the world and supports order; in Hindu law, the duties and qualifications of an individual according to his social class (*varna*) and stage of life (*āśrama*)

dīn "practice, custom, law," glossed as "religion" in Islam

fatwa Islamic opinion, sometimes a legal decree

gotong royong working together for collective community work

hajj the Muslim pilgrimage to Mecca

halal legally allowed in shari'a law

hukum "law," specifically Islamic law

Imlek the Chinese New Year

Islam Berkemajuan Progressive Islam

Islam Nusantara Islam of the Archipelago

jilbab Islamic veil covering women's head and shoulders

Kebalian "Balineseness"; term used in the 1920s by the first generation of Balinese educated in colonial schools to describe themselves

Kebangkitan Hindu Hindu revival triggered by the Islamic resurgence in Indonesia in the 1990s

kemaslahatan benefit, value, goodness

kepercayaan belief(s)

khatam the complete reading of the Qur'an

kommunitas adat terpencil isolated customary communities

Majelis Agama religion councils

Majelis Zikir Nurussalam a religious study group associated with the former president Yudhoyono

mandur migration broker

masyarakat adat indigenous peoples

musyrik idolatrous

niskala unmanifest world that lies beyond the realm of the senses

NU *Garis Lucu* NU's Funny/Humor Brigade

NU *Garis Lurus* NU Straight Path

oknum Misbehaving person(s) whose misconduct does not represent his/her institution/affiliation

Pancasila Indonesia's five-point national philosophy or creed

paraiyar (Tamil) "drummers," name of a cluster of low castes in Tamil Indonesian and Malaysian society

pedanda consecrated *brahmana* high priest

pendatang "outsider"; name given by the Balinese to (mostly) Muslim immigrants in Bali

pengajian Qur'an recitation collectively or individually

penghayat kepercayaan belief practitioner(s)

penolakan "rejection," used to refer to a particular organizing tactic of Islamist groups to mobilize a neighborhood against a particular government policy.

peranakan Chinese who have been living in Indonesia for generations and developed mixed culture and identities with local people through marriage and collaboration

pesantren traditional religious boarding school

petunjuk guidance

politik cuci tangan hand-cleansing politics

putihan normative Muslims

Ramadhan Islamic fasting month

Reformasi period after Suharto stepped down in 1998

rumah inspirasi house of inspiration

sakala manifest world that lies within the bounds of human sensorial perception

sakti feminine godly power; feminine energy; divine power

Sampradaya neo-Hindu devotional movement

sedekah offerings

selametan Javanese traditional ceremonies

shari'a Islamic law

sholat lima waktu five obligatory prayers in Islam

sila principle

suku terasing isolated, estranged tribe or ethnic group(s)

suku tribe; tribal or ethnic group or lineage

tahajud Islamic midnight prayer, usually conducted when one has a serious problem to solve and/or special request to God

tauhid oneness of God
tayub erotic Javanese folk dance
tradisi leluhur ancestral tradition
transmigrasi setempat local transmigration
tuak palm wine
Ulama/Kiai traditional Islamic scholars/teachers
Ustadh Islamic teacher
Vreemde Oosterlingen Eastern Foreigners, consisted of the Chinese, Arabs, and Indians.
    They were the second class citizens during the Dutch colonization in East Indies.
Wali Songo nine Islamic saints who spread Islam in Java
warung small vendors, where food or snacks are sold

Contributors

Lorraine V. Aragon is an adjunct associate professor at the Departments of Anthropology and Asian Studies, the University of North Carolina, Chapel Hill. She is the author of *Fields of the Lord: Animism, Christian Minorities, and State Development in Indonesia* (2000) and other publications on Indonesian religious minorities, "outer island" arts, religious conflicts, language, law, and national development. Her current book project examines how models of individualistic intellectual property law and collective property rights are being adopted by nations such as Indonesia with scant recognition of local creators' perspectives or regional producers' values, customary practices, and community service beyond the market.

Christopher R. Duncan is an associate professor of anthropology at Rutgers University-Newark. He is the author of *Violence and Vengeance: Religious Violence and Its Aftermath in Eastern Indonesia* (2013) and editor of *Civilizing the Margins: Southeast Asian Government Policies for the Development of Minorities* (2004). His areas of research include religious violence, peace and reconciliation, religious pluralism, and indigenous rights with a focus on Southeast Asia.

Chiara Formichi is an associate professor in Southeast Asian Studies at Cornell University. Her work focuses on Islam as a lived religion and political ideology in twentieth-century Indonesia and Southeast Asia more broadly. Publications have addressed the role of Islam in the making of the Indonesian nation-state, the history and status of Muslims minorities in Southeast Asia, and the relationship between Asian Studies and Islamic Studies. Her most recent publication is *Islam and Asia: A History* (2020).

Kikue Hamayotsu is an associate professor in the Department of Political Science and Faculty Associate at the Center for Southeast Asian Studies, Northern Illinois University. Her primary research and publications focus on politics and religion, identity politics, and democratization in Muslim-majority societies, especially Indonesia and Malaysia.

Robert (Bob) W. Hefner is a professor of anthropology and global studies at the Pardee School of World Affairs at Boston University. He has authored or edited twenty books on Islam, religion, and modernity. With Zainal Abidin Bagir, he is currently producing six films on religion, gender, and the politics of plurality in Indonesia.

James B. Hoesterey is the Winship Distinguished Research Professor of Religion at Emory University. His first book chronicles the rise and fall of one of the world's most popular Muslim televangelists (*Rebranding Islam: Piety, Prosperity, and a Self-Help Guru*), and he is currently leading a Henry Luce Foundation-funded project about public diplomacy, soft power, and the making of "moderate Islam."

Sidney Jones has been the founder and director of the Institute for Policy Analysis of Conflict in Jakarta, Indonesia, since 2013 and is a recognized authority on conflict and extremism in Southeast Asia, with a particular focus on Indonesia and the Philippines. She previously worked for the International Crisis Group, Human Rights Watch, Amnesty International, and the Ford Foundation.

Mona Lohanda has degrees from the Universitas Indonesia and the Department of History, School of Oriental and African Studies, University of London. She worked at Arsip Nasional Repubik Indonesia for more than forty years, retiring as senior researcher in 2013. Her publications include *The Kapitan Cina of Batavia, 1837–1942*; a history of Chinese establishment in colonial society (1996, 2001); *Growing Pains: the Chinese and the Dutch in colonial Java 1890–1942* (2002); *Membaca Sumber Menulis Sejarah* (2011); and various articles on the colonial history of Batavia, peranakan-Chinese, and historical sources for Indonesian history.

Michel Picard is a retired researcher at the French National Center for Scientific Research (CNRS) and a founding member of the Centre Asie du Sud-Est in Paris. He holds a PhD from the École des Hautes Études en Sciences Sociales. He has published extensively in the field of Balinese studies, specifically on tourism, culture, identity, ethnicity, and religion. He is the author of *Kebalian: La construction dialogique de l'identité balinaise* (2017) and *Bali: Cultural Tourism and Touristic Culture* (1996), and has edited several collective volumes, the most recent being *The Appropriation of Religion in Southeast Asia and Beyond* (2017) and *The Politics of Religion in Indonesia: Syncretism, Orthodoxy, and Religious Contention in Java and Bali* (2011).

Evi Lina Sutrisno did her PhD on Confucianism and its transformation into the Confucian religion in Indonesia. She currently works as a lecturer at the Political and Social Sciences Faculty, the Gadjah Mada University, Yogyakarta. She is also a research fellow at the Center of Religious and Cross-Cultural Study (CRCS) and Indonesian Consortium for Religious Studies (ICRS) in Yogyakarta. She conducts research on ethnic Chinese-Indonesians, Chinese religions, and ethnic conflicts in the reformation period (1998–present).

Silvia Vignato is an associate professor in anthropology at the Università di Milano-Bicocca (UNIMIB). In addition to a monograph about Sumatranese Hinduism (*Au nom de l'hindouisme*, L'Harmattan, 2001) and numerous articles on the subject, she has published about Malaysian factory workers and about postconflict and postdisaster experiences of young Acehenese people (children, teenagers, and young parents). She has recently edited *Dreams of Prosperity: Inequality and Integration in Southeast Asia* (2018) and *Searching for Work: Small-scale Mobility and Unskilled Labor in Southeast Asia* (2019) and directed two films: *Rezeki. Gold and stone mining in Aceh* (2016) and *Aceh, After* (2020).

Index

Organizations are listed alphabetically according to their Indonesian names. Indonesian names are listed alphabetically following first name-surname order; honorific titles follow the surname.

CPSIA information can be obtained
at www.ICGtesting.com
Printed in the USA
LVHW090429031121
702322LV00003B/290